Dec 1st 2002.

Dear Uncle Charles

I do hope you will enjoy this book as it is for an un-birthday present, meant for the

Lots of Love,

Mary -

THE SPIRIT OF
LICHFIELD
THE 20TH CENTURY IN PHOTOGRAPHS

Howard Clayton and Kathy Simmons

To A.P.

History with its flickering lamp stumbles along the trail of the past,
trying to reconstruct its themes, to revive its echoes and kindle
with pale gleams the passion of former days

Sir Winston Spencer Churchill

THE SPIRIT OF LICHFIELD

THE 20TH CENTURY IN PHOTOGRAPHS

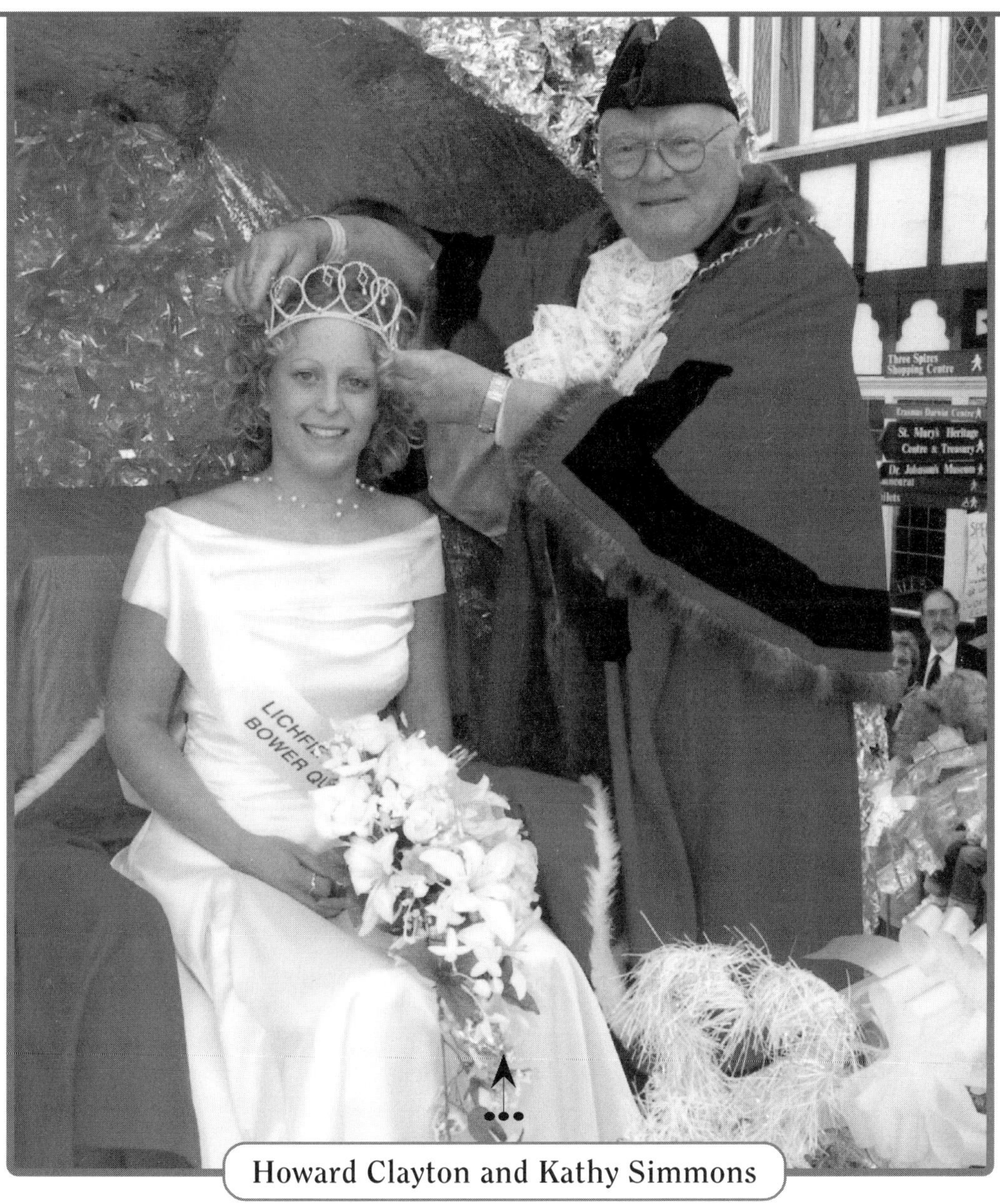

Howard Clayton and Kathy Simmons

Published by

Landmark Publishing Ltd,

Waterloo House, 12 Compton, Ashbourne, Derbyshire DE6 1DA England
Tel: (01335) 347349 Fax: (01335) 347303
e-mail: landmark@clara.net www.landmark publishing.co.uk

1st edition

ISBN 1 901522-78-4

British Library Cataloguing in Publication Data: a catalogue record for this book is available from the British Library.

Print: MPG Ltd, Bodmin, Cornwall
Cover by James Allsopp

Front cover: The Bower Procession led by the "Citizen on horseback" passing the Guildhall in the 1970's.

Back cover: Top - In 1988 the Queen and the Duke of Edinburgh attended the Maundy Service in Lichfield Cathedral.
Middle - A 'Litter Pick' was organised by the Lichfield Guide Association and the Lichfield City Council in 1984.
Bottom - A group of ARP wardens, from Hammerwich. They wore a dark blue uniform with chrome buttons and the insignia "Civil Defence".

Title page: The Mayor of Lichfield crowns this year's Bower Queen Nicola Hewitt from Hammerwich.

Contents

Introduction

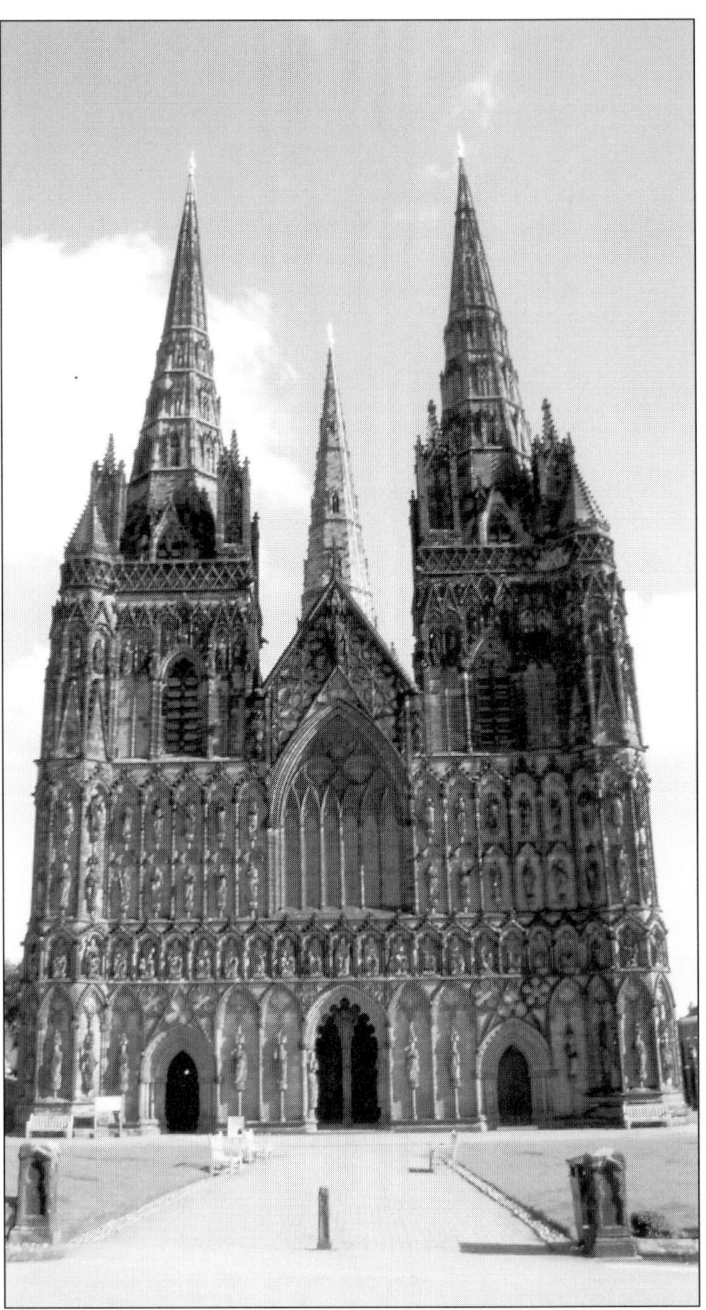

A present day photograph of Lichfield Cathedral.

Lichfield came into existence with the building of the first cathedral in 700AD.Thirteen centuries have passed since then, and much has changed during that time, but of all those centuries none has seen so much change as the last one, the twentieth century.

In 1900 Lichfield was a small cathedral city of some 9,000 inhabitants. It was a very self-contained community, a municipal corporation with its own City Council (created by a Charter of Edward VI), a Mayor and a Sheriff, a Recorder who presided over a court of quarter sessions, a Magistrate's court and a county court for hearing civil causes. Today, out of all these, only the Mayor and Sheriff remain, the latter only as an "office of dignity".

By the end of the century the population of Lichfield has increased to nearly 40,000 as more and more houses have been built, until today the city is in danger of becoming a dormitory town for the Midlands Conurbation. Add to this the effect of two world wars and there is little doubt that the twentieth century has left its mark on the face of Lichfield.

In this book we have attempted to show something of these changes through the eye of the camera, and this has only been possible through the co-operation and kindness of the many people who have responded to our appeals for photographs (a full list of these is acknowledged elsewhere). Inevitably there must be events which we have not covered, but we can only of course, utilise photographs which are available.

We hope that as a result of our efforts we have put before our readers a picture of Lichfield in the twentieth century and the changes that have occurred, so that newcomers to the city can learn something of its past and those who have spent most of their life here can look back and recall, incidents in their lives.

Acknowledgements

Lichfield Joint Record Office
Staffordshire Yeomanry Museum, Stafford
Museum of the Staffordshire Regiment, Whittingham
Lichfield City Council
Lichfield District Council Leisure Services
Alan Williamson - Group Chief Photographer
John Crowe - Photographer, Lichfield Mercury
Trevor Roberts - Lichfield Post Photographer, Birmingham Post and Mail Group
The Friary High School
Central Independent Newspapers
John Rackham LBIPP, President
David Wood
St Mary's Heritage Centre
Terry Finn, Chairman of L.D.C
John Wilson, Past Chairman of Johnson Society
John Sanders M.B.E.
Lorna Bushell
Linda MacCormack
Jean Bird
Mr & Mrs V. Andrews
Graham Beckley LBIPP
Rachel White LBIPP
Jean Quance
Hugh Skemp
Commune de Trieste, Civico Museo
Pauline Duval
Peter Kenny
Pauline Larkin

The publisher would also like to thank John, David and Laura at The Lichfield Collection (St Mary's Heritage Centre)

Chapter 1 – A New Century

The beginning of the twentieth century was a sombre time, not only for Lichfield, but also for the whole nation. In October 1899, war had broken out in South Africa between the British and the Boers. From the start it had gone badly for the British, culminating in the "Black Week" of the 9th to 15th of December, when they suffered three defeats including the Battle of Colenso in which the British suffered 1,127 casualties and the Boers 28.

To help the regular army, the reserves were called up. For the first time in their history the Staffordshire Yeomanry, whose headquarters was at the Friary, Lichfield, were called upon to serve overseas, providing a contingent of 120 men for the Imperial Yeomanry, a regiment formed from volunteers of the various county yeomanry regiments. On a raw winter's evening in January 1900 the contingent, now Number 6 Company of the 4th Battalion, Imperial Yeomanry, paraded at the Friary to entrain at Lichfield City Station for active service in South Africa.

Not long afterwards they were followed by the two militia infantry battalions of the South Staffordshire Regiment, the 3rd and 4th Battalions, in which many Lichfield men served.

As the year 1900 drew to its close, other dark clouds gathered on the horizon. Queen Victoria, who had reigned over the British people for sixty three years, was nearing the end of her life. Soon after the commencement of the new century she passed away on January 22nd, 1901. The feelings of the country, and the people of Lichfield in particular, were typified by the following entry in the minute book of the Lichfield St.John's Lodge of Freemasons, meeting the day after the Queen's death.

"The Worshipful Master most feelingly alluded to the great calamity that had fallen on the nation through the death of our beloved Queen on the previous evening. She would be remembered in the hearts of her people for her wisdom, love of duty, piety and devotion to her country's welfare...."

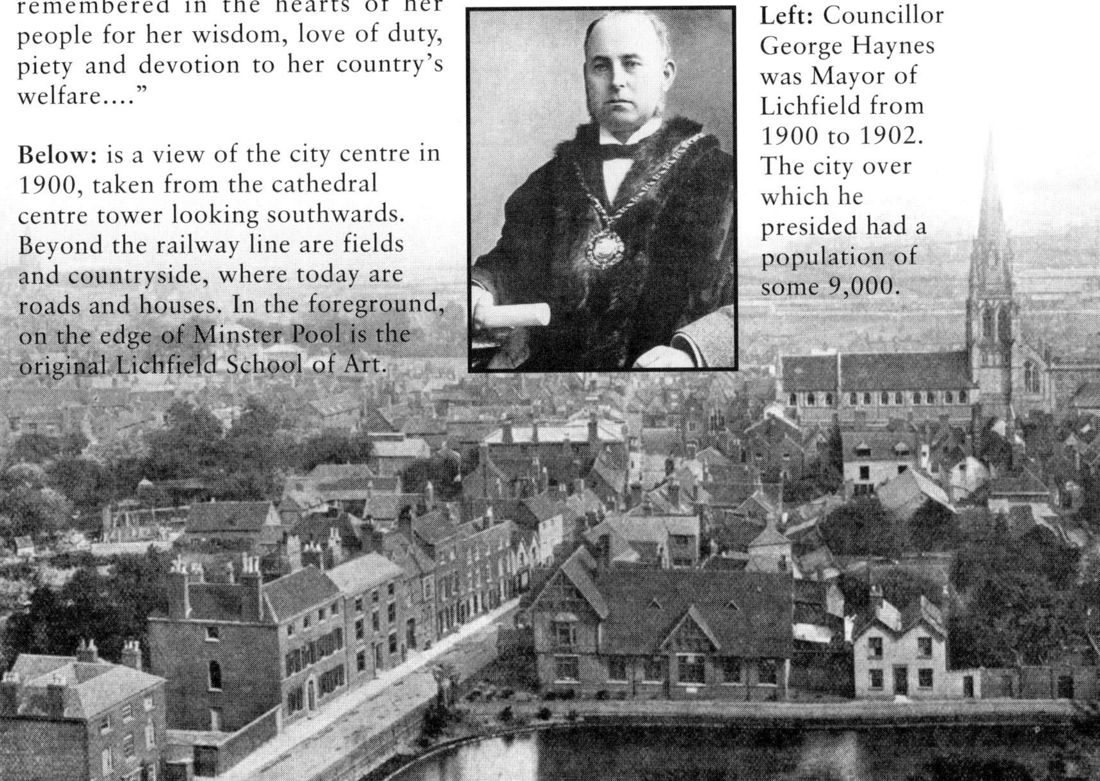

Left: Councillor George Haynes was Mayor of Lichfield from 1900 to 1902. The city over which he presided had a population of some 9,000.

Below: is a view of the city centre in 1900, taken from the cathedral centre tower looking southwards. Beyond the railway line are fields and countryside, where today are roads and houses. In the foreground, on the edge of Minster Pool is the original Lichfield School of Art.

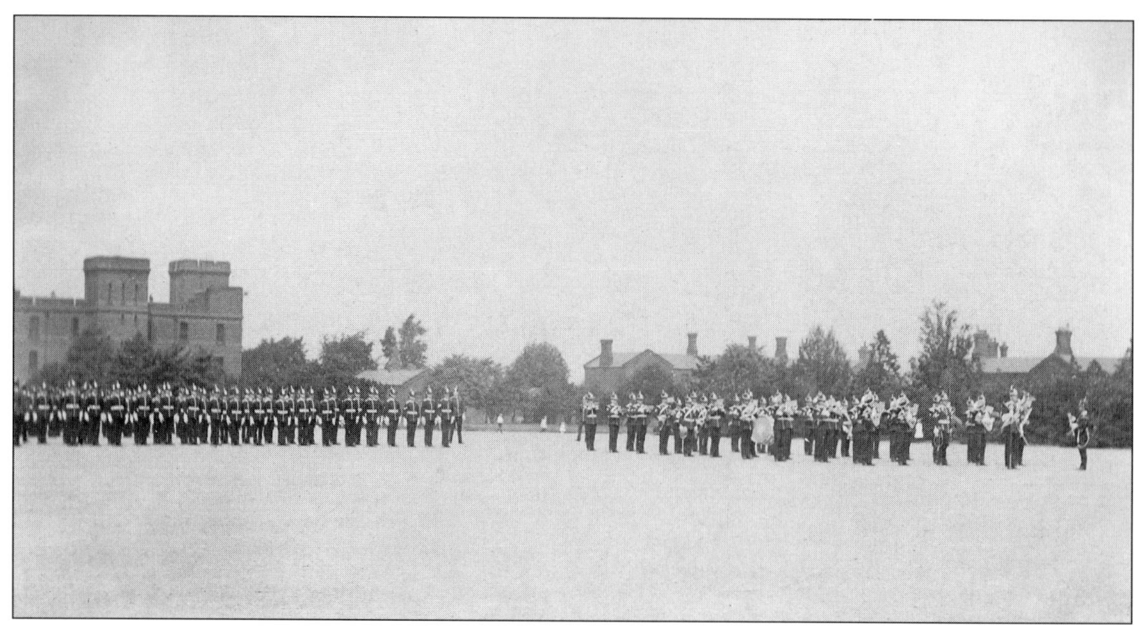

Church Parade at Whittington Barracks, c 1898. The troops are in full dress uniform of helmet, scarlet tunic and dark blue trousers, with white gloves. The regimental band is in attendance.

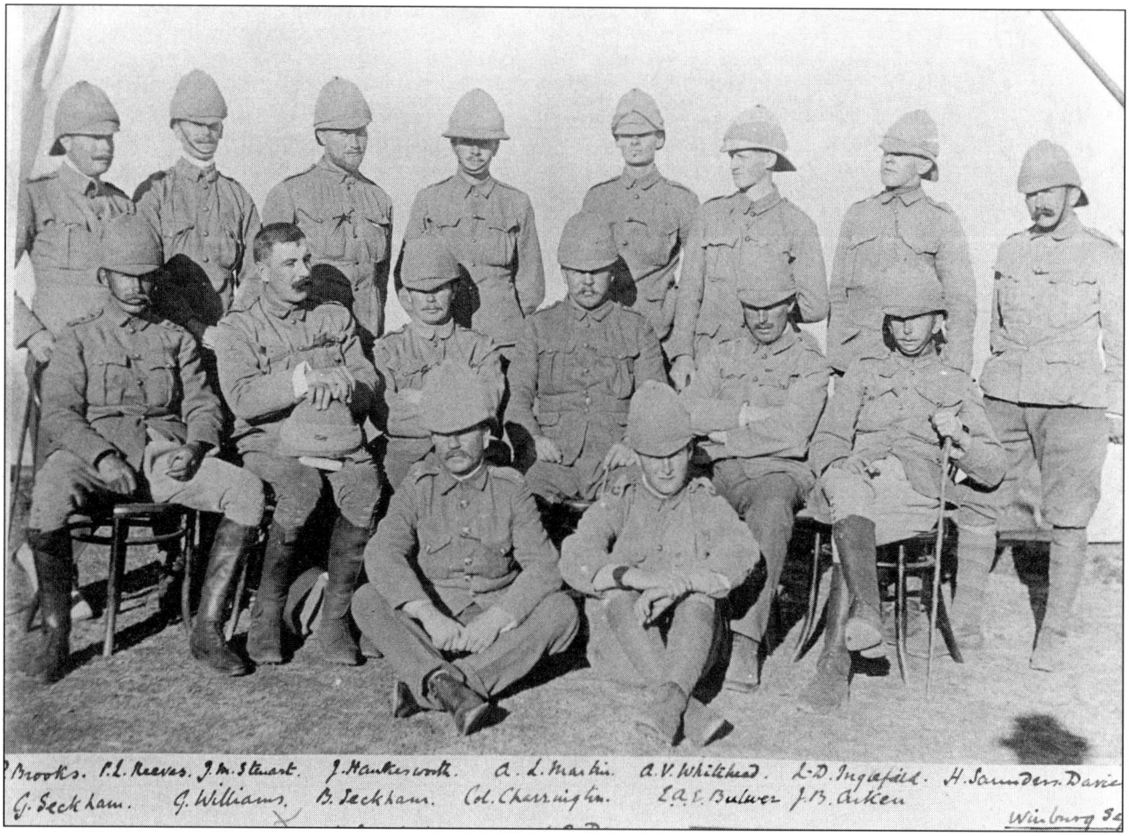

Brooks. P.L. Reeves. J.M. Stewart. J. Hankesworth. A. L. Martin. A.V. Whitehead. L.D. Ingafell. H. Saunders Davies
G. Seckham. G. Williams. B. Seckham. Col. Charrington. E.A.E. Bulwer J.B. Aiken

A group of officers of the 4th (Militia) Battalion, South Staffordshire Regiment on active service in South Africa, 1901. In the group are two sons of Samuel Upscombe Seckham, of Beacon Place, Lichfield.

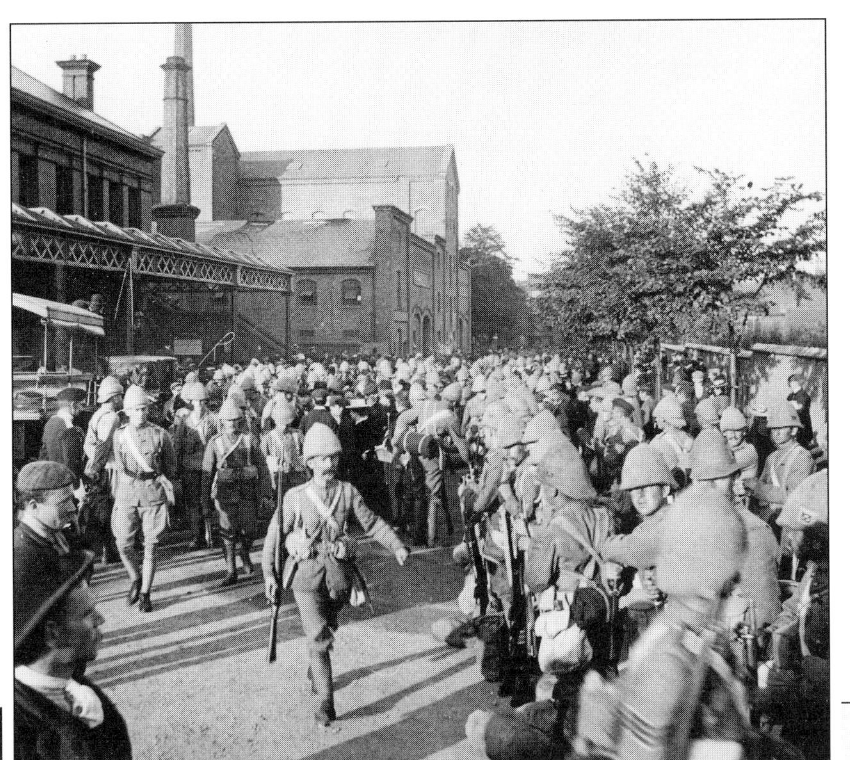

Left: Men of the 4th Battalion, which included many from Lichfield, arriving at Lichfield City Station at 7.15 am in June 1901 on return from service in South Africa.

Below: The troops fell in and marched up St John Street and Bird Street to the Museum Gardens where they were entertained to a breakfast of bacon butties and ale, provided by Lichfield people.

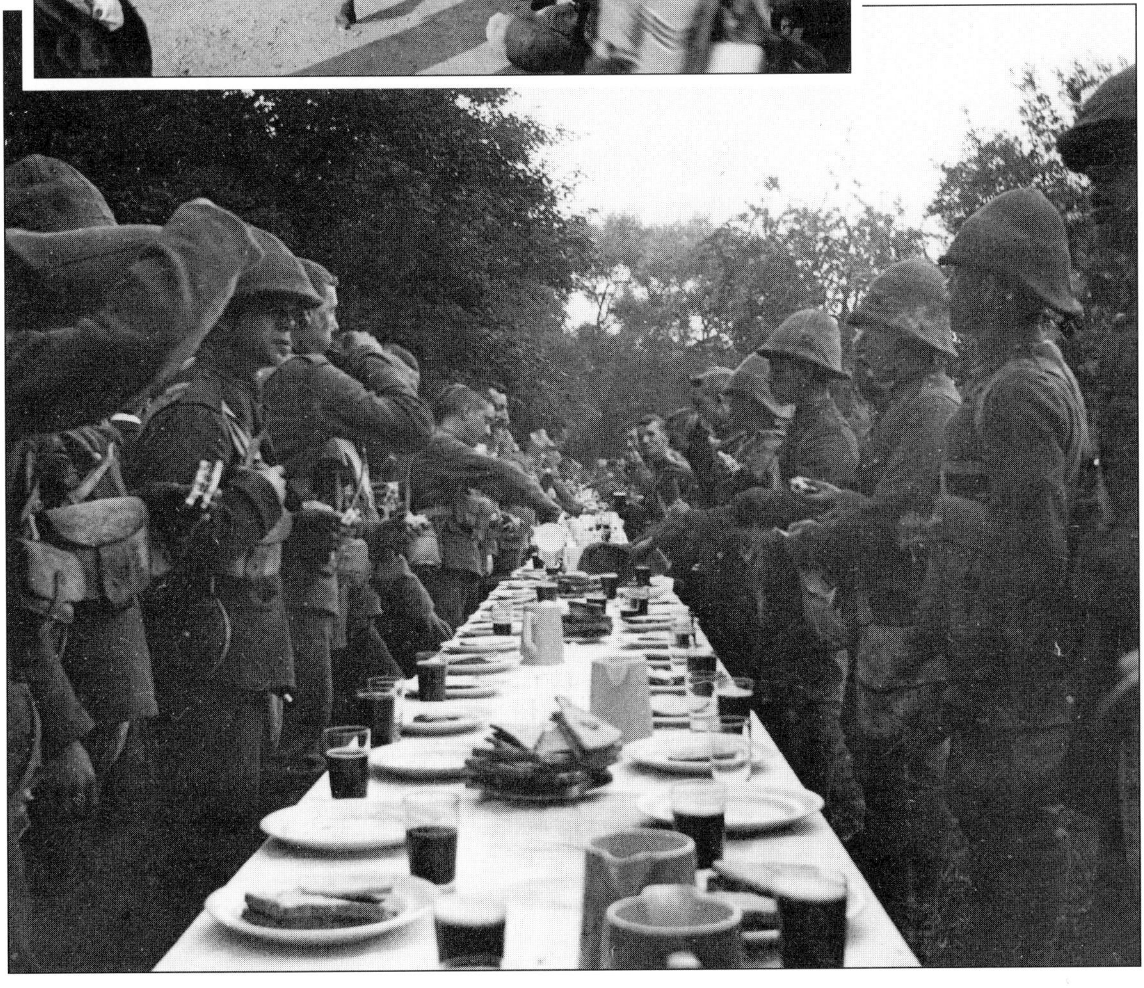

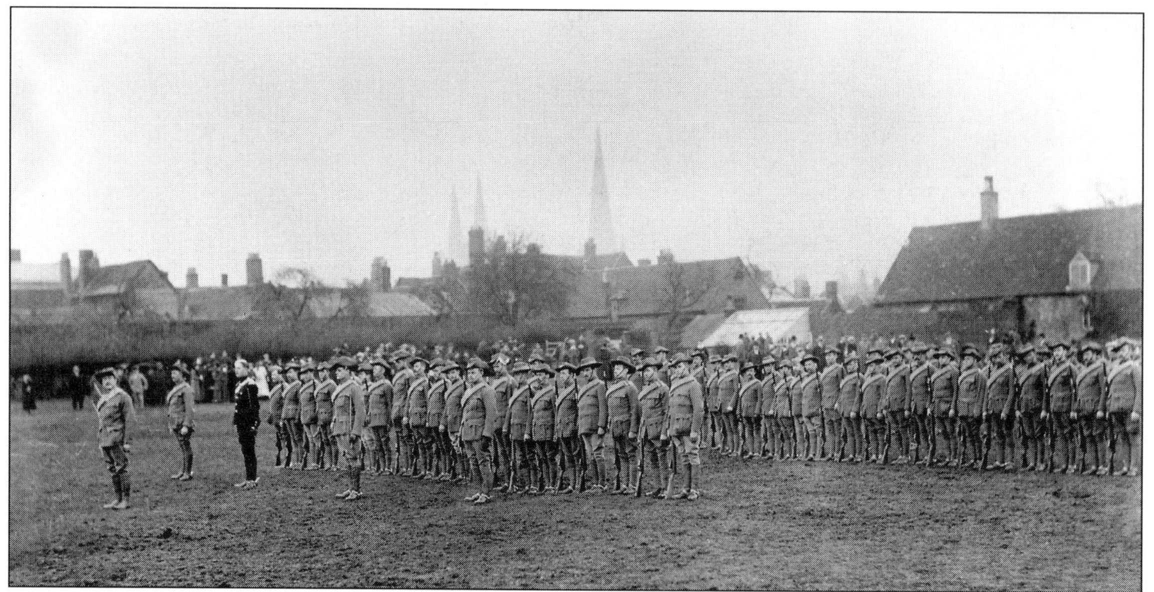

On a dismal January day, 1900, volunteers from the Staffordshire Yeomanry contingent of the Imperial Yeomanry paraded outside their H.Q. at the Friary, Lichfield before entraining at the City Station for service in South Africa. Among the 120 volunteers were several Lichfield men.

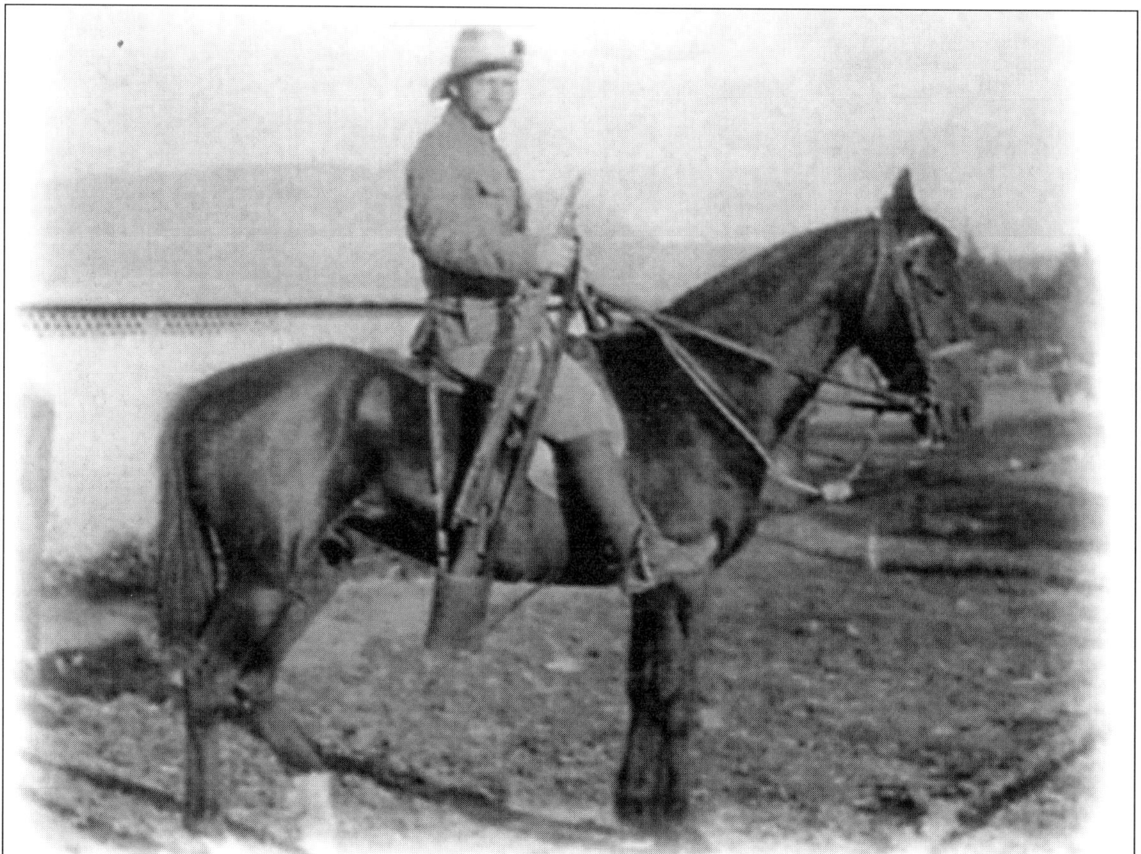

One of the contingent on service in South Africa. The Imperial Yeomanry acted as mounted infantry and were armed with the Long Lee Enfield rifle as shown here.

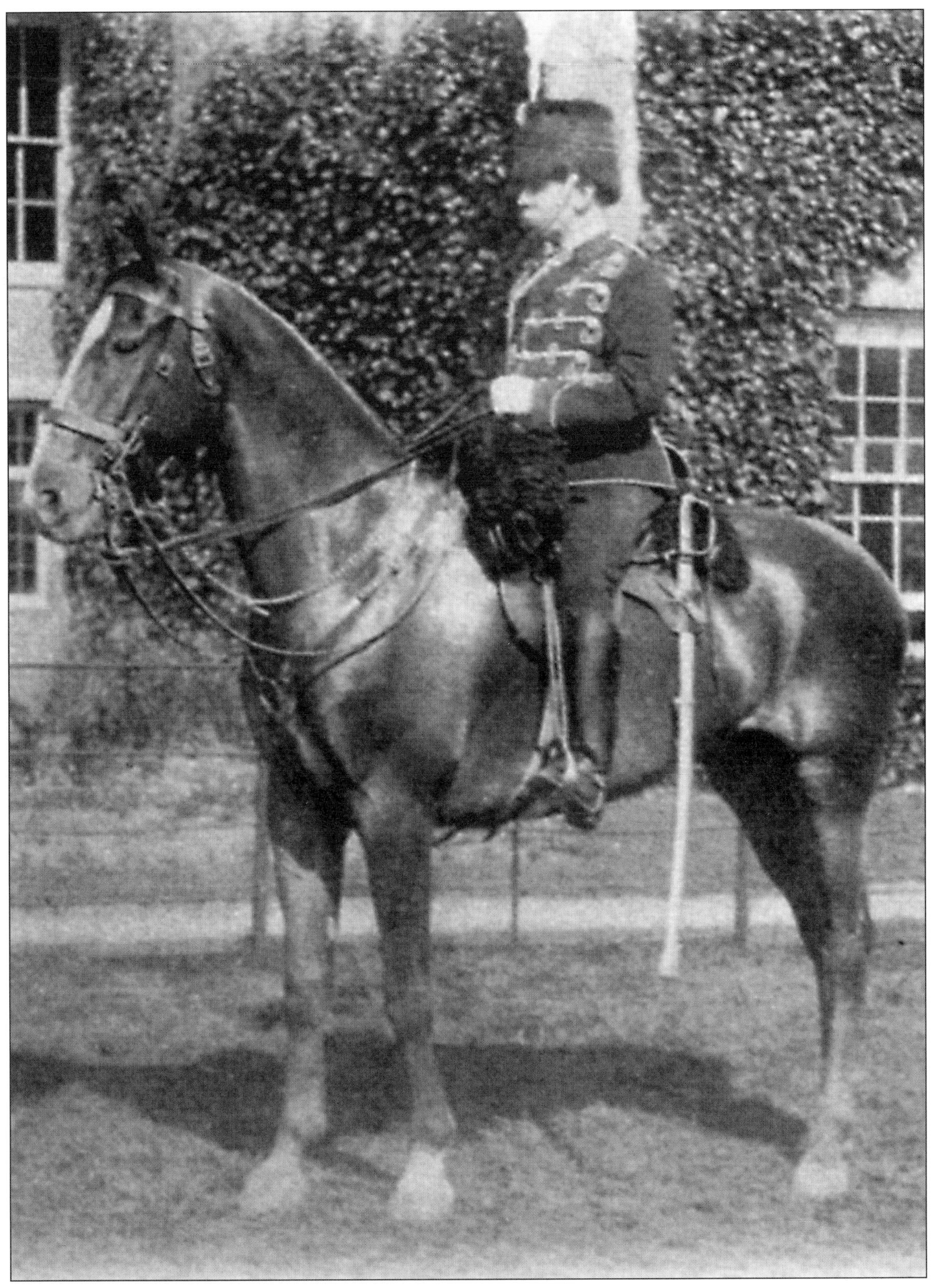

R.S.M. (Regimental Sergeant Major) Brown, Staffordshire Yeomanry. c 1900.

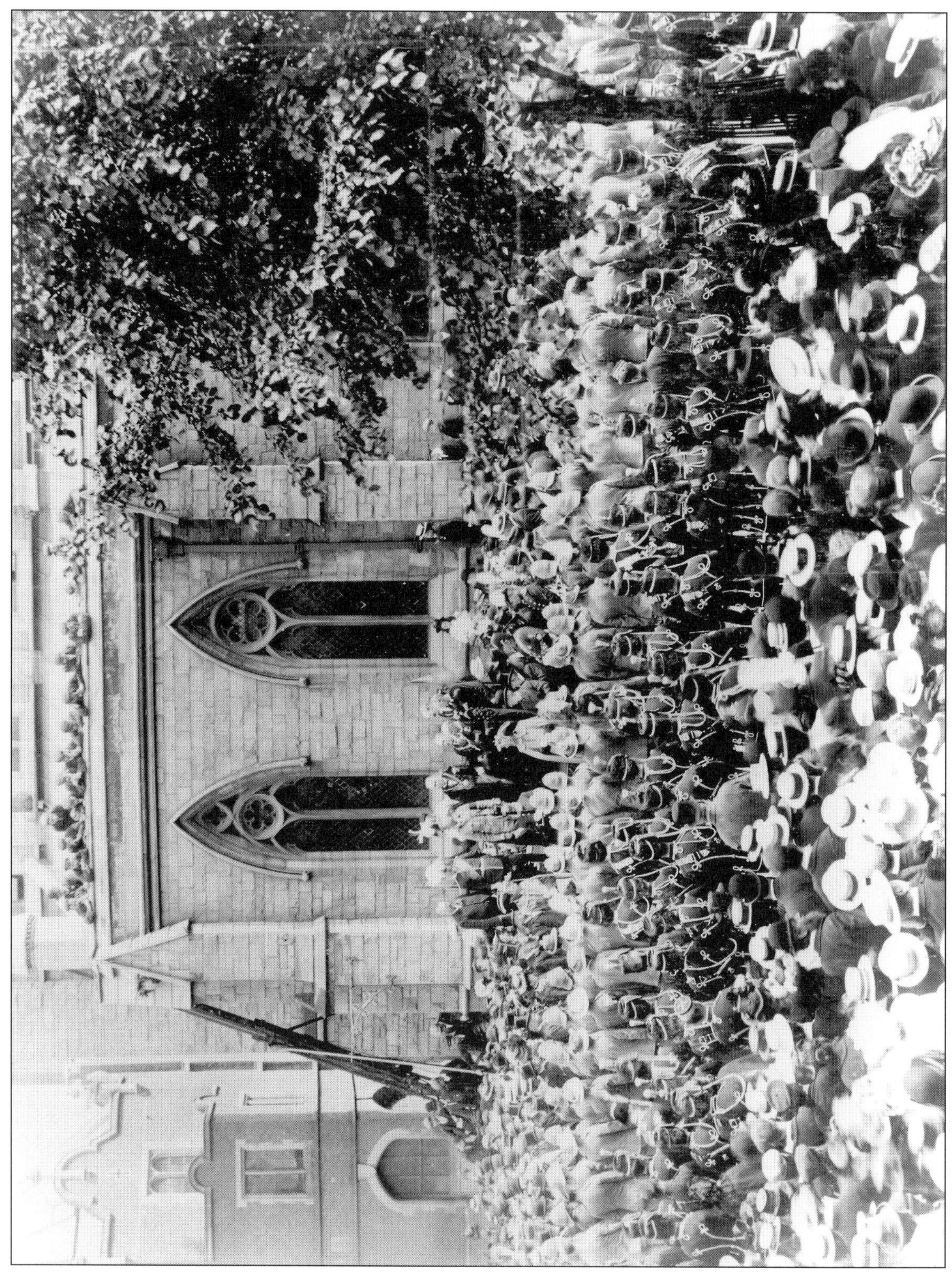

Below: The High Sheriff of Staffordshire gave a luncheon to the contingent of Staffordshire Yeomanry, in Lichfield Guildhall.

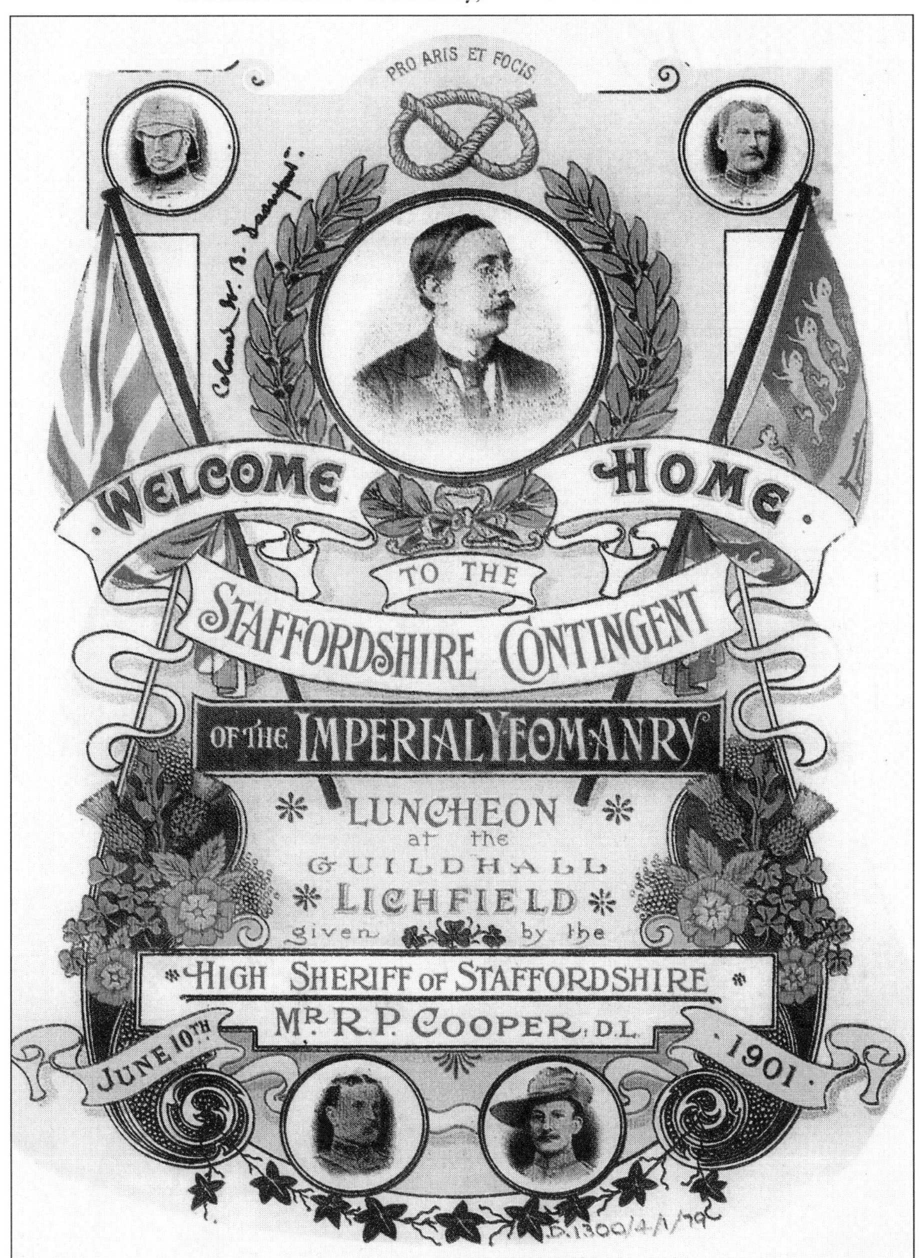

Opposite page: The return from active service in South Africa of the Staffordshire Yeomanry contingent They are being welcomed formally by the High Sheriff of Staffordshire, Mr Richard Powell Cooper, D.L. This interesting scene, in Lichfield Market Place, shows in the foreground the general public (straw boater hats seem to be fashionable). Beyond them, is the Yeomany band in full dress uniform, having just marched the troops from the City Station. Then come the volunteers themselves, still in their khaki service dress, and facing them are the V.I.Ps on a platform. Most interesting of all is the group of small boys watching the proceedings from the roof of St. Mary's church. How did they get there? The answer is on the left where the city fire brigade used to park their escape ladder – a challange to any enterprising youth. As a result the fire brigade later moved their ladder to the west end of the church where there was no access to the roof.

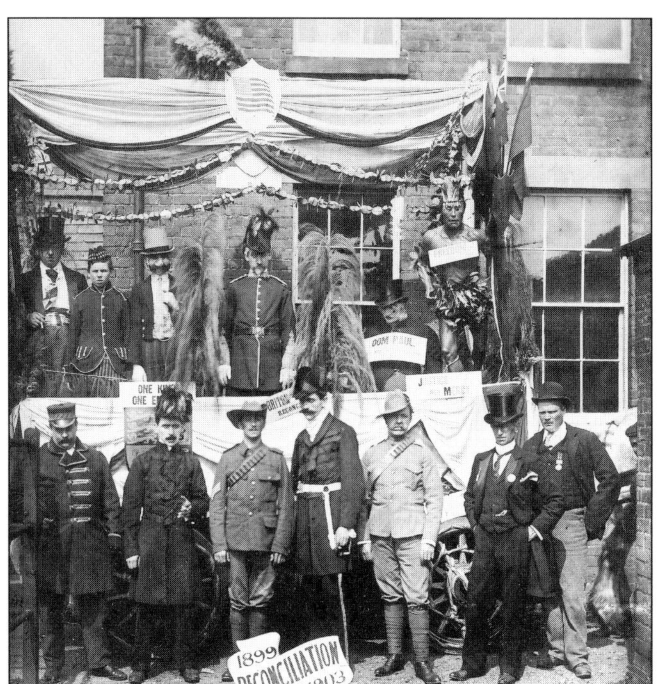

The Lichfield Bower is an occasion peculiar to Lichfield, based on the mediaeval Arraye of Arms. It takes place on Whit Monday and includes a procession through the streets of the city.

In 1903 the procession included this float commemorating peace in South Africa.

Among the motley collection of uniforms that are being worn are two of the Imperial Yeomanry – khaki service dress with bandolier and slouch hat (turned up at one side so that the wearer can slope arms). But why the stars and stripes at the top of the float? This was one war which the United States was not involved in.

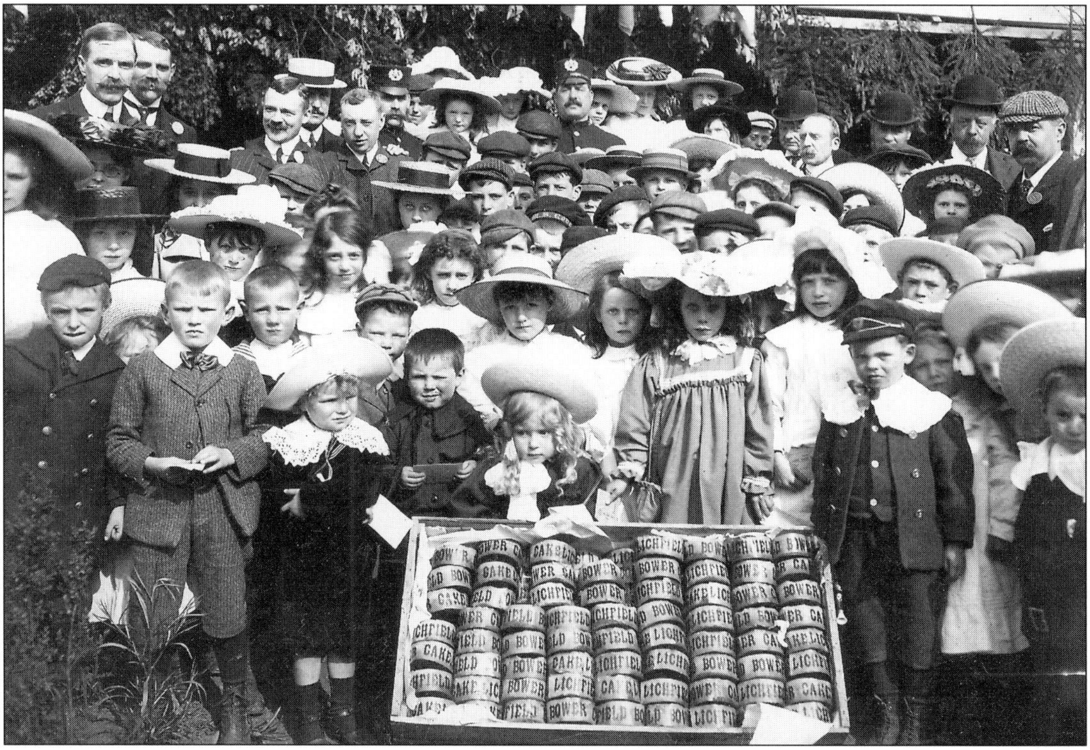

Another picture of the 1903 Bower. Originally visitors to the Bower were entertained to roast beef and wine. Later this was reduced to cakes and ale. By 1903 there were just cakes, distributed to a few favoured children, seen here. About 1980 even this was discontinued on the grounds of economy. The cakes were baked to a secret receipe, still jealously guarded by the Bower Committee.

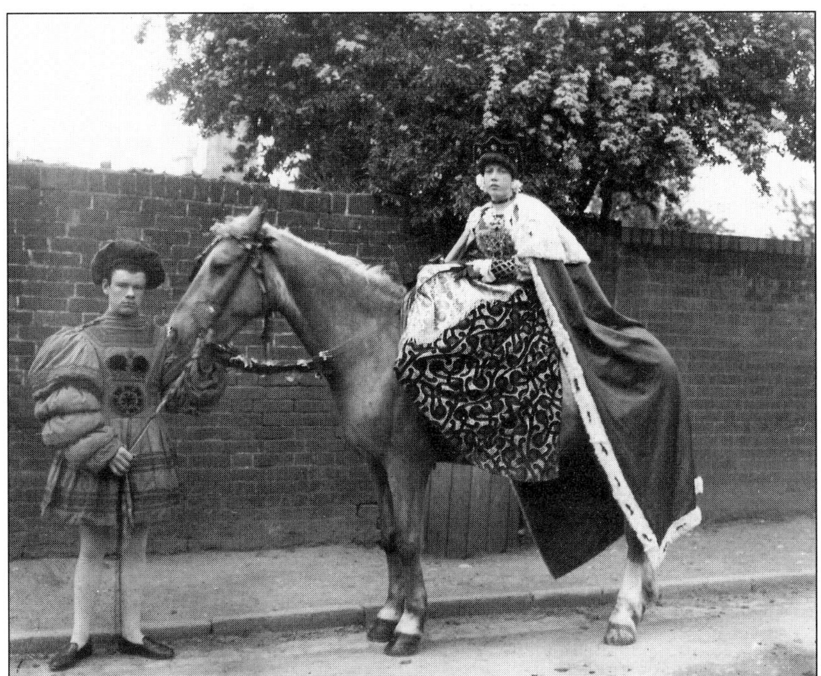

In the same procession was this young lady as "Queen of the May", standing appropriately in front of a may tree in blossom. The Bower has always had a mediaeval atmosphere about it.

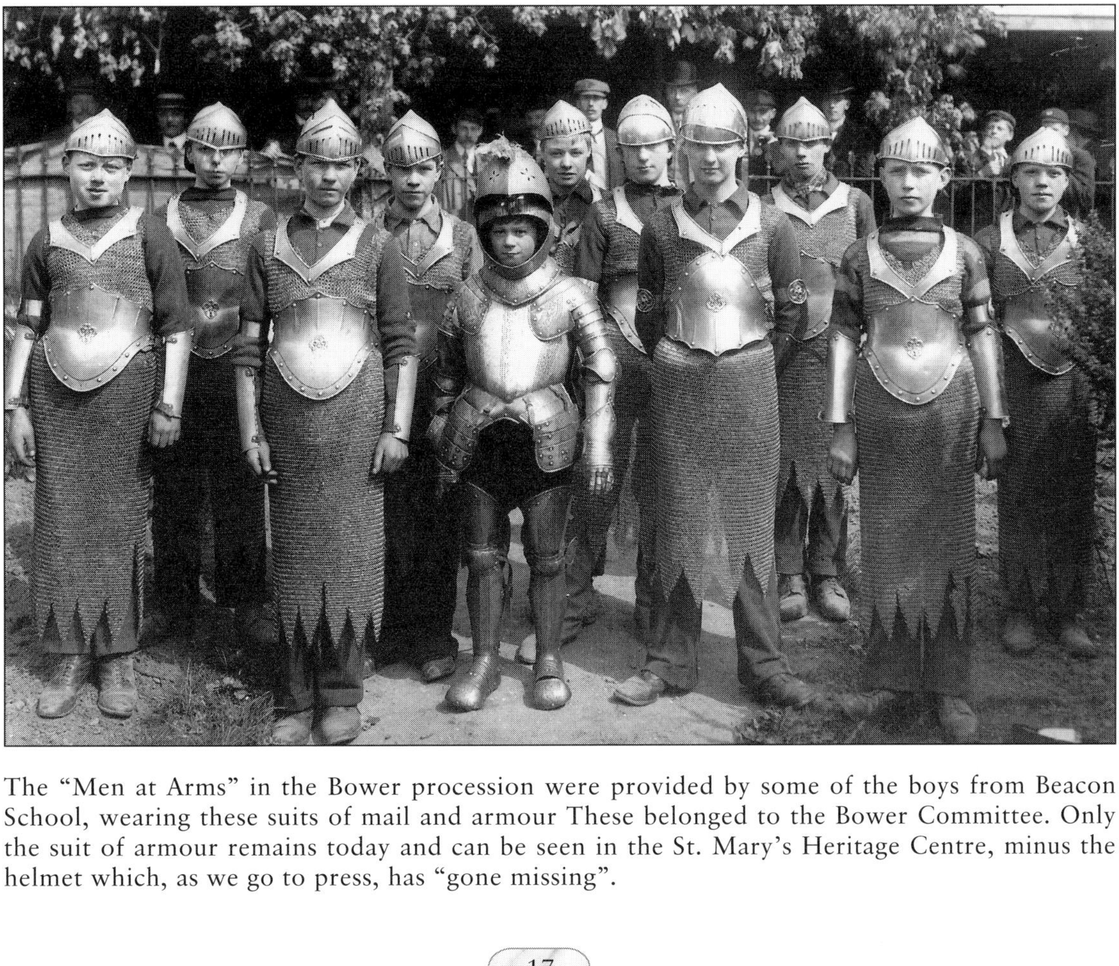

The "Men at Arms" in the Bower procession were provided by some of the boys from Beacon School, wearing these suits of mail and armour These belonged to the Bower Committee. Only the suit of armour remains today and can be seen in the St. Mary's Heritage Centre, minus the helmet which, as we go to press, has "gone missing".

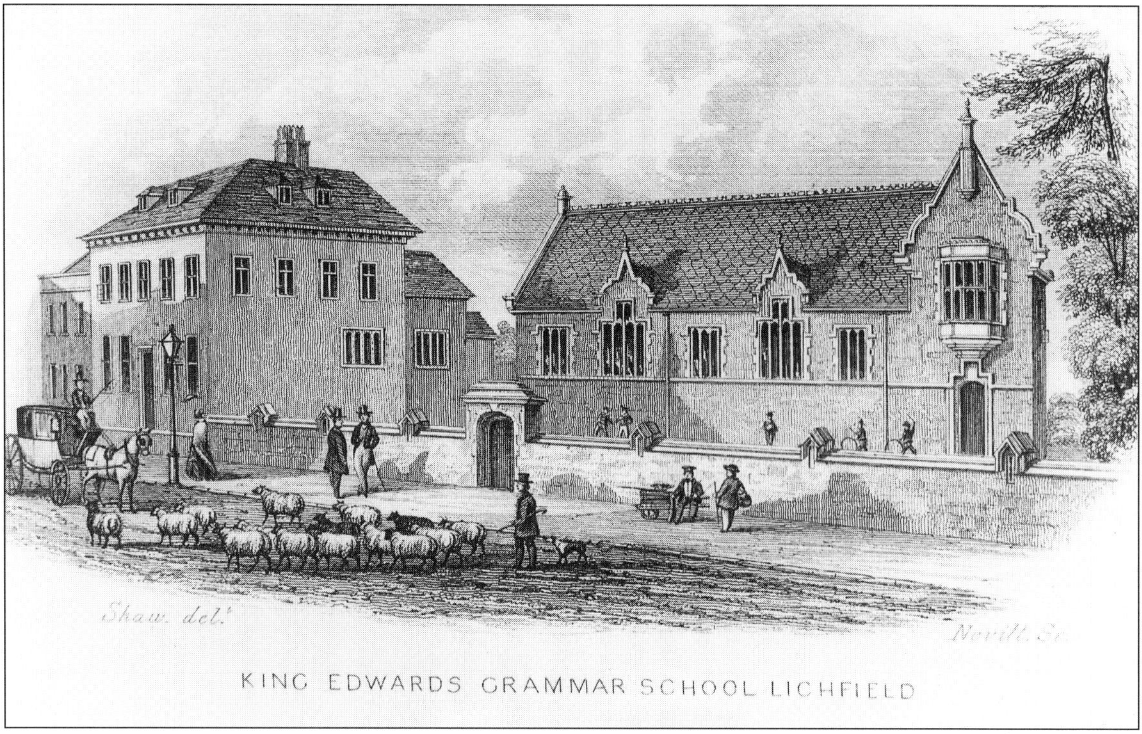

Shaw. del.

Novill. Sc.

KING EDWARDS GRAMMAR SCHOOL LICHFIELD

King Edward's Grammar School, Lichfield, has an ancient lineage, dating from 1497. Two school buildings occupied this site, but by 1902, with some 100 pupils, it had outgrown its town centre position.

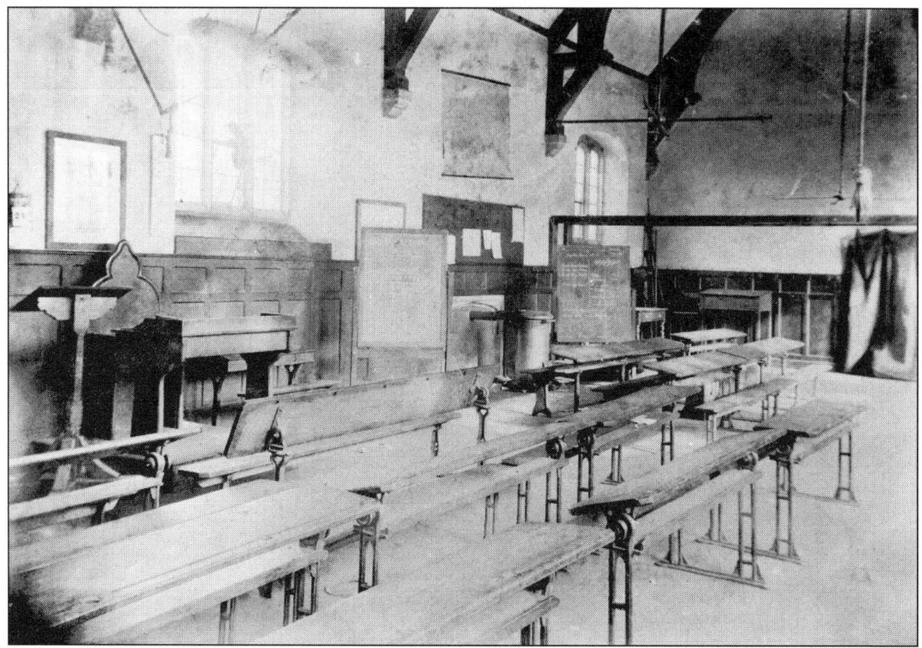

This picture of the interior of the school vividly illustrates the cramped conditions. Fortunately that great Lichfield institution, the Conduit Lands Trust, came to the rescue with a gift of five acres of land at Borrowcop Hill on the outskirts of the city together with £5,200 towards the cost of a new building.

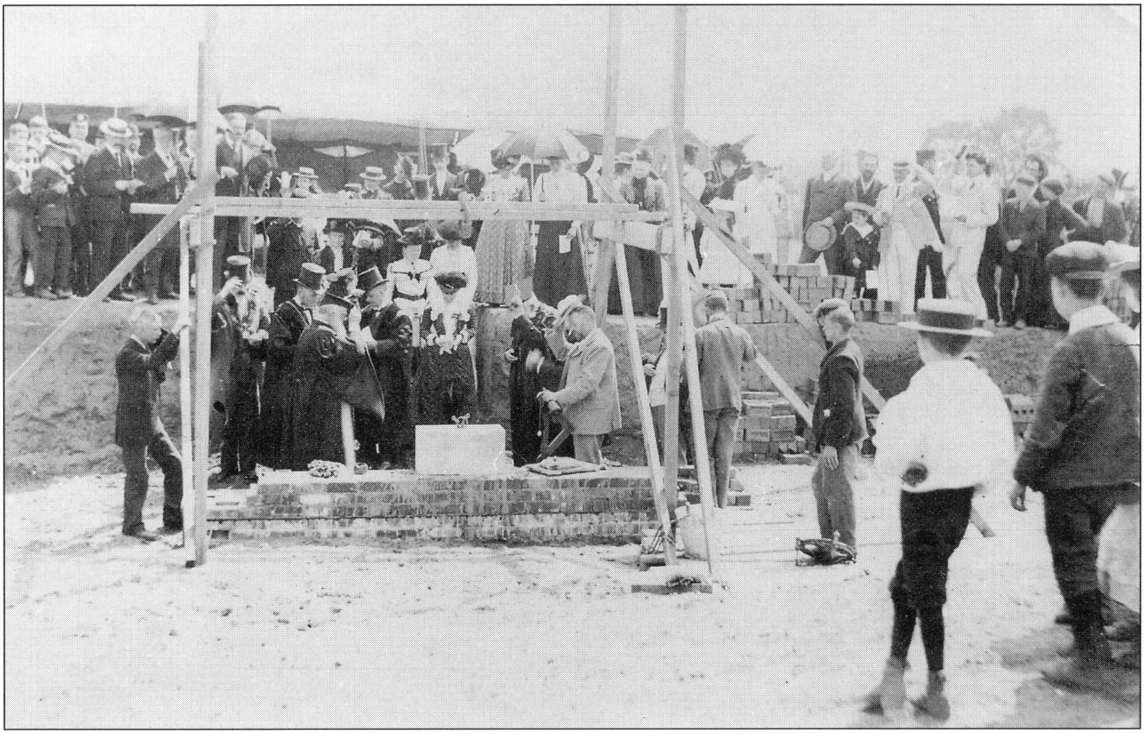

The foundation stone of the new school was laid in 1901, and the building was ready for occupation in January 1903.

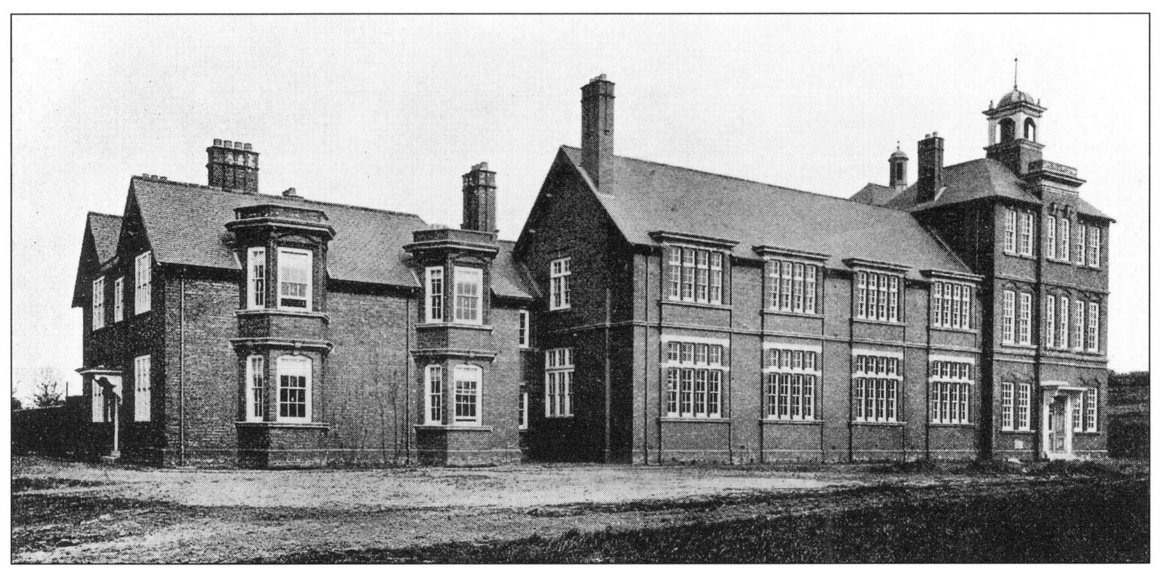

This photograph of the new school from the south immediately brings to mind the similarity in plan of the old and new buildings. In each case there is a headmaster's house and a large schoolroom ("Big School") adjoining. At the other end of the schoolroom is an additional block higher and wider, containing smaller rooms as well as the main entrance and lobby. The new school is the old school writ large. The "Big School" now has an upper floor containing dormitories, while the entrance block has three floors and contains science labs and a staff common room (full time staff at this stage was the headmaster and two assistants).

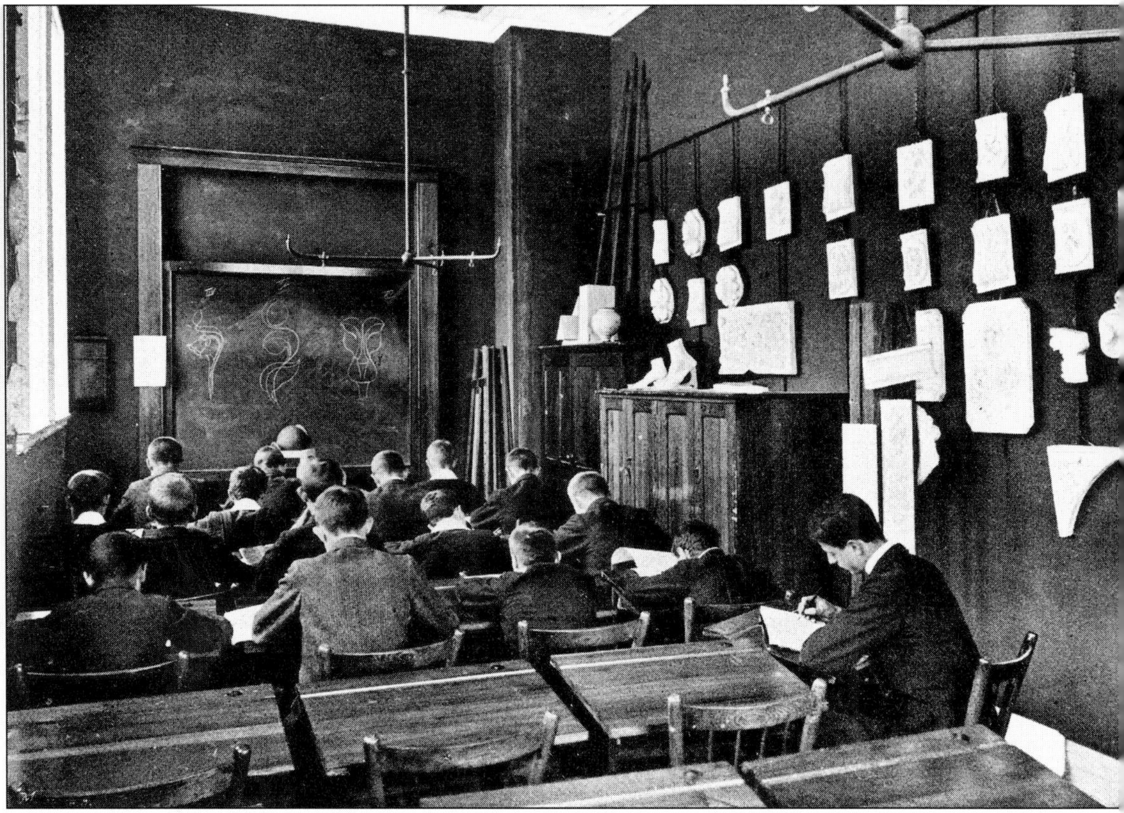

The Art Room, with a class in progress – its size would make any teacher of today envious.

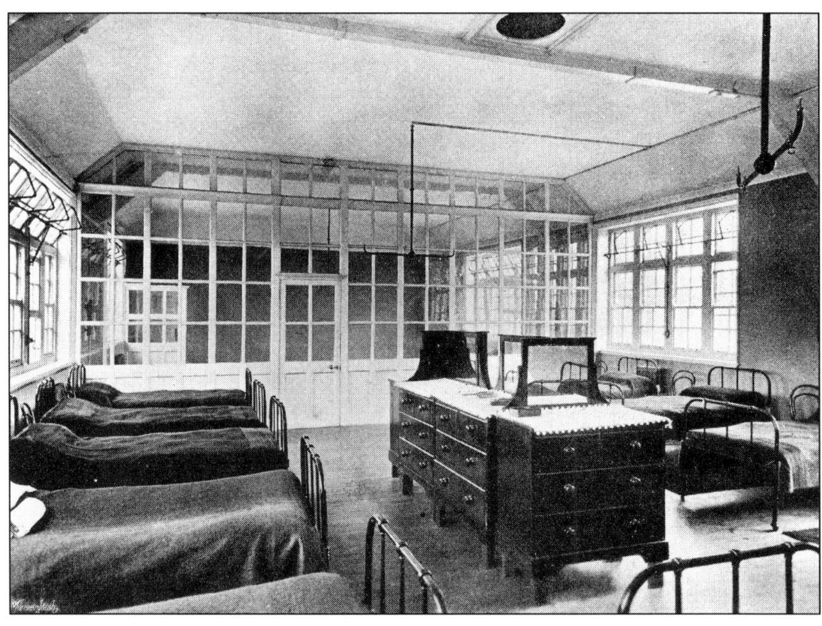

The dormitory, above Big School.

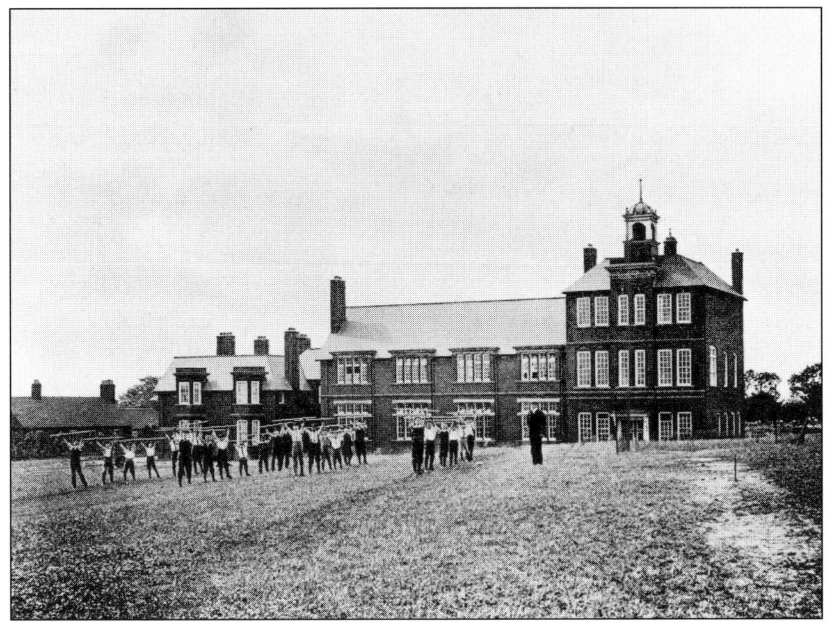

Physical training on the cricket field. The first century to be scored here was in 1907, a fact recorded on a stone nearby.

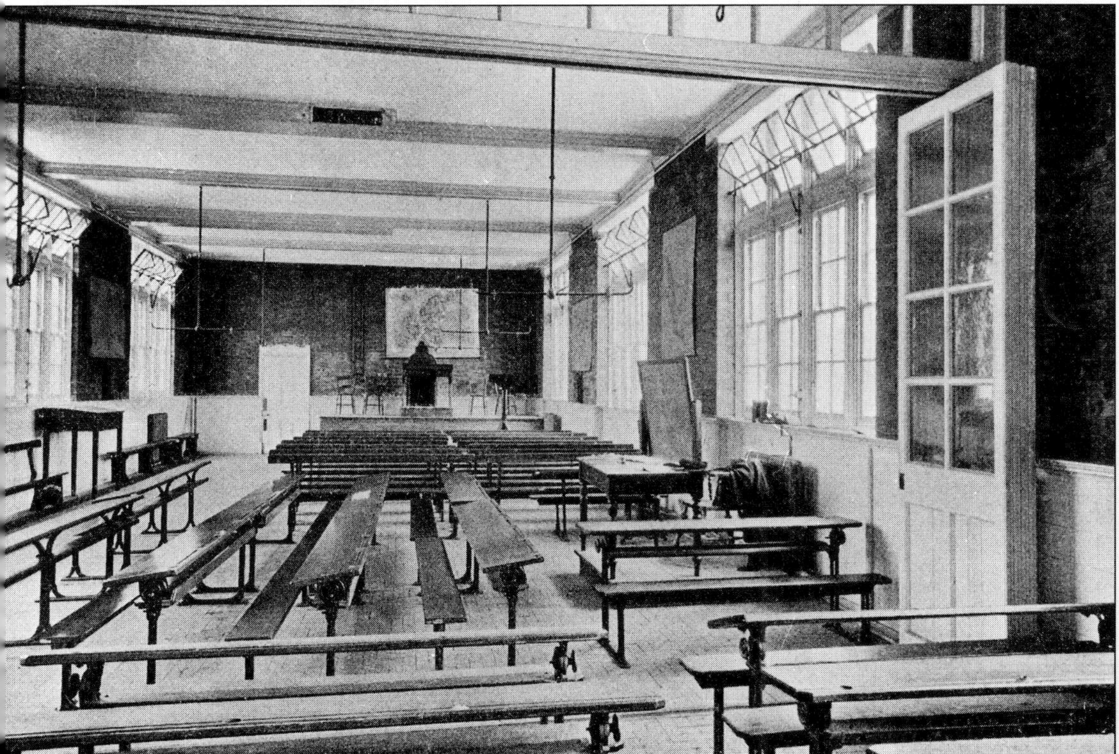

Big School. Here were held school assemblies, Speech Days, concerts and any special occasion. At other times it served as three classrooms.

Previous Performances by the Society:

SHERWOOD'S QUEEN, 1896. THE MANDARIN, 1897—*and a repeat Performance by general request.*
H. M. S. PINAFORE, 1898. PIRATES OF PENZANCE, 1899. THE YEOMAN OF THE GUARD, 1900.
IOLANTHE, 1901. THE MIKADO, 1902. PATIENCE, 1903.
THE SORCERER, 1904.

St. James's Hall, Lichfield.

The Lichfield Amateur Opera Society

(Affiliated to the National Amateur Operatic & Dramatic Association),

WILL GIVE THREE PERFORMANCES ON

Wednesday, Thursday & Friday in Easter Week,

APRIL 26th, 27th & 28th, 1905,

OF

THE CELEBRATED ORIGINAL COMIC OPERA,

The Gondoliers,

OR

THE KING OF BARATARIA,

Written by W. S. GILBERT. Music by SIR A. SULLIVAN.

IN AID OF THE LICHFIELD VICTORIA NURSING HOME.

SPECIAL ENGAGEMENT OF

MISS EDITH WELLING.

Orchestra & Chorus of about Seventy.

HON. CONDUCTOR - - - MR. J. GLADMAN.

These performances will be given by special permission of Mrs. H. D'Oyly Carte, who also kindly allows the Orchestral parts used at the Savoy Theatre.

Doors Open at 7 30. Commence at 8 (Overture at 7-55). Carriages at 10-30. Doors open to Ticket Holders at 7-15.

PRICES OF ADMISSION.

Reserved Floor, 3s. 6d. and 2s.; Reserved Centre Balcony, 2s. 6d.;
Reserved Side Balcony, 2s.; Unreserved Balcony and Floor, 1s.

Plan of Reserved Seats, and Tickets, at A. C. Lomax's Successors. The Plan will be open on Tuesday. April 11th.
One Shilling Tickets may also be had from Members of the Society.

SPECIAL SCENERY.

Splendid Costumes & Wigs by Messrs. B. & H. Drury, of Brighton.

LIMELIGHT BY MR. W. G. PORTER, TAMWORTH.

Above: Lichfield Operatic Society's offering for 1903.

Opposite page: At the beginning of the twentieth century Lichfield had a flourishing amateur operatic society which every year produced a show (generally Gilbert & Sullivan). In 1905 it was *The Gondoliers*. Edith Welling who frequently took the leading role was the prima donna of the Brighton and Hove Amateur Operatic Society who kept up her semi-professional career long enough to appear on BBC television. She can be seen in the front row of the photograph, the only one not in costume.

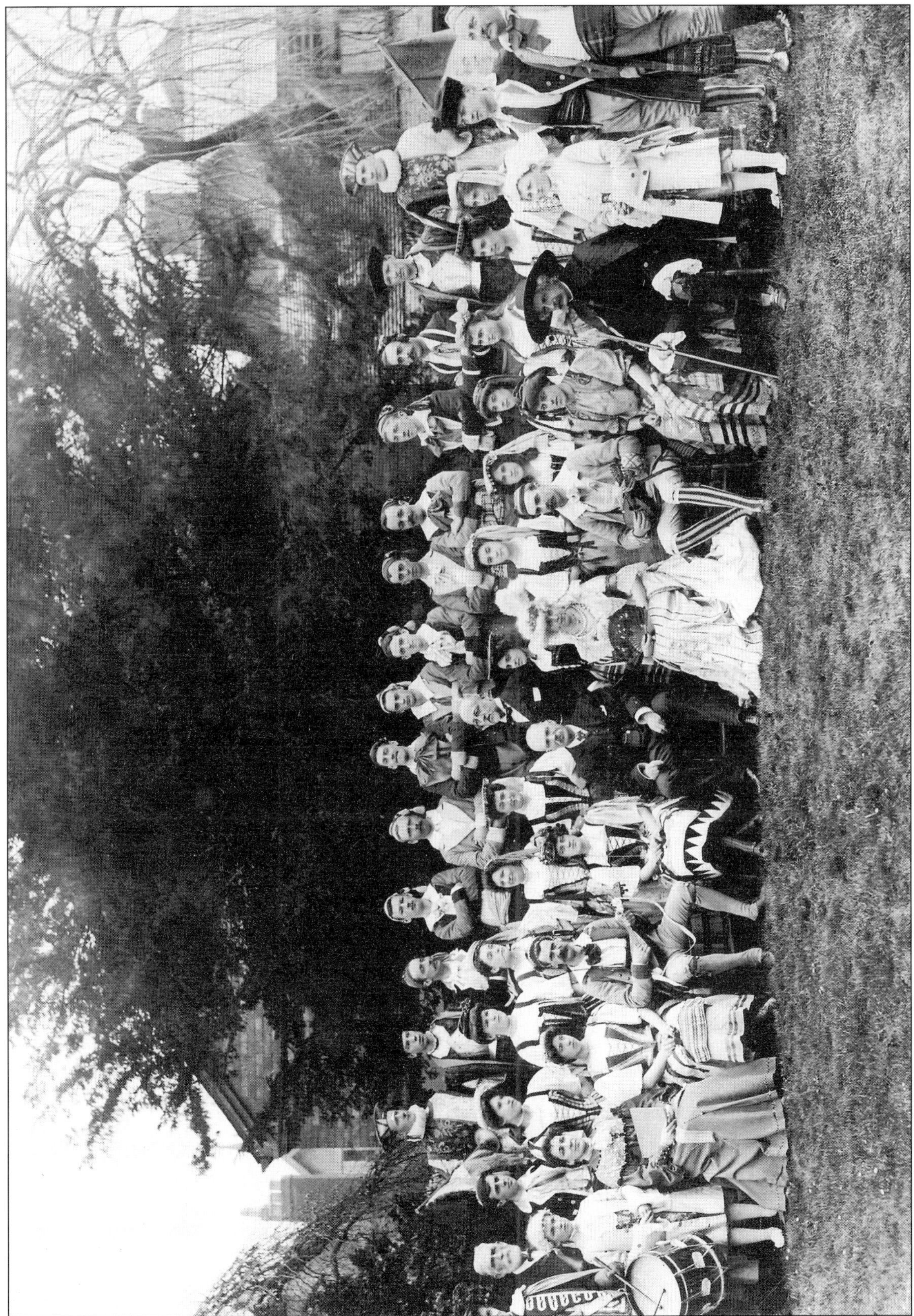

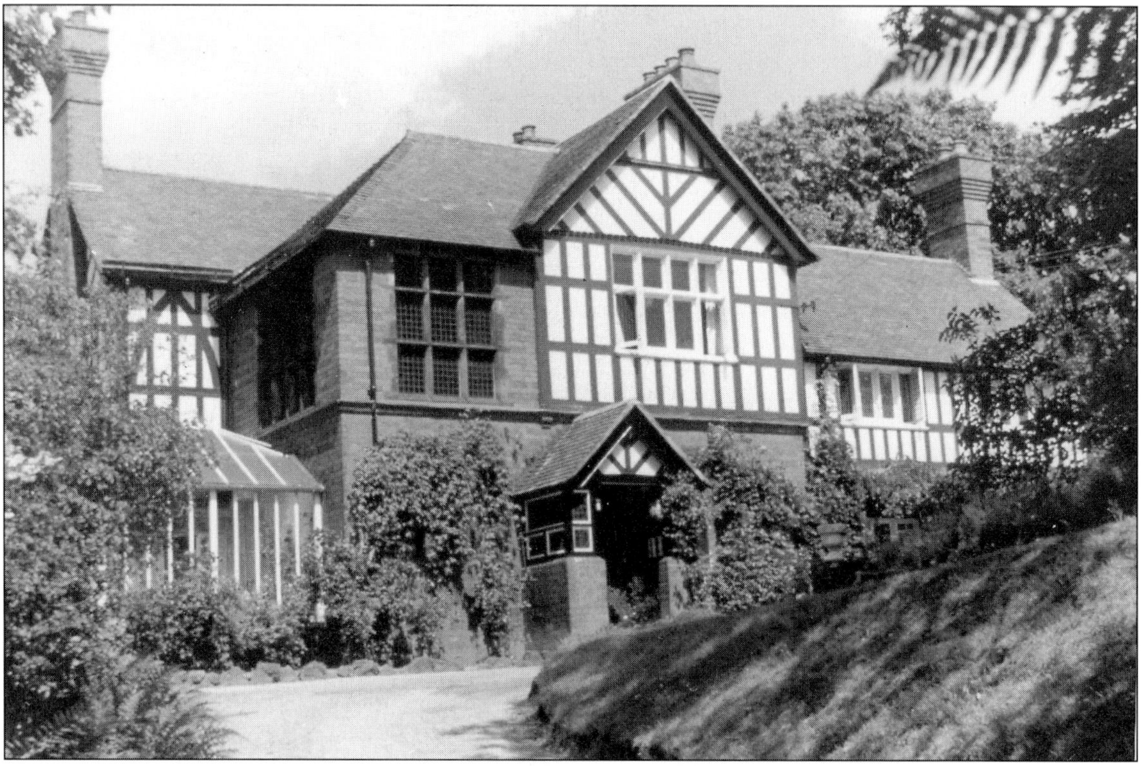

In 1907, the Mayor of Lichfield, Cllr. Reginald Coleridge Roberts, gave a dinner party for his fellow councillors at his home at Rocklands (above). It is interesting to see what a typical Edwardian menu contained and what music they listened to. There were 24 councillors and the Town Clerk, and the mystery is how they all got into the dining room. Rocklands is now a children's day nursery.

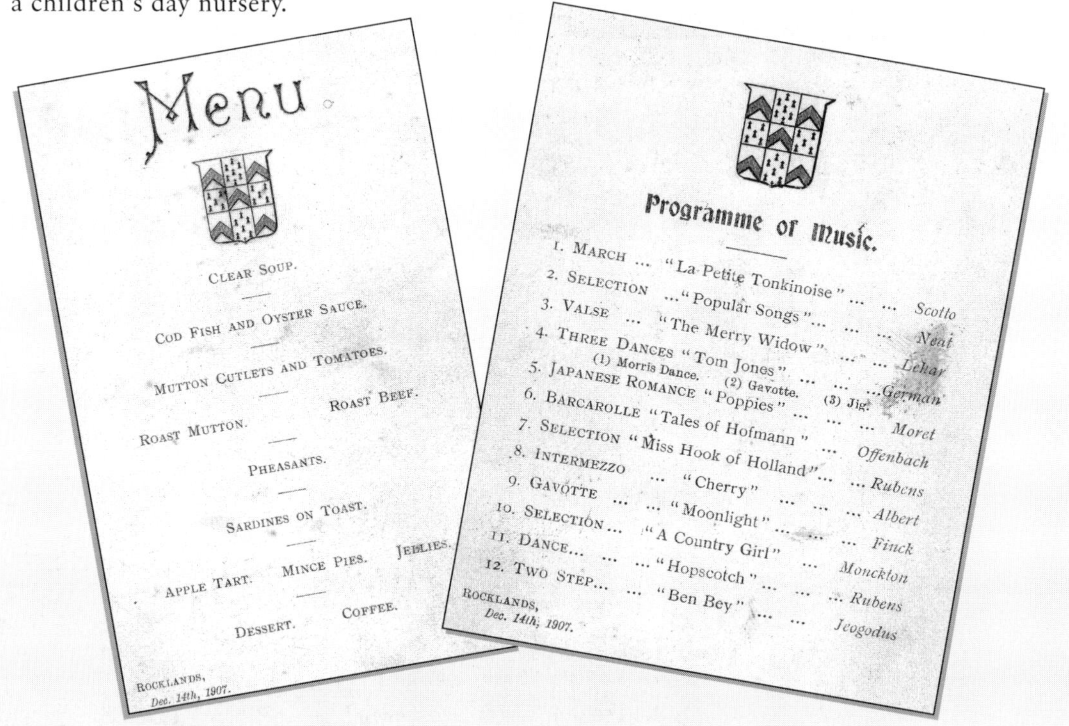

Menu

Clear Soup.

Cod Fish and Oyster Sauce.

Mutton Cutlets and Tomatoes.

Roast Mutton. Roast Beef.

Pheasants.

Sardines on Toast.

Apple Tart. Mince Pies. Jellies.

Dessert. Coffee.

Rocklands,
Dec. 14th, 1907.

Programme of Music.

1. March ... "La Petite Tonkinoise" ... ... Scotto
2. Selection ... "Popular Songs" ... ... Neat
3. Valse ... "The Merry Widow" ... ... Lehar
4. Three Dances "Tom Jones" ... ... German
(1) Morris Dance. (2) Gavotte. (3) Jig.
5. Japanese Romance "Poppies" ... ... Moret
6. Barcarolle "Tales of Hofmann" ... Offenbach
7. Selection "Miss Hook of Holland" ... ... Rubens
8. Intermezzo ... "Cherry" ... ... Albert
9. Gavotte ... ... "Moonlight" ... ... Finck
10. Selection ... "A Country Girl" ... Monckton
11. Dance ... ... "Hopscotch" ... ... Rubens
12. Two Step ... ... "Ben Bey" ... ... Jeogodus

Rocklands,
Dec. 14th, 1907.

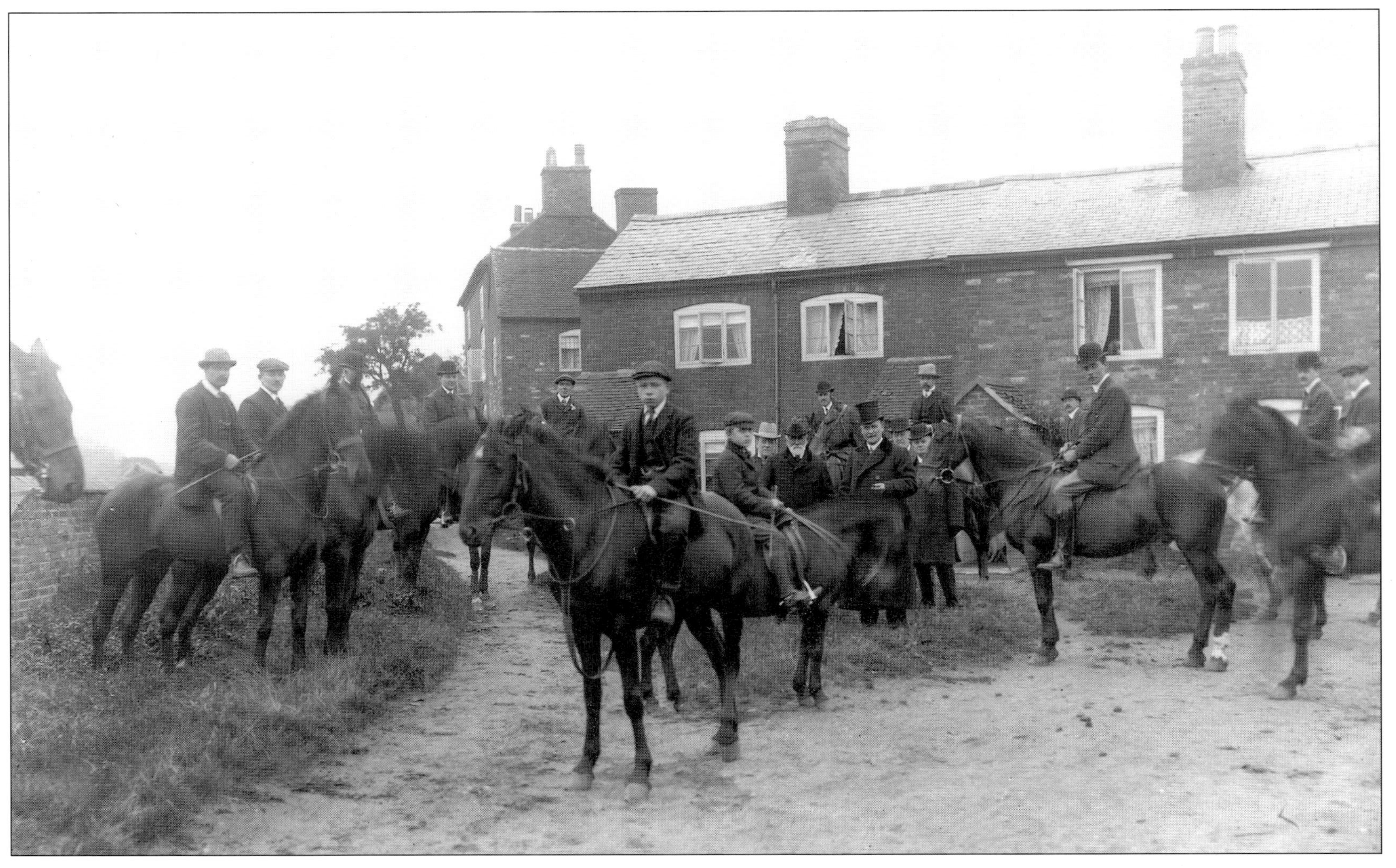

The Sheriff's Ride is a traditional part of Lichfield's civic life. In 1553, Queen Mary granted a charter to the city which gave it the status of a county, 'The City and County of the City of Lichfield". As such it had a Sheriff, an office still in force today, and once a year the Sheriff is required to perambulate the bounds of the city on horseback. This takes place in September, and has been carried out every year since 1553.

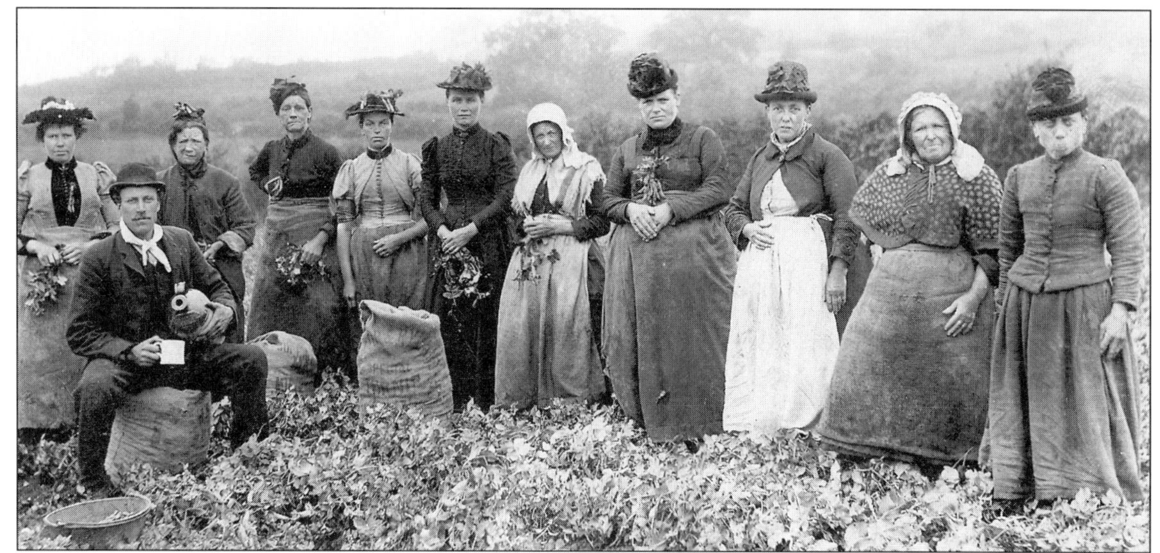

The area around Lichfield was, and still is, famous for its horticultural products, which supplied the markets in Birmingham and Wolverhampton. Peas, beans, broccoli and root crops are the staple produce. Here a party of pea-pickers of around 1900 is assembled.

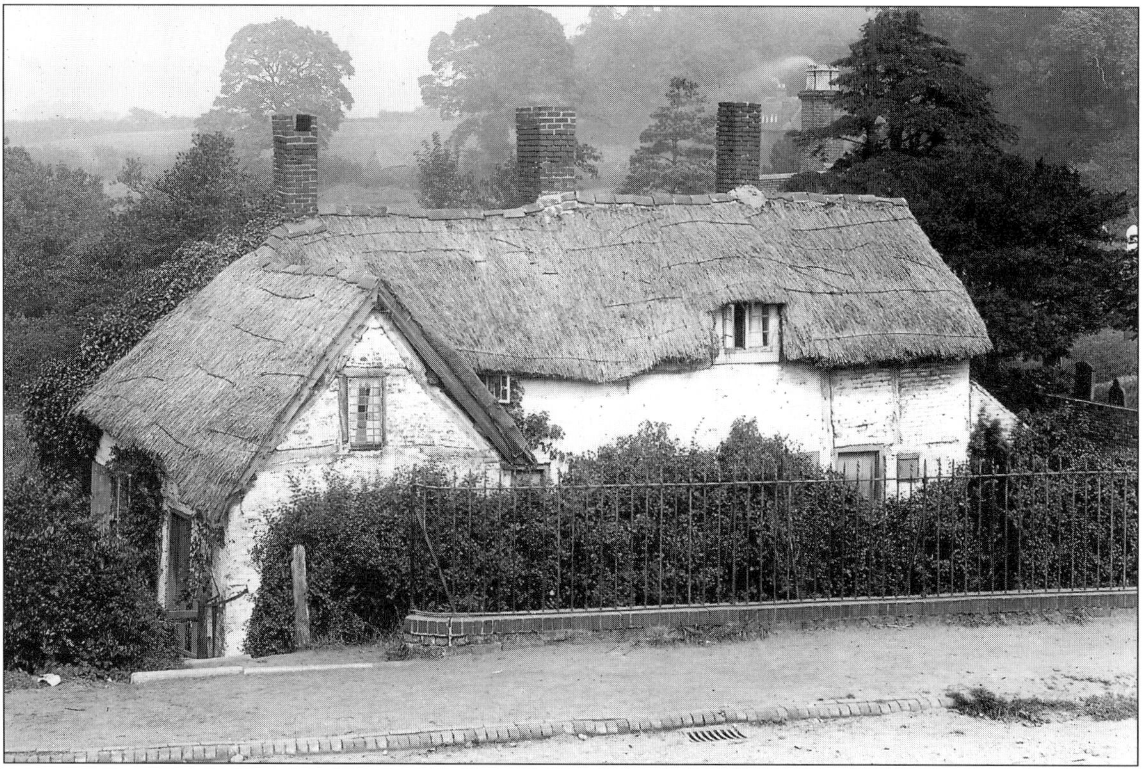

Before the days of municipal housing, many of the pea-pickers shown above may have lived in dwellings similar to those seen here. Situated in St. Chad's churchyard, they were built by the contractor who restored the church after the civil war of 1642–1646, for use by his workmen. Having finished the job, he handed over the cottages to the Rector with the words: 'They are of little worth'. So they became known as *Littleworth Cottages* from then until they were condemned and demolished in 1949.

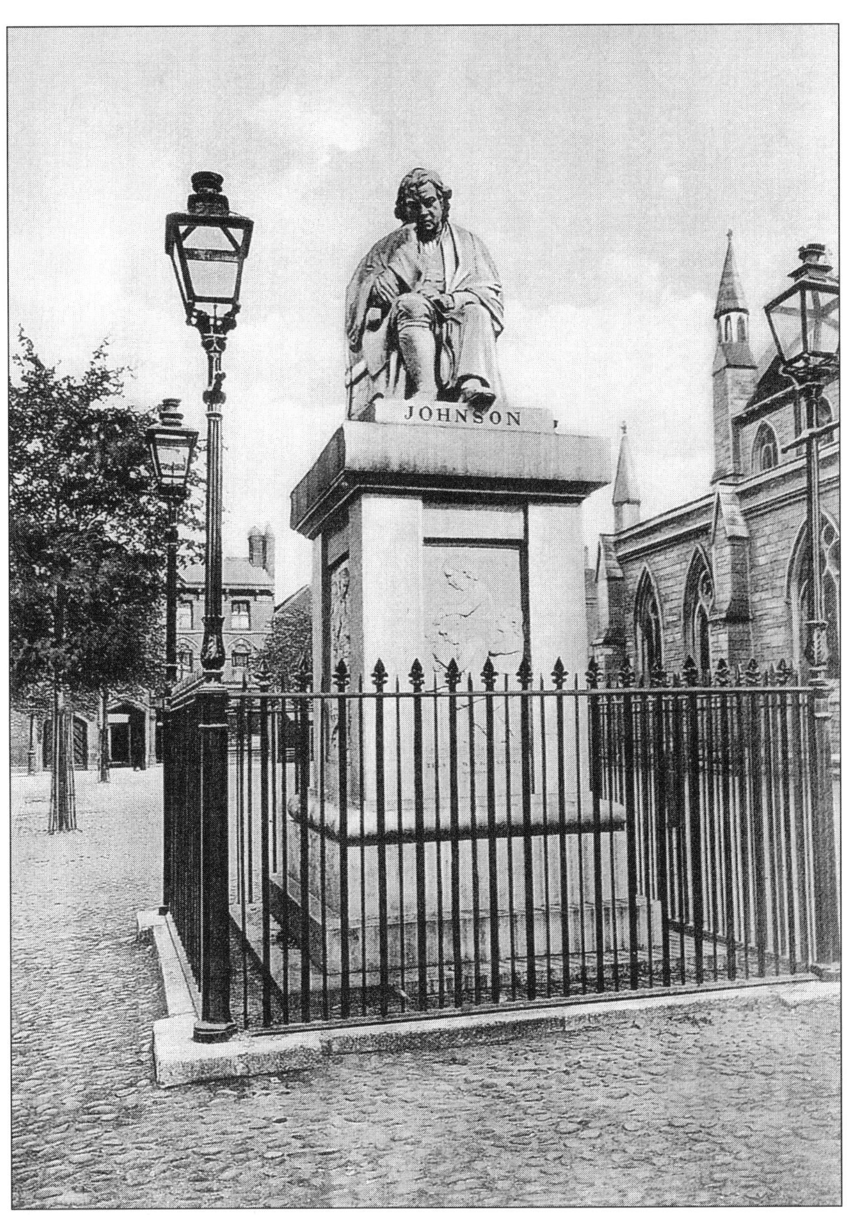

Samuel Johnson 'The Great Lexicographer" has always been held in high esteem by the people of Lichfield, as one of their greatest sons. From the time of his death in 1784 people came from afar as pilgrims to his birthplace in the Market Square, and in 1838 James Law, Chancellor of the Diocese of Lichfield, presented to the city the statue of Johnson which stands facing his house.

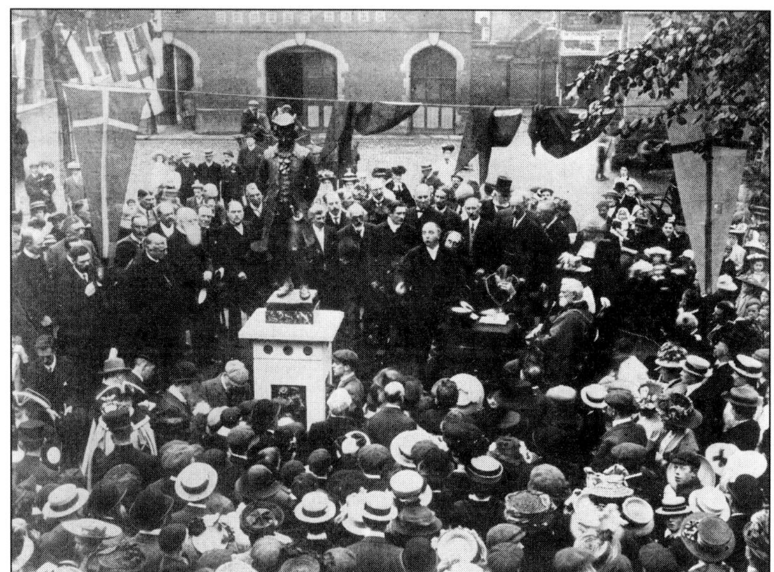

The year 1908 was a very special year for Johnsonians, for it saw the unveiling of a second statue in the Market Square: that of James Boswell, Johnson's friend and biographer. This was executed by Percy Fitzgerald and presented by him to the city, being unveiled, as seen here, on September 18th, 1908.

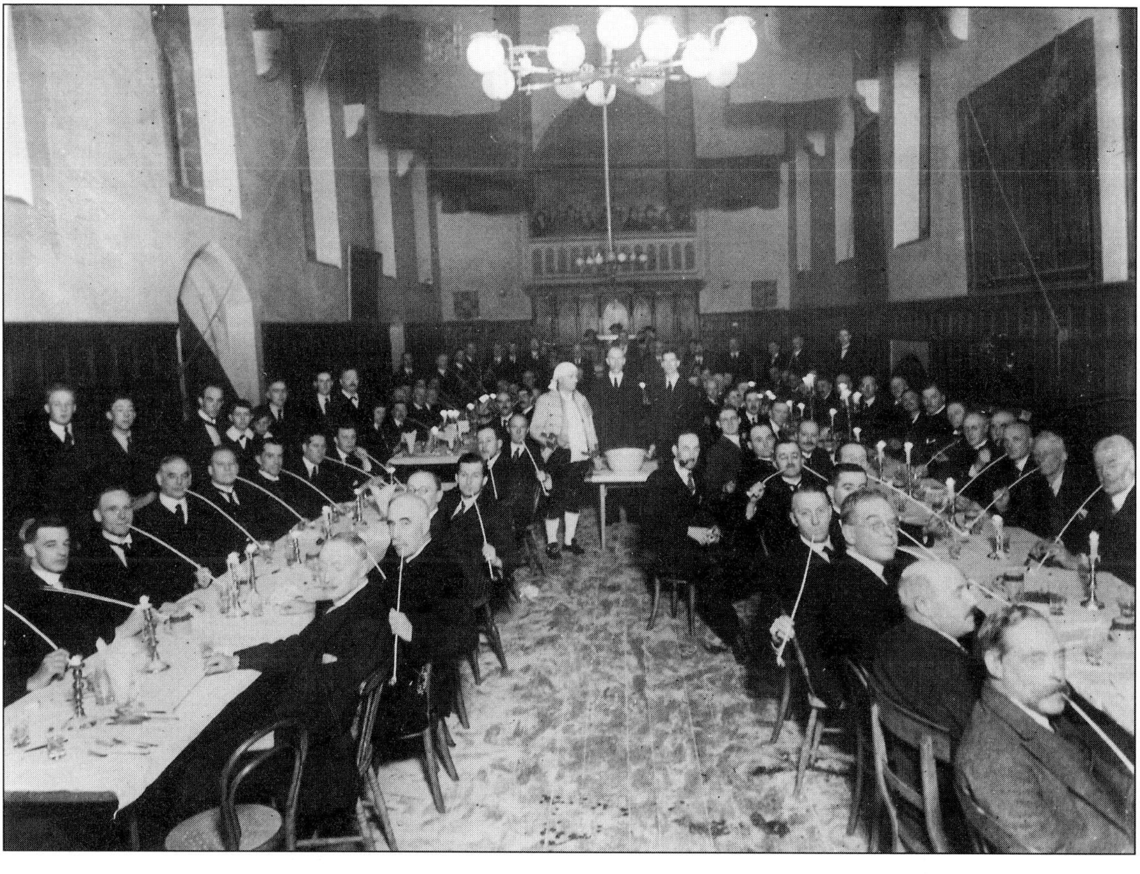

In 1908 the practice of holding a Johnson supper on his birthday was started. At first it took place in the Three Crowns, Johnson's favourite inn when in Lichfield, but it has proved so popular ever since that it was moved to the Guildhall, with all its features of lighted candles, sanded floor, ale, churchwarden pipes and punch. The Toast of the evening is always "The Immortal Memory of Dr. Samuel Johnson". This picture is c 1920.

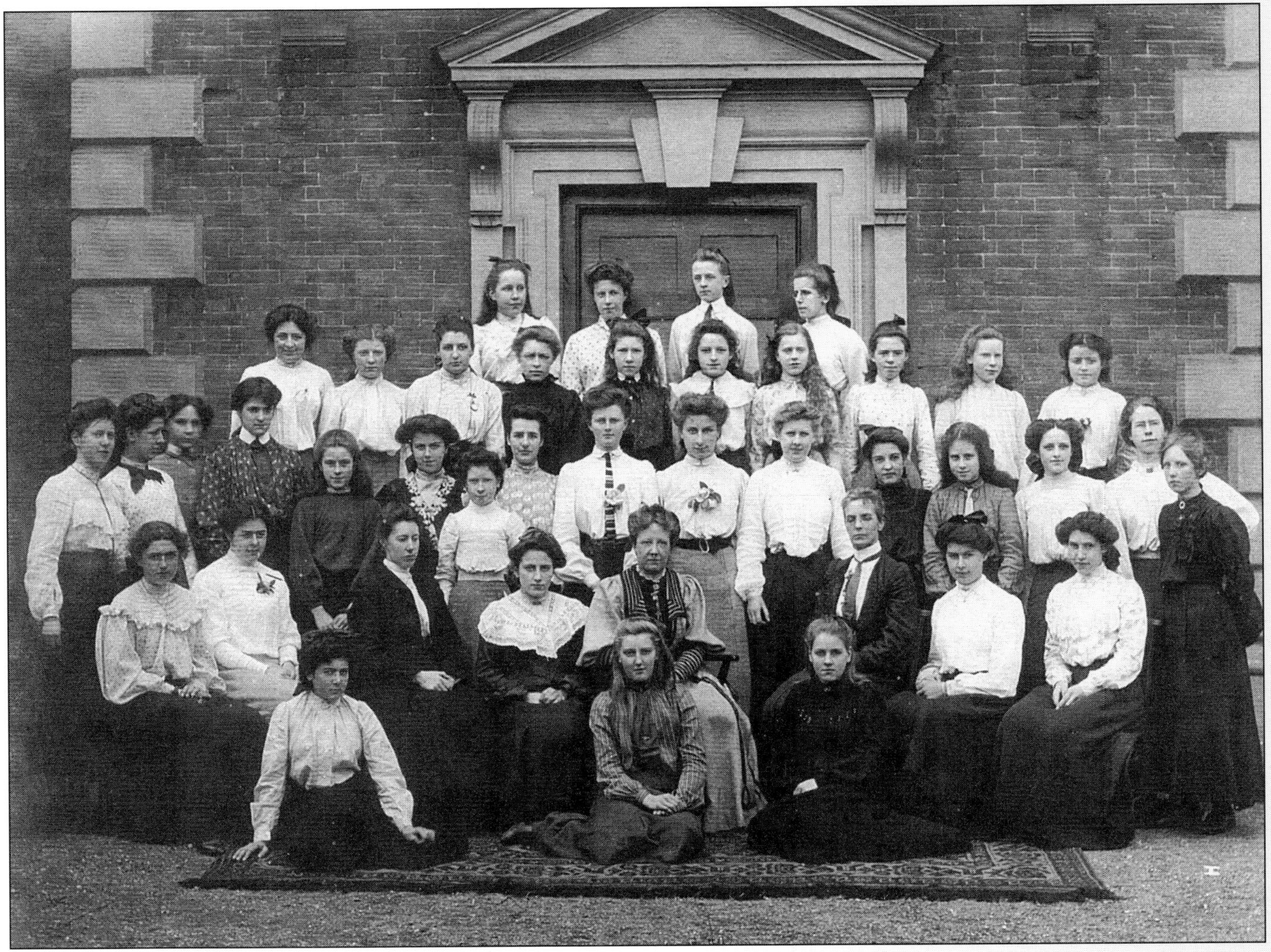

Yeomanry House, Lichfield, was a fine Georgian House at the corner of St John Street and Station road, on the site of the present Kenning's Garage. Up until 1896 it had been the H.Q. of the Staffordshire Yeomanry, but in that year the Yeomanry moved to the Friary and Yeomanry House became the home of Lichfield Girl's High School. The school had been founded some years before at premises in Market Street. This photograph was taken about 1902. Yeomanry House had been the home of the Levett family and at this time was owned by Sir Robert Levett, to whom the school paid £150 per annum rent.

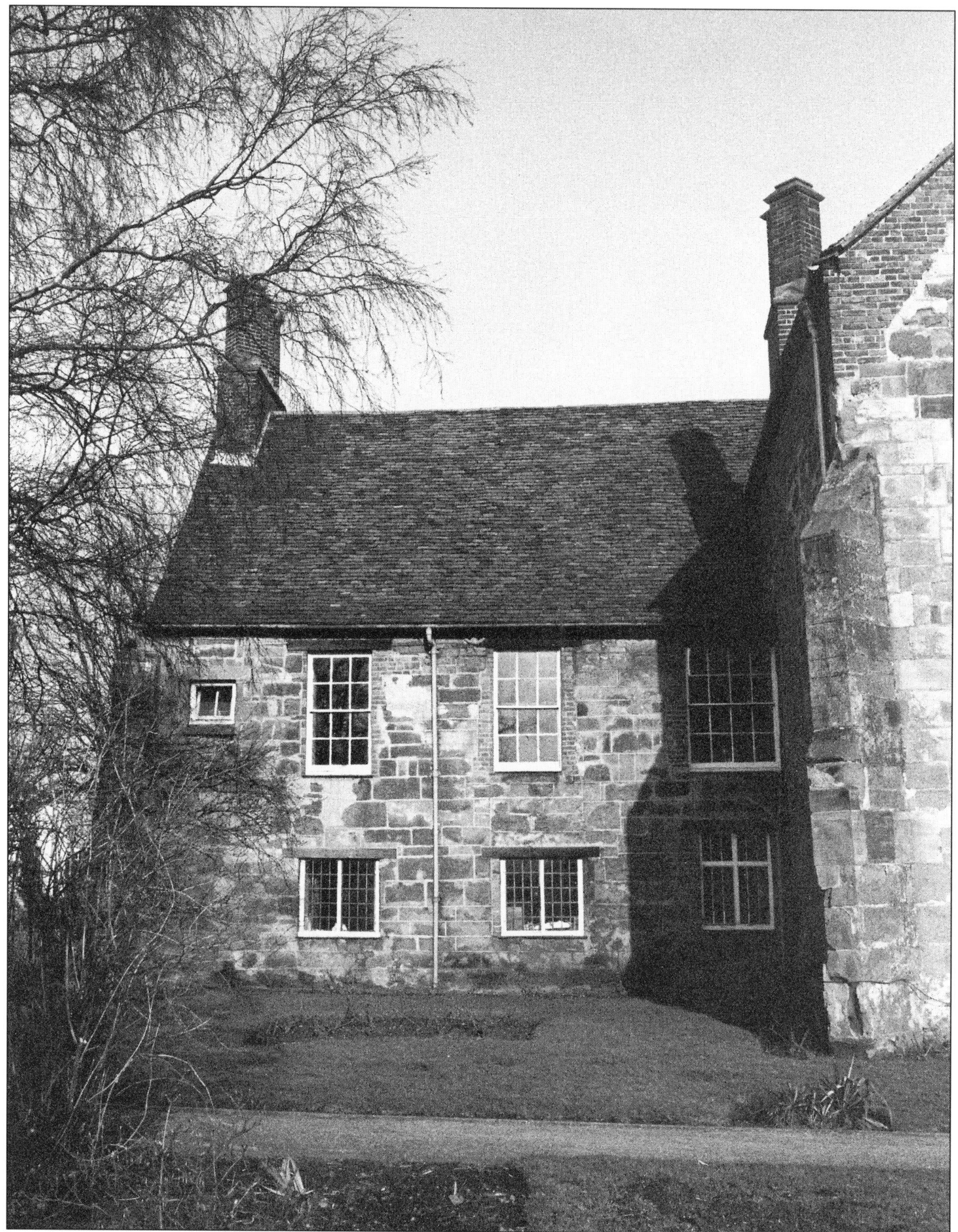

The Friary, to which the Staffordshire Yeomanry had moved their headquarters was the remains of a Franciscan friary which had been a private house since the dissolution of the monastries. It was situated right in the middle of Lichfield. In this view of it from the west its mediaeval origin shows up well.

Chapter 2 – The Great War

Once again a new decade brought with it a new monarch. Edward VII died in May 1910. It had been a short reign by comparison with his mother, but he had his admirers and one of these was Robert Bridgeman of Lichfield, the head of the firm of church furnishers in Quonians Lane, off Dam Street.

During his term of office as Sheriff in 1908 he had executed and then presented to the city the statue of King Edward which stands in the Museum Gardens.

Edward was succeeded by George V whose reign was signified by the carved heads of King George and his consort Queen Mary being placed on the front of the Guildhall. These were presented to the city by the wife of the Mayor for 1910, Godfrey Rathbone Benson (later Lord Charnwood) who lived at Stowe House.

In 1914 war broke out once again, but this time involving much more the people of Britain including, of course, the inhabitants of Lichfield. There are few photographs of this period and of the later second world war, for photography of any matter to do with the defence of the Realm was forbidden, and anyone wielding a camera would be suspect as an enemy spy.

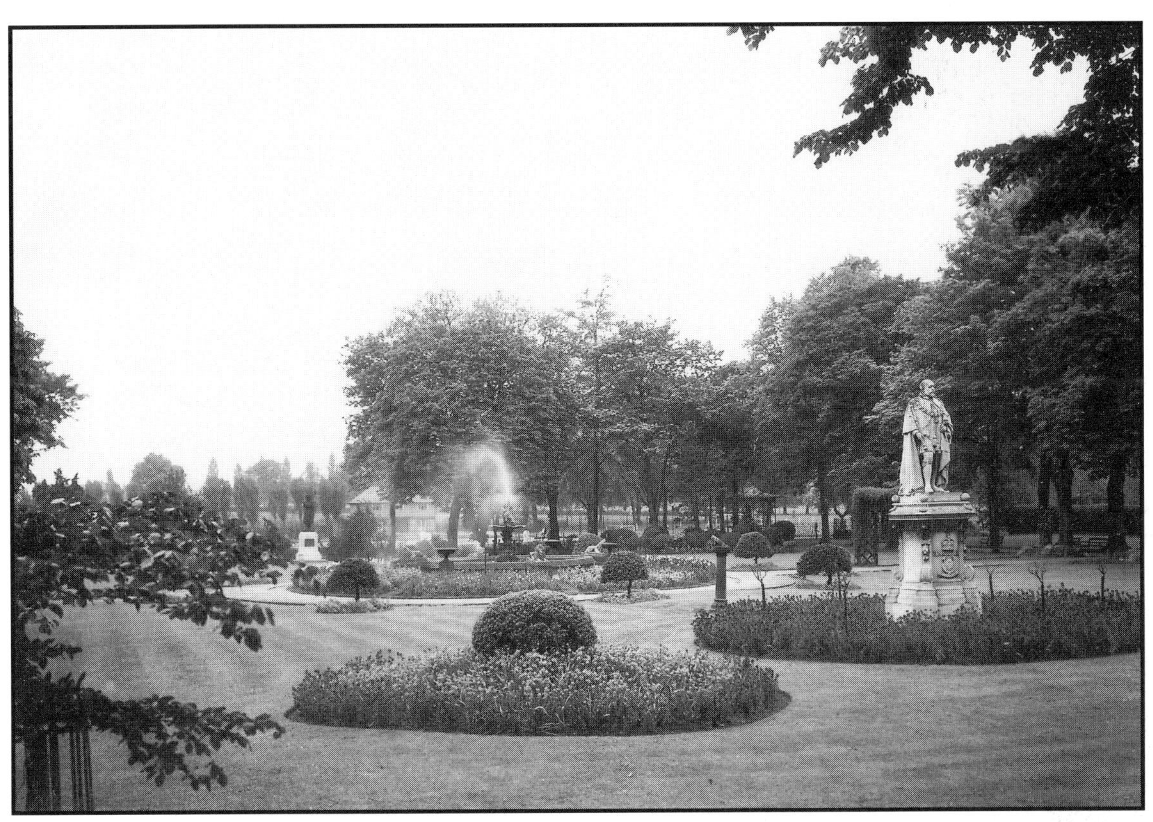

Mr Bridgeman's statue of King Edward VII in the Museum Gardens.

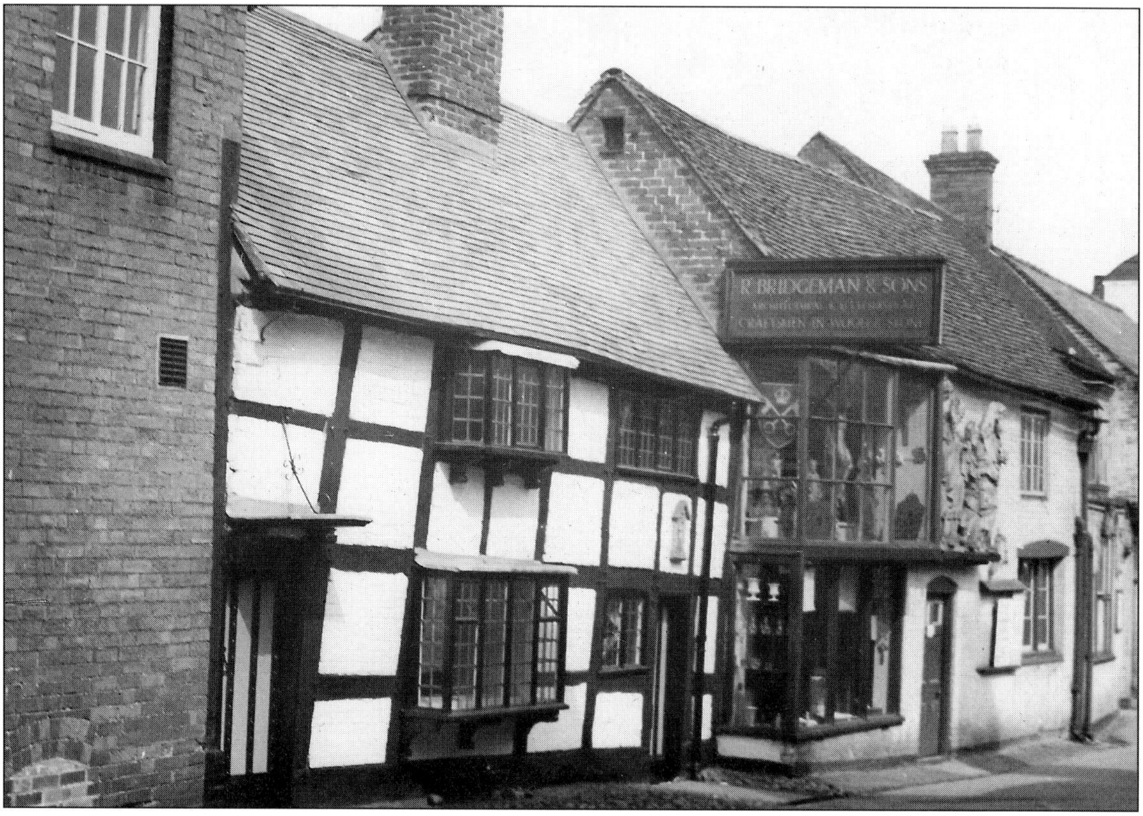

Bridgeman's works in Quonians Lane, off Dam Street.

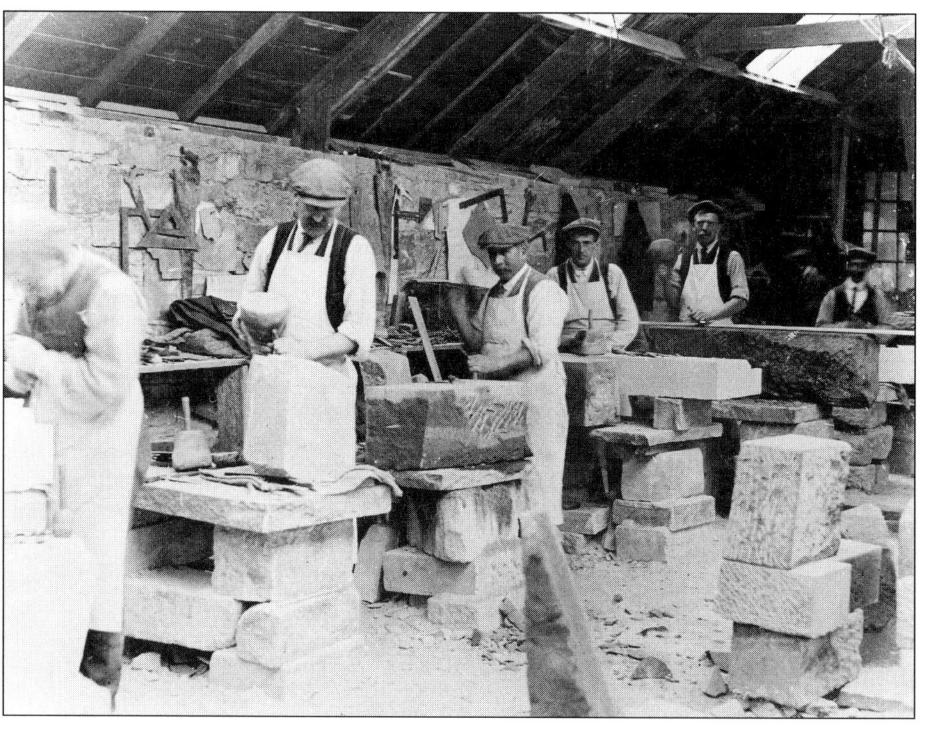

Stonemasons at work. Bridgemans became famed world wide for their work as church furnishers and restorers.

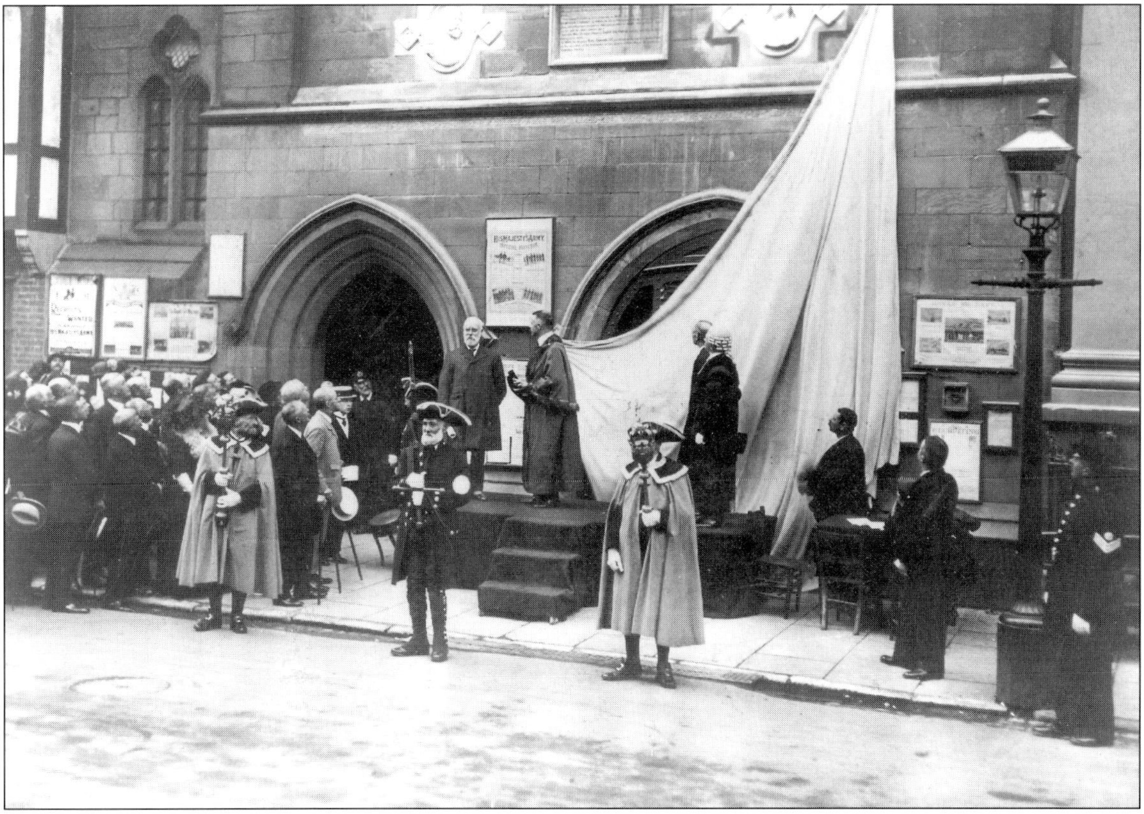

Above: Unveiling of the heads of King George V and Queen Mary on the outside of the Guildhall, 1910, the gift of the Mayoress, Mrs Benson.

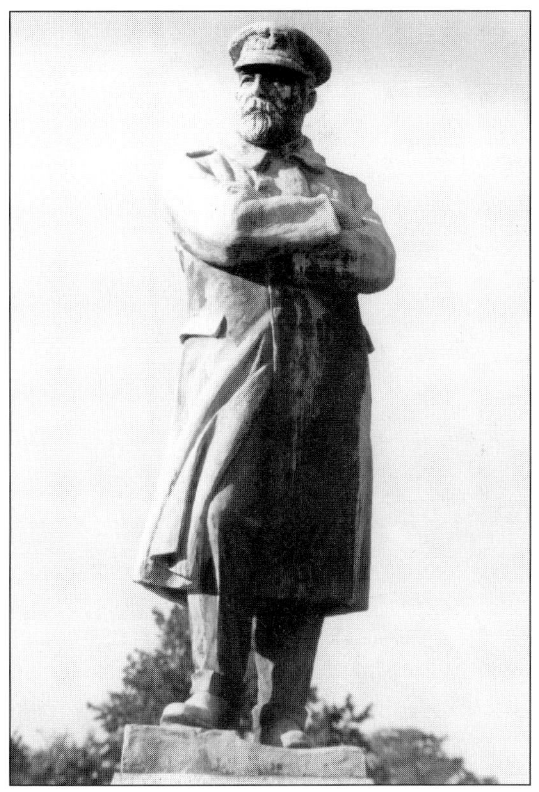

Left: Also in the Museum Gardens, a short distance from King Edward's statue, is another figure in bronze of a man in naval uniform. This is a memorial to Captain Edward Smith, Commander of the ill-fated liner *Titanic* which sank on the 15th April, 1912, after striking an iceberg in the North Atlantic. Captain Smith went down with his ship. The sculptor of the statue was Lady Scott, widow of Captain Scott the Antarctic explorer. The statue was unveiled in August 1914, a few days before the outbreak of war. Over the years, a myth grew up in Lichfield to the effect that the statue was originally intended to be placed in Hanley, the place of Captain Smith's birth. The people of Hanley, incensed at the idea of a memorial to a man who had lost his ship, refused to accept the statue which was then offered to Lichfield. Reference to the minutes of Lichfield City Council for 1912, however, show that Lichfield had always been the chosen place for this fine memorial.

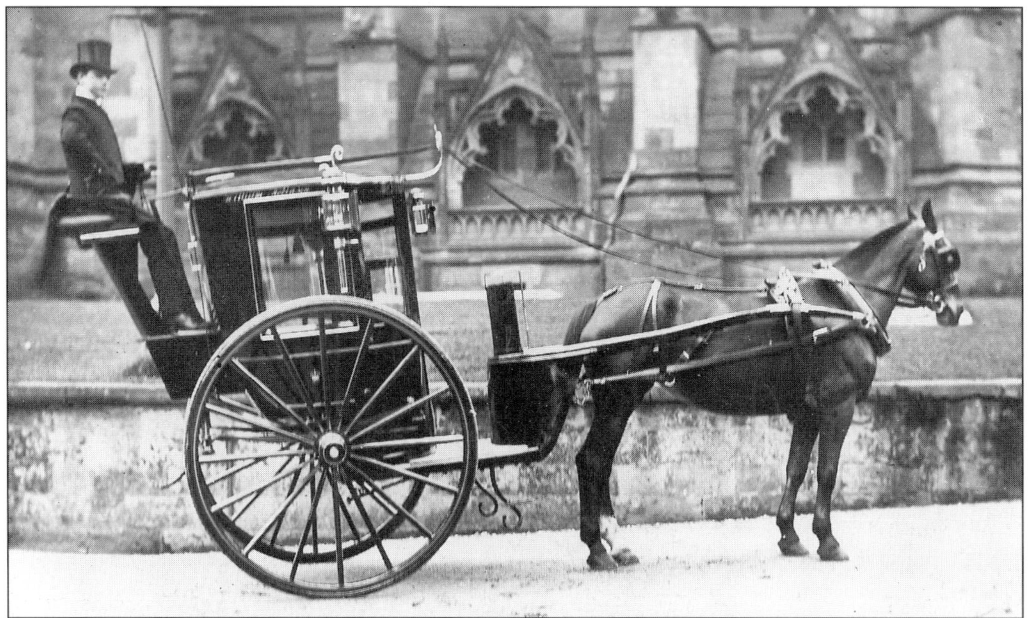

Above and below: Horse transport was still the most common means of carrying goods and people, apart from the railways. Here are two fine examples, a hansom cab of Smallwoods who operated from The Scales in Market Street. It is waiting outside the house of a canon in the Close, and the London North Western parcels van which worked from Lichfield City Station. In each case the horse is well turned out – railway horses usually were.

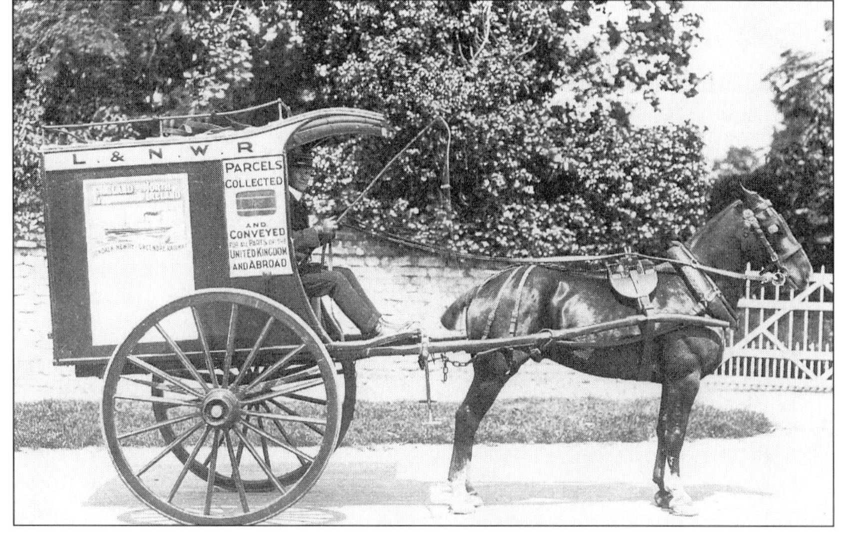

Opposite page: The first decade of the century had also seen the appearance on the roads of the motor car. This fine Daimler tourer was available for hire from Jones's Garage in 1913. One of the leading businesses in Lichfield during the first half of the century, Jones' Garage was founded in 1896 as a hardware and ironmongers, situated at the corner of Bird Street and Bore Street in what had been the Talbot Inn. With the cycling craze of the 1900s, Mr Jones moved into selling bicycles, then sent his son Herbert to serve an apprenticeship at the Daimler factory at Coventry, where he worked alongside Herbert Austin. When he finished his training, he returned to Lichfield and started up the motor side of the business, which became "Jones's Garage" from then on. In 1913 they sold petroleum at one shilling (25p) a gallon. They also sold electricity generating equipment to large country houses and businesses at a time when Lichfield had no public electricity supply.

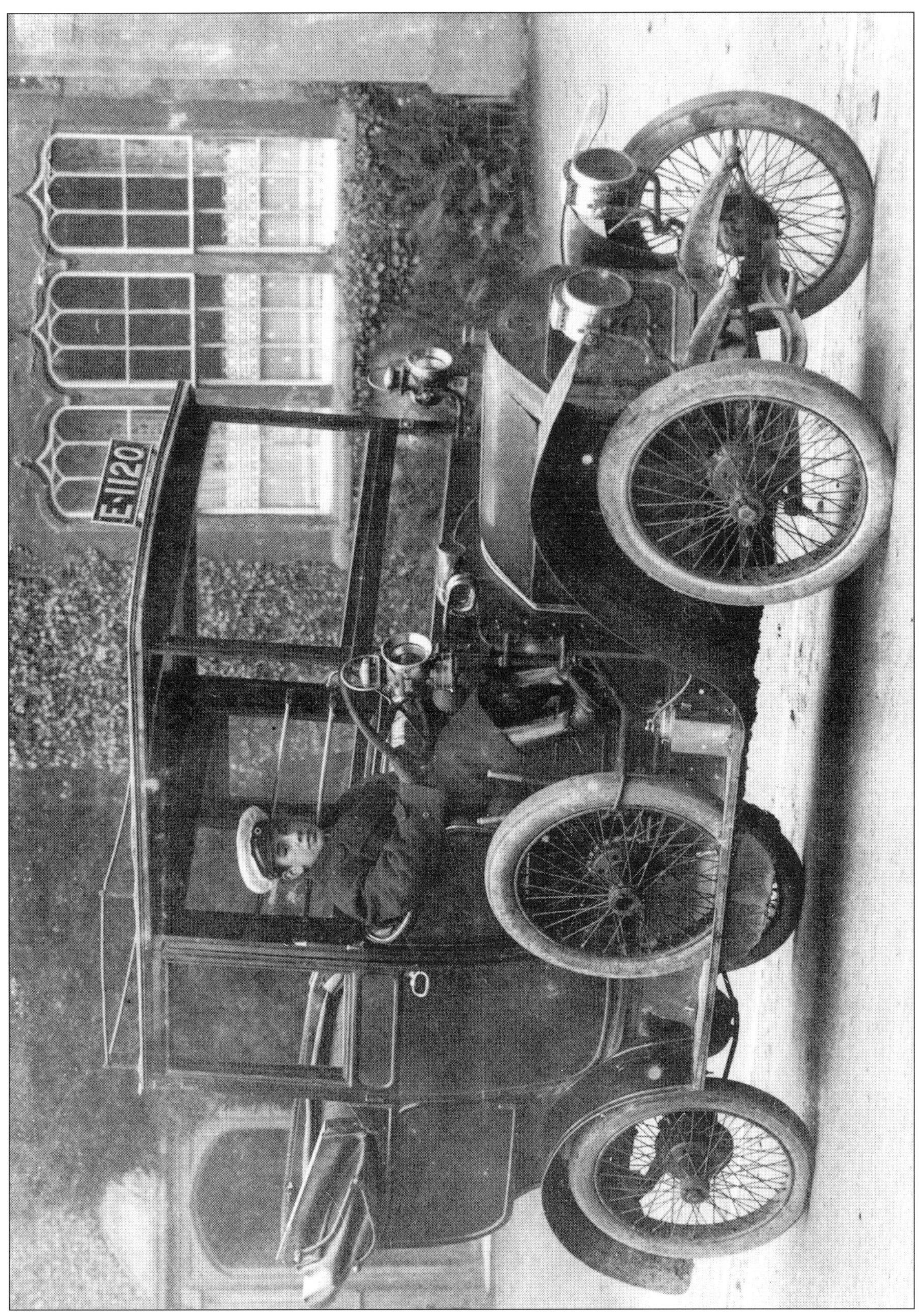
E 1120

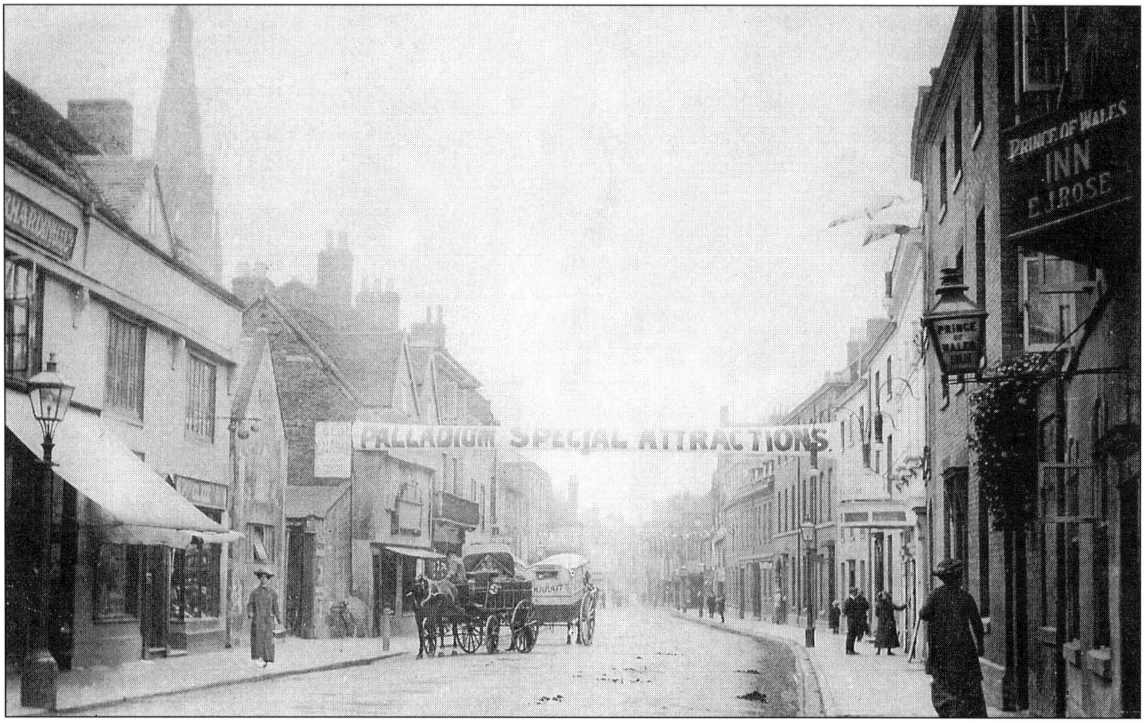

Bore Street in 1912. The St James's Hall became a full-time cinema in 1911. But cinemas require a supply of electricity, and Lichfield had no public supply. So a cable was stretched across Bore Street to Jones's Garage and a supply obtained from the garage generator, a Siemen's dynamo driven by a 10hp Tangye gas engine. The cable was also used to advertise the cinema's attractions.

The coming of the cinema meant the end of the Operatic Society, the Amateur Dramatics, the County Balls and many other functions which depended on the St James's Hall for a venue.

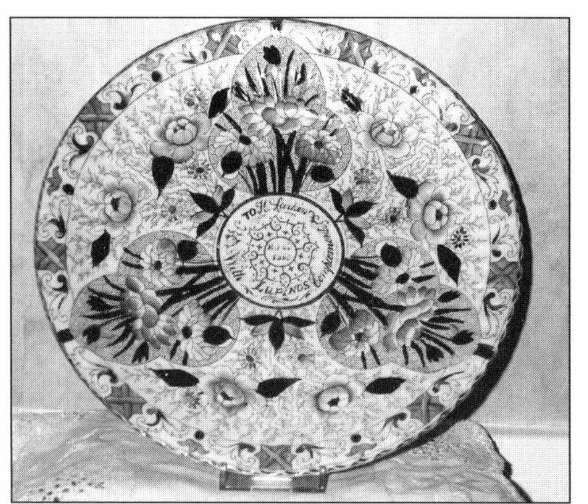

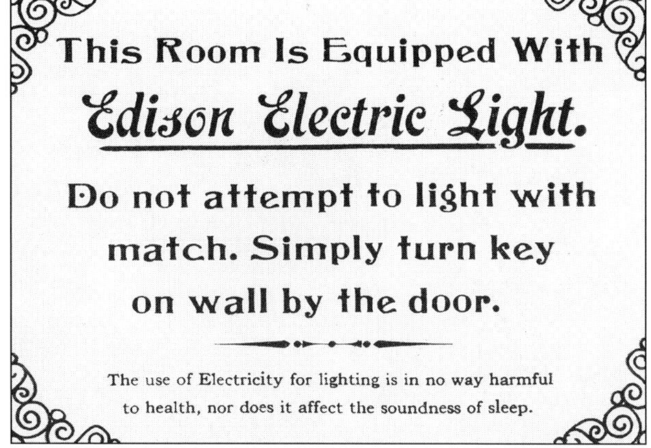

Above left: Mr H.Larkin was Secretary of St. James's Hall and must have received many gifts similar to this plate, which is inscribed "To Mr Larkin, with Lupinos compliments, May 1900". The Lupinos were a famous family of entertainers. **Above right:** When Jones's Garage supplied electric lighting sets to private houses they provided copies of this notice to hang in each room.

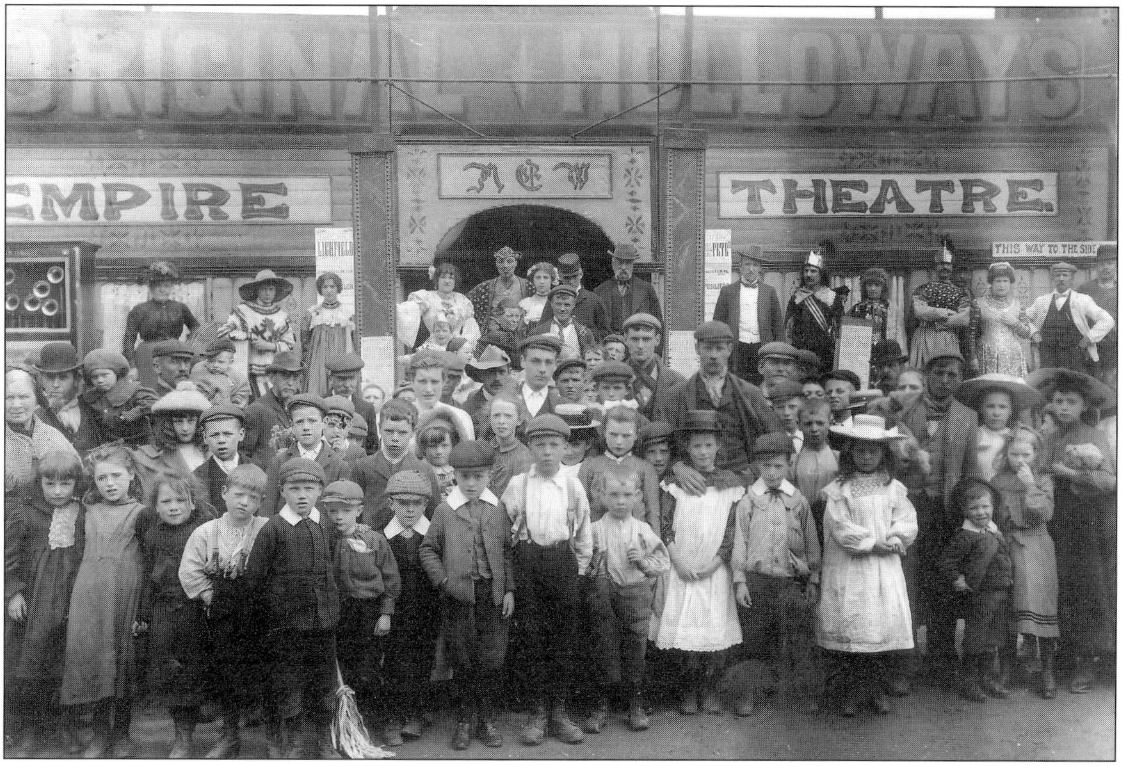

When the St James's Hall became the Palladium Cinema the only form of live entertainment, apart from travelling circuses, were travelling theatres. There were two of these, Holloway's and Richardson's, both of which came regularly, setting up their mobile theatres at the Cross Keys public house in Lombard Street. This scene shows Holloway's, with performers and audience. Plays consisted of their own versions of Shakespeare and old melodramas such as *Maria Martin and the Red Barn* – anything, in fact, that was out of copyright.

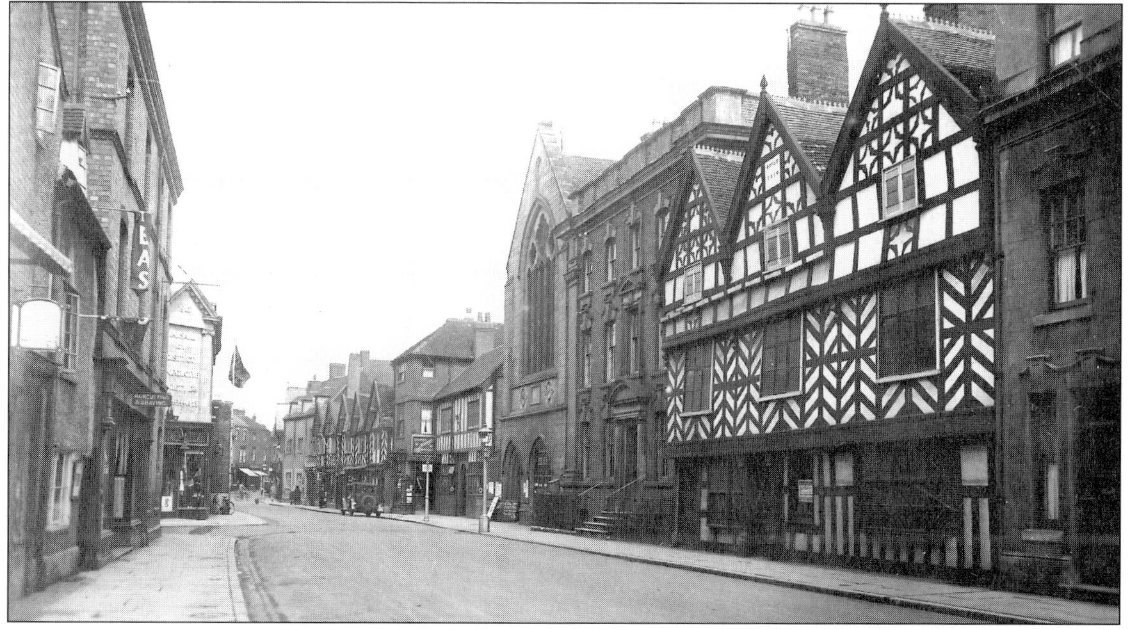

Here we see Boswell House now the Tudor Café in its setting of Bore Street, about 1920.

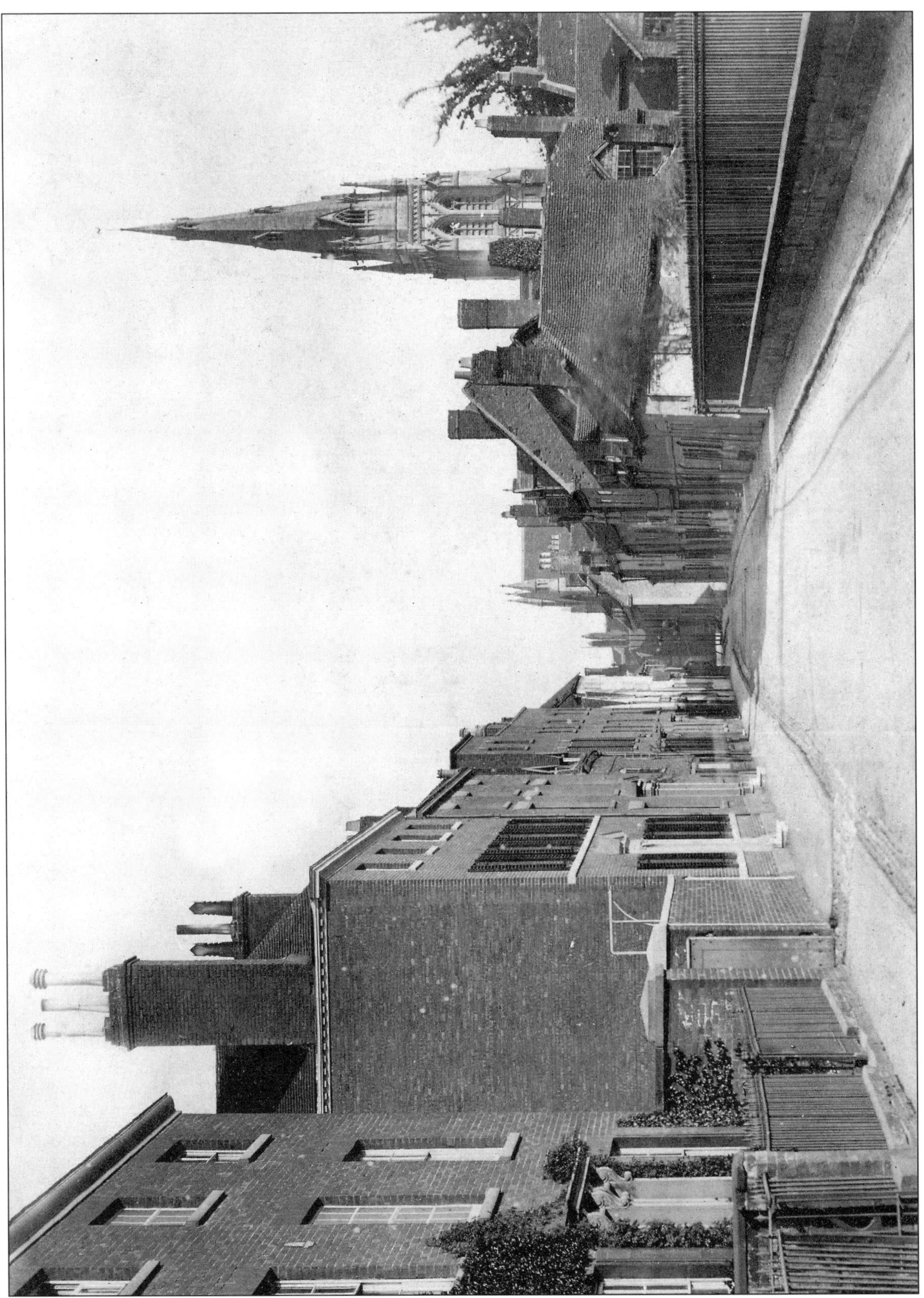

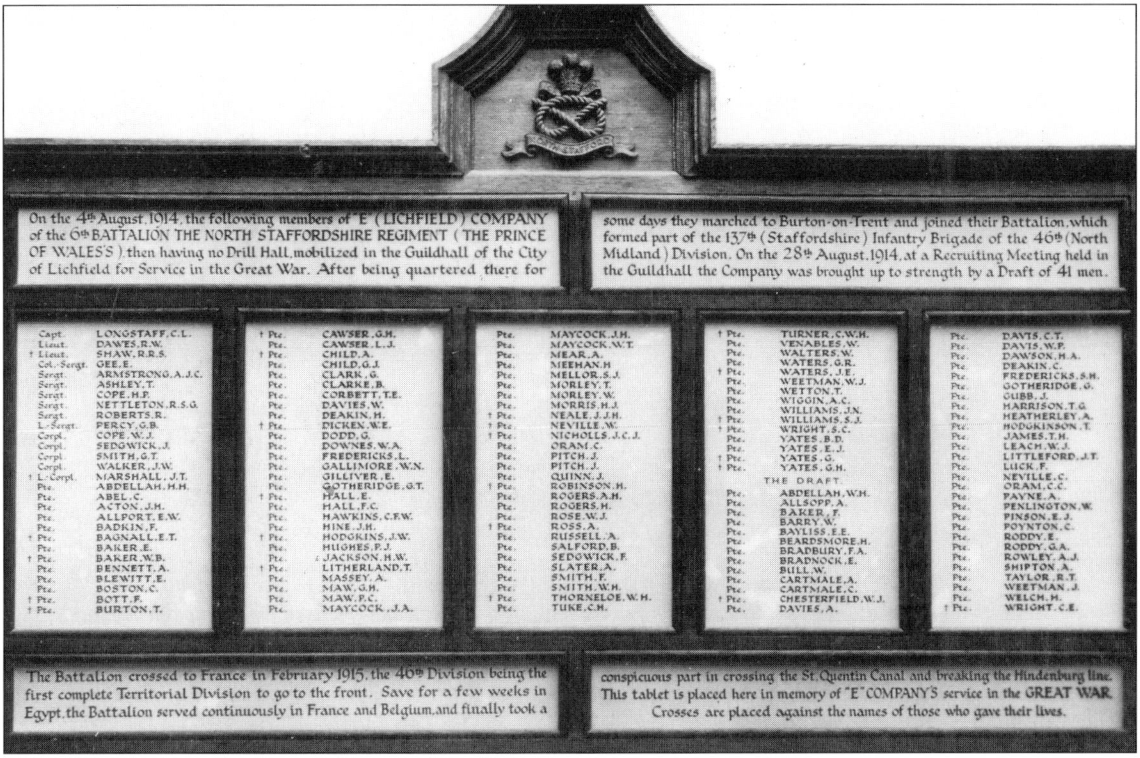

On the 4th August, 1914, the following members of "E" (LICHFIELD) COMPANY of the 6th BATTALION THE NORTH STAFFORDSHIRE REGIMENT (THE PRINCE OF WALES'S), then having no Drill Hall, mobilized in the Guildhall of the City of Lichfield for Service in the Great War. After being quartered there for some days they marched to Burton-on-Trent and joined their Battalion, which formed part of the 137th (Staffordshire) Infantry Brigade of the 46th (North Midland) Division. On the 28th August, 1914, at a Recruiting Meeting held in the Guildhall the Company was brought up to strength by a Draft of 41 men.

Capt. LONGSTAFF, C.L.
Lieut. DAWES, R.W.
† Lieut. SHAW, R.R.S.
Col.-Sergt. GEE, E.
Sergt. ARMSTRONG, A.J.C.
Sergt. ASHLEY, T.
Sergt. COPE, H.P.
Sergt. NETTLETON, R.S.G.
Sergt. ROBERTS, R.
L.-Sergt. PERCY, G.B.
Corpl. COPE, W.J.
Corpl. SEDGWICK, J.
Corpl. SMITH, G.T.
Corpl. WALKER, J.W.
† L.-Corpl. MARSHALL, J.T.
Pte. ABDELLAH, H.H.
Pte. ABEL, C.
Pte. ACTON, J.H.
Pte. ALLPORT, E.W.
Pte. BADKIN, F.
† Pte. BAGNALL, E.T.
Pte. BAKER, E.
† Pte. BAKER, W.B.
Pte. BENNETT, A.
Pte. BLEWITT, E.
Pte. BOSTON, C.
† Pte. BOTT, F.
† Pte. BURTON, T.

† Pte. CAWSER, G.H.
Pte. CAWSER, L.J.
† Pte. CHILD, A.
Pte. CHILD, G.J.
Pte. CLARK, G.
Pte. CLARKE, B.
Pte. CORBETT, T.E.
Pte. DAVIES, W.
Pte. DEAKIN, H.
† Pte. DICKEN, W.E.
Pte. DODD, G.
Pte. DOWNES, W.A.
Pte. FREDERICKS, L.
Pte. GALLIMORE, W.N.
Pte. GILLIVER, E.
Pte. GOTHERIDGE, G.T.
† Pte. HALL, E.
Pte. HALL, F.C.
Pte. HAWKINS, C.F.W.
Pte. HINE, J.H.
† Pte. HODGKINS, J.W.
Pte. HUGHES, P.J.
Pte. JACKSON, H.W.
† Pte. LITHERLAND, T.
Pte. MASSEY, A.
Pte. MAW, G.H.
Pte. MAW, P.C.
Pte. MAYCOCK, J.A.

Pte. MAYCOCK, J.H.
Pte. MAYCOCK, W.T.
Pte. MEAR, A.
Pte. MEEHAN, H.
Pte. MELLOR, S.J.
Pte. MORLEY, T.
Pte. MORLEY, W.
Pte. MORRIS, H.J.
† Pte. NEALE, J.J.H.
† Pte. NEVILLE, W.
† Pte. NICHOLLS, J.C.J.
Pte. ORAM, C.
Pte. PITCH, J.
Pte. PITCH, J.
Pte. QUINN, J.
† Pte. ROBINSON, H.
Pte. ROGERS, A.H.
Pte. ROGERS, H.
Pte. ROSE, W.J.
† Pte. ROSS, A.
Pte. RUSSELL, A.
Pte. SALFORD, B.
Pte. SEDGWICK, F.
Pte. SLATER, A.
Pte. SMITH, F.
Pte. SMITH, W.H.
† Pte. THORNELOE, W.H.
Pte. TUKE, C.H.

† Pte. TURNER, C.W.H.
Pte. VENABLES, W.
Pte. WALTERS, W.
Pte. WATERS, G.R.
† Pte. WATERS, J.E.
Pte. WEETMAN, W.J.
Pte. WETTON, T.
Pte. WIGGIN, A.C.
Pte. WILLIAMS, J.N.
† Pte. WILLIAMS, S.J.
† Pte. WRIGHT, S.C.
Pte. YATES, B.D.
Pte. YATES, E.J.
† Pte. YATES, G.
† Pte. YATES, G.H.

THE DRAFT.

Pte. ABDELLAH, W.H.
Pte. ALLSOPP, A.
Pte. BAKER, F.
Pte. BARRY, W.
Pte. BAYLISS, E.E.
Pte. BEARDSMORE, H.
Pte. BRADBURY, F.A.
Pte. BRADNOCK, E.
Pte. BULL, W.
Pte. CARTMALE, A.
Pte. CARTMALE, C.
† Pte. CHESTERFIELD, W.J.
Pte. DAVIES, A.

Pte. DAVIS, C.T.
Pte. DAVIS, W.P.
Pte. DAWSON, H.A.
Pte. DEAKIN, C.
Pte. FREDERICKS, S.H.
Pte. GOTHERIDGE, G.
Pte. GUBB, J.
Pte. HARRISON, T.G.
Pte. HEATHERLEY, A.
Pte. HODGKINSON, T.
Pte. JAMES, T.H.
Pte. LEACH, W.J.
Pte. LITTLEFORD, J.T.
Pte. LUCK, F.
Pte. NEVILLE, C.
Pte. ORAM, C.C.
Pte. PAYNE, A.
Pte. PENLINGTON, W.
Pte. PINSON, E.J.
Pte. POYNTON, C.
Pte. RODDY, E.
Pte. RODDY, G.A.
Pte. ROWLEY, A.J.
Pte. SHIPTON, A.
Pte. TAYLOR, R.T.
Pte. WEETMAN, J.
Pte. WELCH, H.
† Pte. WRIGHT, C.E.

The Battalion crossed to France in February 1915, the 46th Division being the first complete Territorial Division to go to the front. Save for a few weeks in Egypt, the Battalion served continuously in France and Belgium, and finally took a conspicuous part in crossing the St. Quentin Canal and breaking the Hindenburg line. This tablet is placed here in memory of "E" COMPANY'S service in the GREAT WAR. Crosses are placed against the names of those who gave their lives.

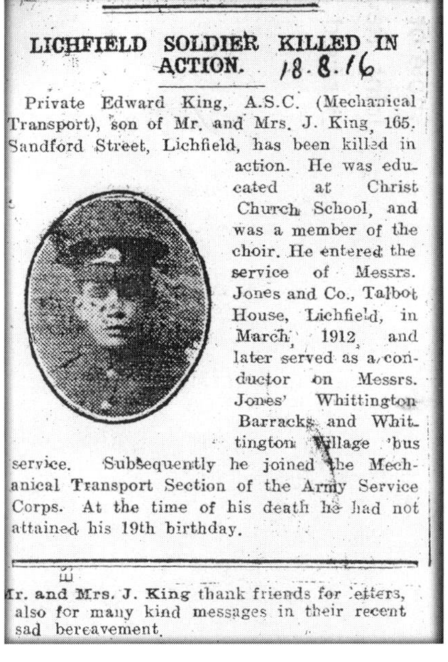

LICHFIELD SOLDIER KILLED IN ACTION. 18.8.16

Private Edward King, A.S.C. (Mechanical Transport), son of Mr. and Mrs. J. King, 165, Sandford Street, Lichfield, has been killed in action. He was educated at Christ Church School, and was a member of the choir. He entered the service of Messrs. Jones and Co., Talbot House, Lichfield, in March, 1912, and later served as a conductor on Messrs. Jones' Whittington Barracks and Whittington Village 'bus service. Subsequently he joined the Mechanical Transport Section of the Army Service Corps. At the time of his death he had not attained his 19th birthday.

Mr. and Mrs. J. King thank friends for letters, also for many kind messages in their recent sad bereavement.

Above: War came in August 1914. Many people thought it would be over by Christmas, but four terrible years of Armageddon were to follow. The Territorial Army had been created by Act of Parliament in 1908 replacing the old militia, and now Lichfield volunteers found themselves serving in the 6th Battalion, North Staffordshire Regiment. When war was declared, the Territorial Army was immediately embodied. The Lichfield Territorials were at training camp and returned to the city, where they were housed in the Guildhall before marching off to Burton to join their unit. The names of these men are recorded on this plaque which now hangs in the Guildhall.

Left: During the war of 1914 – 1918 the number of Lichfield men who gave their lives was 220. Many notices such as the one above appeared in newspapers; in this case the man who died was the driver of the hire car from Jones's Garage, seen in an earlier photograph.

Opposite page: This tranquil scene in Dam Street, looking south could be any time between 1900 and 1941 when the iron railings were removed and taken away for scrap to help the war effort. The railings on the right hand side of the road were removed c 1980 by vandals.

POLICE WARNING.

WHAT TO DO WHEN THE

ZEPPELINS COME.

Sir Edward Henry, the Commissioner of the Metropolitan Police, has issued a series of valuable instructions and suggestions as to the action that should be taken by the ordinary householder or resident in the event of an air raid over London.

New Scotland Yard, S.W.
June 26, 1915.

In all probability if an air raid is made it will take place at a time when most people are in bed. The only intimation the public are likely to get will be the reports of the anti-aircraft guns or the noise of falling bombs.

The public are advised not to go into the street, where they might be struck by falling missiles; moreover, the streets being required for the passage of fire engines, etc., should not be obstructed by pedestrians.

In many houses there are no facilities for procuring water on the upper floors. It is suggested, therefore, that a supply of water and sand might be kept there, so that any fire breaking out on a small scale can at once be dealt with. Everyone should know the position of the fire alarm post nearest to his house.

All windows and doors on the lower floor should be closed to prevent the admission of noxious gases. An indication that poison gas is being used will be that a peculiar and irritating smell may be noticed following on the dropping of the bomb.

Gas should not be turned off at the meter at night, as this practice involves a risk of subsequent fire and of explosion from burners left on when the meter was shut off. This risk outweighs any advantage that might accrue from the gas being shut off at the time of a night raid by aircraft.

Persons purchasing portable chemical fire extinguishers should require a written guarantee that they comply with the specifications of the Boardof Trade, Office of Works, Metropolitan Police, or some approved Fire Prevention Committee.

No bomb of any description should be handled unless it has shown itself to be of incendiary type. In this case it may be possible to remove it without undue risk. In all other cases a bomb should be left alone, and the police informed.

E. R. HENRY.

EXTRACT FROM

LATEST POLICE WARNING:

KEEP SAND AND WATER HANDY.

Press Bureau.

In view of the possibility of further attacks by hostile aircraft, the Commissioner of Police deems it advisable to call attention to the public warning published on June 26 recommending residents to remain under cover, and advising them for dealing with incendiary fires to keep a supply of water and sand readily available.

* * * * * *

(Signed) E. R. HENRY,
Commissioner of Police of the
Metropolis.

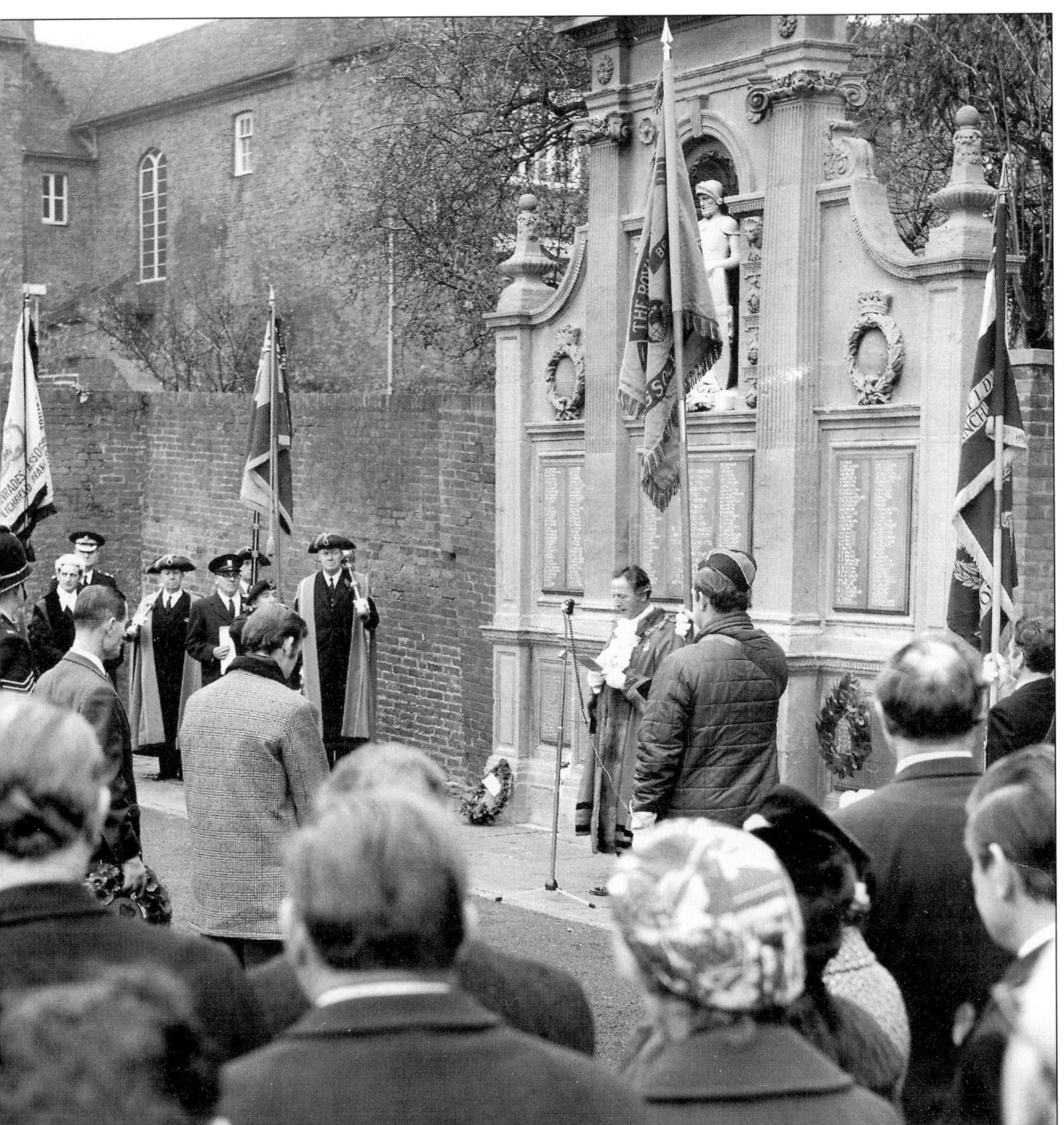

The City War Memorial contains the 220 names of all the men of the city who gave their lives in the Great War. Every Armistice Day since 1923 a ceremony of wreath laying by the Mayor of Lichfield is held. This one is from the 1970s.

Opposite page: Zeppelins were dirigible airships, named after their inventor, Count Zeppelin. In 1915 they began a bombing offensive against Britain, coming as close to Lichfield as Walsall (where in one raid the Mayoress of Walsall was killed) and Burton-on-Trent (mistaken for Sheffield). In view of this warnings were issued to householders and businesses.

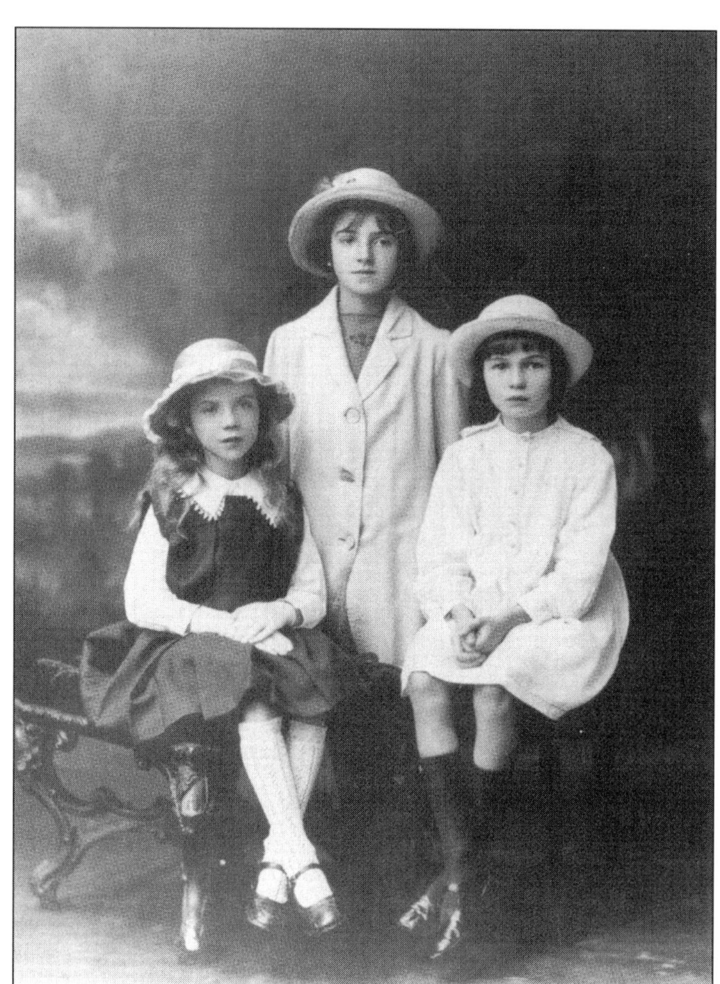

Left: Before the 1944 Education Act secondary schools such as King Edward's and the Friary were fee-paying establishments, but provision was made for admitting a certain proportion of children to free places. Selection was made by an examination taken at the primary school and known as a "Minor Scholarship". These scholarships were highly prized by the primary schools and one school with a consistently good record was Christ Church School, Lichfield. In 1919, these "three little maids from school" from Christ Church all won scholarships to, presumably, the Girls' High School then at Yeomanry House. Unfortunately we do not know their names.

Below: Lichfield Girls' High School, 1920. By now the school under the Headship of Miss D.V.M. Hodge M.A. had outgrown its home at Yeomanry House and was looking for new premises. The three little girls from the last picture are presumably somewhere in the front row.

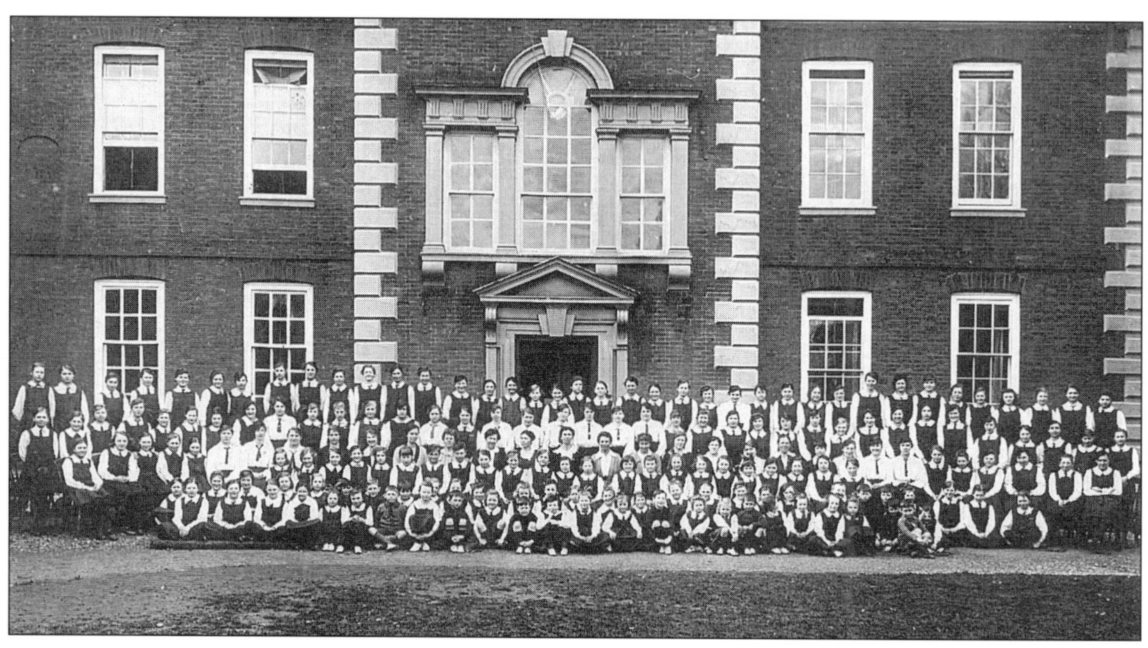

Chapter 3 – The Twenties

The decade of the Twenties in Lichfield was one of change, most of it in the development of the Friary, in the centre of the city. This estate was, before the dissolution of the monasteries, a Franciscan monastery founded by Bishop Stavenby in 1224. After the dissolution it became a private house, with spacious grounds, right in the middle of the city. Its last tenants were the Staffordshire Yeomanry, who moved their Head Quarters there from Yeomanry House in 1896. Now, in 1921, they moved again, to Stafford, when the Friary came on the market. It was purchased by a local landowner, Sir Richard Ashmole Cooper, M.P. of Shenstone Court, Shenstone. His father, the first Baronet (1905) had tried unsuccessfully to acquire the estate with a view to presenting it to the City of Lichfield. Now his son was able to carry out his father's wish, and by this generosity Lichfield acquired a wonderful asset.

It was decided that the first use to be made of this acquisition was as a new home for Lichfield Girls' High School, which by now was bursting at the seams in Yeomanry House. Accordingly, the City Council leased the premises of the Friary to Staffordshire County Council for a term of five years. for use as "a temporary school" until a new school could be built at Cherry Orchard; and so the Friary School came into existence.

In 1925 Lichfield City Council decided to make further use of the Friary estate by building through it a road system that would take traffic from Birmingham and Walsall into the centre of the city. At the same time it was decided by the Education Authority to abandon the idea of building a new school at Cherry Orchard and instead to expand the existing Friary School. This was done and both the new road and the new school were completed by 1928.

Below: Aerial photographs were now in fashion and this one of Lichfield Cathedral was taken about this time. Above the two western Spires can be seen Beacon Place, former home of the Seckham family.

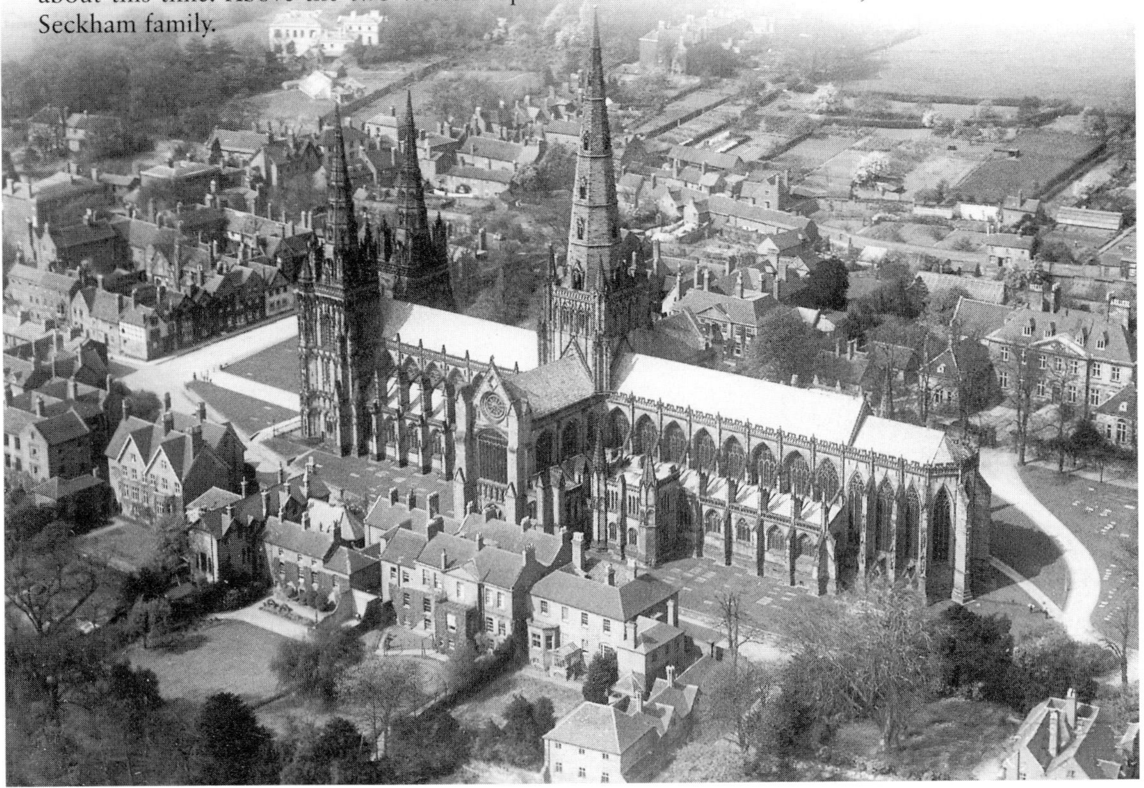

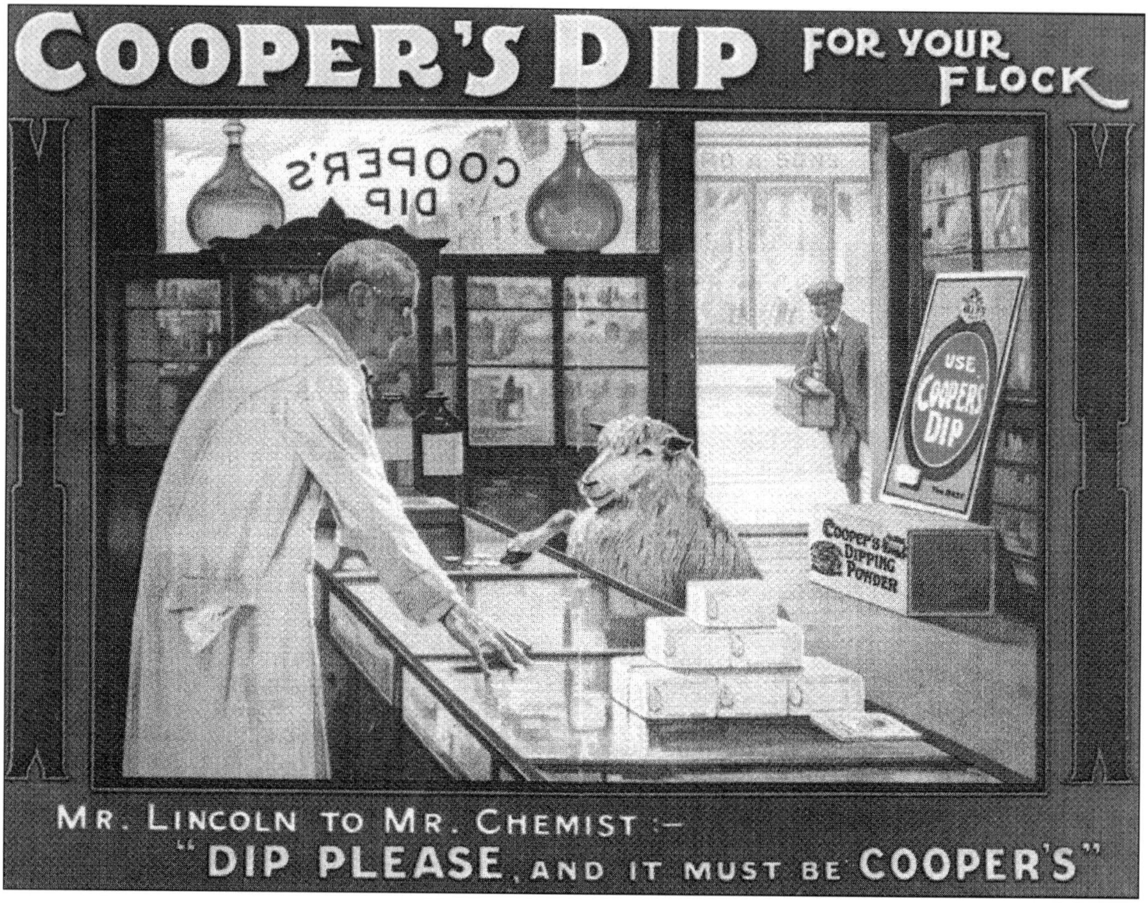

COOPER'S DIP FOR YOUR FLOCK

MR. LINCOLN TO MR. CHEMIST :–
"DIP PLEASE, AND IT MUST BE COOPER'S"

Walter Cooper was one of the first veterinary surgeons to be registered in 1847. He invented and developed a sheep dip which bore his name and made him a fortune, enabling his son, Richard Powell, to adopt the life of a country landowner at Shenstone, near Lichfield. One of his greatest wishes was to purchase the Friary estate.

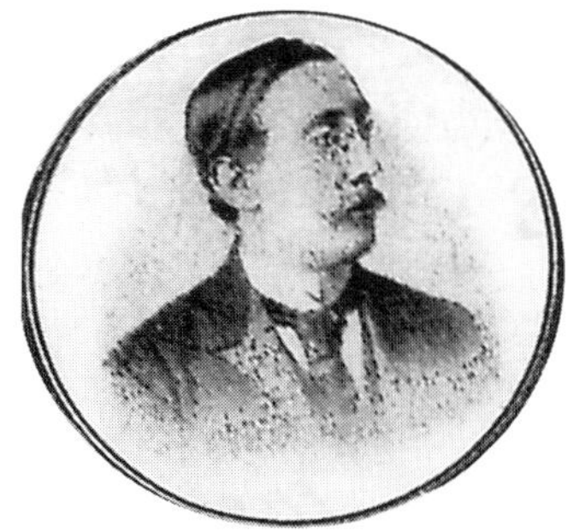

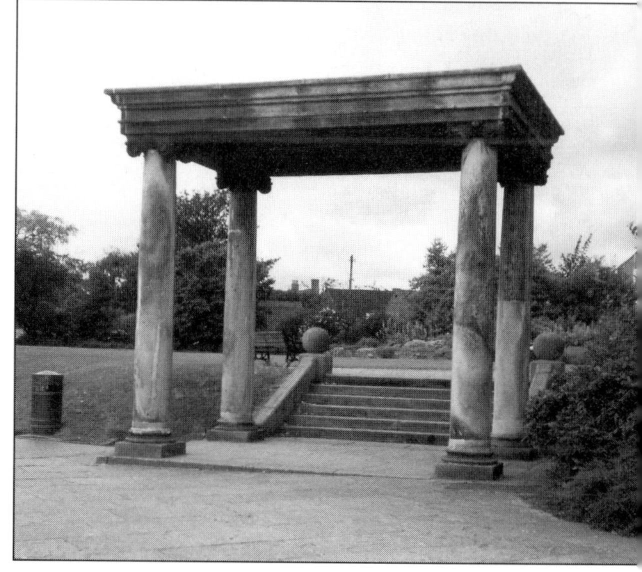

Above: Sir Richard Powell Cooper, Bt. D.L., of Shenstone Court, Staffordshire.

Right: This stone portico came from Shenstone Court when it was demolished in 1935. It was purchased by Lichfield City Council and re-erected on its present site opposite the Friary School.

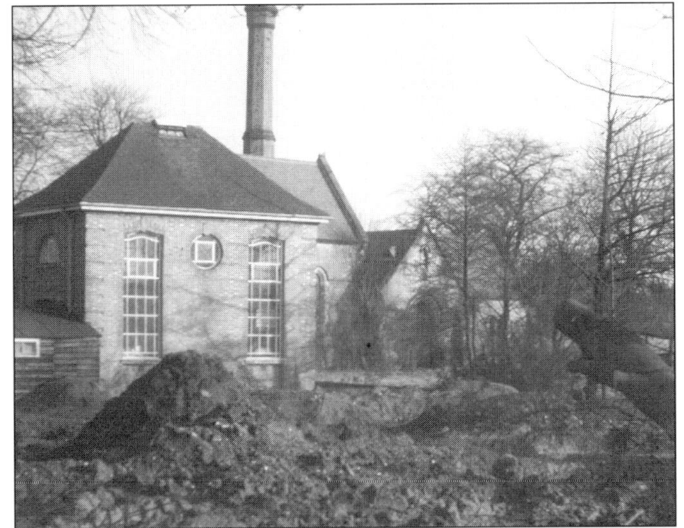

The Conduit Lands Trust, which for centuries had supplied Lichfield with clean water, operated this pumping station in the Friary, close to the junction with Walsall Road. It closed down on November 7th 1923, when the supplying of water to the city of Lichfield was taken over by the South Staffordshire Waterworks Co.

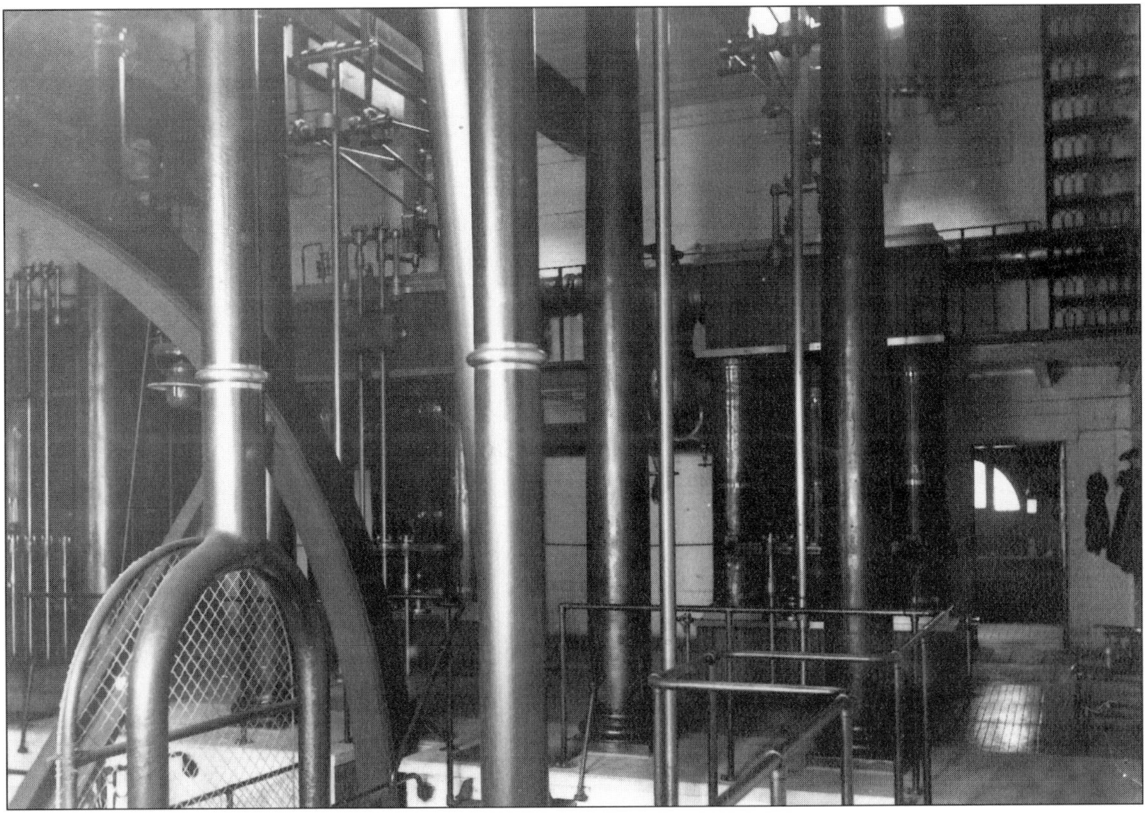

These engines, at one time installed in the Sandfields Pumping Station of the South Staffordshire Waterworks Company, are of some historic interest They were made by Boulton & Watt of Soho Works, Birmingham, for the South Devon Atmospheric Railway, in 1846. Before they were installed, the railway company decided to abandon the atmospheric system and so the engines were left on the makers hands. In 1856 they sold them to the waterworks company who installed them at Lichfield from where they pumped water for many years to the Black Country.

In 1924, these historic engines were replaced by more modern equipment.

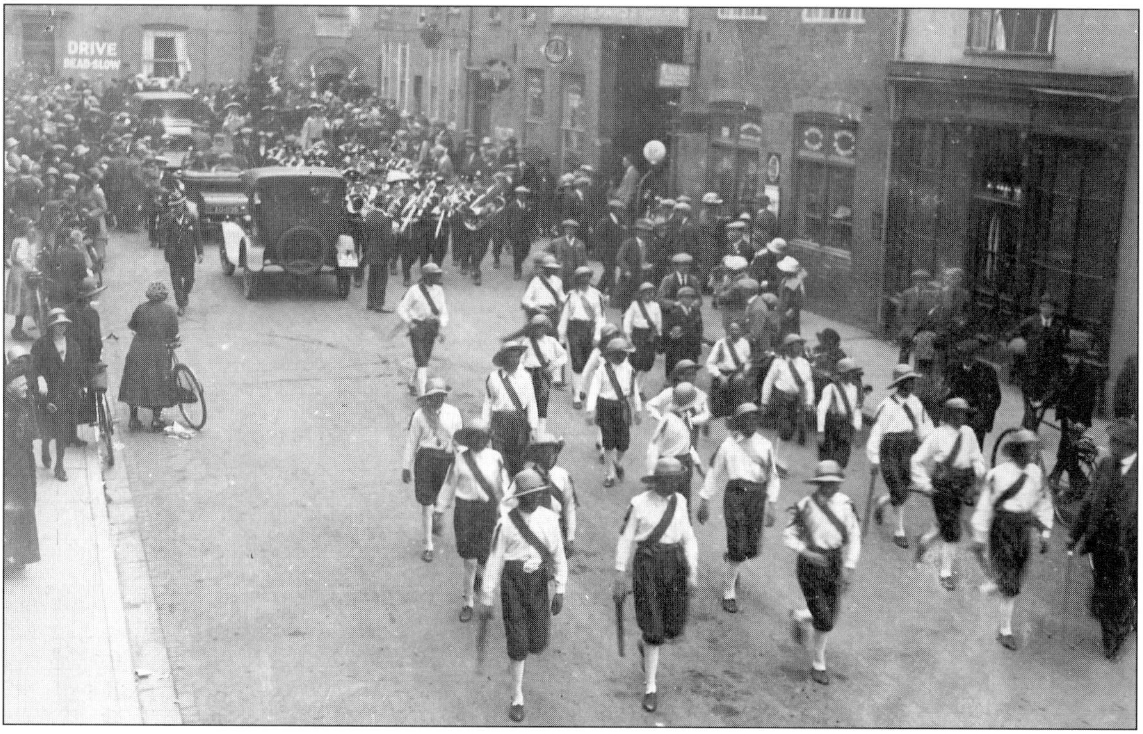

At the Bower of 1925, the boys from Beacon School in these two photographs danced Lancashire Morrice led by their trainer Mr Gallimore (the man with the big whip).

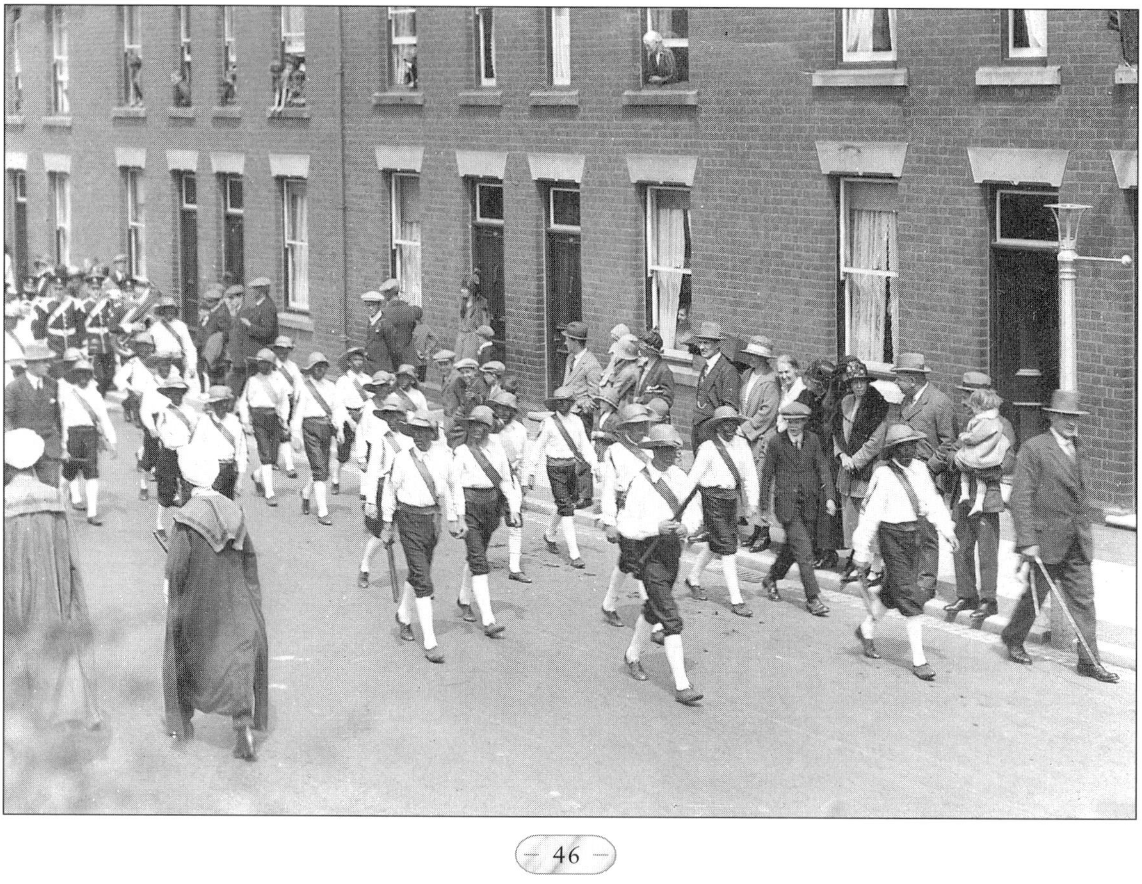

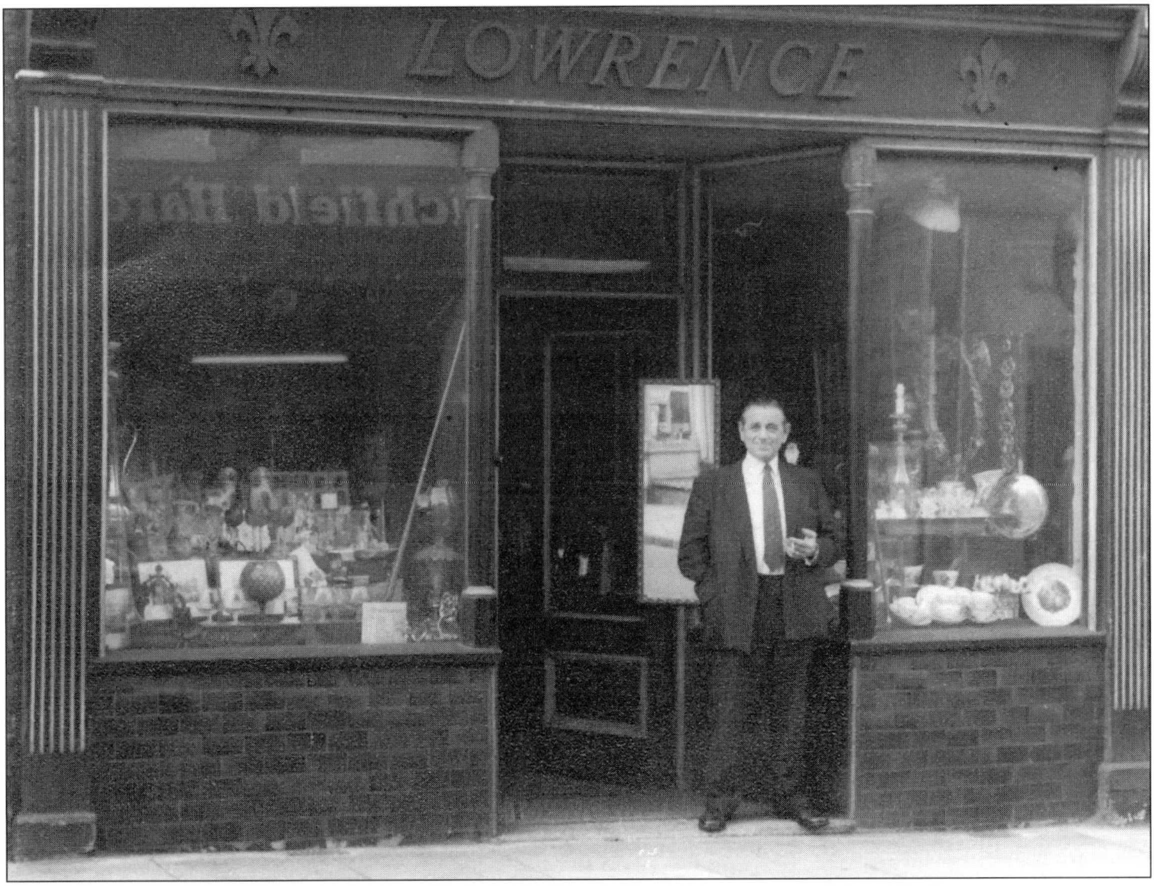

By 1925 Mr Lowrance, the antique dealer, had moved his business from Boswell House to a shop in Bird Street, and had been succeeded by his son, here outside the new shop.

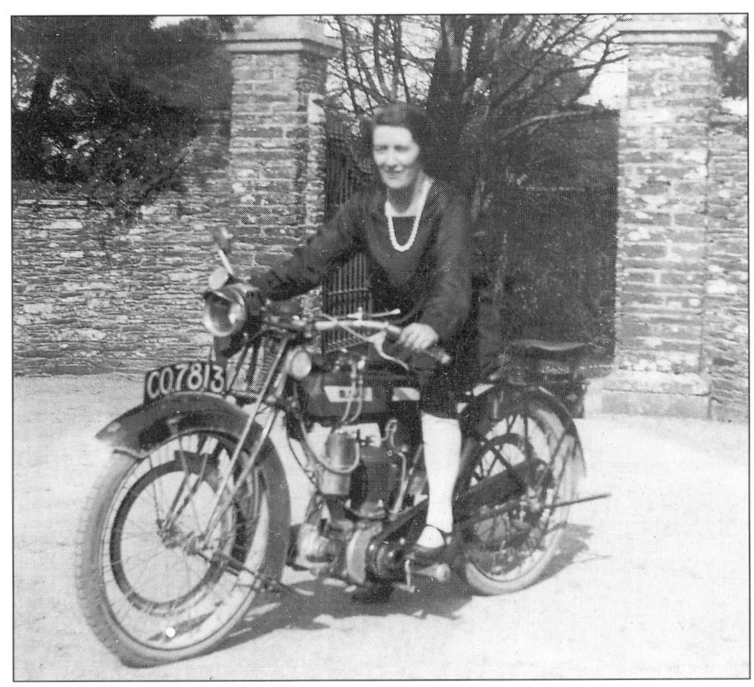

This was the age of the motorbike, and the lady who was to become Mrs Lowrance thought nothing of riding her bike from Devonshire to Lichfield for week ends, while she trained to be a teacher. She married and settled down in Lichfield. She is remembered with affection by many people whom she taught in their primary schools.

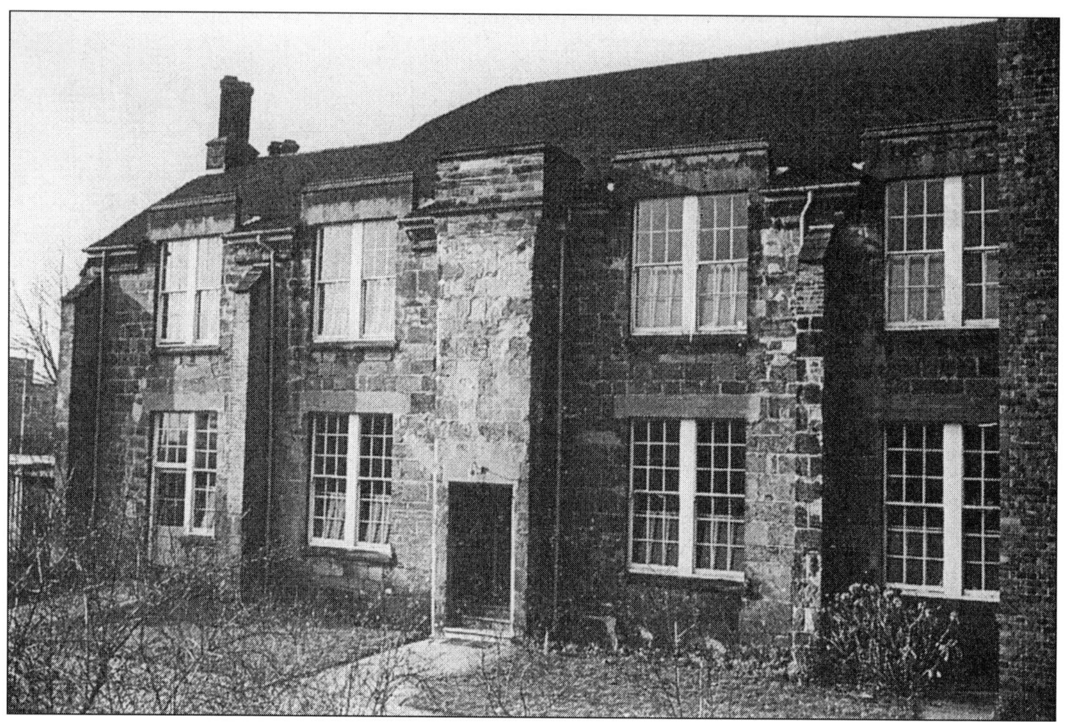

The friary – remains of the original Franciscan friary H.Q of Staffordshire Yeomanry 1896-1921 and home of the Friary School 1921-75.

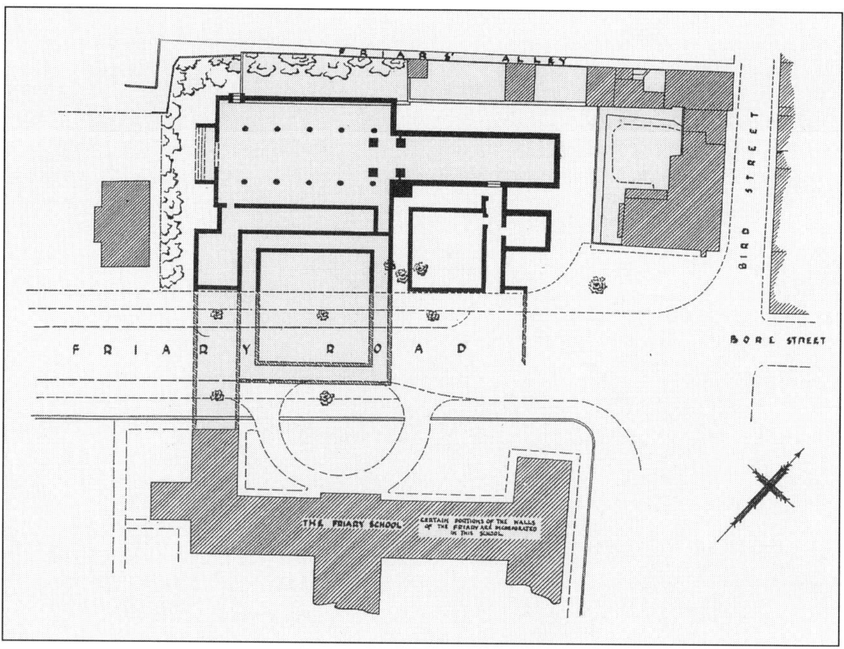

Plan of the site of the Franciscan Friary, Lichfield, showing the present Friary Road and the former Friary School (now the Public Library and former Art School).

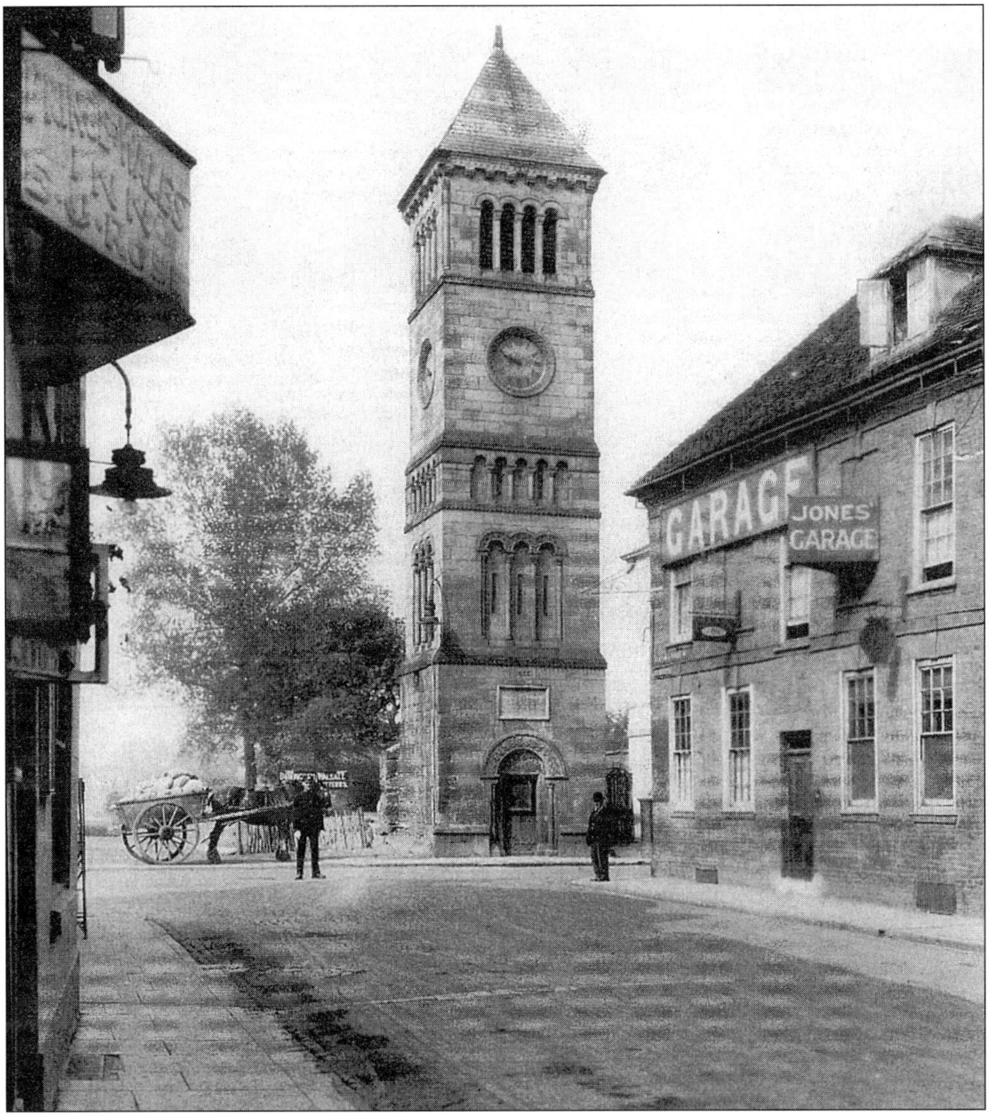

Above: The Clock Tower in its original position, seen from Bore Street. This gives an excellent view of Jones's Garage.

As part of the Friary Road development it became necessary to remove the ClockTower, a monument to the Conduit Lands Trust, which had supplied the city with clean water for centuries. The City Council had decided to demolish it, but Sir Richard Cooper came once again to the rescue and met the cost of moving it to it present position.

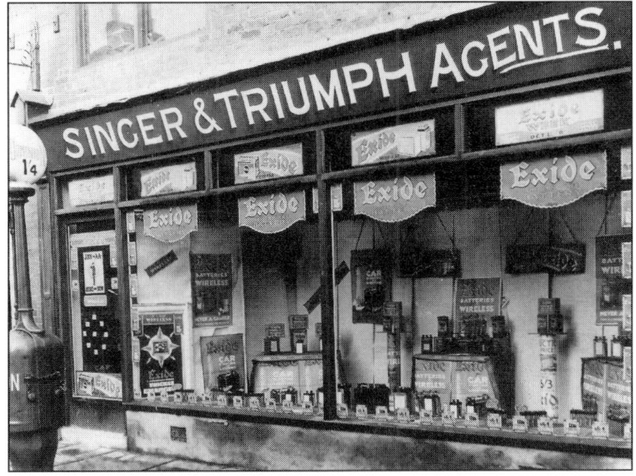

Right: Jones's Garage again c 1925. Petrol at 1/4d (13p) a gallon and batteries for the newly arrived "wireless" were available.

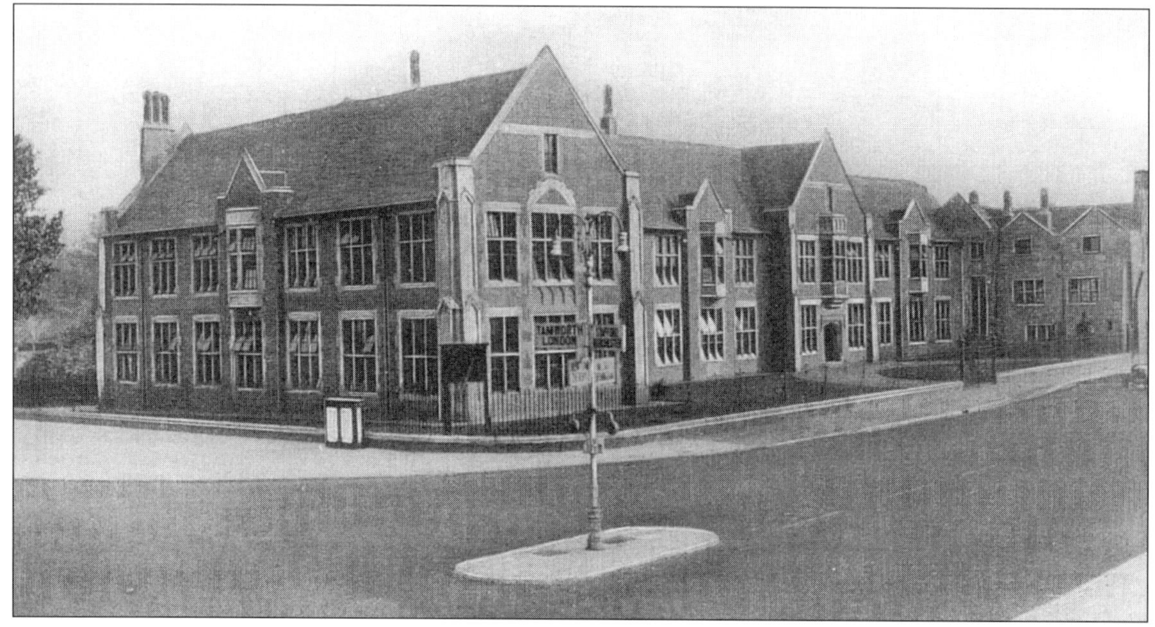

The Friary, with new Friary School and new road.

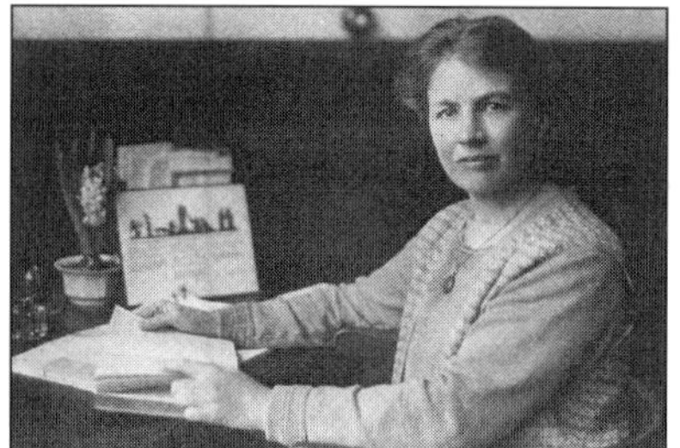

Miss D.V.M. Hodge, MA., Headmistress of the Friary School, 1911 to 1945.

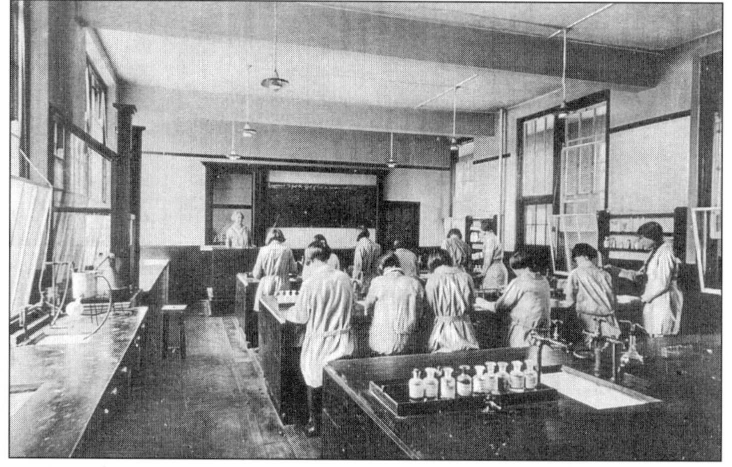

The Chemistry Laboratory.

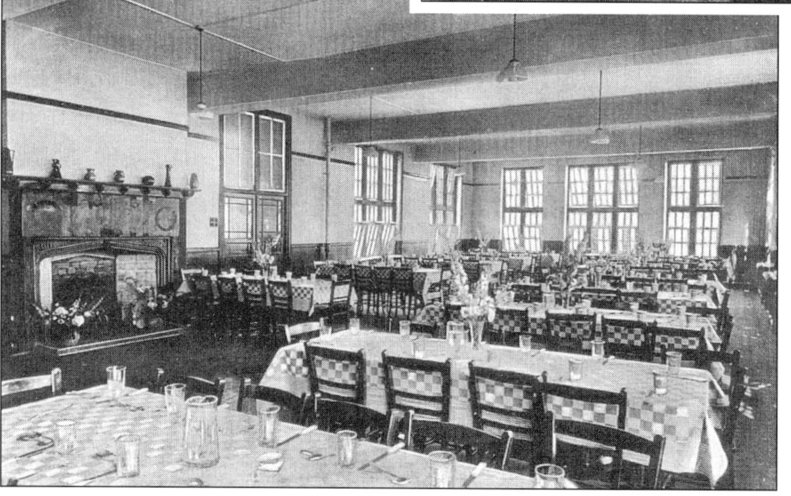

The Refectory, with its Tudor fireplace.

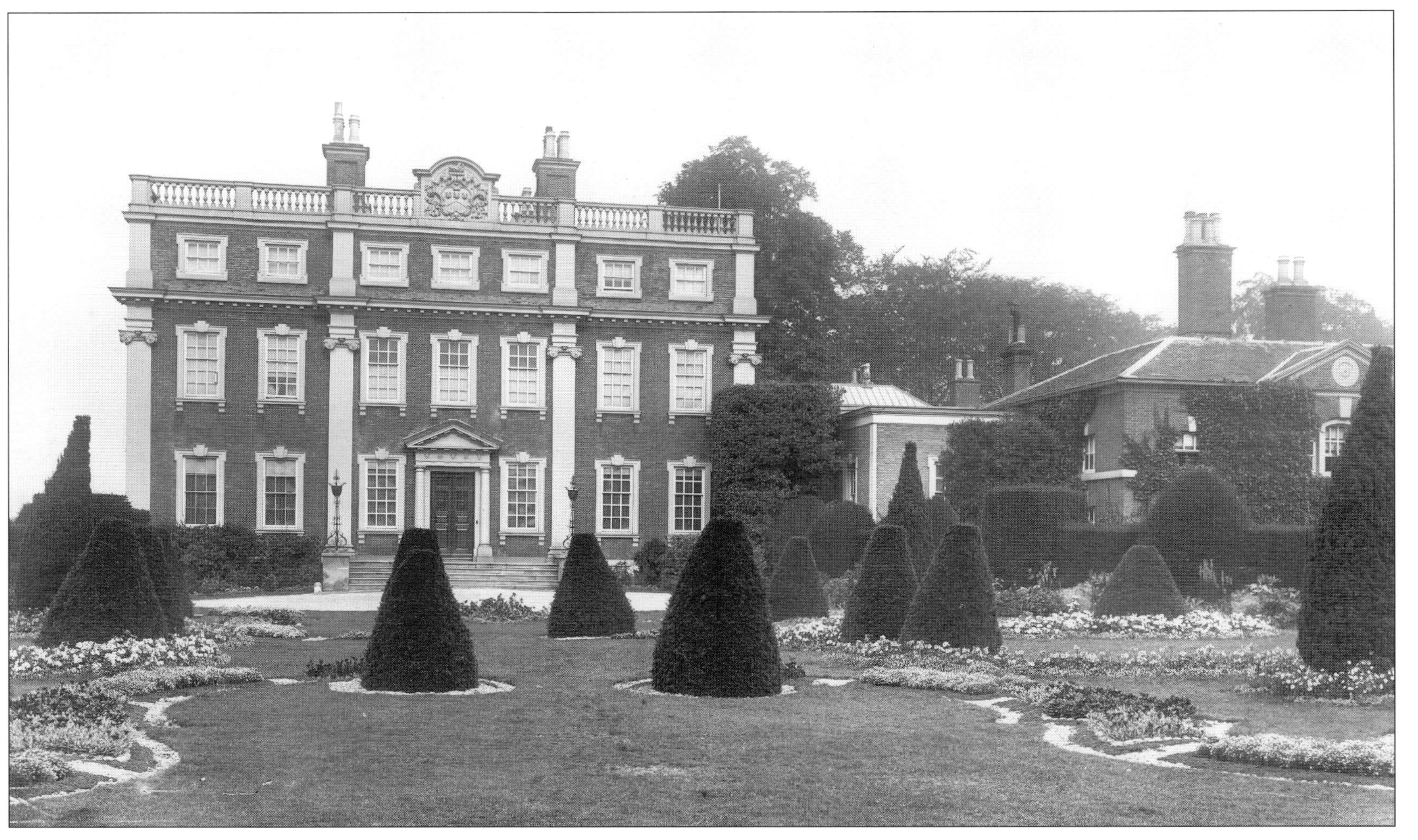

A name which will always be remembered in Lichfield is that of Colonel Swinfen Broun of Swinfen Hall, an estate about three miles out of the city, which he inherited from his stepmother, Mrs Patience Swinfen, who in the previous century had acquired it after protracted litigation in the courts. During the South African War, Colonel Swinfen Broun had commanded the 3rd (Militia) Battalion, South Staffordshire Regiment, and in the years just after the Great War he returned many times to the continent of Africa in pursuit of big game. (His trophies were later donated to Lichfield Museum).

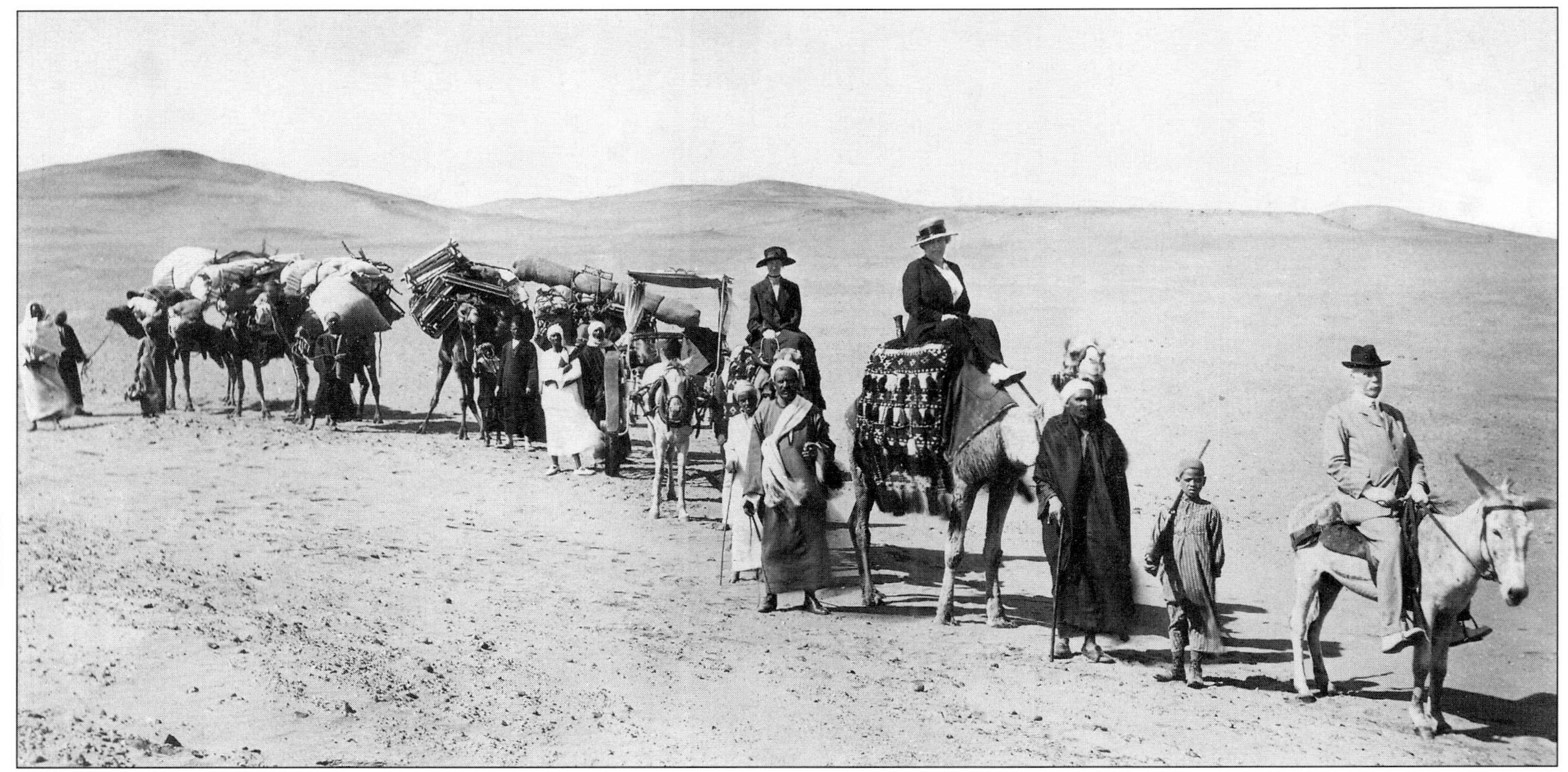

Opposite page: Setting out for a day's shooting (the ladies wearing gloves).

Opposite page: On Safari. From right to left: Headman, Colonel Swinfen Broun, Mrs Swinfen Broun, Miss Allen (of Alrewas), Lady's Maid to Mrs Swinfen Broun.

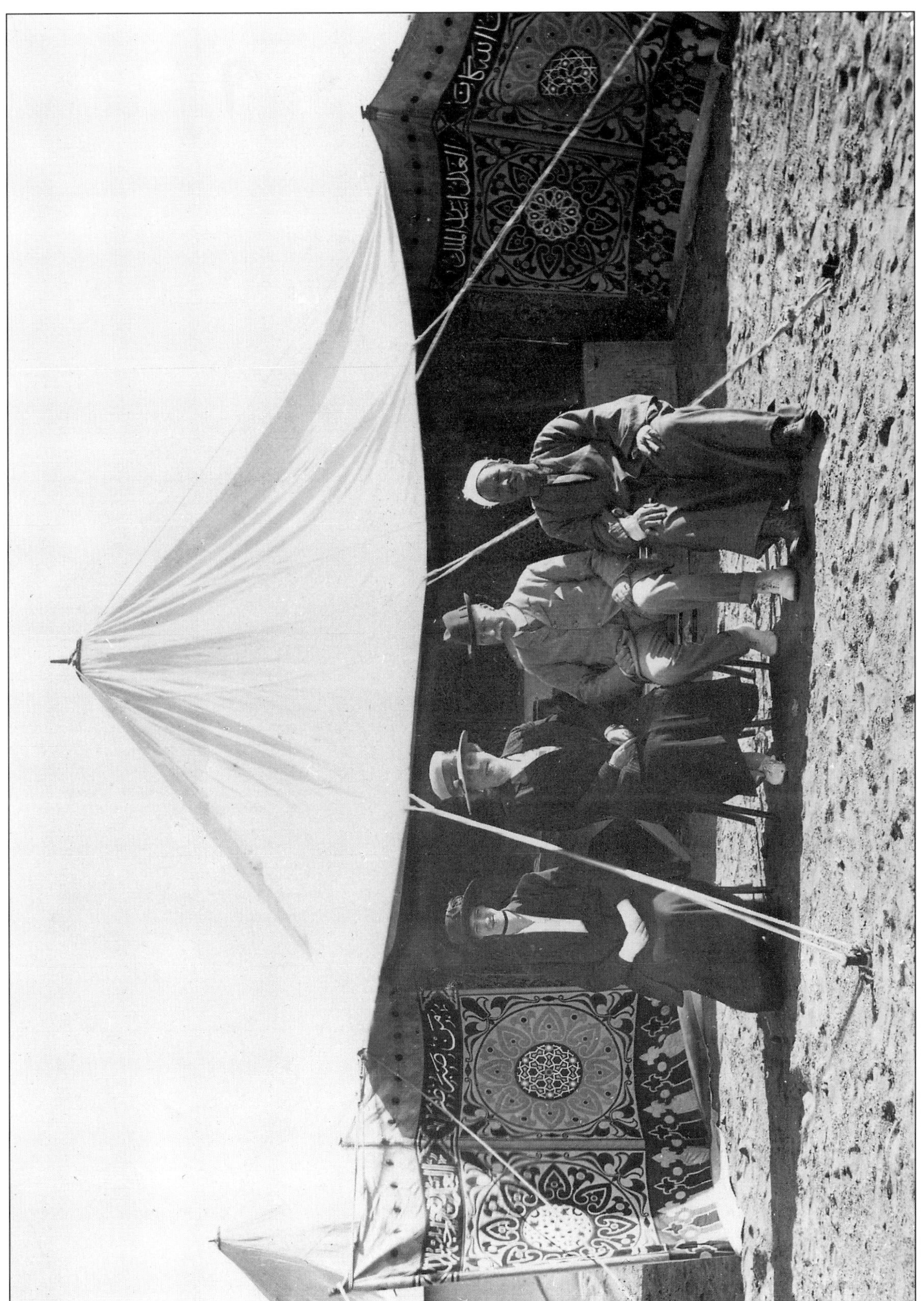

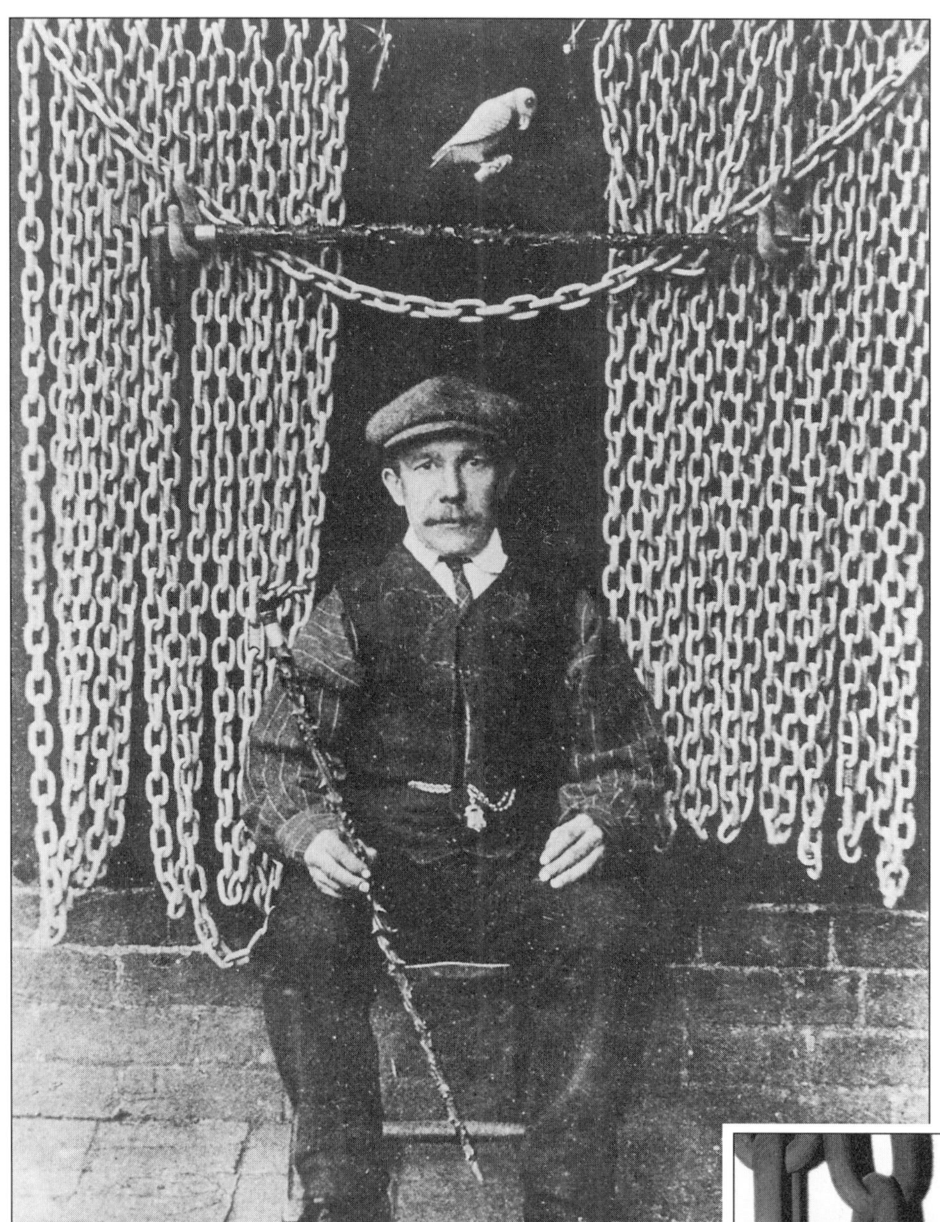

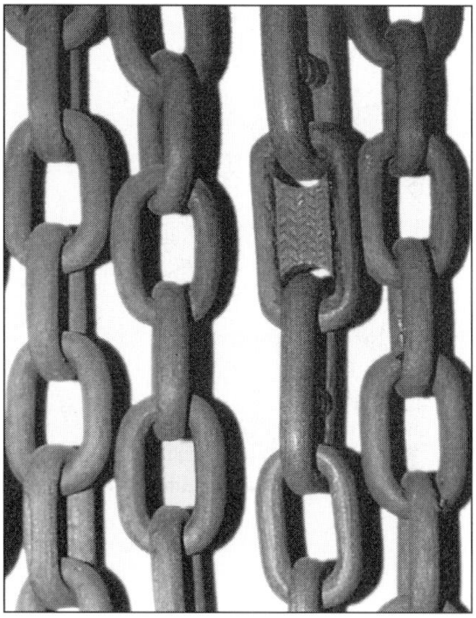

This is Edward Buckley of Heath Hayes, wood carver extraordinary. He lived at a time (probably near the beginning of the century) when the value of a work of art was judged by the amount of work which went into it. The chain which hangs behind him is of wood, carved from a single plank of timber, each link being separate from the others – a work requiring enormous patience. **Inset:** The chain can be seen today in St Mary's Heritage Centre, Lichfield.

Chapter 4 – The Thirties

The Thirties were noticeable in Britain for technological advances which put the country in the forefront of world achievement. We produced the fastest and largest ships on the North Atlantic run with the *Mauritania*, the *Queen Mary* and the *Queen Elizabeth*, all holders of the Blue Riband. In the air, we produced the winner of the Schneider Trophy with the forerunner of the wartime Spitfire. On the ground, we had speed records broken by Sir Henry Seagrave and Sir Malcolm Campbell in their motor cars. On the railways, we had the fastest steam locomotives in the world. We were the first country in the world to have television, and among our other achievements was the R101, the largest airship in the world. On its second voyage it passed over Lichfield, admired by all the citizens. A year later it lay in a field at Beauvais, in France, a tangled wreck of burnt out metal.

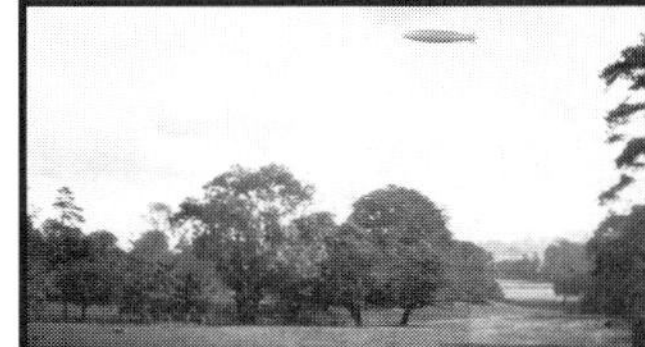

Above: The airship R10l on its second flight, in the autumn of 1929. Photographed from Abnalls House, Lichfield.

Below: The Bower procession, in the early 1930s, passing the Five Gables, Bore Street The float is entered by Garratts, the principal bakers in the city and the windmill is made of bread. Note the American style trilby hats (men) and the cloche hats (women).

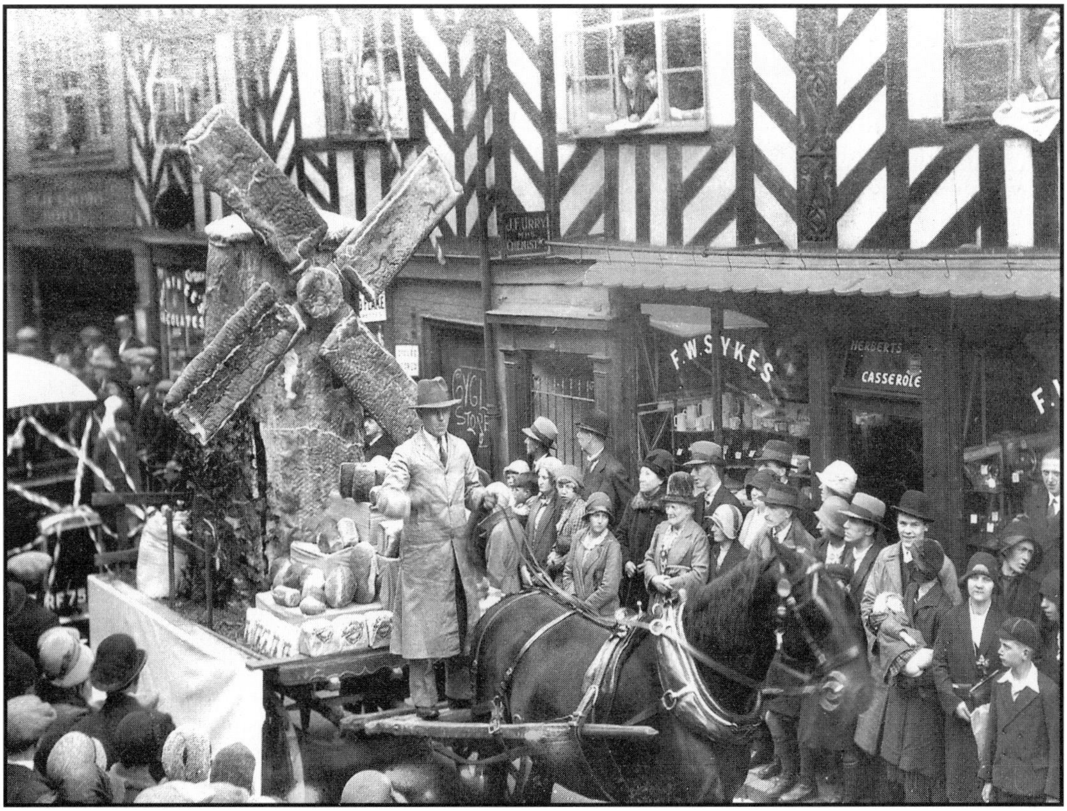

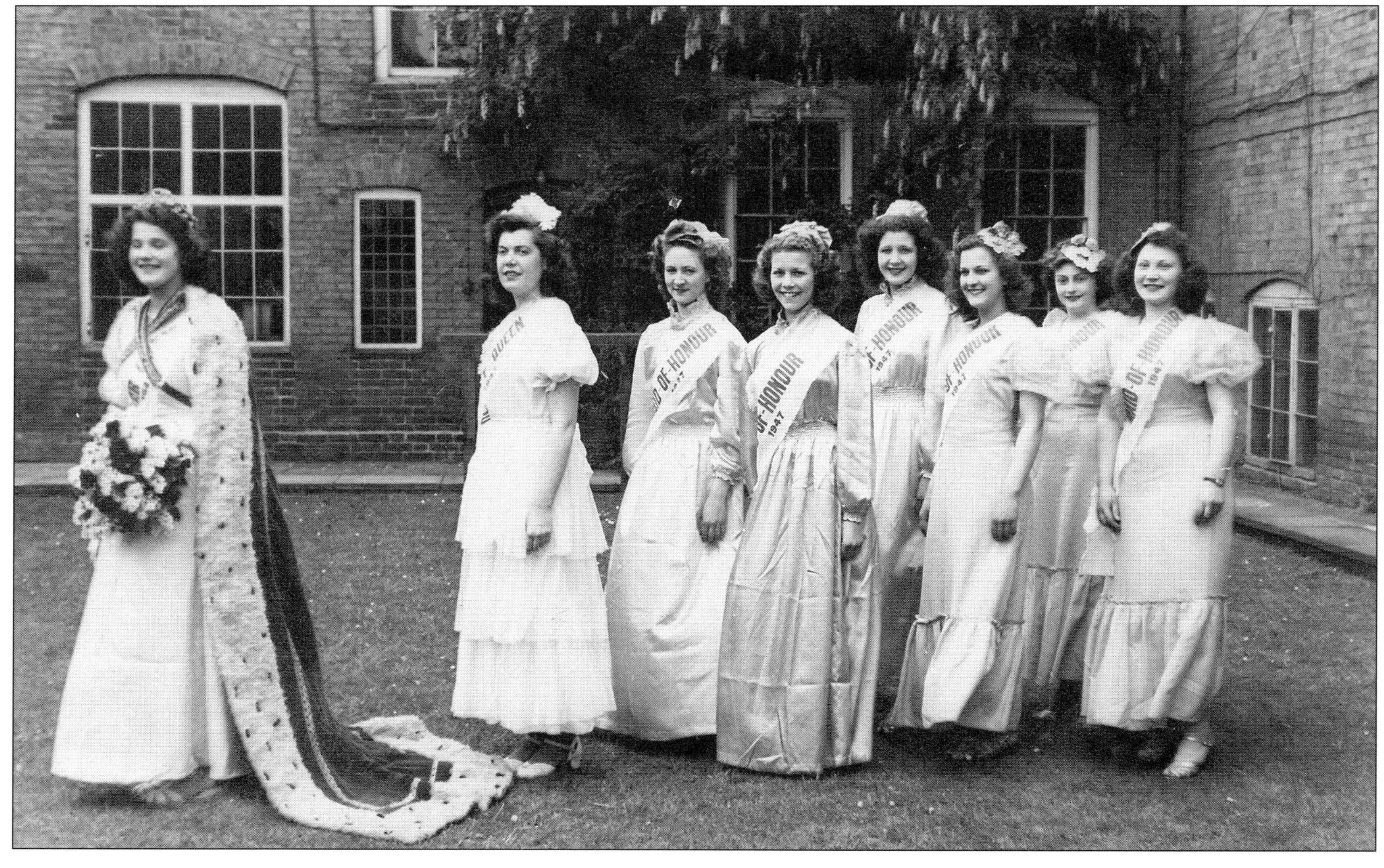

The influence of American culture on Britain became more obvious in the thirties. “Beauty Queens” were all the rage as young ladies in bathing costumes and high -heeled shoes paraded before judges for the coveted winner’s sash. In Lichfield the beauty queen cult was assimilated into the annual Bower procession, in which the Mayor crowned the Bower Queen who rode in a specially decorated vehicle at the front of the procession.

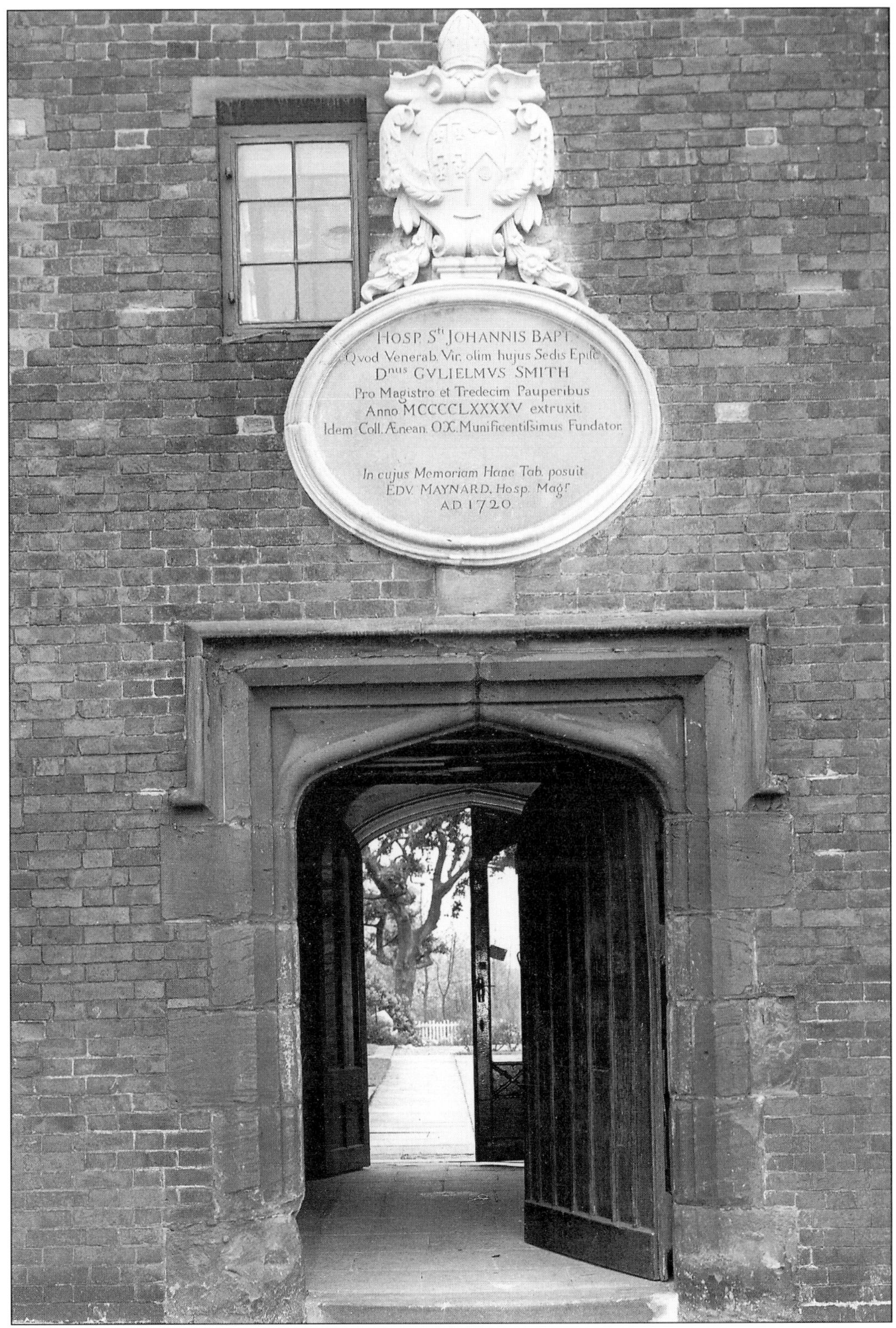

The view through the doorway of St. John's Hospital, a venerable 500 year old almshouse for old men, gives an inviting welcome to the passer by.

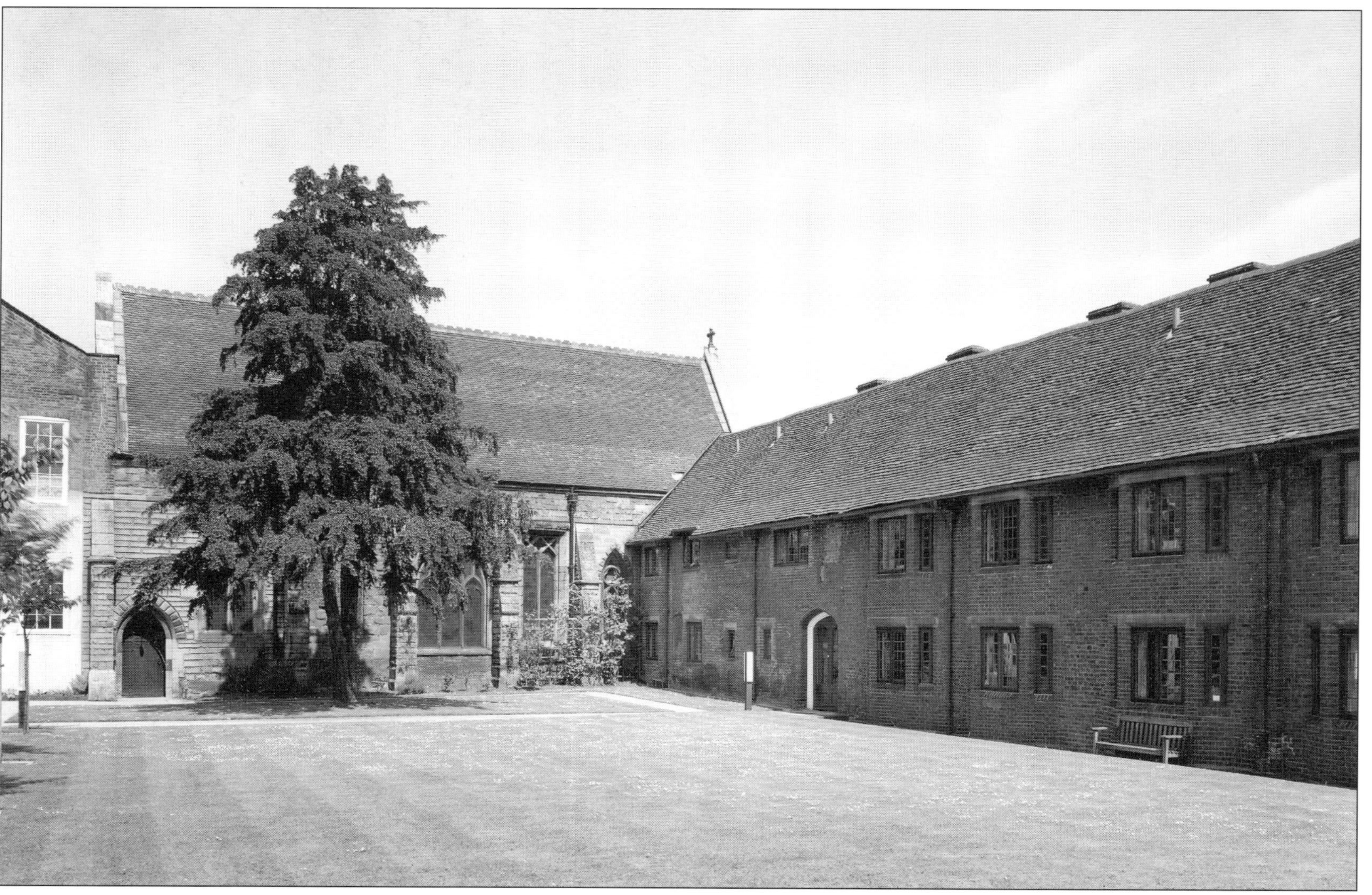

This is the scene inside.

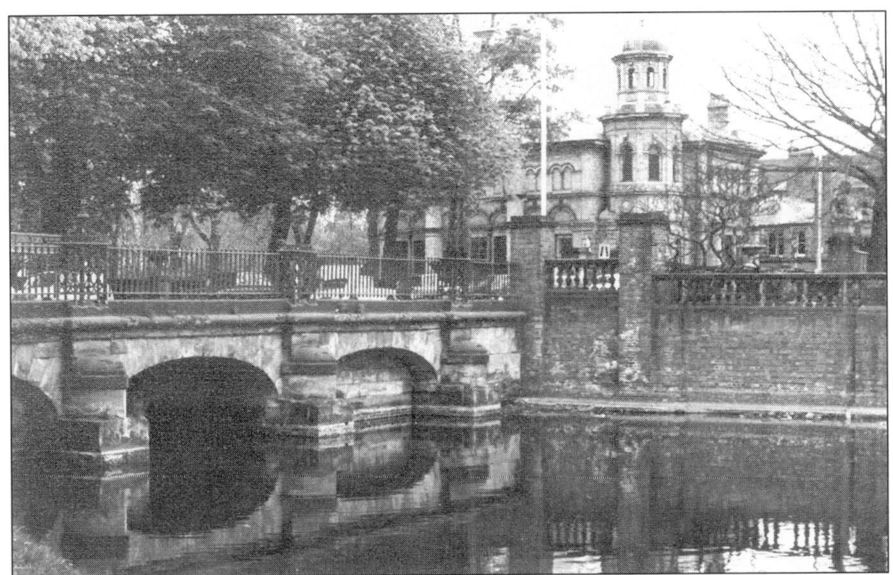

During this period a number of buildings built on the marshy ground around the Minster Pool began to subside; the Post Office, the Art School and the Library, shown here. Of these three only the Library has survived, thanks to the efforts of Mr Leslie Straw, the City Surveyor, and his staff of the former City Council. But the age old pastime of angling in the Pool still went on (below).

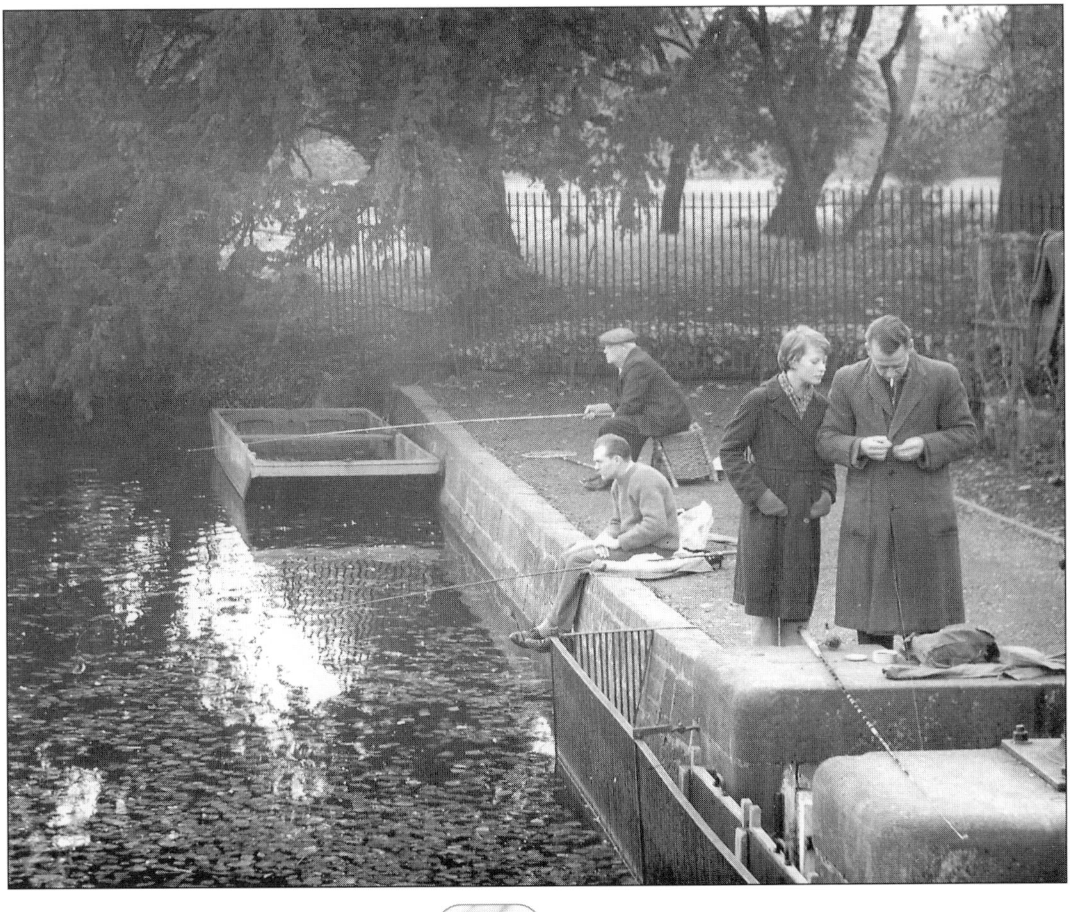

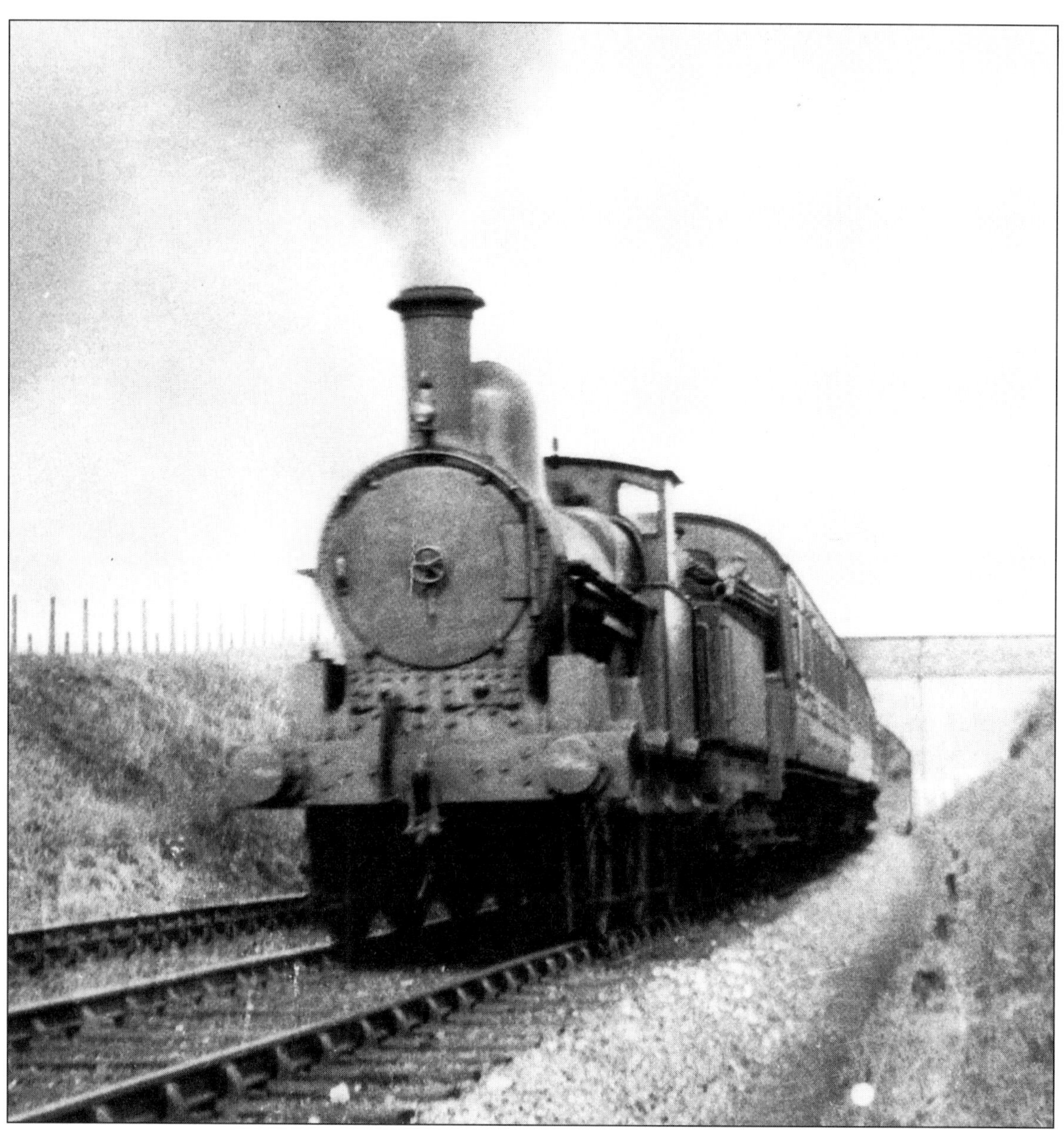

Above: During the 1930s, Lichfield City Station was a busy place. As well as the commuter lines to Sutton and Birmingham New Street, the line from Walsall and Wolverhampton in one direction and Burton and Derby in the other all passed through Lichfield City. All of these lines were worked by steam, usually with locomotives of the late Victorian period such as this Webb 0-6-0 pictured entering Hammerwich station with the 08.45 for Lichfield.

Opposite page top: The Palladium cinema in the post war period.presented a very run-down appearance. So too, did their entry for the Bower Procession.

Opposite page bottom: By 1930, they had smartened up considerably. Perhaps competition had something to do with it.

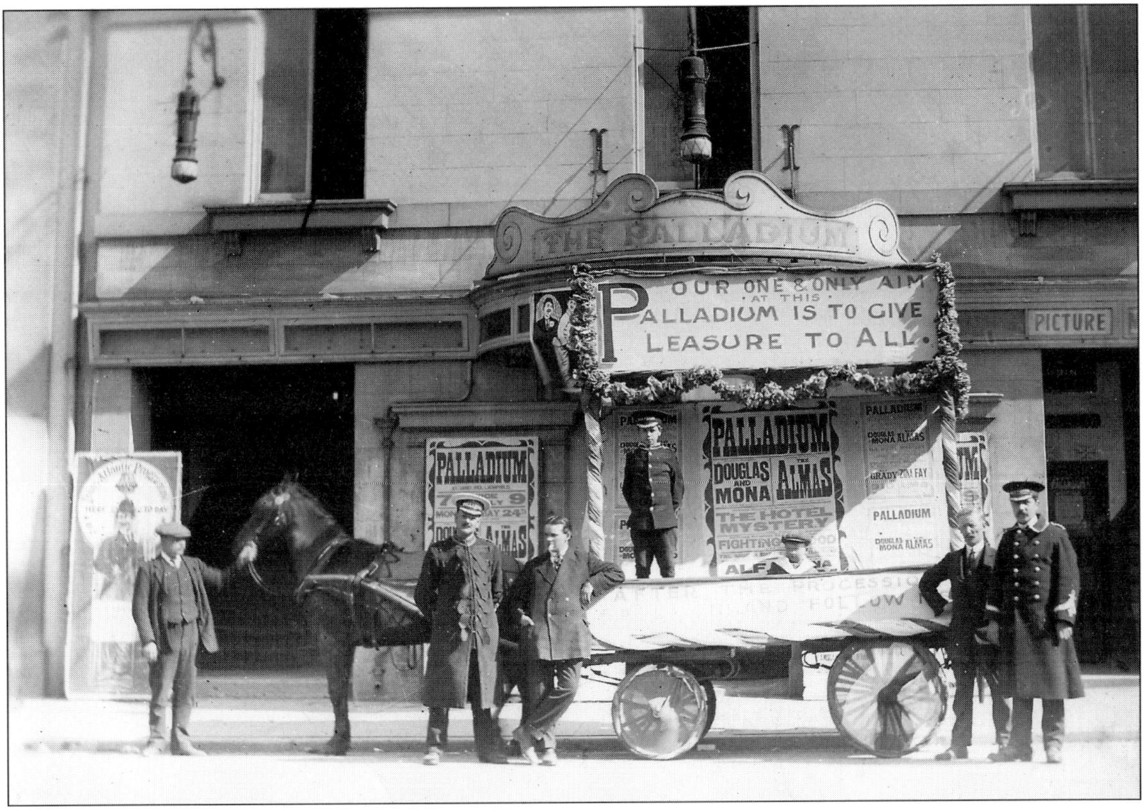
THE PALLADIUM
OUR ONE & ONLY AIM
AT THIS
PALLADIUM IS TO GIVE
PLEASURE TO ALL.
PICTURE
PALLADIUM
DOUGLAS AND MONA
THE ALMAS
THE HOTEL MYSTERY
PALLADIUM

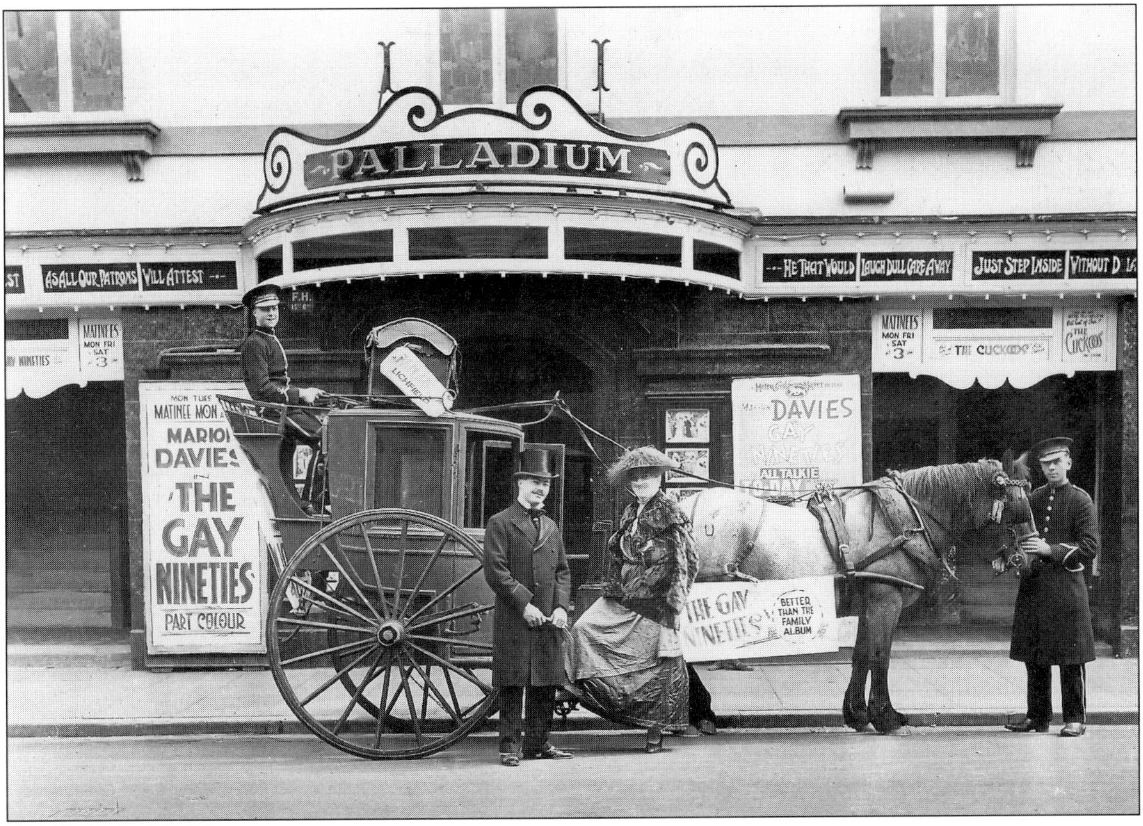
PALLADIUM
AS ALL OUR PATRONS WILL ATTEST
HE THAT WOULD LAUGH DULL CARE AWAY
JUST STEP INSIDE
MATINEES MON FRI SAT 3
THE CUCKOOS
DAVIES
THE GAY NINETIES
PART COLOUR
DAVIES GAY NINETIES
ALL TALKIE
LICHFIELD
THE GAY NINETIES
BETTER THAN THE FAMILY ALBUM

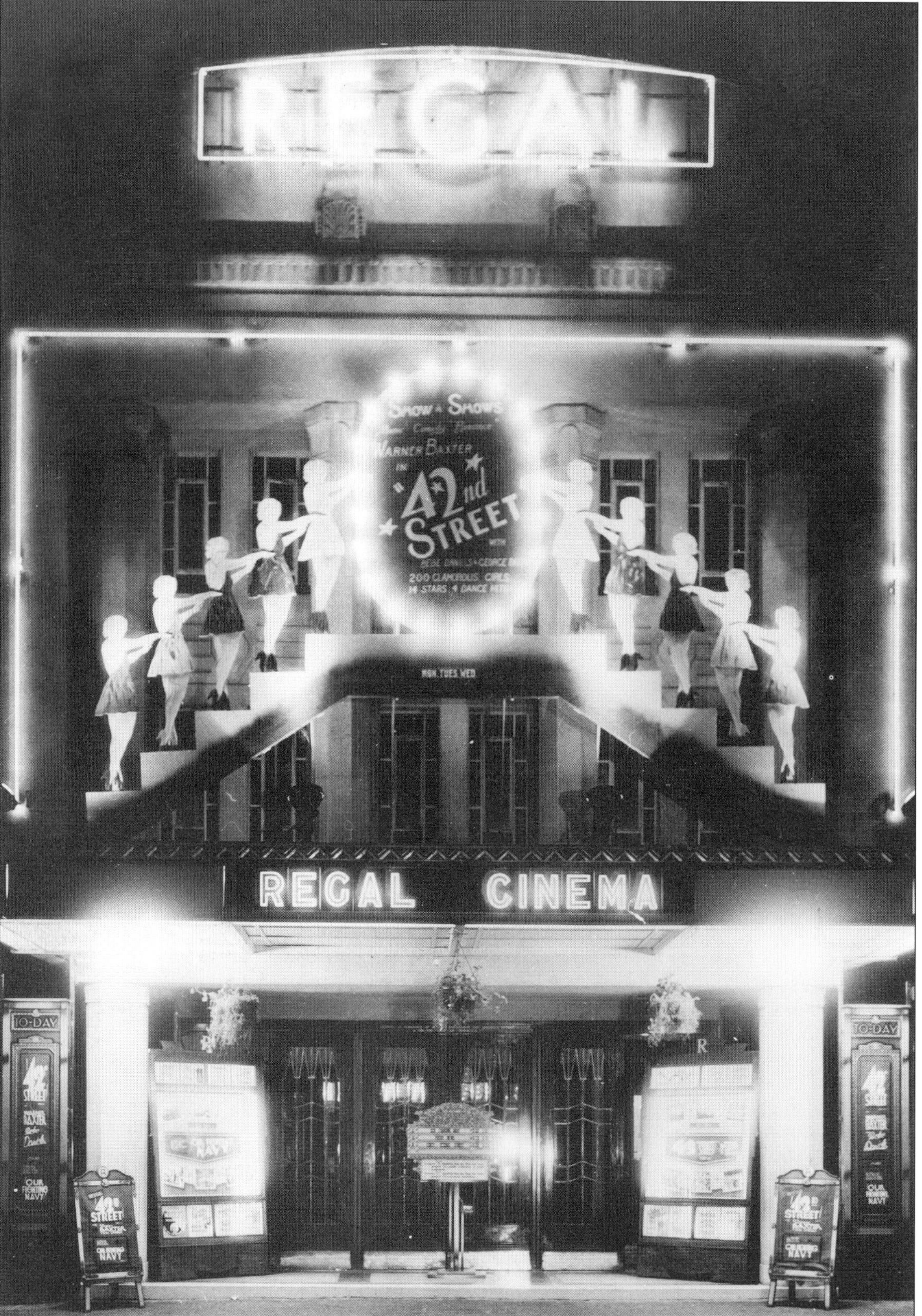
REGAL
WARNER BAXTER
IN
42nd STREET
200 GLAMOROUS GIRLS
MON. TUES. WED
REGAL CINEMA
TO-DAY
OUR FIGHTING NAVY
TO-DAY
OUR FIGHTING NAVY

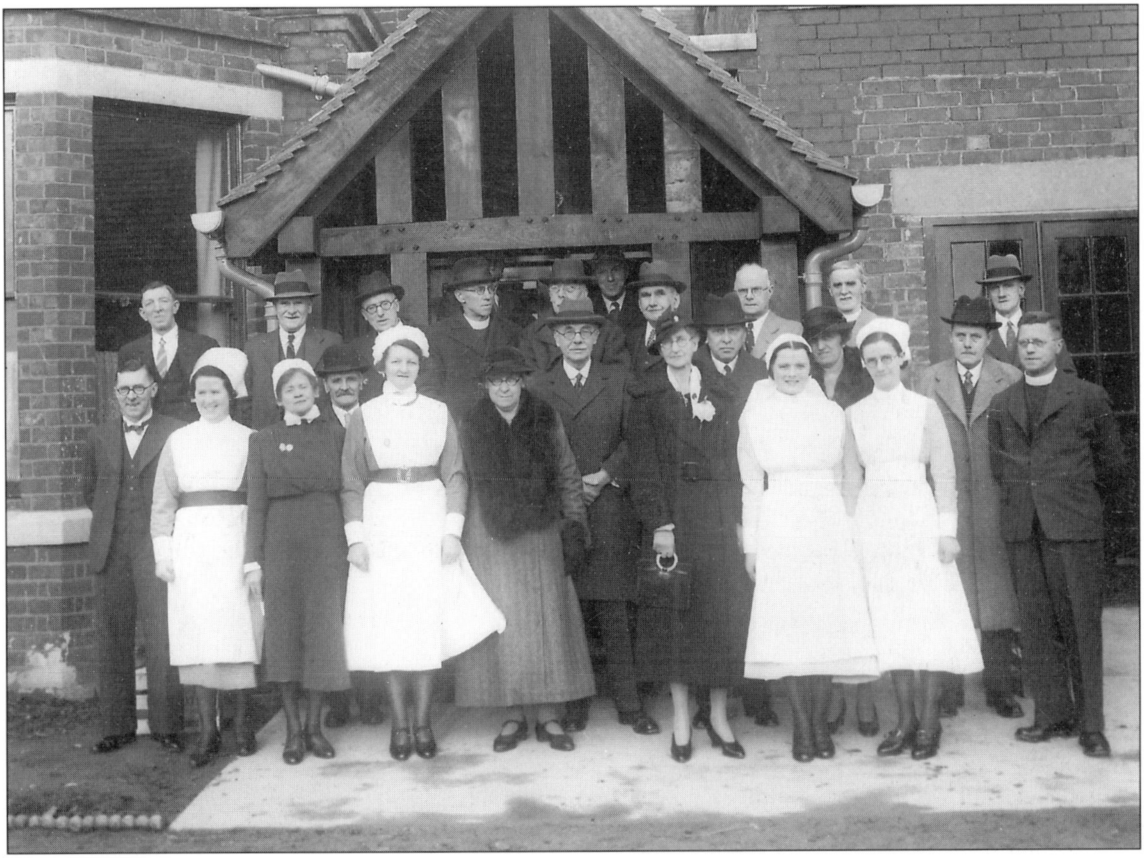

Above: In the 1930s the NHS had not yet been thought of and hospitals were either municipal (based on the Union Workhouses) or private such as Hammerwich Hospital, here shown with staff (including Matron, third from left), committee and chaplains.

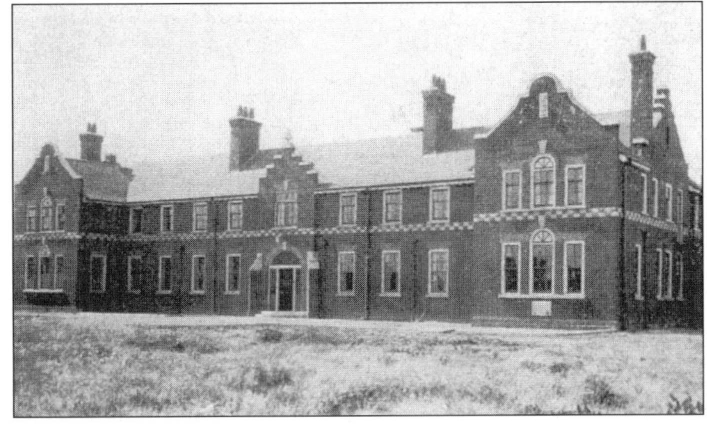

Right: Lichfield had had its own hospital since the year 1899 when the Victoria Hospital was opened to commemorate Queen Victoria's Diamond Jubilee. In 1933, a new hospital was opened and like the first one, the money for it was raised by public subscriptions. Prominent among the subscribers were Colonel and Mrs Swinfen Broun, but contributions came from all sections of Lichfield people. Because of this, and also because of the close association between the people and their hospital, it has always had a firm place in the hearts of the community. Today, as we go to press, the Victoria Hospital is under threat from the beaurocrats of the Health Authority and its future is uncertain.

Opposite page: The full force of Hollywood's influence was being felt in Lichfield by 1930 in the form of the Regal Cinema, custom built and with all the glitz and glamour of the American film industry.

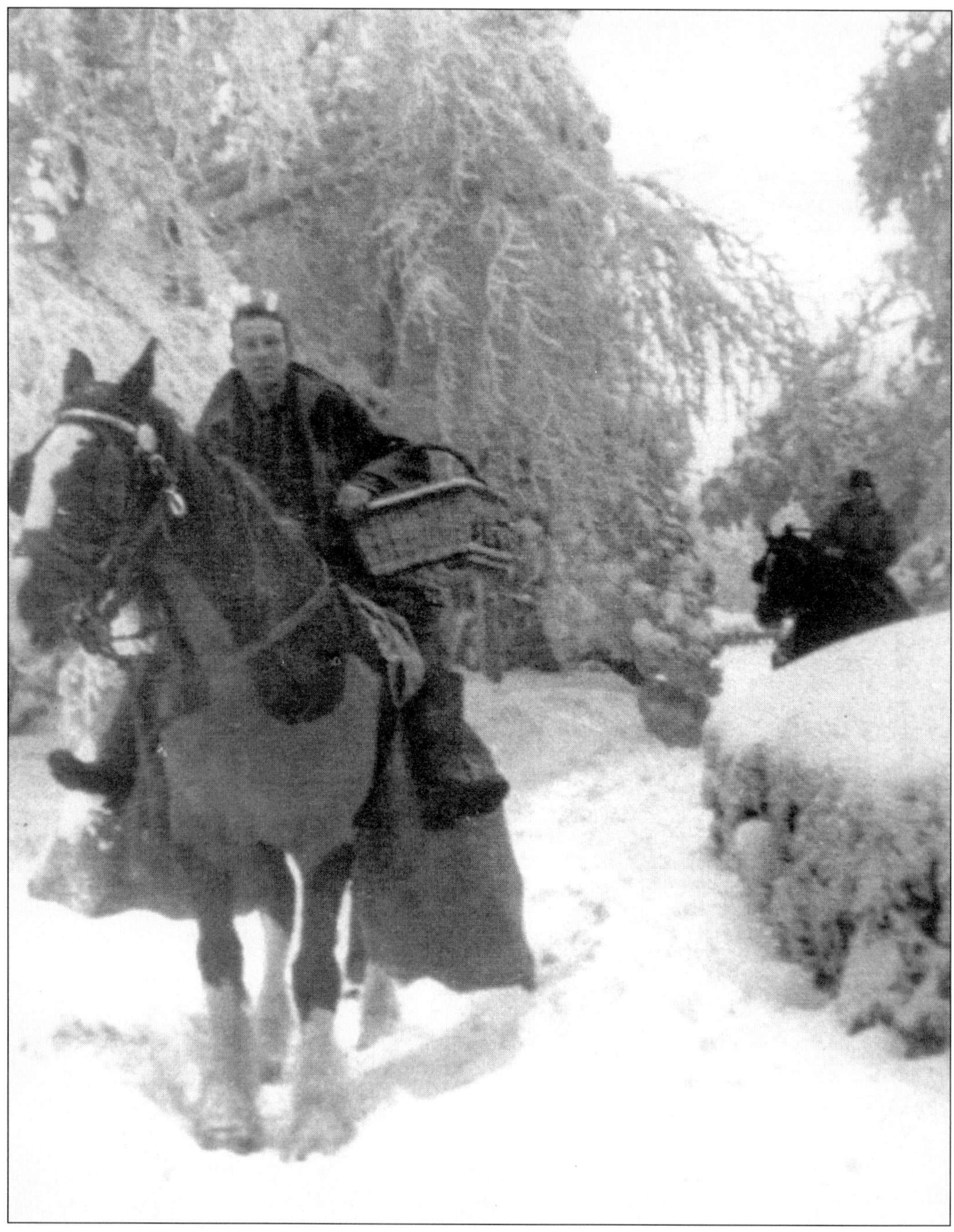

The last days of the decade saw the country under snow to an extent rarely experienced. This picture, taken by the Revd Sharples, Vicar of Gentleshaw, records the valiant efforts of Garratt's Bakery to reach the more remote parts of the district. Here we see Syd Bennett and Patch the horse delivering bread in Gentleshaw on December 29th, 1939.

Chapter 5 – Second World War

The Forties opened with the country at war with Germany. As with previous wars, photographs of wartime activities are scarce, so it is appropriate that our first picture is an ARP blackout notice. ARP (Air Raid Precautions) was the civilian organization set up to counter the effects of air raids. It had two branches – Air Raid Wardens, who dealt with people, and the rescue services who had to cope with the damage from bombs. In Lichfield the ARP services operated from a control centre in the basement of the public library.

By the time the war ended there had been 312 alerts, seventeen bombs had fallen in the area but fortunately no damage or casualties occurred.

At Fradley, three miles to the east of the city the Royal Air Force had a training airfield and RAF and RAAF were frequently to be seen in the city. So too, were members of the American army from 1942, as they took over the whole of Whittington Barracks.

The worst occurrence of this decade took place after the war was over, when on 1st January 1946 a collision occurred between a slow train waiting at the up platform and a fish train moving through Trent Valley Station. For some reason the points were not set properly for the fish train and it ran into the platform road smashing into the passenger train. A number of people was killed or injured.

On a happier note, 1949 saw the return of live theatre to Lichfield, with the setting up of the David Garrick Repertory Theatre in the old St James's Hall.

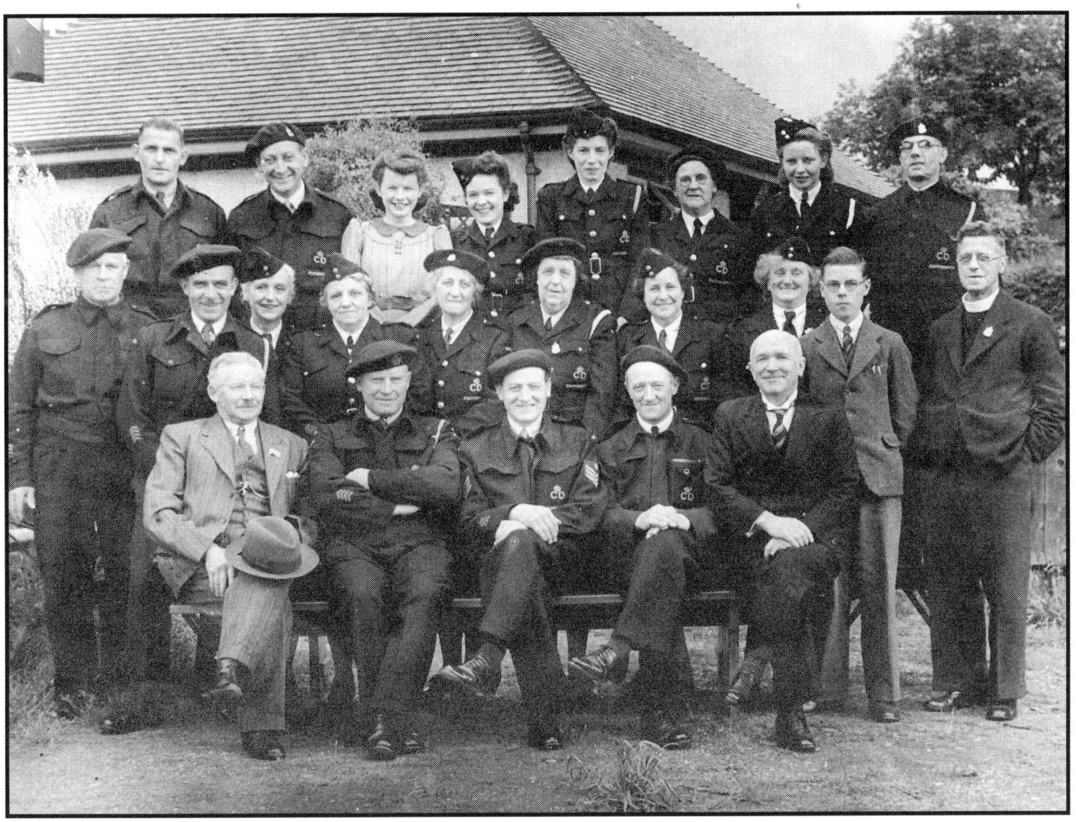

A group of ARP wardens, from Hammerwich. They wore a dark blue uniform with chrome buttons and the insignia "Civil Defence".

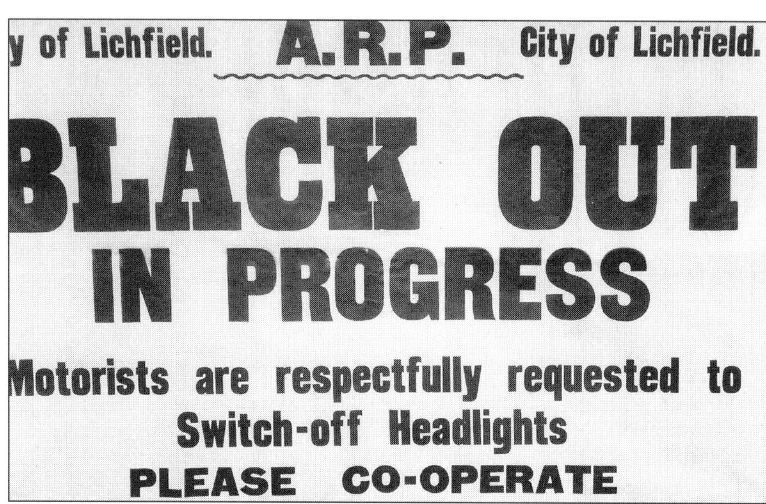

These signs were used for ARP exercises before war broke out. After the commencement of hostilities requests gave way to more peremptory orders.

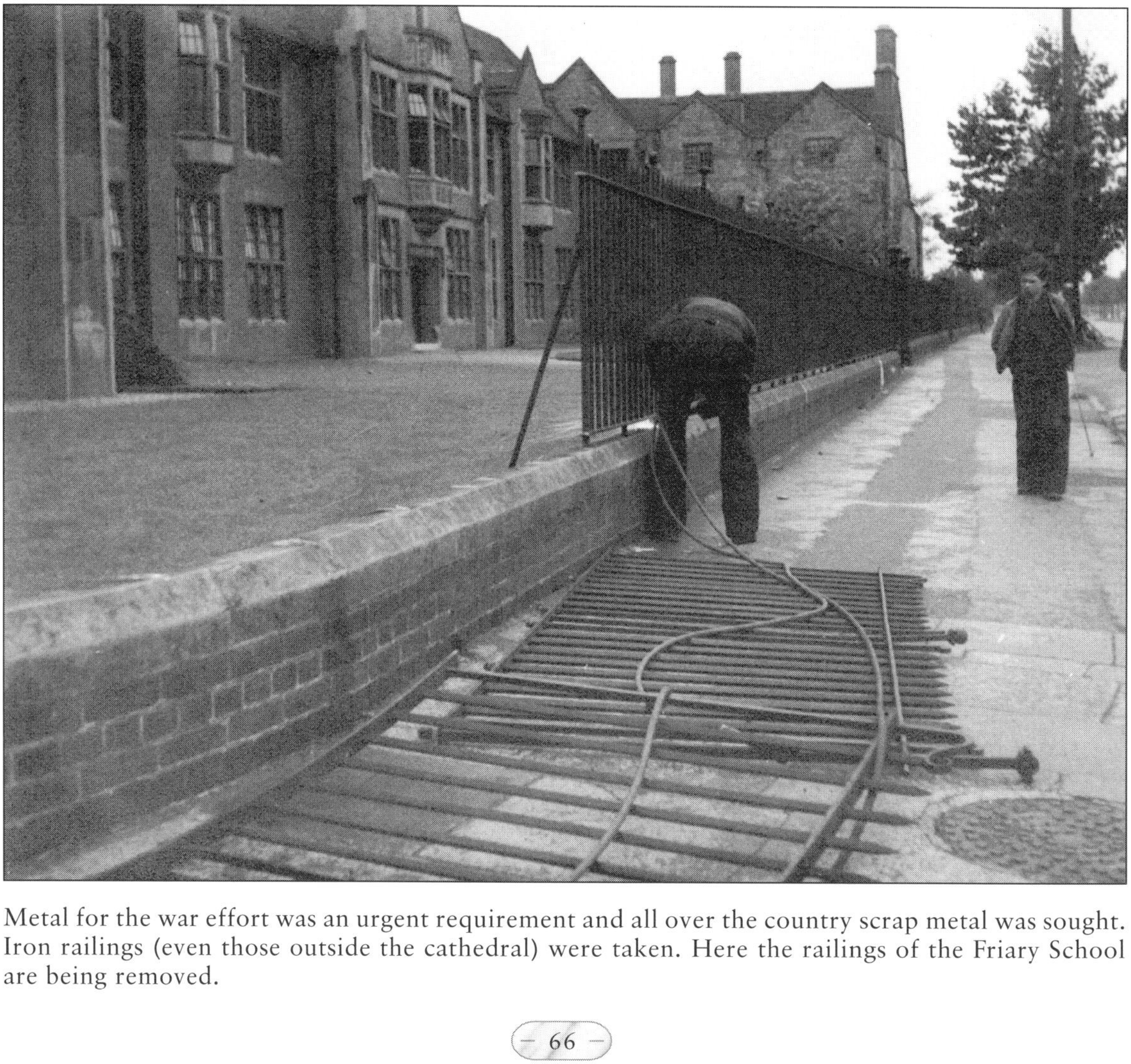

Metal for the war effort was an urgent requirement and all over the country scrap metal was sought. Iron railings (even those outside the cathedral) were taken. Here the railings of the Friary School are being removed.

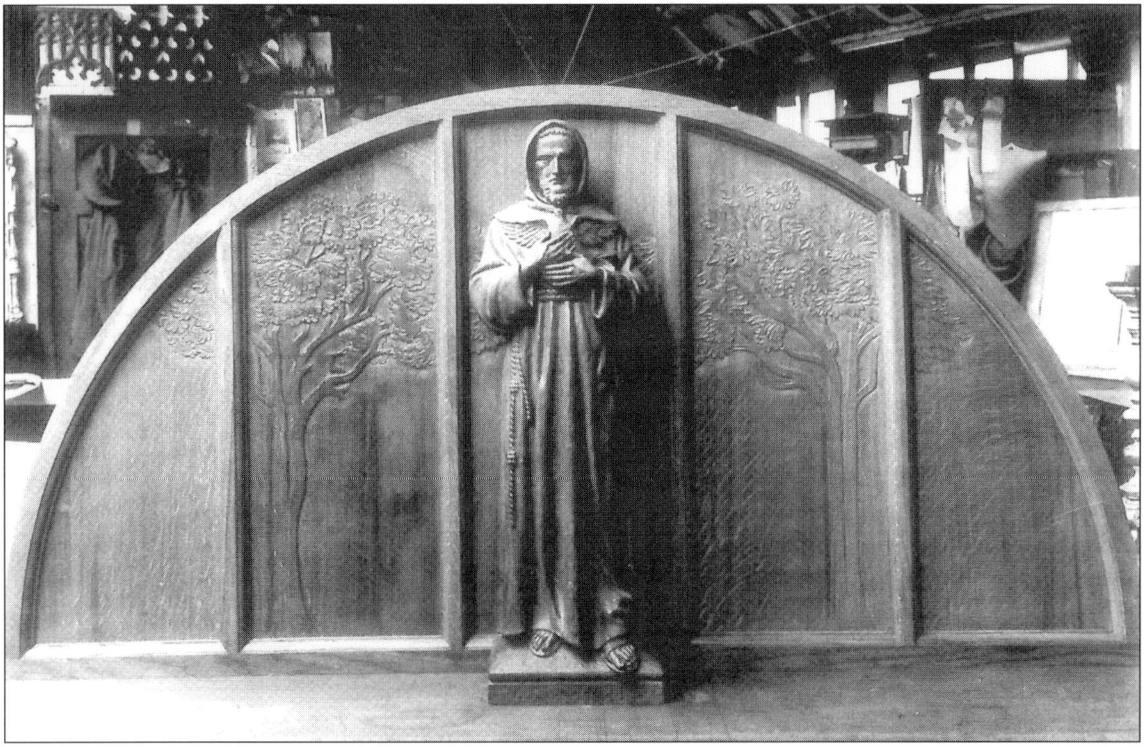

In 1944 the Friary School received from Mr and Mrs Stanton the gift of a statue of St Francis, beautifully carved in oak, which for the remaining life of the school, stood in the hall to welcome all who entered. Today it stands in the hall of Friary Grange School.

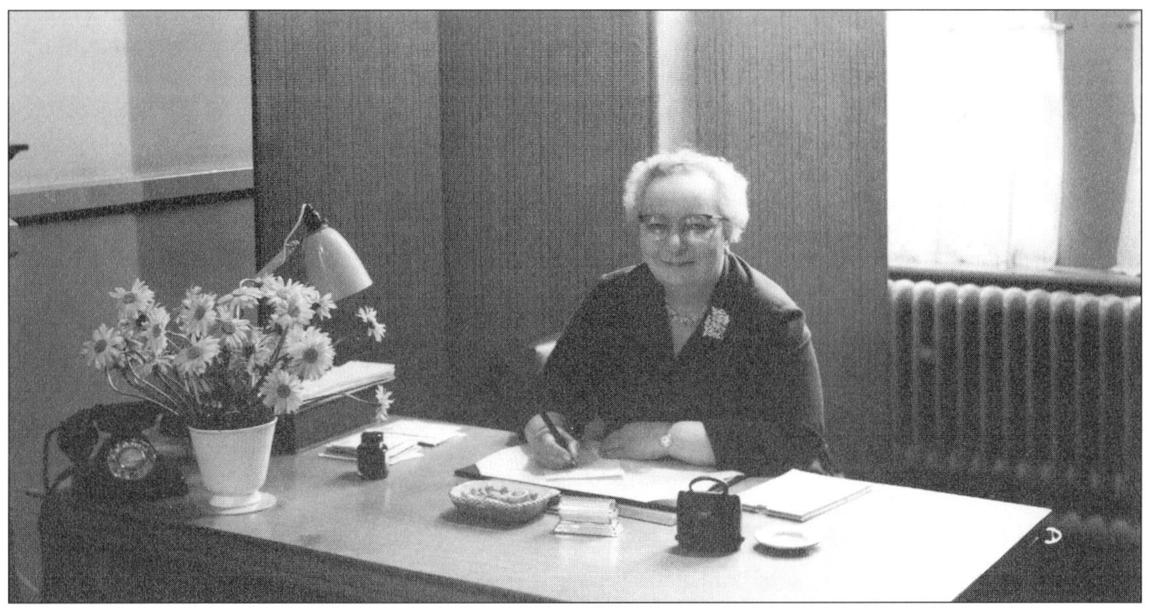

1945 saw the retirement of Miss Hodge, who had been Headmistress of the Friary School since 1911. Her place was taken by Miss K. C. M. Gent, M.A.

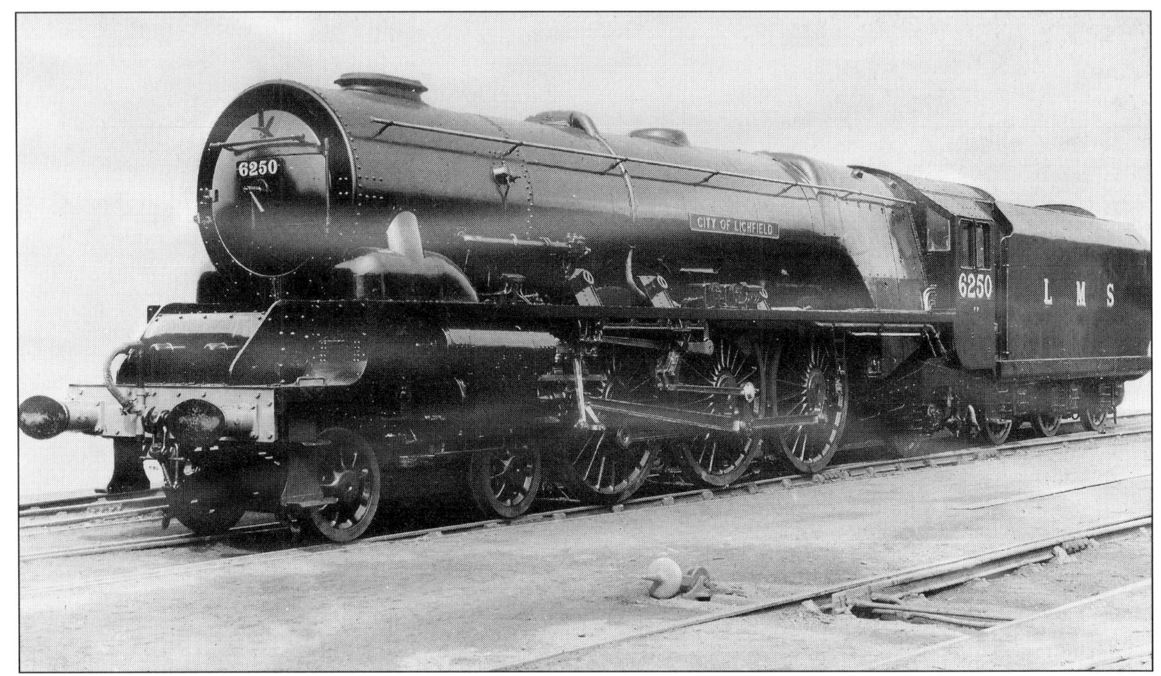

During the war, the manufacture of all but the most essential requirements was prohibited, but this included railway locomotives, and among the new engines built in 1943 was this superb example of a 4-6-2 express passenger locomotive. Constructed at Crewe for the London Midland and Scottish Railway, it bore the proud name *City of Lichfield*, the third to carry that name.

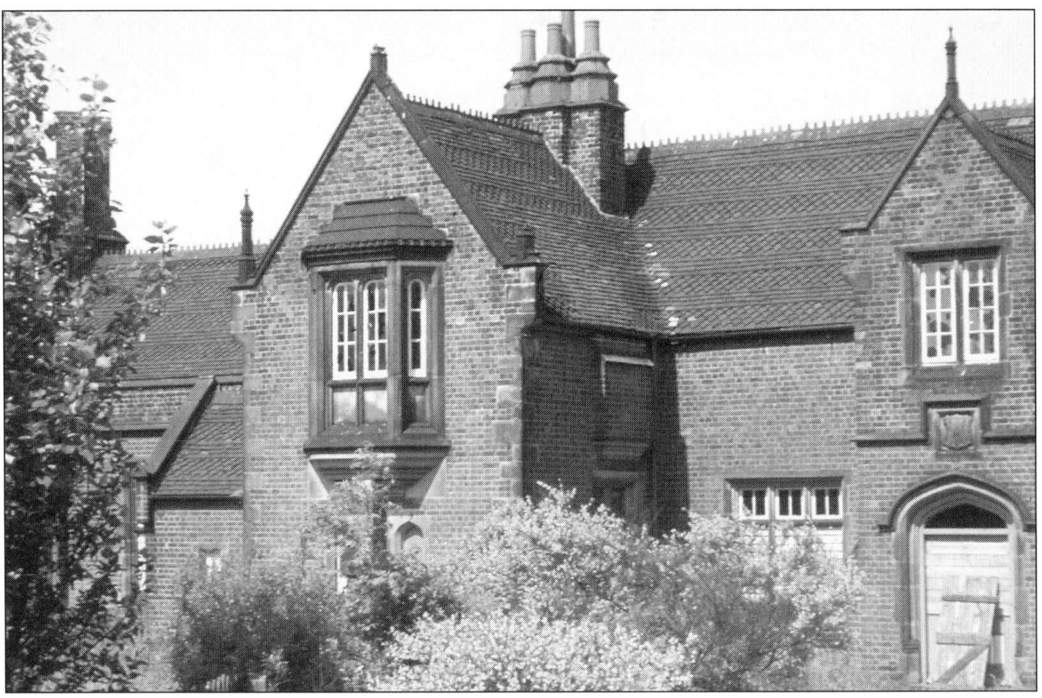

During its lifetime *City of Lichfield* must have passed this building many times. It is not a country manor but in fact the old Lichfield Trent Valley station, erected by the Trent Valley Railway in 1846 and demolished by British Rail at the time of electricfication.

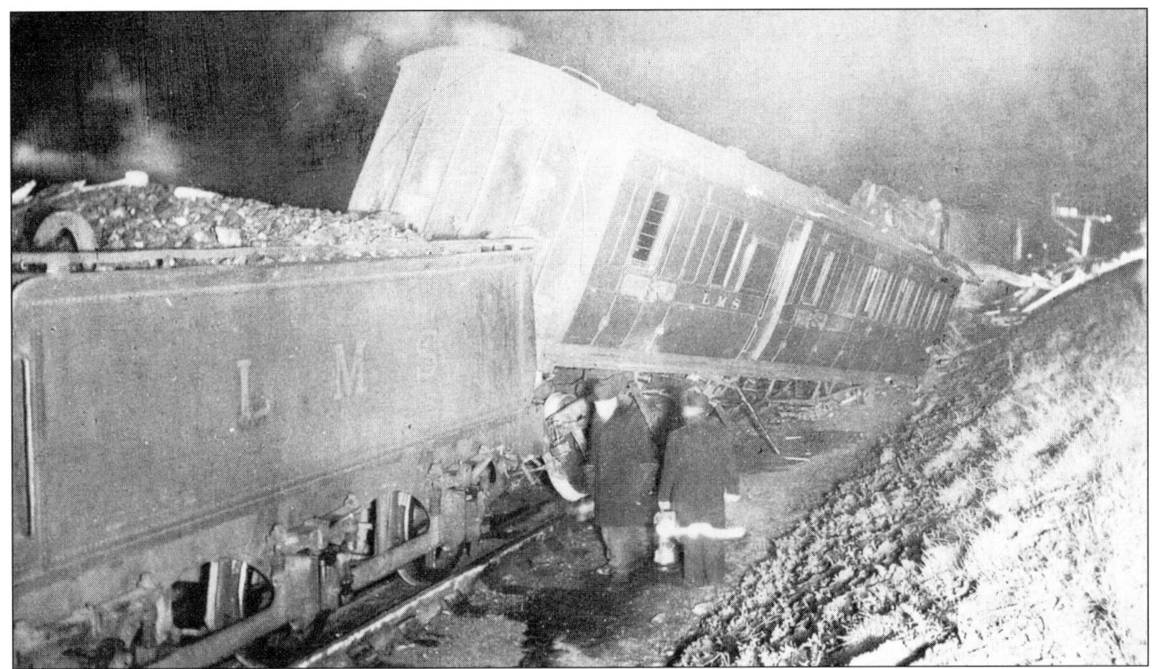

The collision at Lichfield Trent Valley station on January 1st 1946.

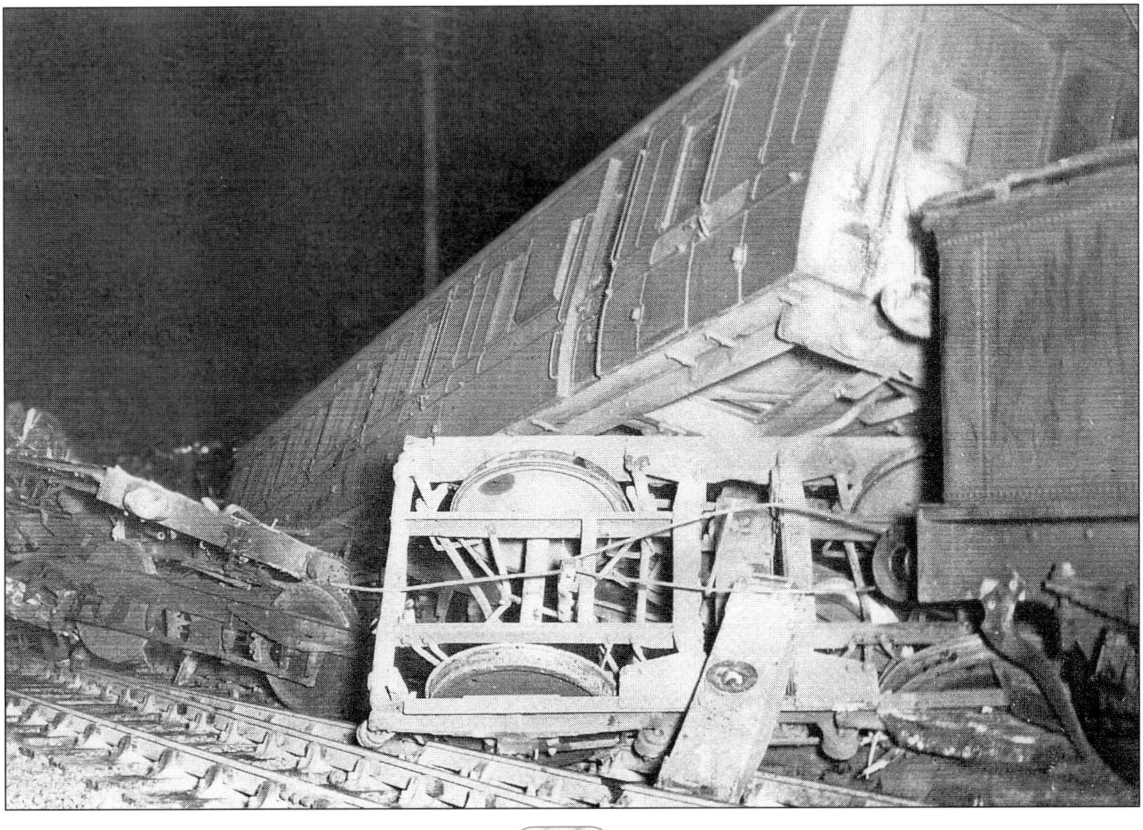

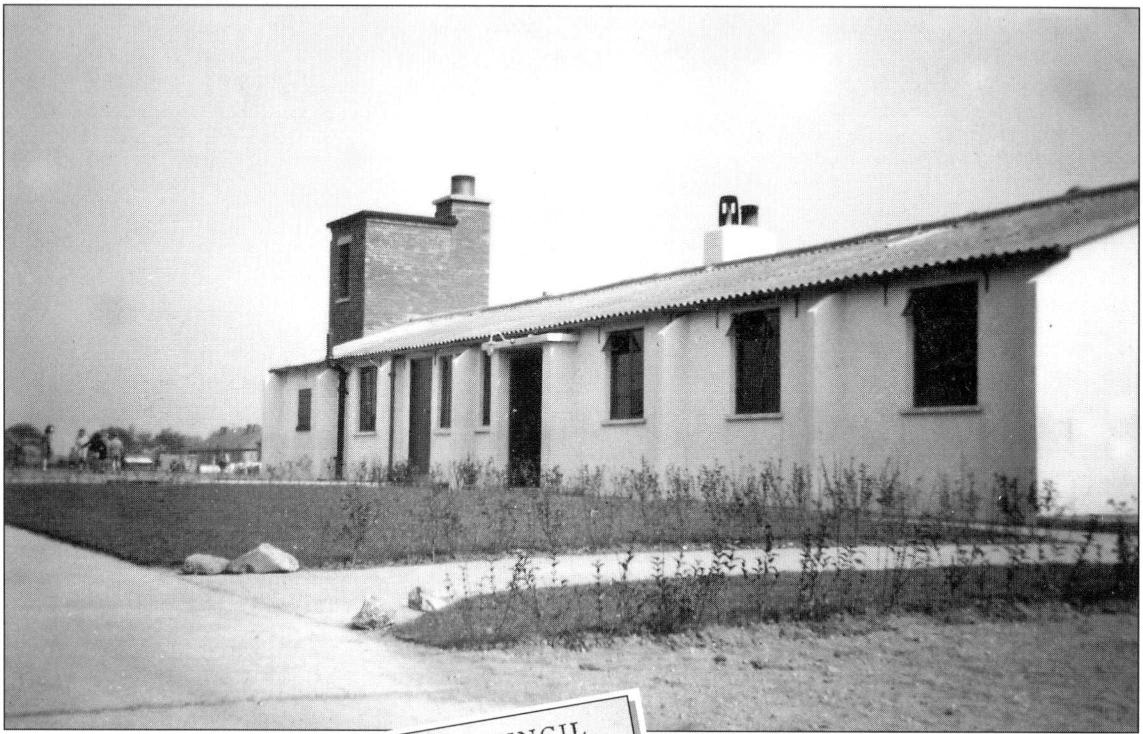

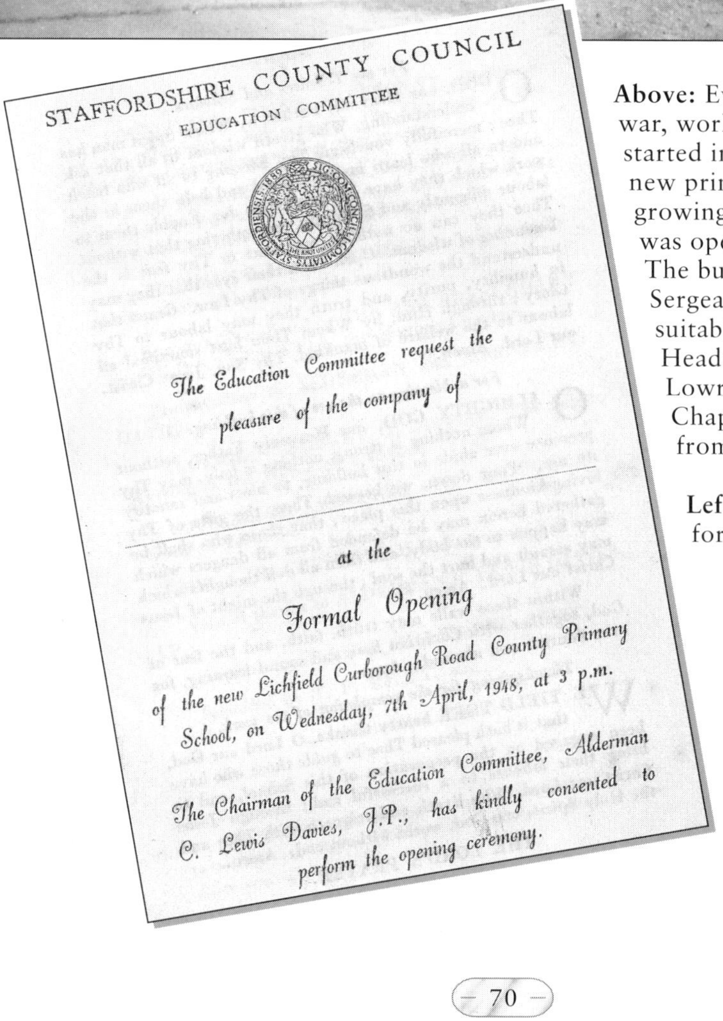

STAFFORDSHIRE COUNTY COUNCIL

EDUCATION COMMITTEE

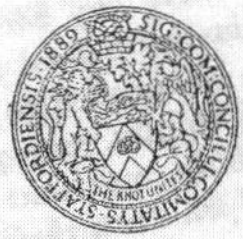

The Education Committee request the pleasure of the company of

at the

Formal Opening

of the new Lichfield Curborough Road County Primary School, on Wednesday, 7th April, 1948, at 3 p.m.

The Chairman of the Education Committee, Alderman C. Lewis Davies, J.P., has kindly consented to perform the opening ceremony.

Above: Even before the end of the war, work of reconstruction had started in the field of education. A new primary school for the growing population of Lichfield was opened at Curborough Road. The building was the former Sergeants' Mess of RAF Fradley, suitably adapted. The first Headmistress was Mrs Lowrance, the motorcyclist of Chapter 2, who came here from Pool Walk School.

Left: The invitation to the formal opening.

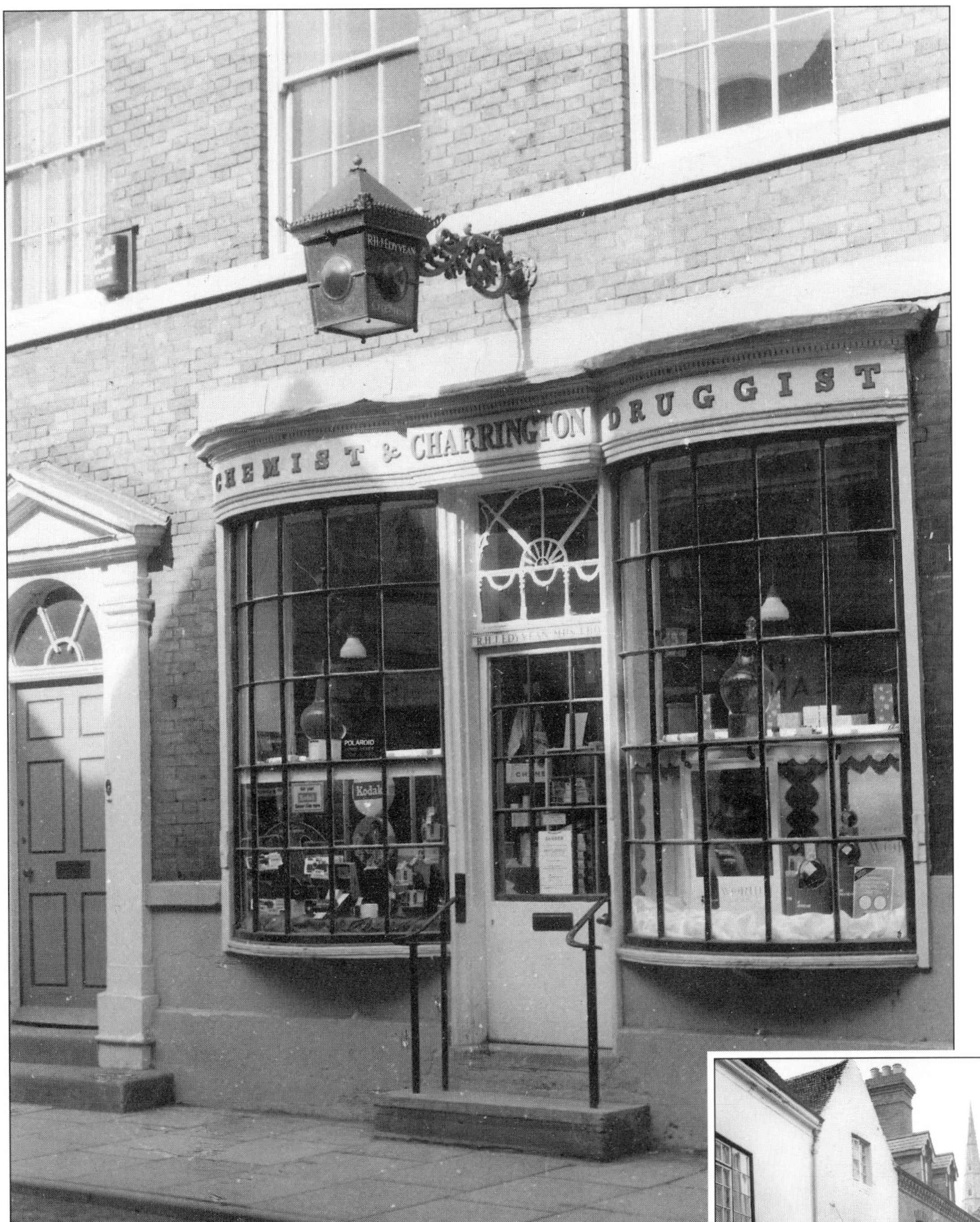

Above: Many will remember the fine Georgian shop front of Robert Edyvean's chemist shop in Market Street

Right: Lichfield still retained many of its small shops such as the cobblers shop of Mr Brown in Dam Street and its neighbouring newsagents.

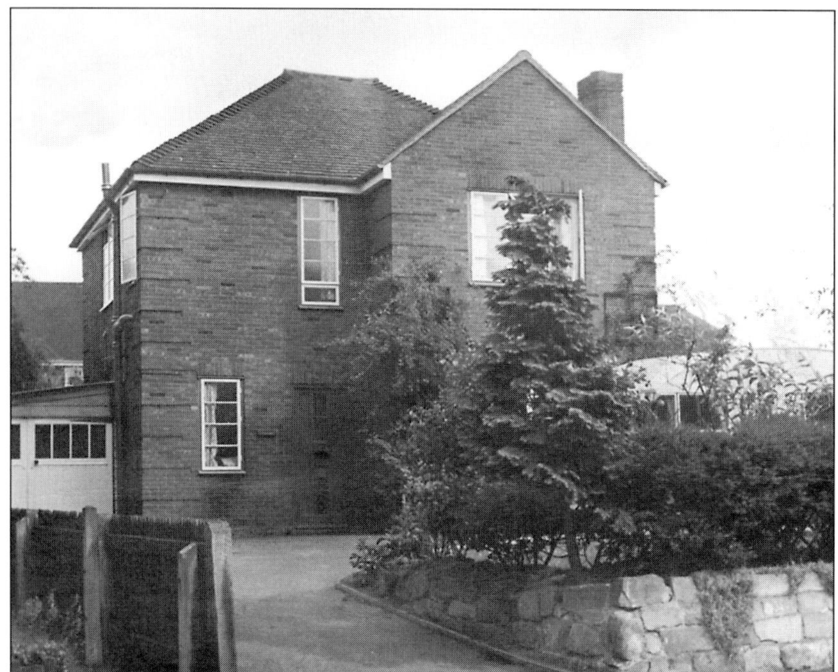

1946 saw the recommencement of house building. This was the first private post-war house, one of a group of six off Gaia Lane. Without the garage (a later edition) it sold for £1,000 plus £60 for road charges.

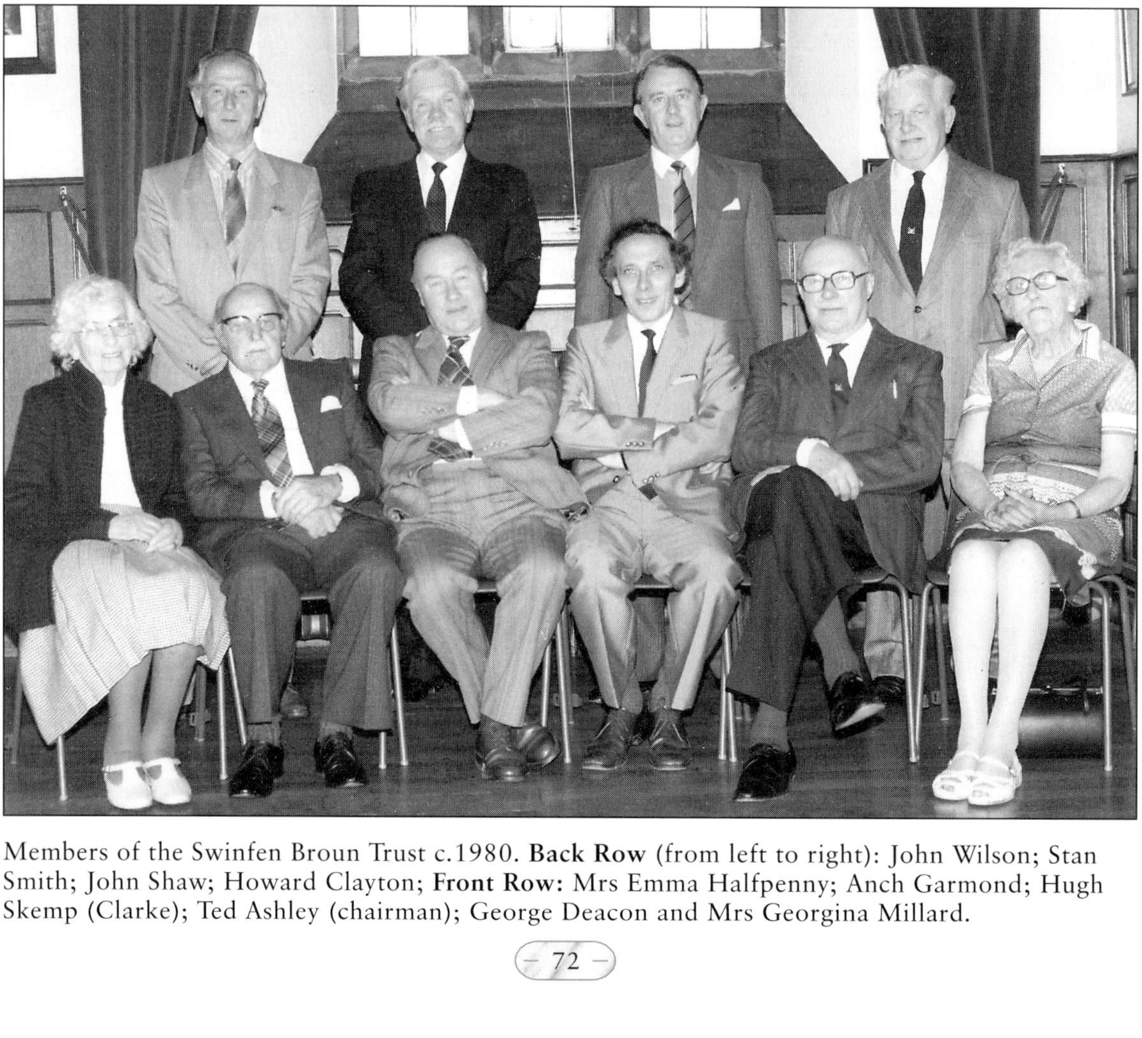

Members of the Swinfen Broun Trust c.1980. **Back Row** (from left to right): John Wilson; Stan Smith; John Shaw; Howard Clayton; **Front Row:** Mrs Emma Halfpenny; Anch Garmond; Hugh Skemp (Clarke); Ted Ashley (chairman); George Deacon and Mrs Georgina Millard.

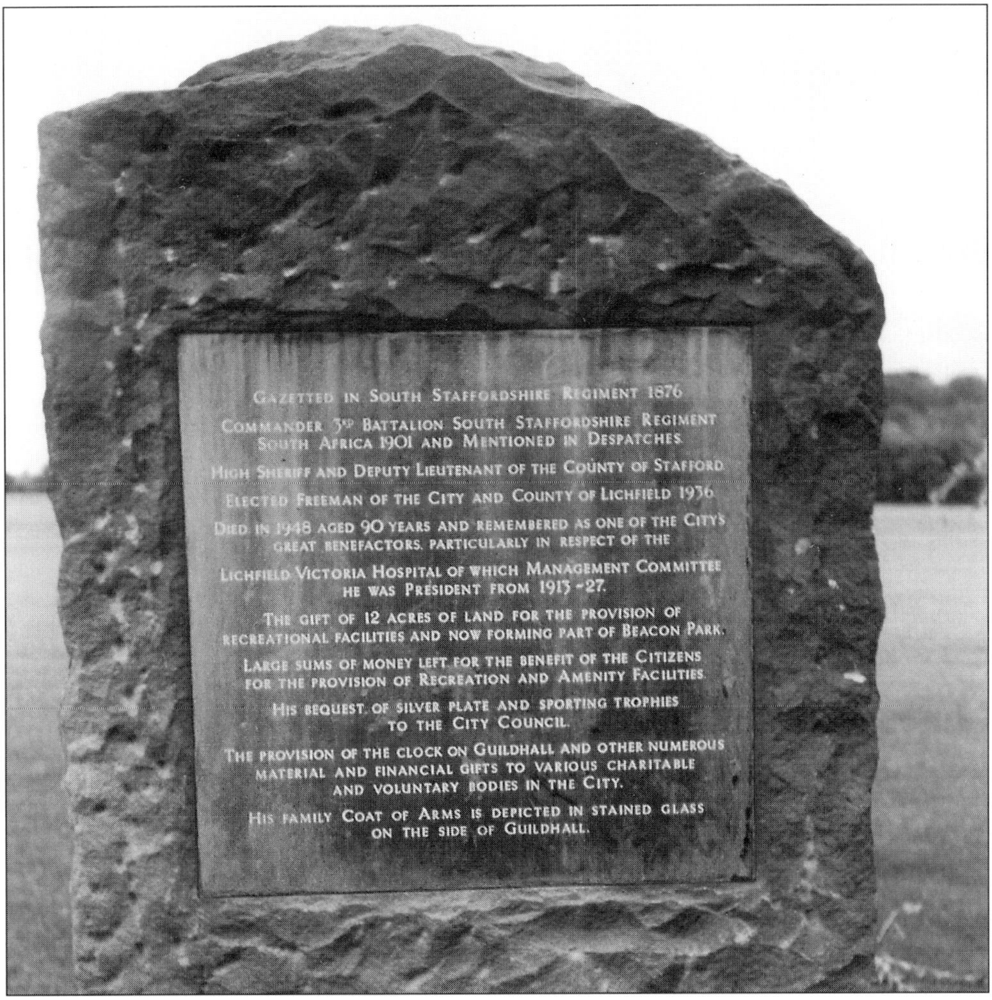

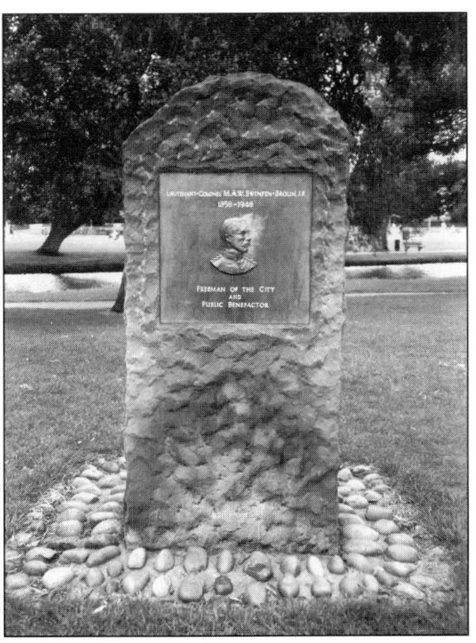

In 1948 Lichfield mourned the loss of one of its most generous benefactors, Colonel Michael Swinfen Broun. He and his wife had paid a large part of the cost of the Victoria Hospital, had given to the city Beacon Place and Beacon Park and numerous other smaller gifts. Now, in his will he left half of the residue of his estate to Lichfield Cathedral and the other half to the Corporation of Lichfield, including his silver.

Before Lichfield Corporation was abolished under the provisions of the Local Government Act, 1972, the council set up a trust, The Swinfen Broun Trust, to which all the assets held by the Corporation were transferred, and which the Trust now administers for the benefit of the citizens of Lichfield.

The pictures show the memorial to Colonel Swinfen Broun in Beacon Park.

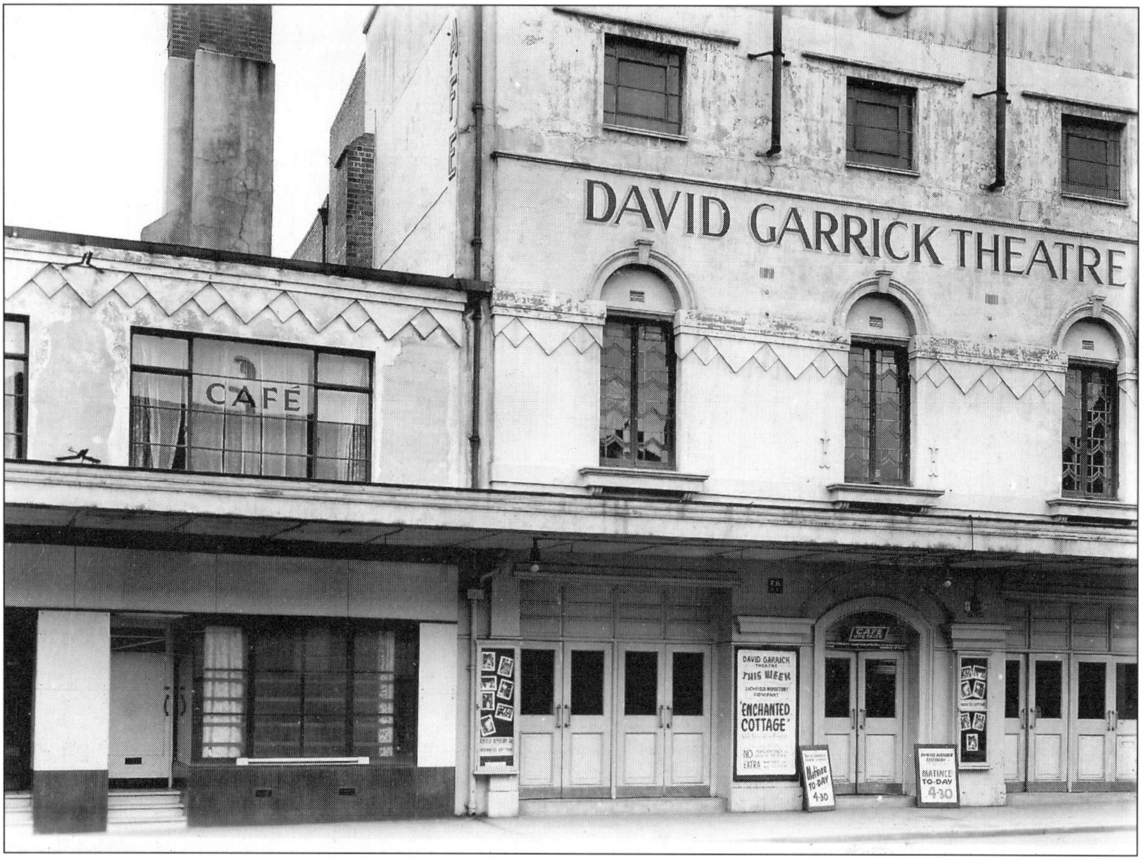

Above: March 14th 1949 marked the beginning of a new era for live theatre in Lichfield. This was the opening of the David Garrick Theatre in Bore Street. In the building which had one been the Palladium Cinema and before that the Theatre Royal, later the St James's Hall, plays were now regularly performed by a full-time repertory company. There were licensed bars, a restaurant and all the amenities of a proper theatre.

Right: The opening play was *Rebecca* by Daphne Du Maurier.

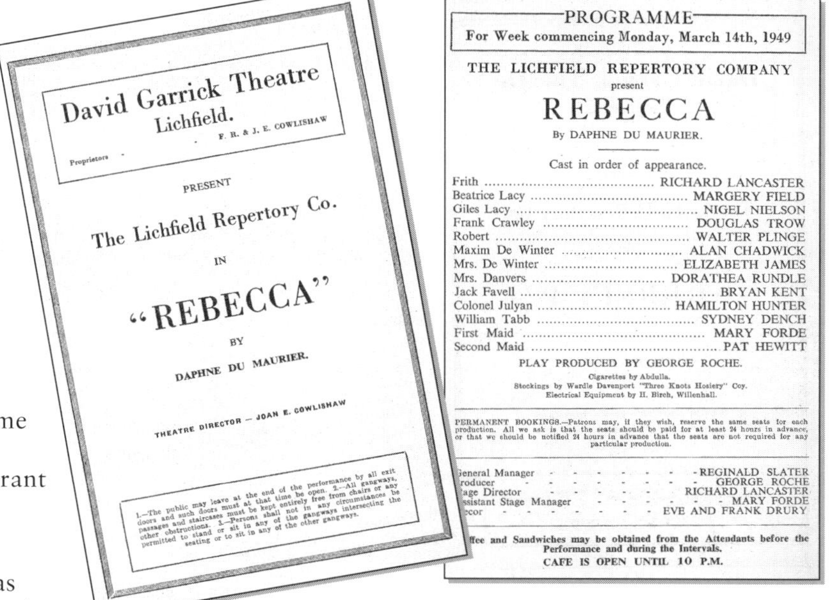

David Garrick Theatre
Lichfield.
Proprietors - F. R. & J. E. COWLISHAW

PRESENT

The Lichfield Repertory Co.

IN

"REBECCA"

BY

DAPHNE DU MAURIER.

THEATRE DIRECTOR — JOAN E. COWLISHAW

1.—The public may leave at the end of the performance by all exit doors and such doors must at that time be open. 2.—All gangways, passages and staircases must be kept entirely free from chairs or any other obstructions. 3.—Persons shall not in any circumstances be permitted to stand or sit in any of the gangways intersecting the seating or to sit in any of the other gangways.

PROGRAMME
For Week commencing Monday, March 14th, 1949

THE LICHFIELD REPERTORY COMPANY
present

REBECCA

By DAPHNE DU MAURIER.

Cast in order of appearance.

Frith	RICHARD LANCASTER
Beatrice Lacy	MARGERY FIELD
Giles Lacy	NIGEL NIELSON
Frank Crawley	DOUGLAS TROW
Robert	WALTER PLINGE
Maxim De Winter	ALAN CHADWICK
Mrs. De Winter	ELIZABETH JAMES
Mrs. Danvers	DORATHEA RUNDLE
Jack Favell	BRYAN KENT
Colonel Julyan	HAMILTON HUNTER
William Tabb	SYDNEY DENCH
First Maid	MARY FORDE
Second Maid	PAT HEWITT

PLAY PRODUCED BY GEORGE ROCHE.

Cigarettes by Abdulla.
Stockings by Wardle Davenport "Three Knots Hosiery" Coy.
Electrical Equipment by H. Birch, Willenhall.

PERMANENT BOOKINGS.—Patrons may, if they wish, reserve the same seats for each production. All we ask is that the seats should be paid for at least 24 hours in advance, or that we should be notified 24 hours in advance that the seats are not required for any particular production.

eneral Manager	REGINALD SLATER
roducer	GEORGE ROCHE
age Director	RICHARD LANCASTER
ssistant Stage Manager	MARY FORDE
ecor	EVE AND FRANK DRURY

ffee and Sandwiches may be obtained from the Attendants before the Performance and during the Intervals.

CAFE IS OPEN UNTIL 10 P.M.

Opposite page: The company twice performed The Beaux' Stratagem, Farquhar's restoration comedy set in Lichfield. The second time the play was produced by Ken Tynan, who also acted in it.

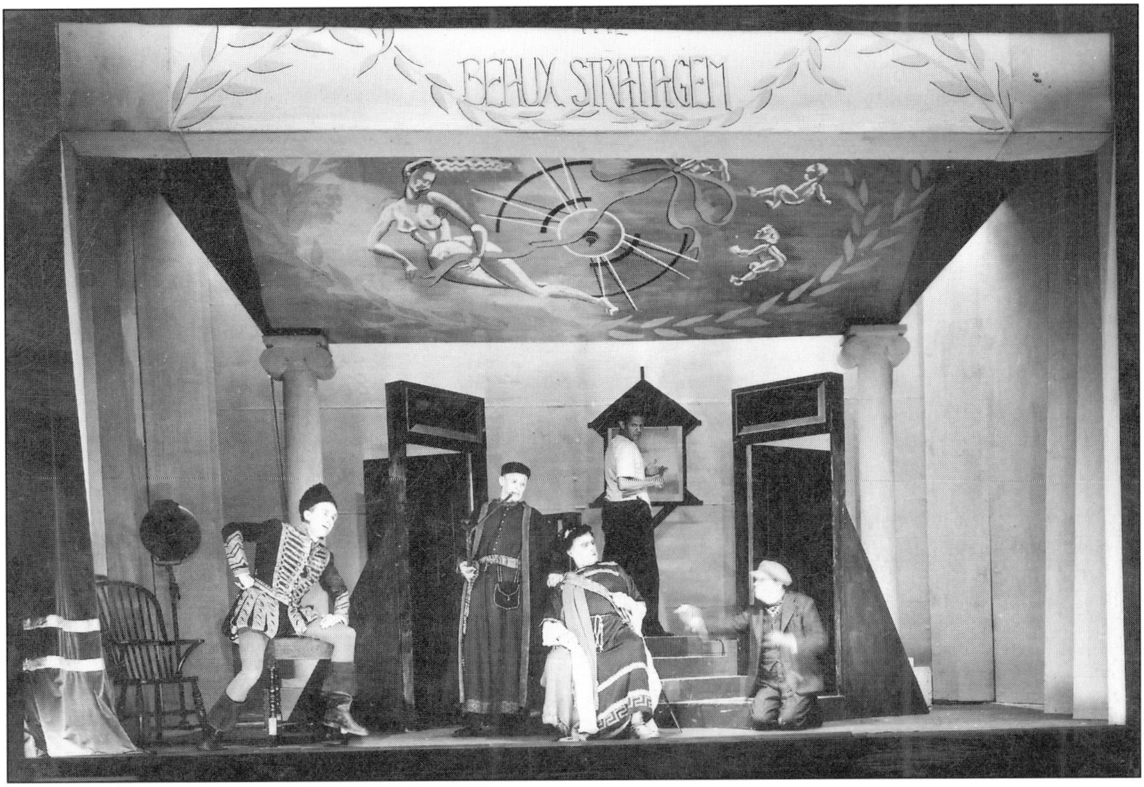
BEAUX STRATAGEM

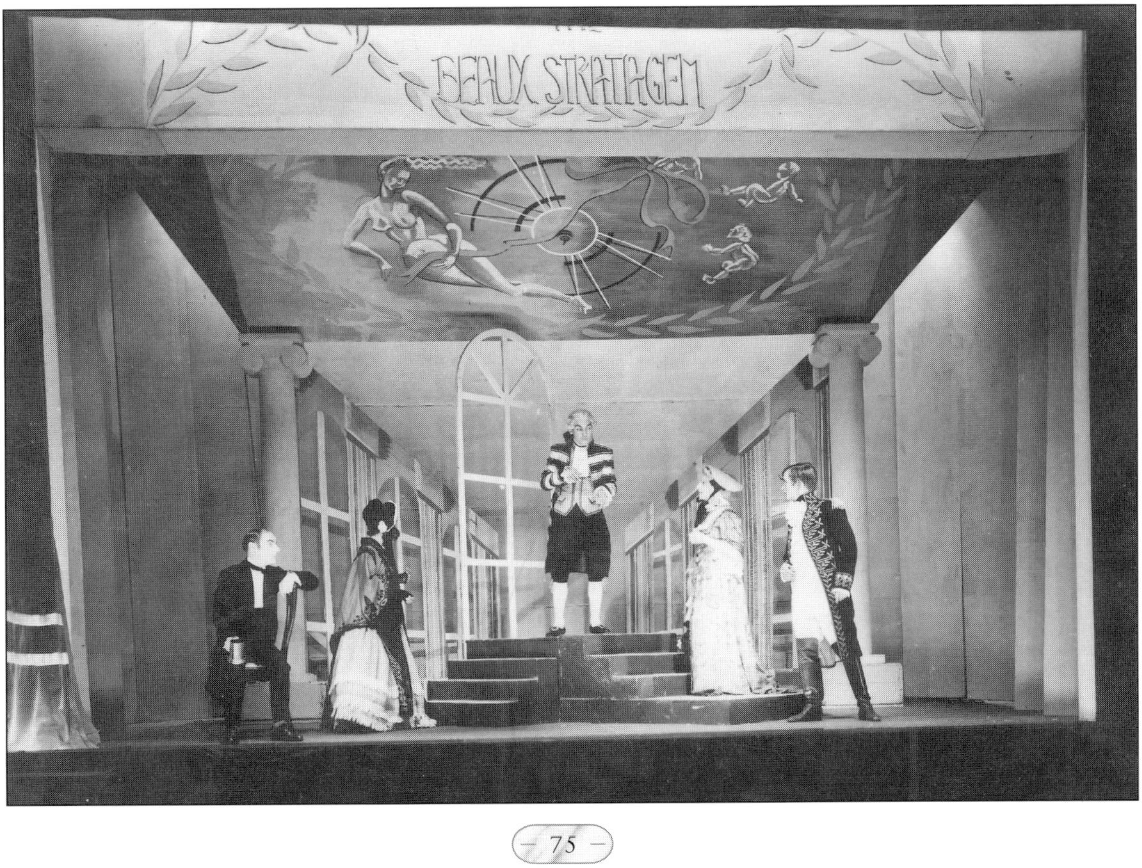
BEAUX STRATAGEM

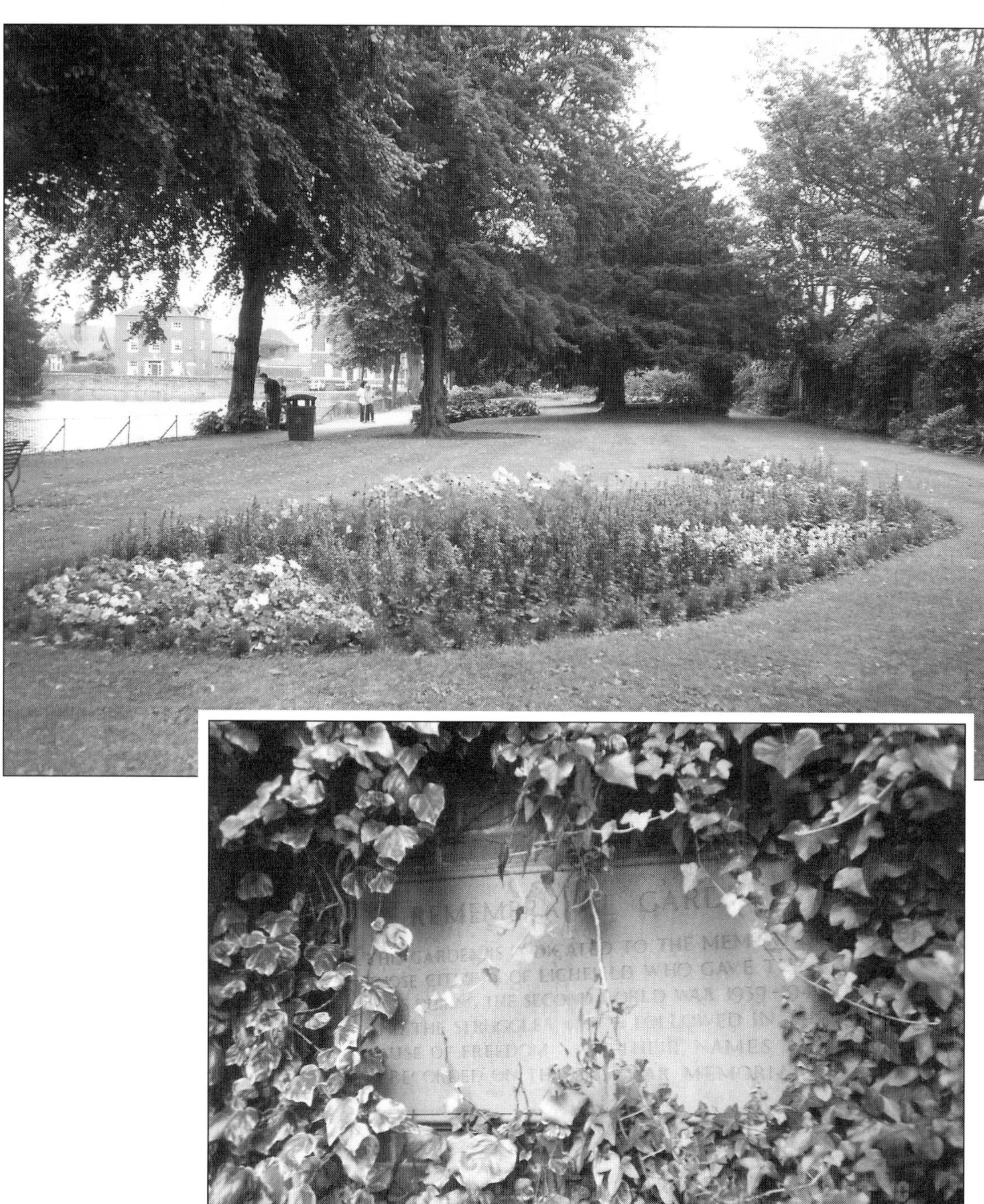

The war memorial to the fallen of the Second World War is the garden on the south side of Minister Pool, where a tablet on the wall records this fact. Names of those who fell are recorded on the 1914 memorial.

Chapter 6 – The Fifties

The Fifties were a comparatively uneventful period for Lichfield. The decade began with wartime austerity still very much to the fore, especially where food, clothing, petrol and cars were concerned. Lichfield expended as more and more houses were built under direction from central government – the St Michael's estate, The Dimbles and Stowe Street for example. The last was a clearance of unsuitable housing, condemned before the war. A large number of what appeared to be eighteenth or nineteenth century houses were found to be much earlier, with timber framed construction behind the brick. One of these, a cruck house, was selected for preservation, while around it Stowe Street became a pedestrianized area of modern municipal housing.

Levetts' Field disappeared as a recreational area where circuses and mobile theatres could perform and instead an extension of the Birmingham Road was driven through it. On one side appeared a bus station and on the other the fire and ambulance stations with some incredibly ugly firemens' houses.

At Lichfield City Station steam - hauled trains became a rarity as diesel multiple units took over passenger services on both the Sutton and Walsall - Burton lines.

And most noteworthy of all, in common with the rest of the country, Lichfield had its first sight of high-rise flats, not the best of architectural additions to the skyline.

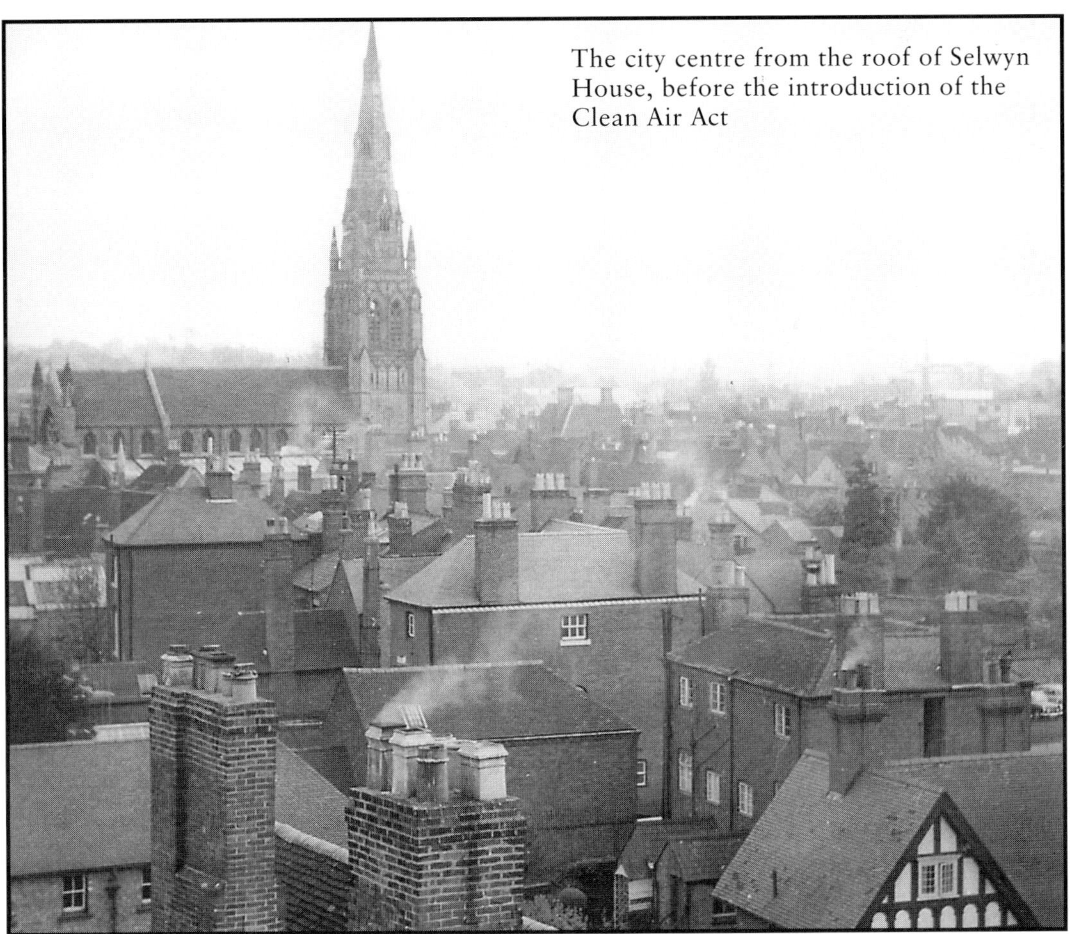

The city centre from the roof of Selwyn House, before the introduction of the Clean Air Act

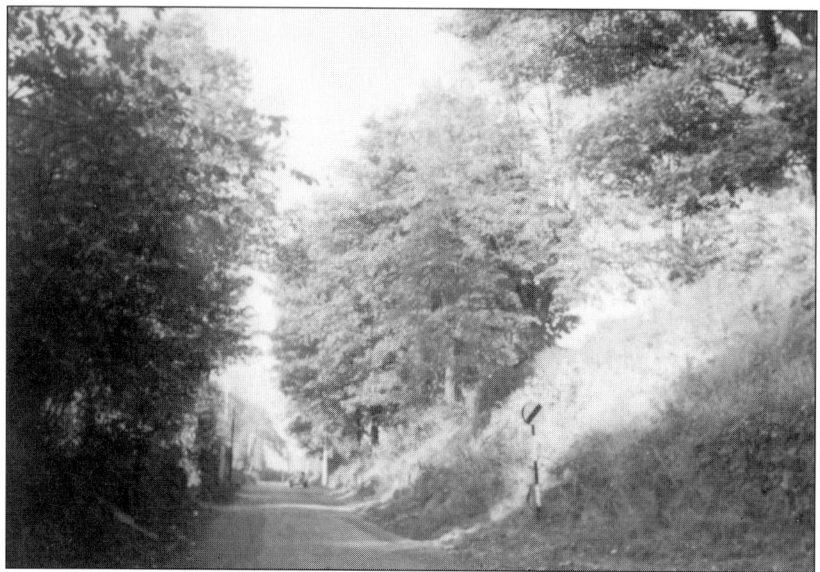

Brownsfield Road, east of the city, in the summer of 1956. Like many other roads and lanes on the outskirts of the city it had a rural aspect, soon to disappear as housing development took over.

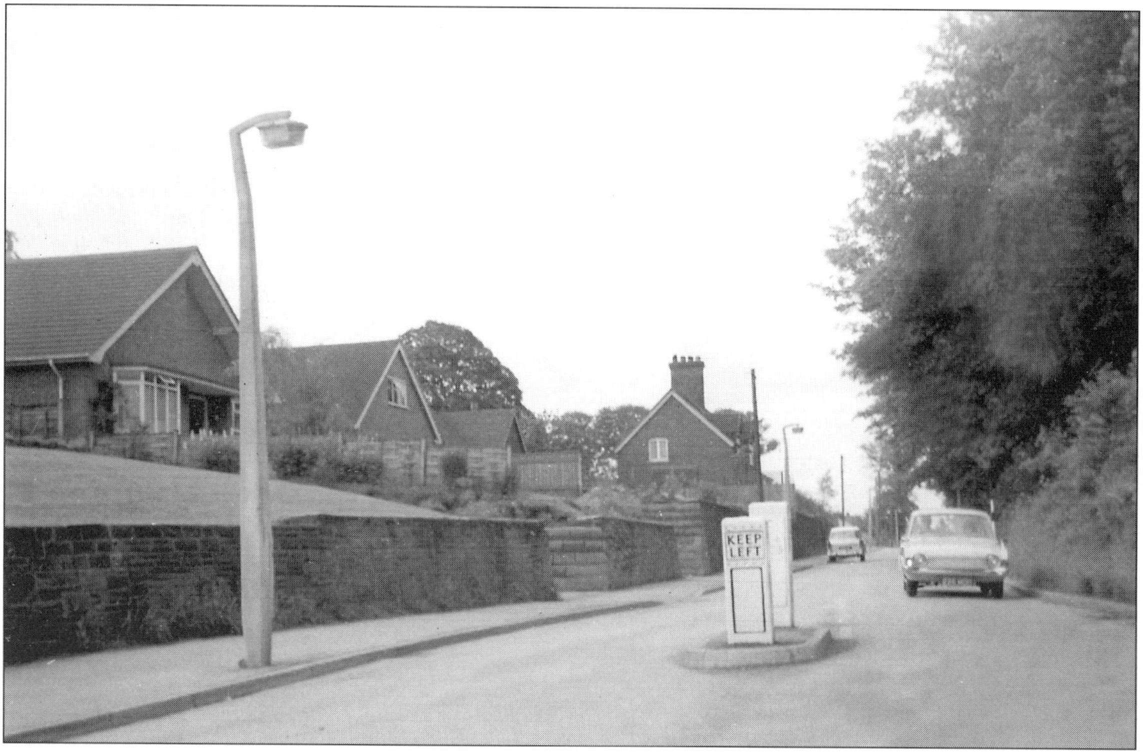

Taken from the exact spot from which the last photograph was taken, only two years later.

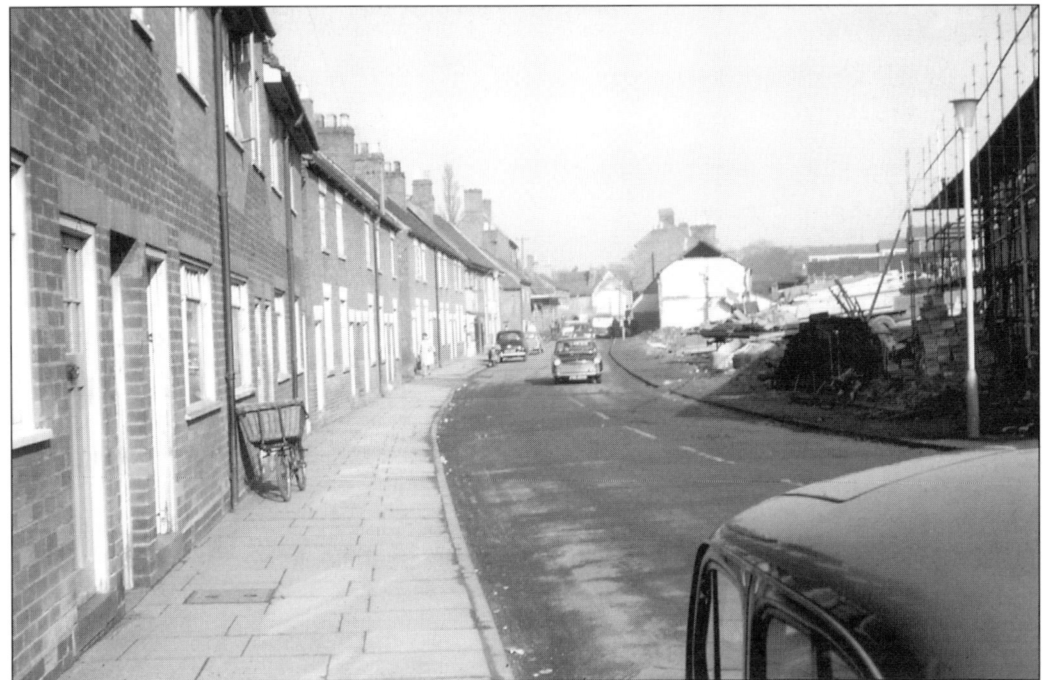

Stowe Street, before redevelopment

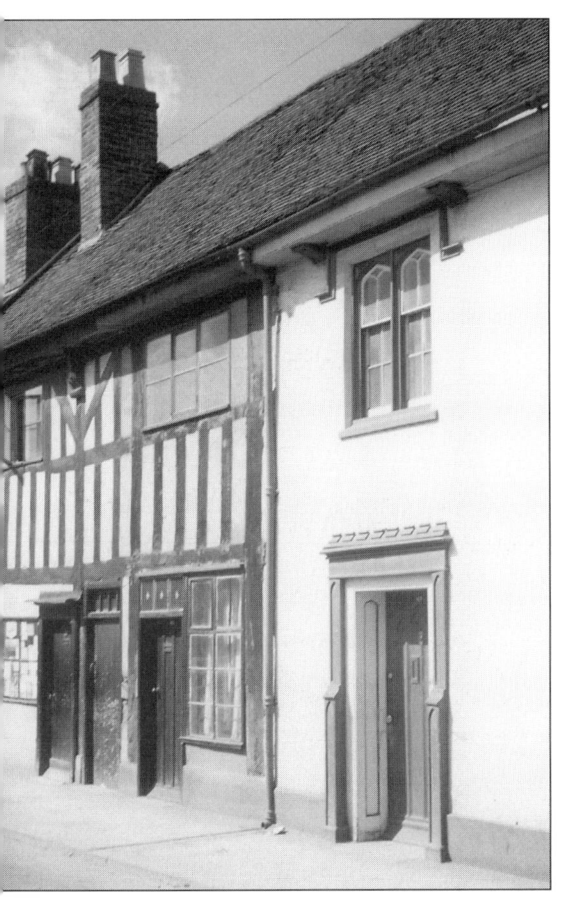

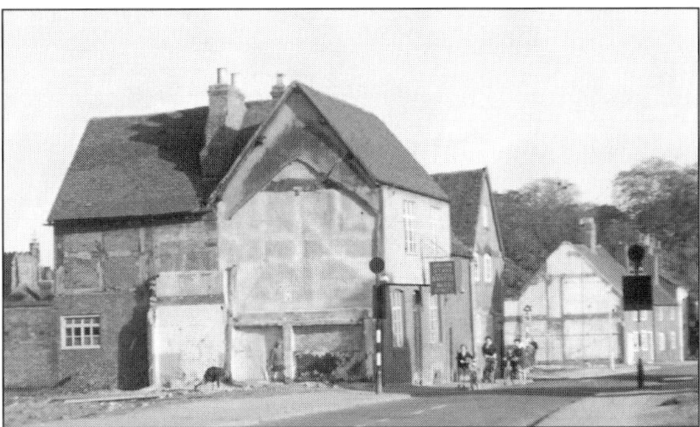

Stowe Street, with demolition under way.

These two buildings were spared from demolition. Both are timber-framed, but the one on the right has been plastered over, to produce a "Strawberry Hill Gothic" effect.

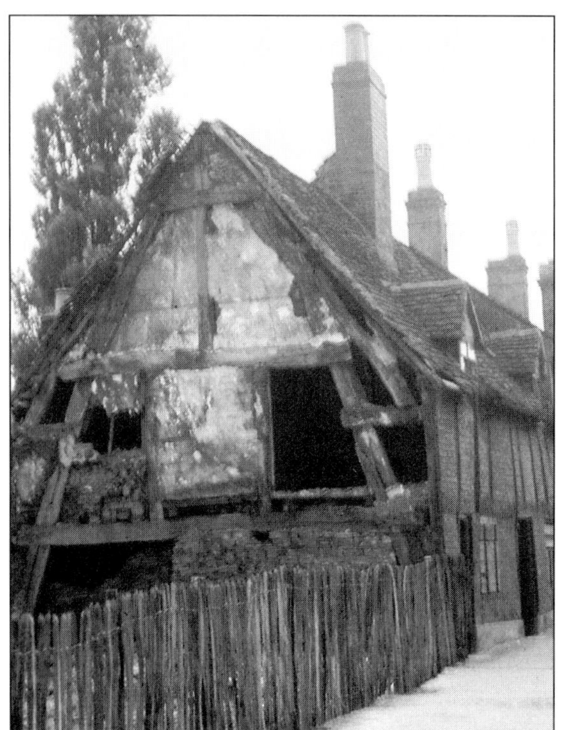

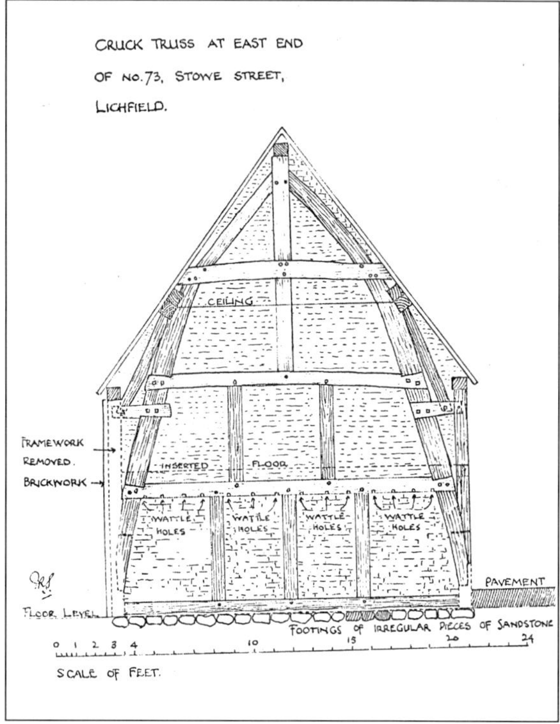

Above left: A Cruck House discovered in Stowe Street. Demolition work disclosed the cruck frame behind the nineteenth century brickwork. **Above right:** An artist's reconstruction of how a cruck house would have been built originally.

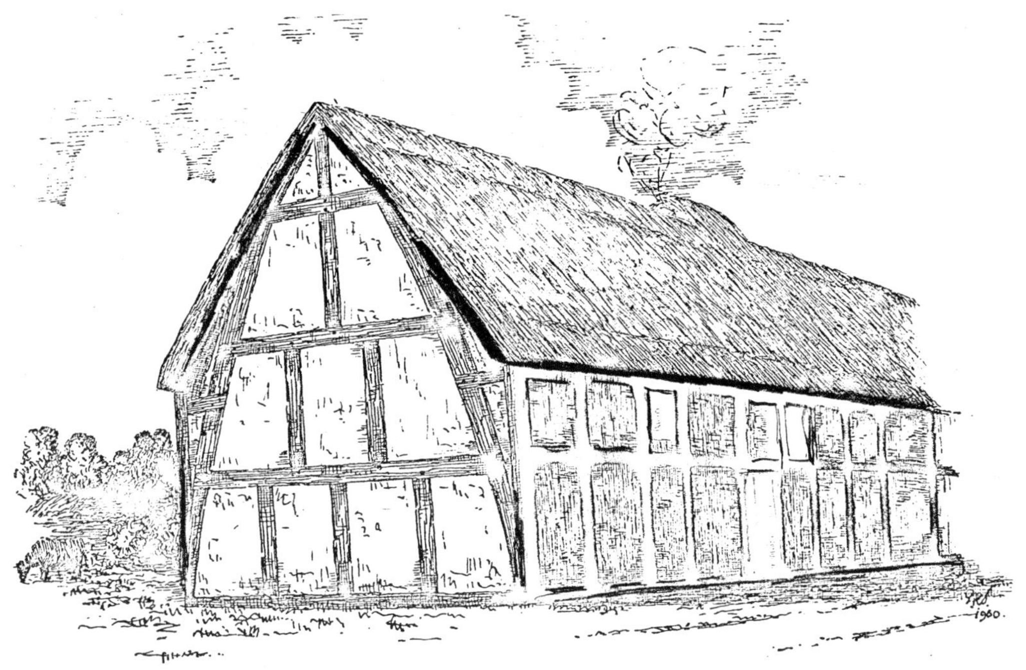

Above: This sketch shows the suggested original structure of the cruck house gable end. **Opposite page:** The Cruck House, following reconstruction.

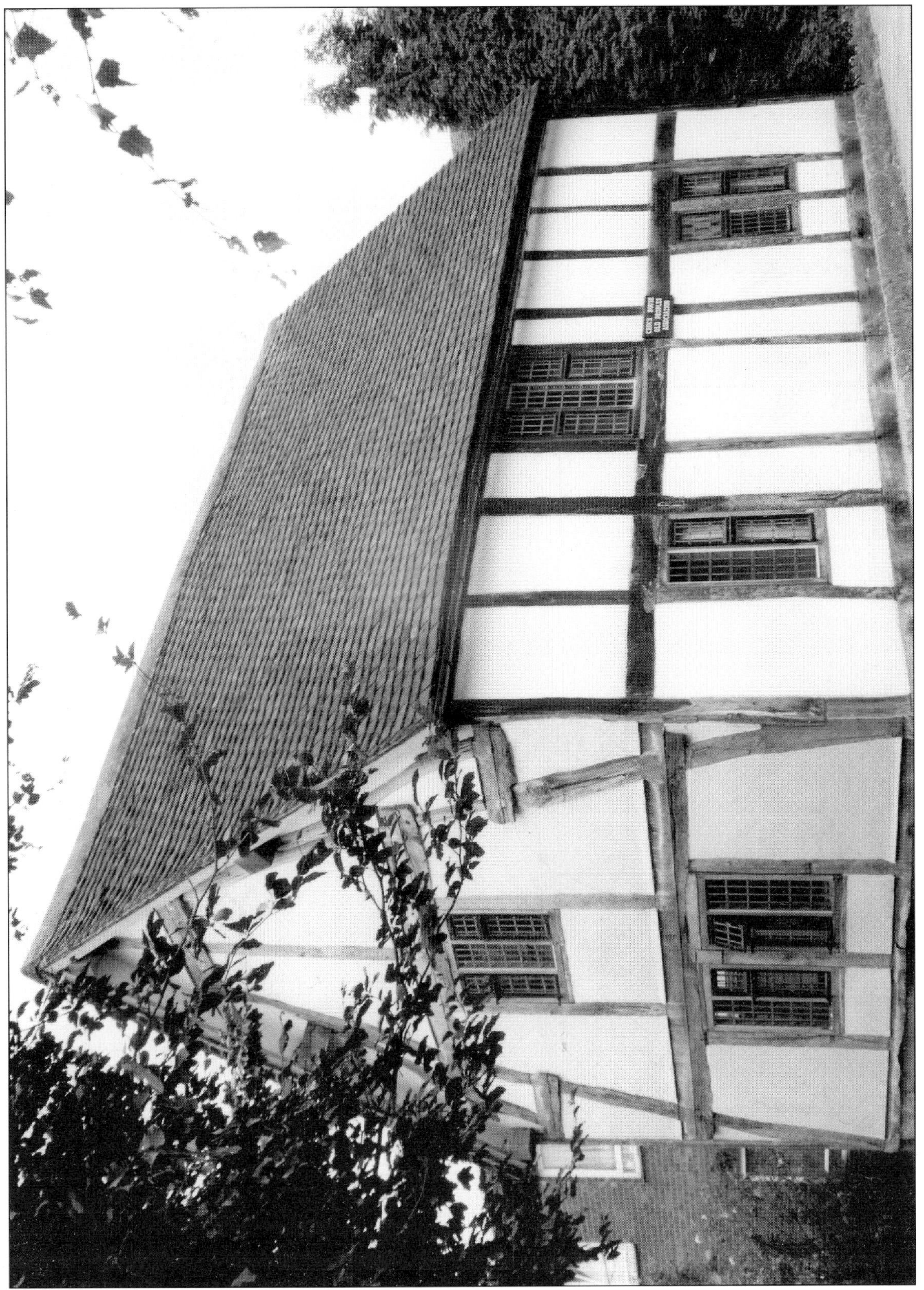

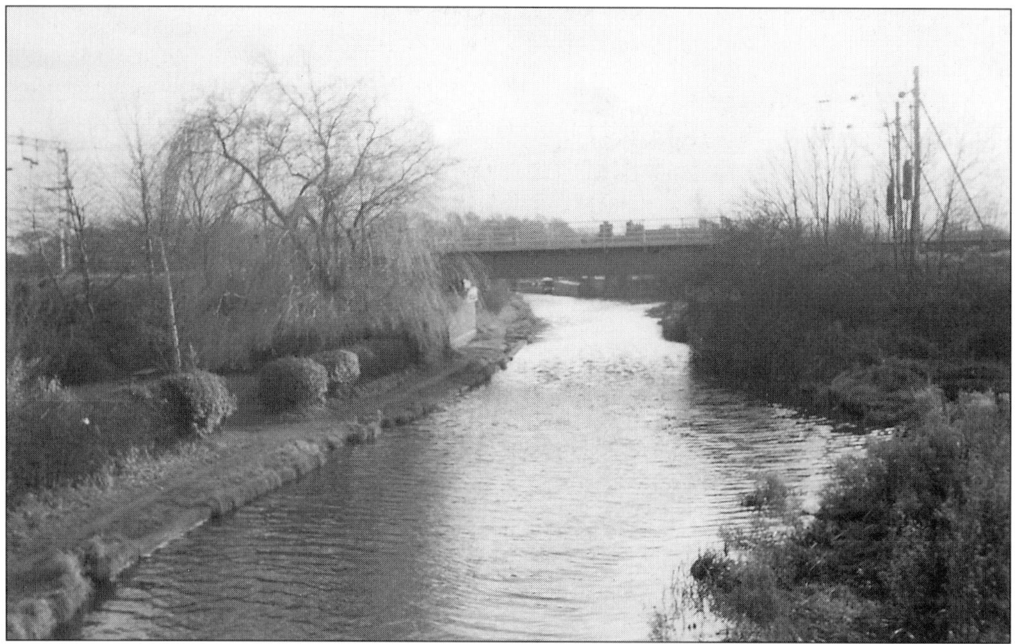

The Lichfield Canal, part of the Wyrley and Essington Canal, ran through the southern part of Lichfield. It was closed in 1954 and drained. A small section was left untouched at Huddlesford, where it joined the Coventry Canal.

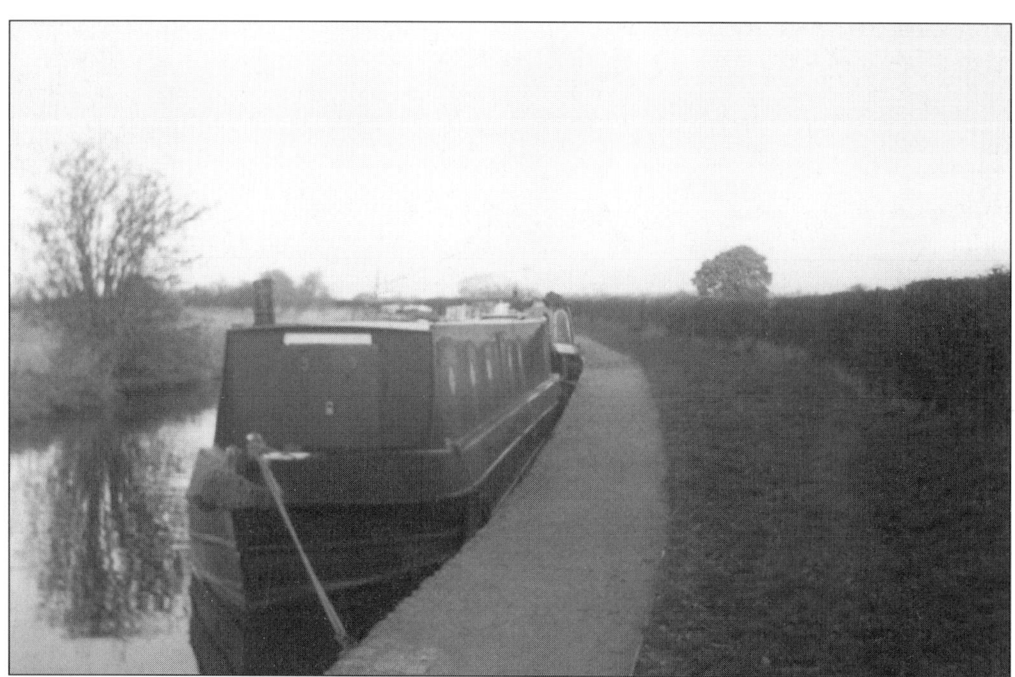

A narrow boat on the Lichfield Canal at Huddlesford.

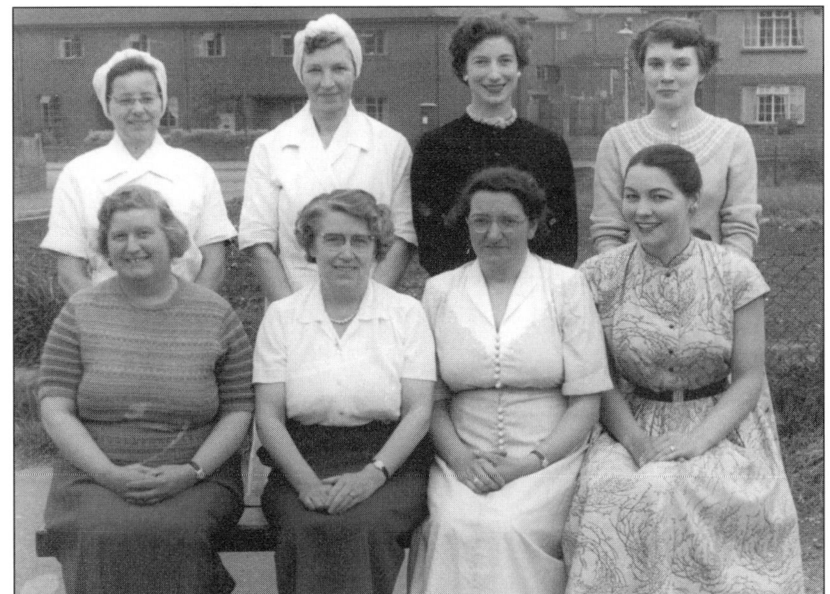

Curborough Road School staff, c 1955 with Mrs Lowrance, the Headmistress, second from left on the front row.

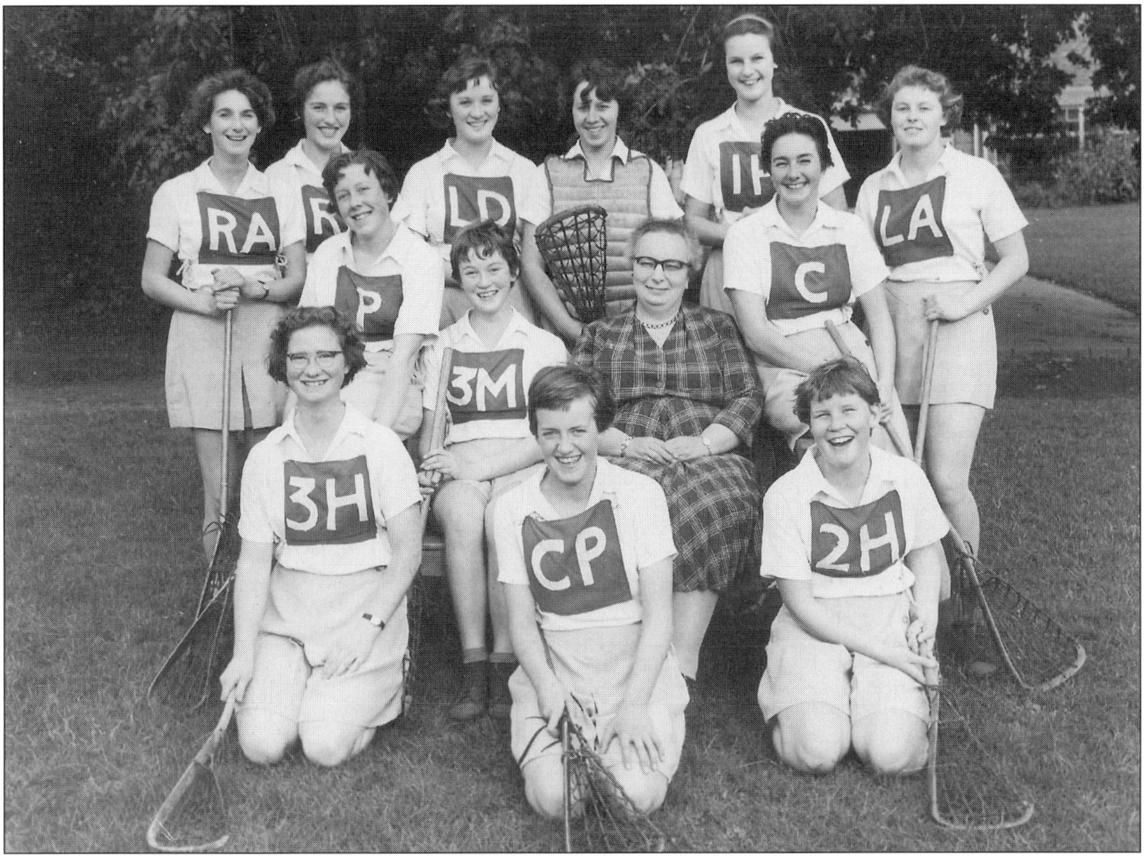

Friary School Lacrosse XI, 1958, and for once someone has put the names on the back, so we give them here: **Back Row:** Anne Brook; ?; Lesley Callender; June Hatterman; Gillian Webb; **Middle Row:** ? ; Rosemary Caddy; Miss Gent; Margaret 0'Reilly; **Front Row:** Joy Wynn; Jacqueline Lees; Wendy Harper.

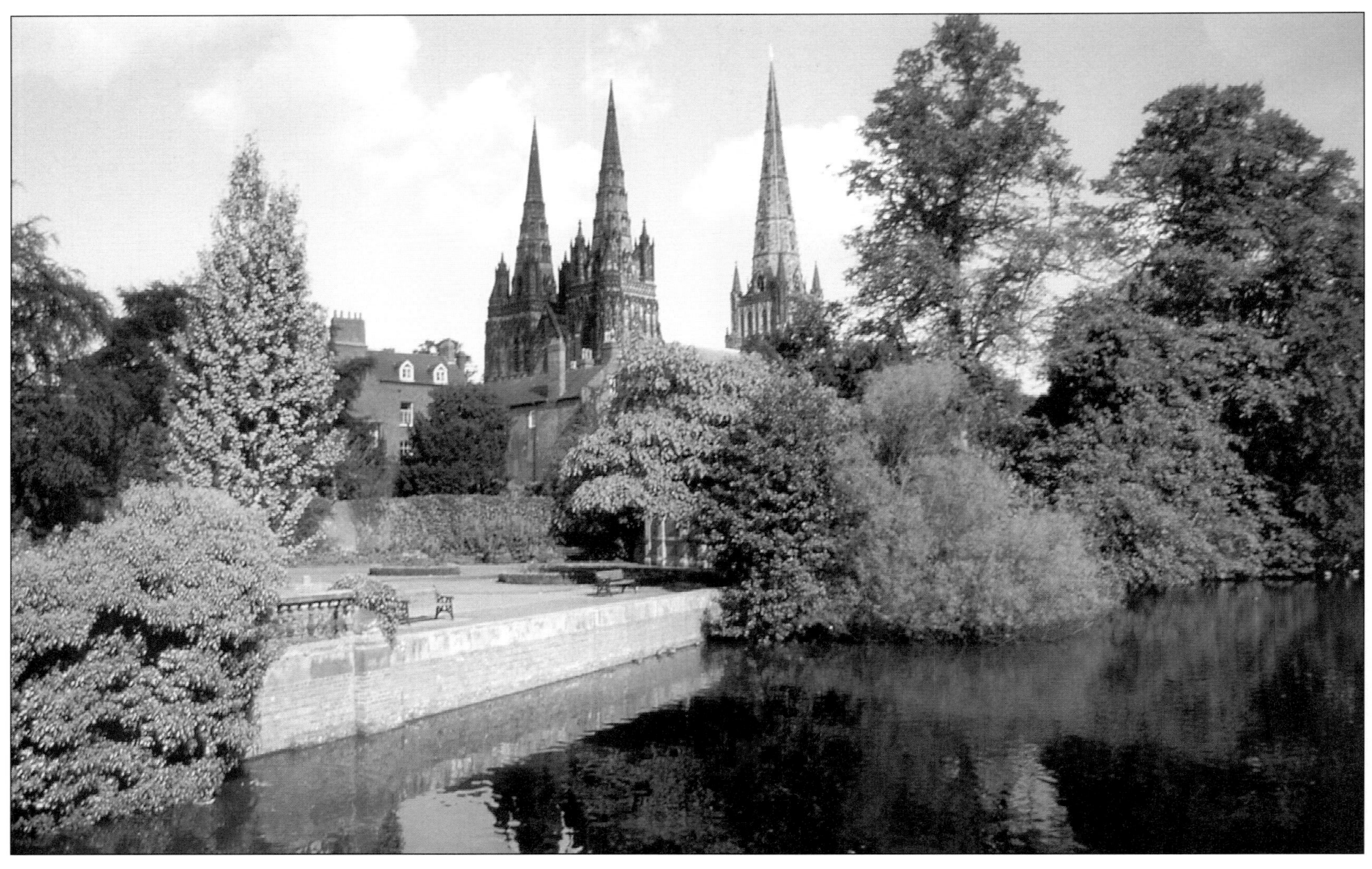

Minster Pool, to the south of the cathedral is one of the glories of Lichfield. Designed by Anna Seward in the eighteenth century in imitation of the Serpentine in Hyde Park, it retains its natural beauty in spite of attempts over the centuries to clutter it up with fountains, statues and even in one case in the 1950s, a floating restaurant.

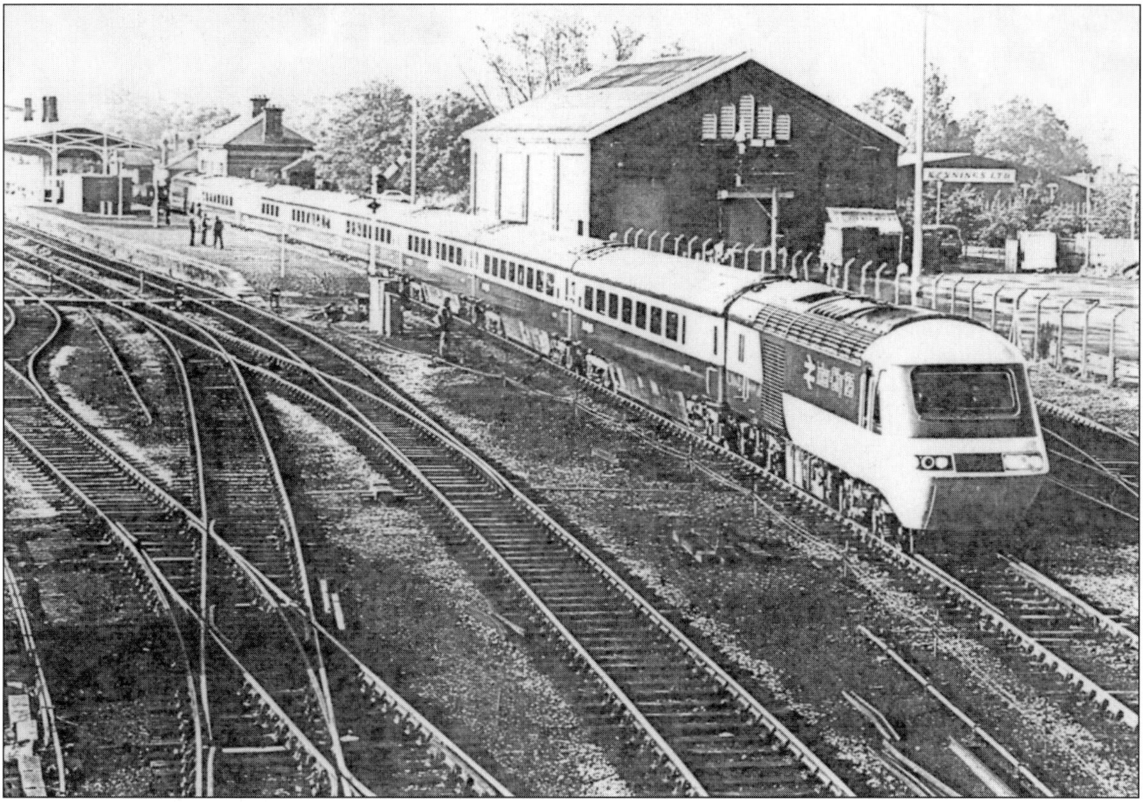

Lichfield City Station c 1960. The No.2 signal box has gone; the goods shed is about to be sold to a car tyre firm.

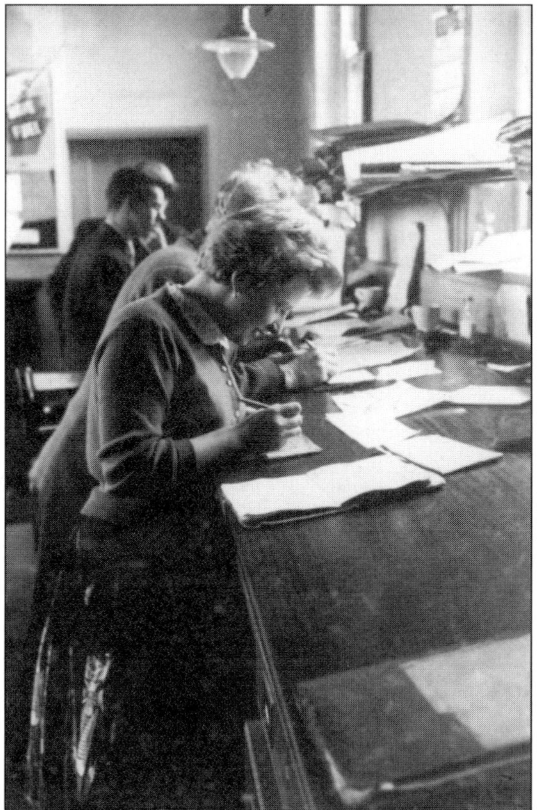

Inside the Goods Shed office in 1957. A relic of Victoriana with high desks and gaslight. The pretty girl nearest the camera is now Mrs Linda MacCormack.

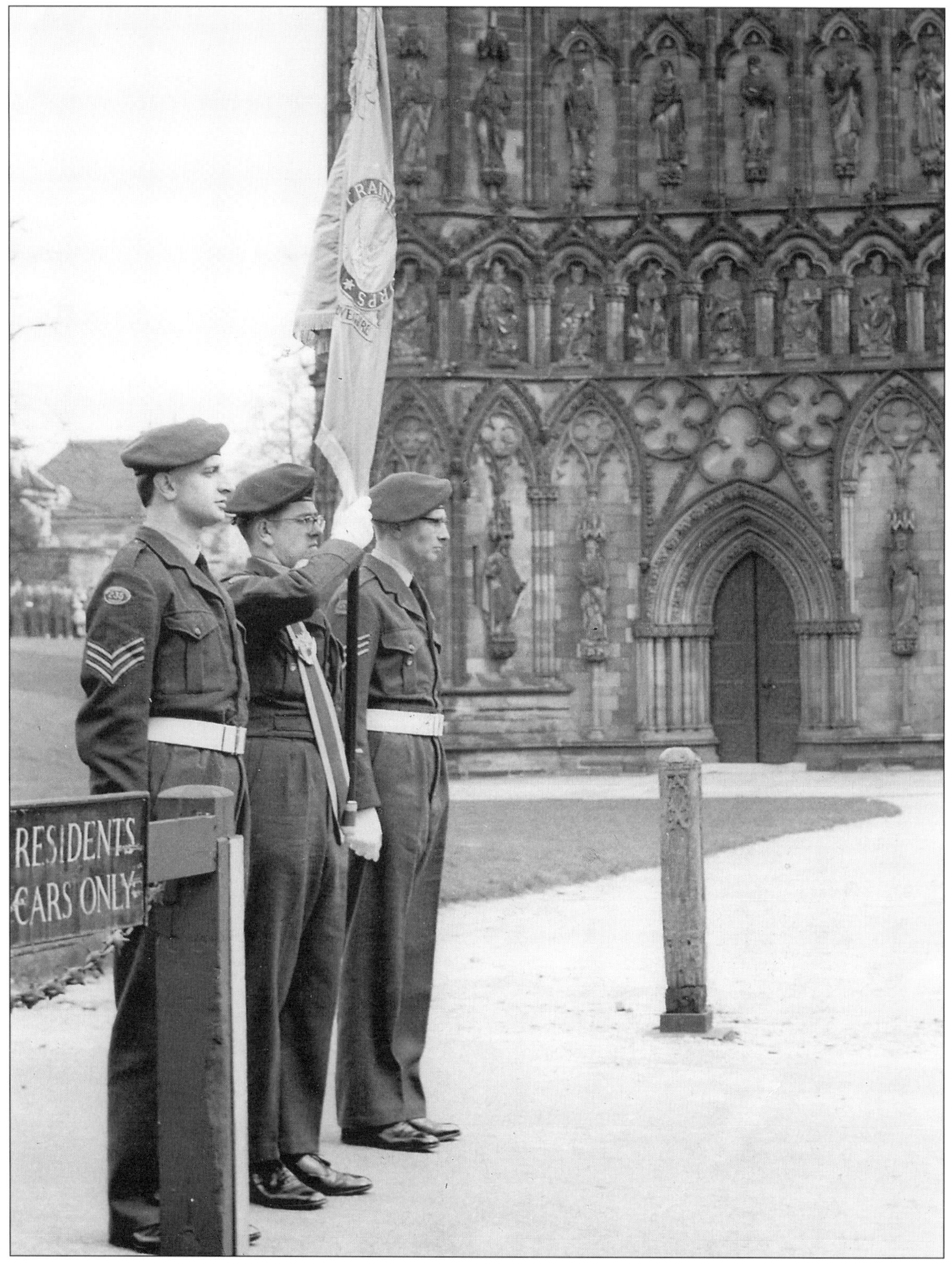

A colour party of the Air Training Corps during a parade of air cadets at Lichfield.

Chapter 7 – The Sixties

The Sixties in Lichfield was a time for the regeneration of the arts. Lichfield had always had a tradition of amateur performers banding together, especially in the realm of music, but as we have seen, the loss of the St James's Hall left only the Guildhall as a suitable venue, and this left much to be desired. In the Sixties, two things happened to change this. One was the formation of a Lichfield Arts Association, under its famous Red Umbrella. The old Post Office became available as a venue for all sorts of ventures; drama, music and the visual arts. At the same time a new secondary school, Netherstowe School, near St Chad's Church, with a fine hall complete with stage, became available for performances such as the Operatic Society and an Orchestral Society.

The latter had been formed in 1957, the Musical Director and Conductor being Donald Cox, Assistant Organist of Lichfield Cathedral. Today it flourishes under the title of The Lichfield Symphonia, a great asset in the musical life of the city.

The Arts Assocation flourished and with the work of volunteers from the various affiliated societies, the old Post Office was fashioned into a thriving centre of the arts and played a vital rôle in the social life of Lichfield.

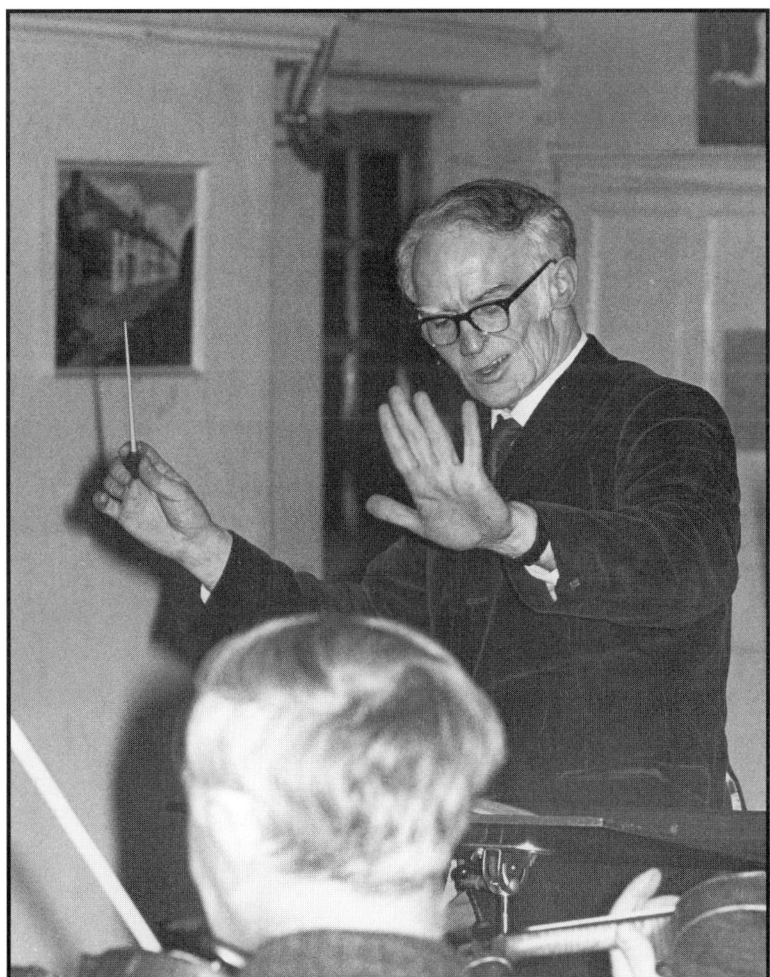

Donald Cox conducting Lichfield Orchestral Society.

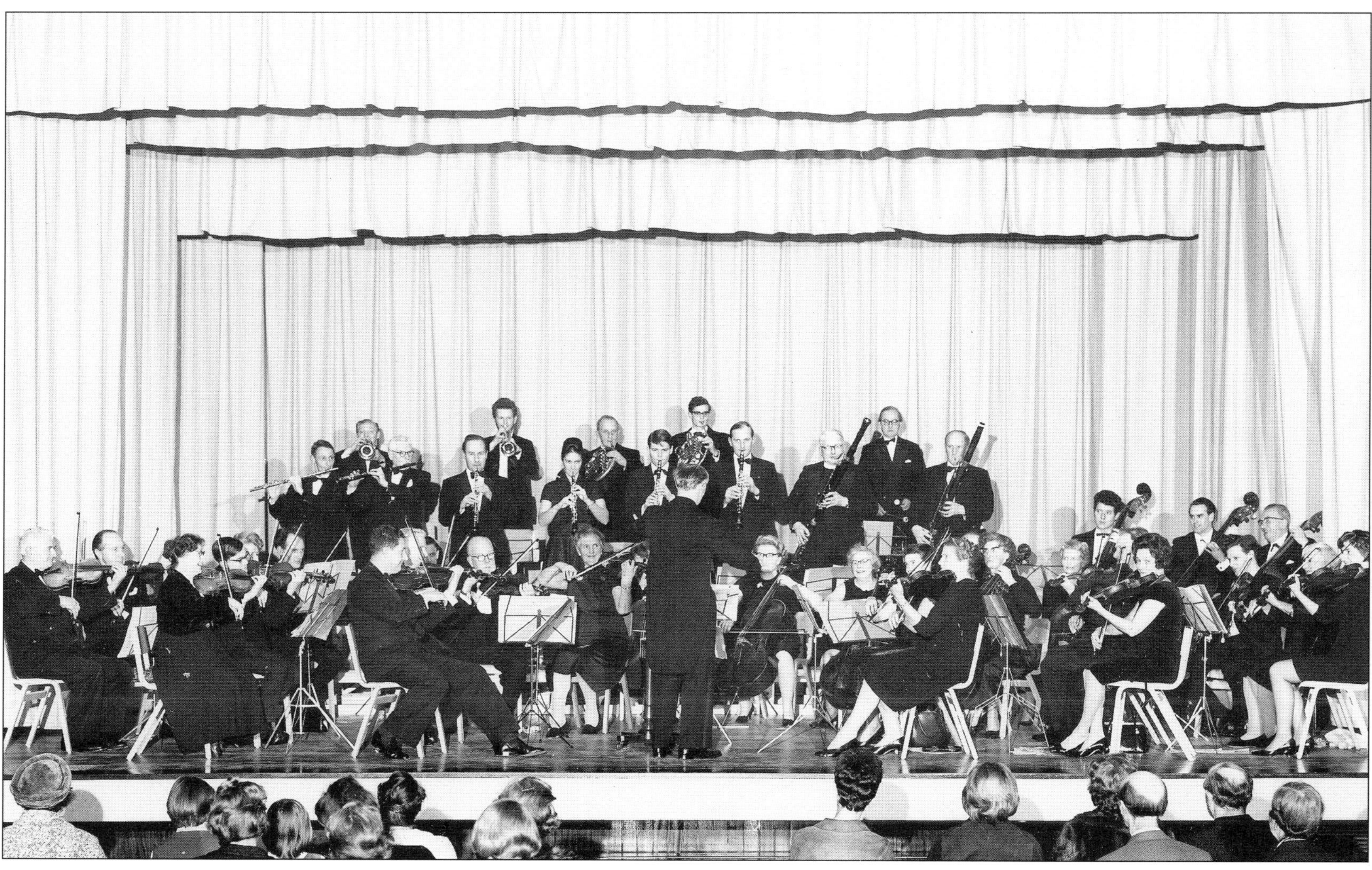

Lichfield Orchestral Society at Netherstowe School c 1960. Donald Cox conductor, John McNulty Leader.

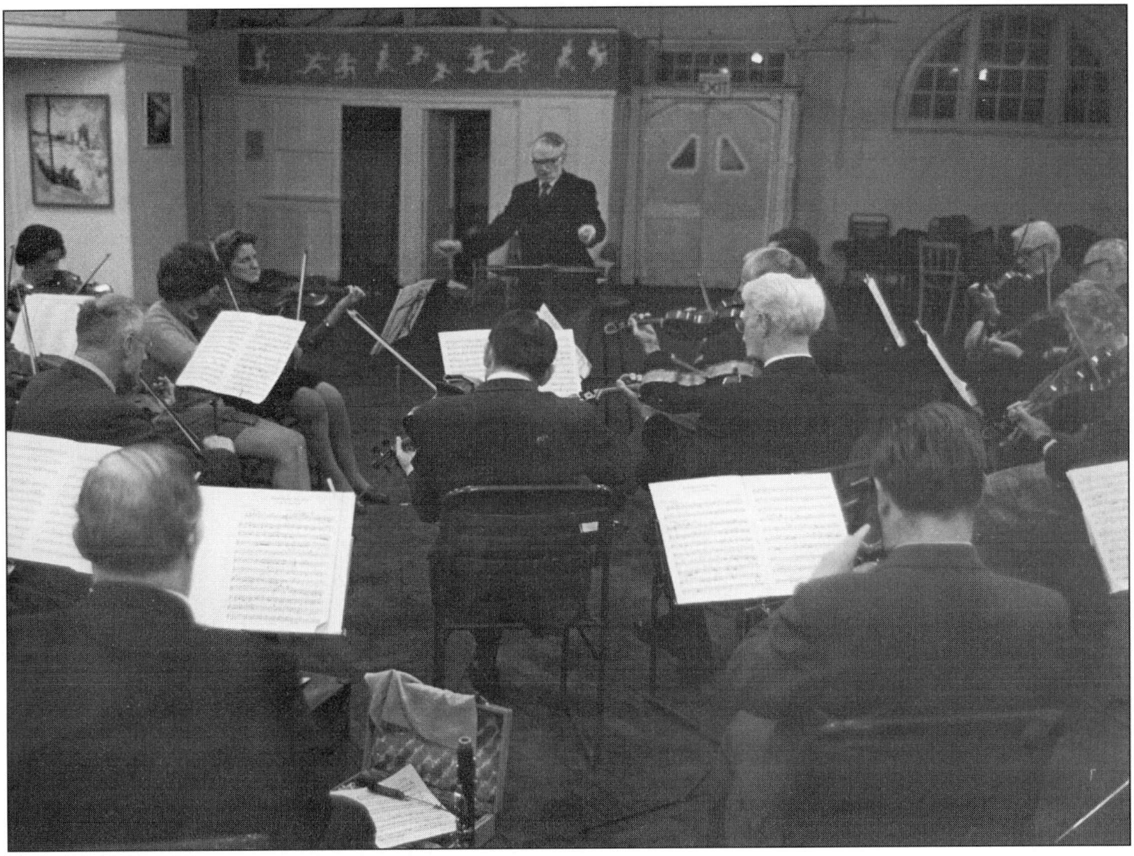

Orchestra rehearsing in Lichfield Arts Centre.

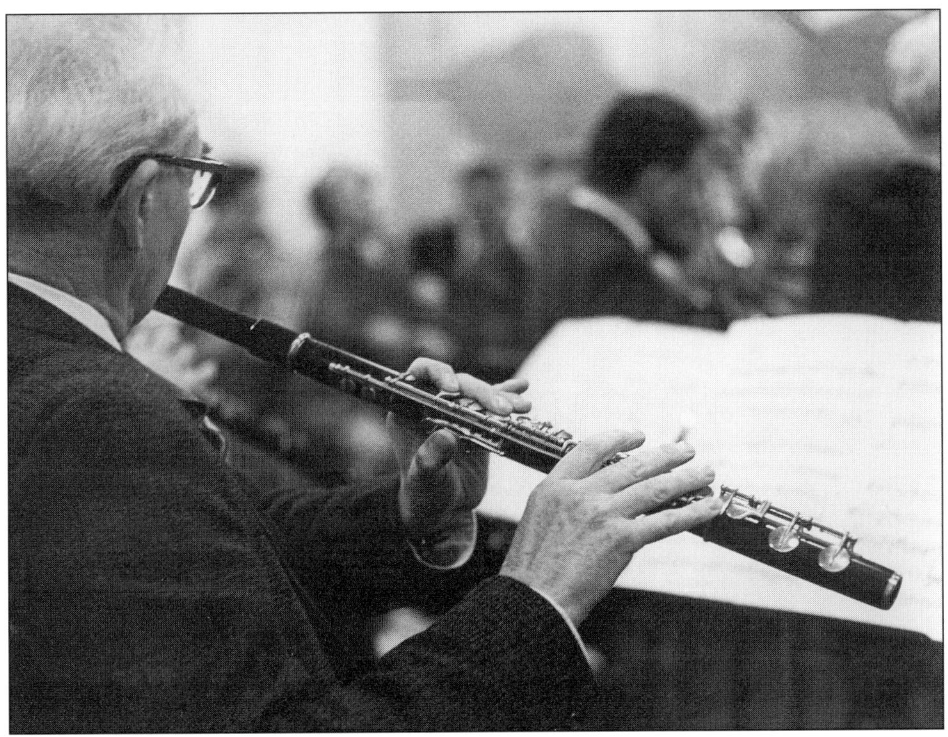

The flautist.

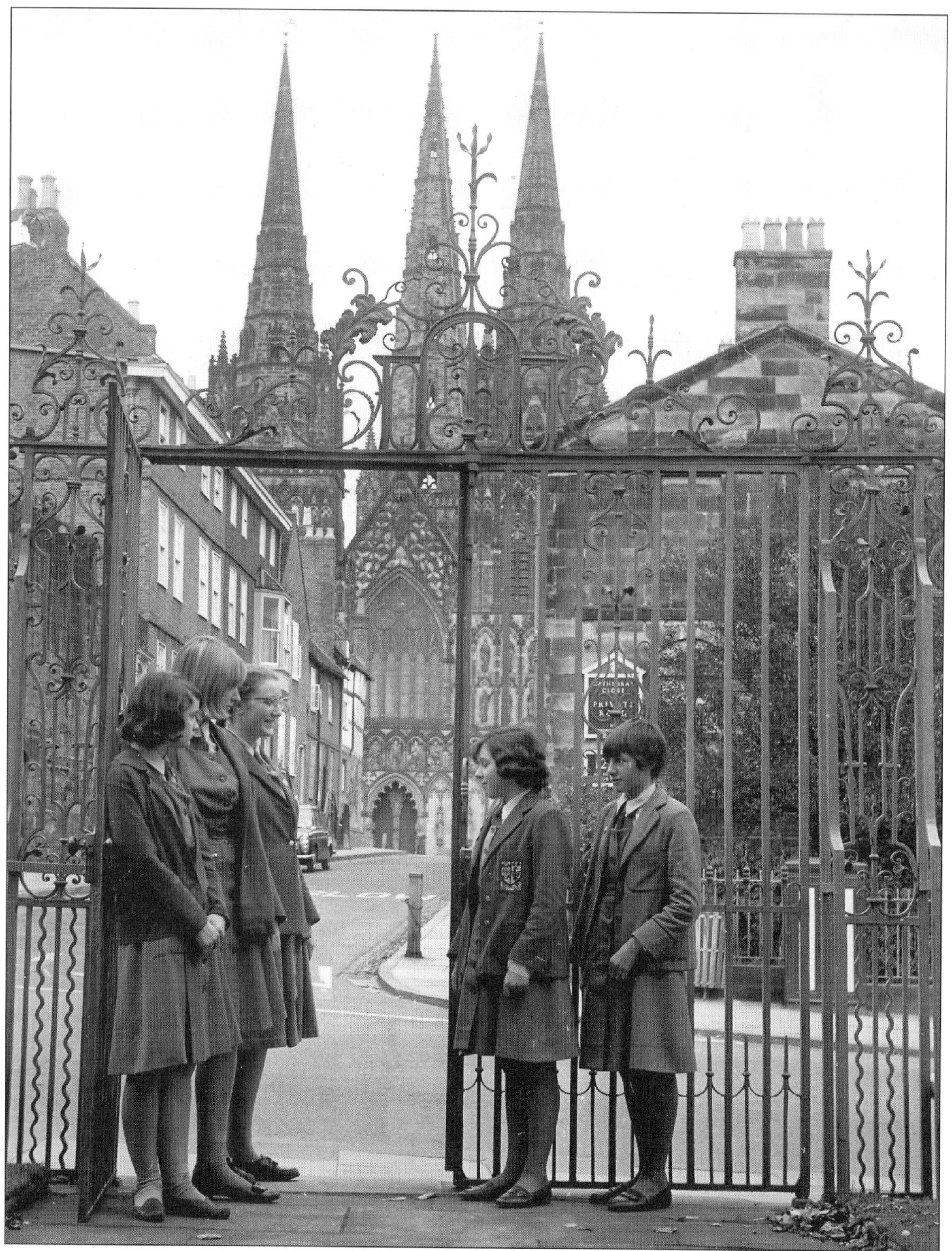

In 1953 the Friary had opened a boarding house at Westgate, opposite the west front of the cathedral, for those girls whose parents wished them to have a boarding school education.

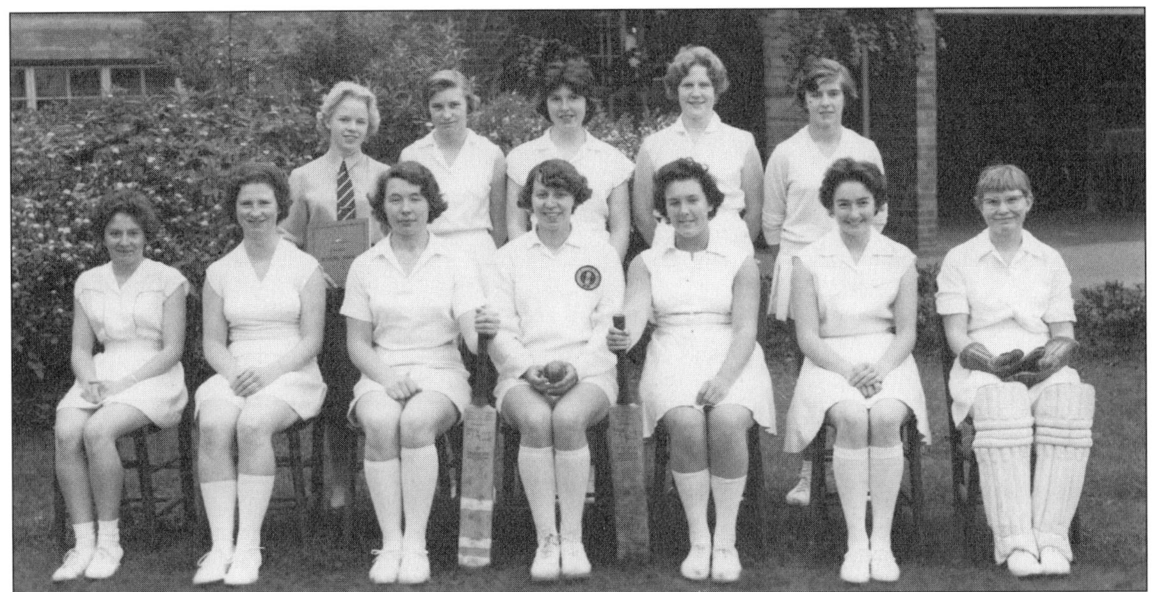

The Friary School Cricket XI, 1963.

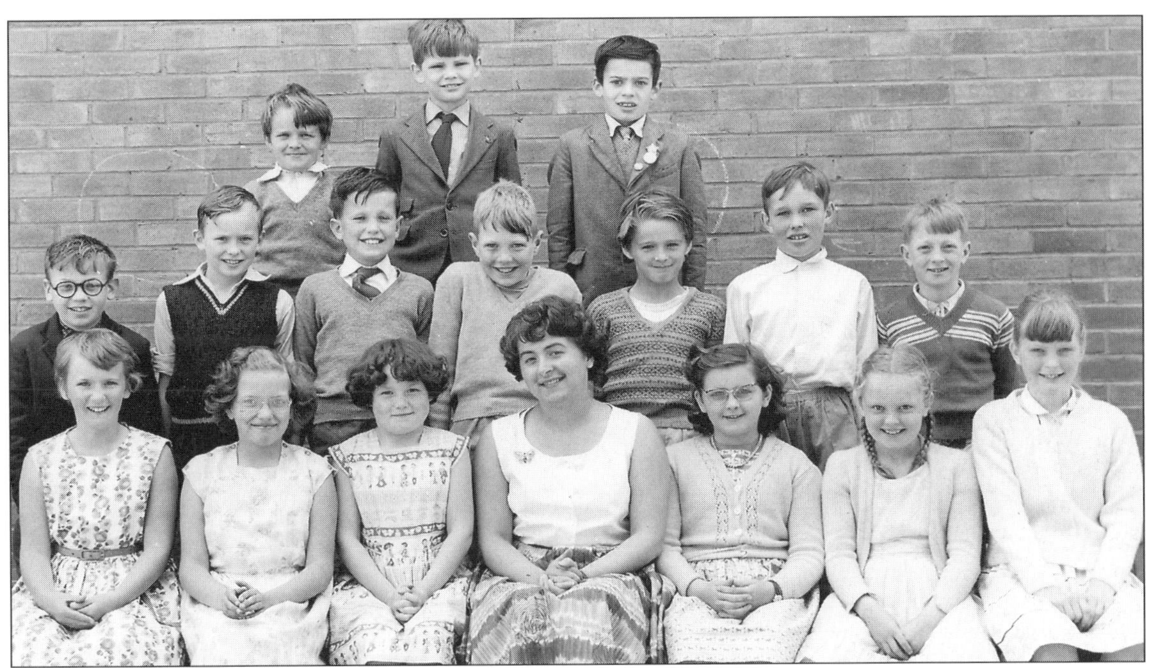

A class from Christ Church Primary School with their teacher Mrs Jean Bird. (Mrs Bird was formerly Miss Lowrance).

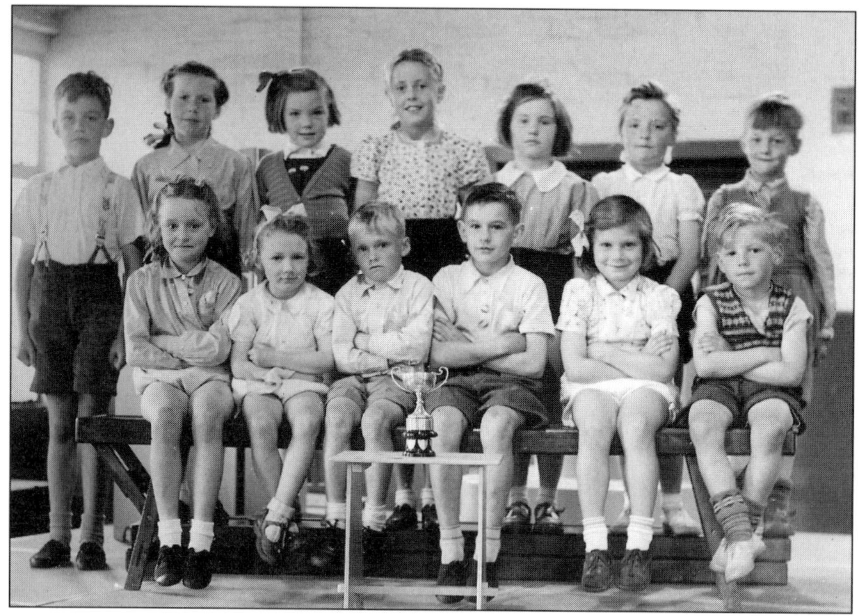

A class at Curborough Road School some time in the sixties. Unfortunately we don't know their names nor the trophy they have won, but they seem very pleased.

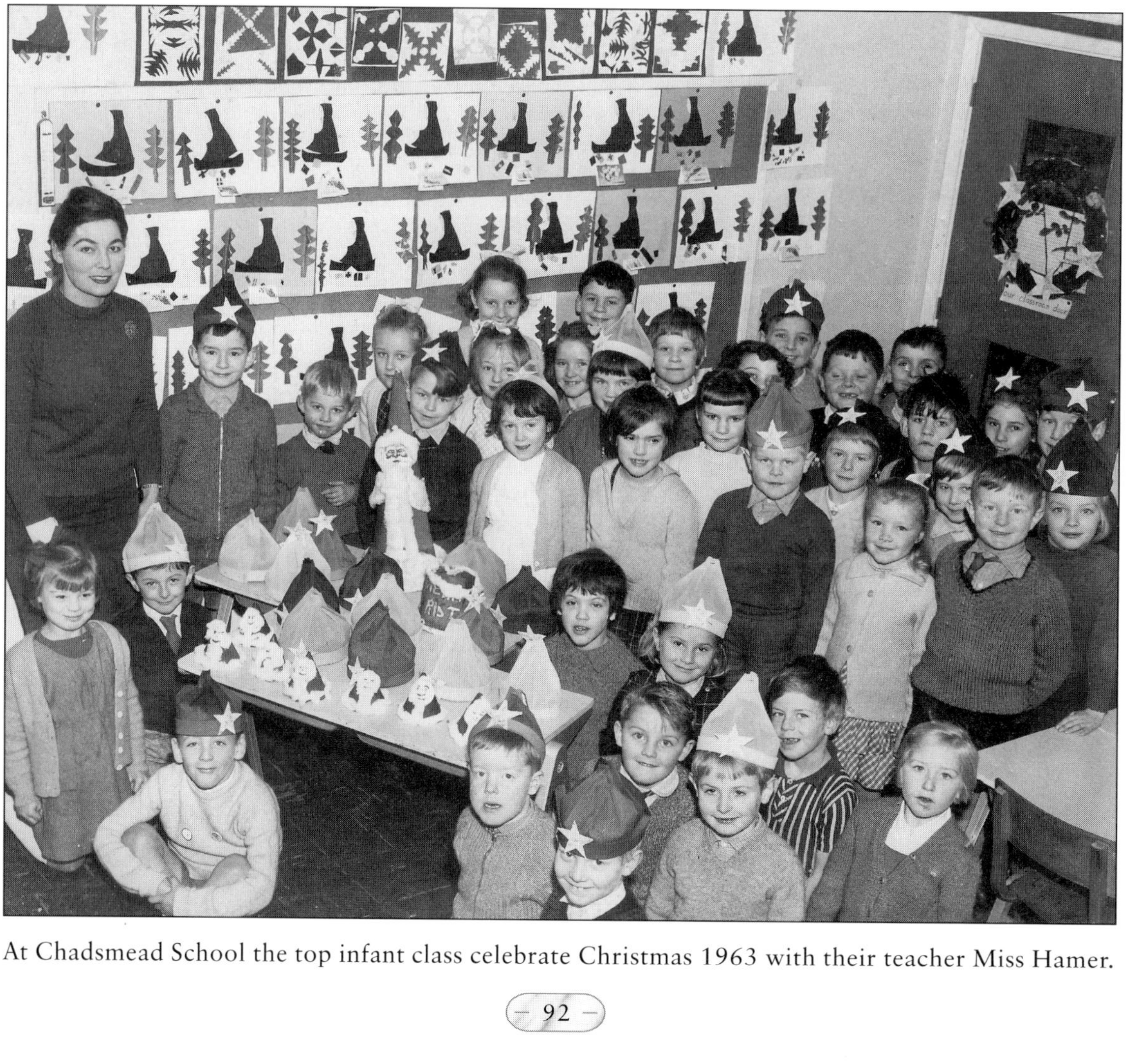

At Chadsmead School the top infant class celebrate Christmas 1963 with their teacher Miss Hamer.

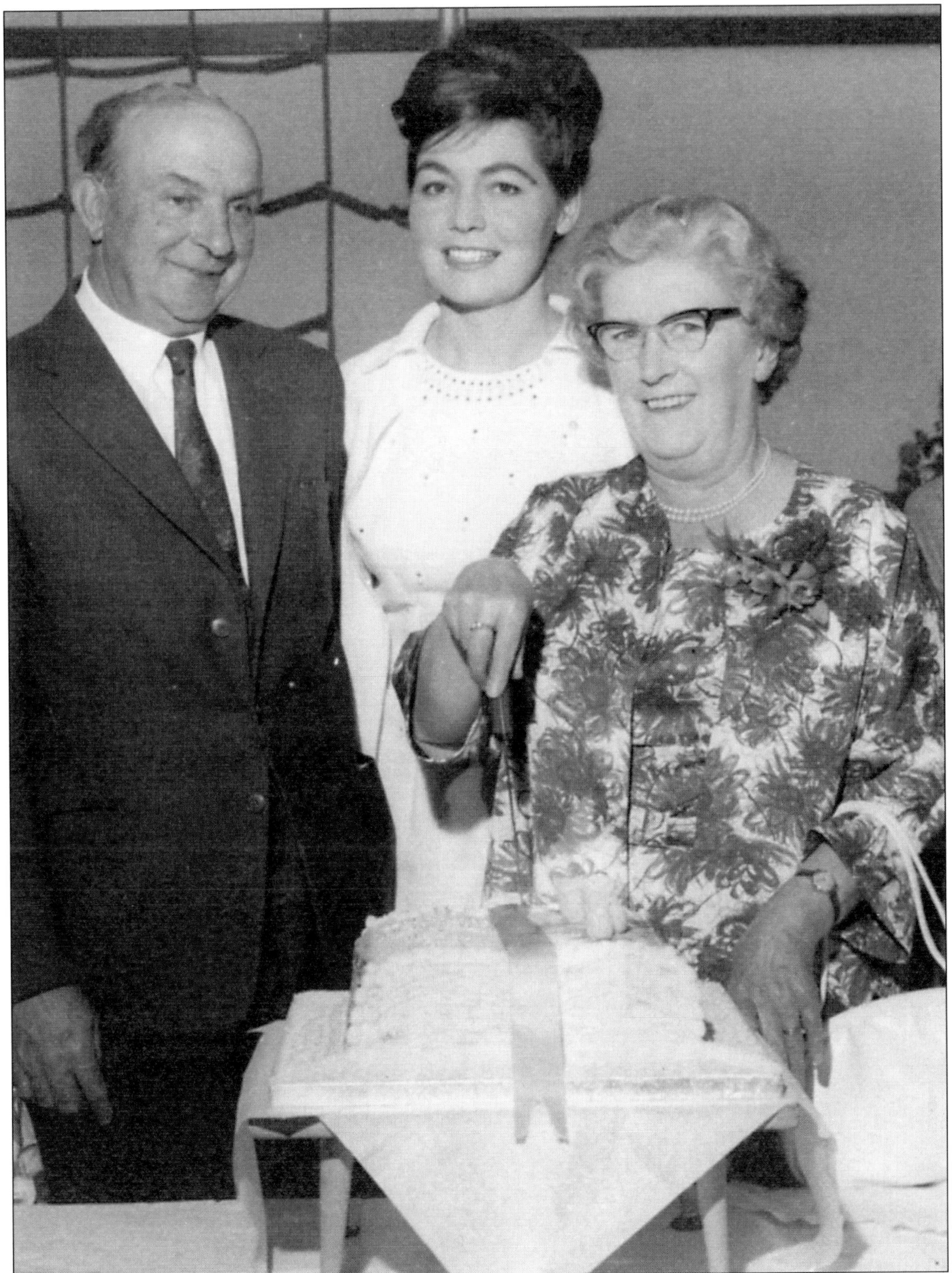

Also at Chadsmead School the Head Teacher (our old friend Mrs Lowrance) cuts a celebratory cake on retirement after 40 years service. During this time she had taught at Stowe School, and served as Head Teacher at St Mary's Pool Walk, Curboorough Road, and Chadsmead Schools.

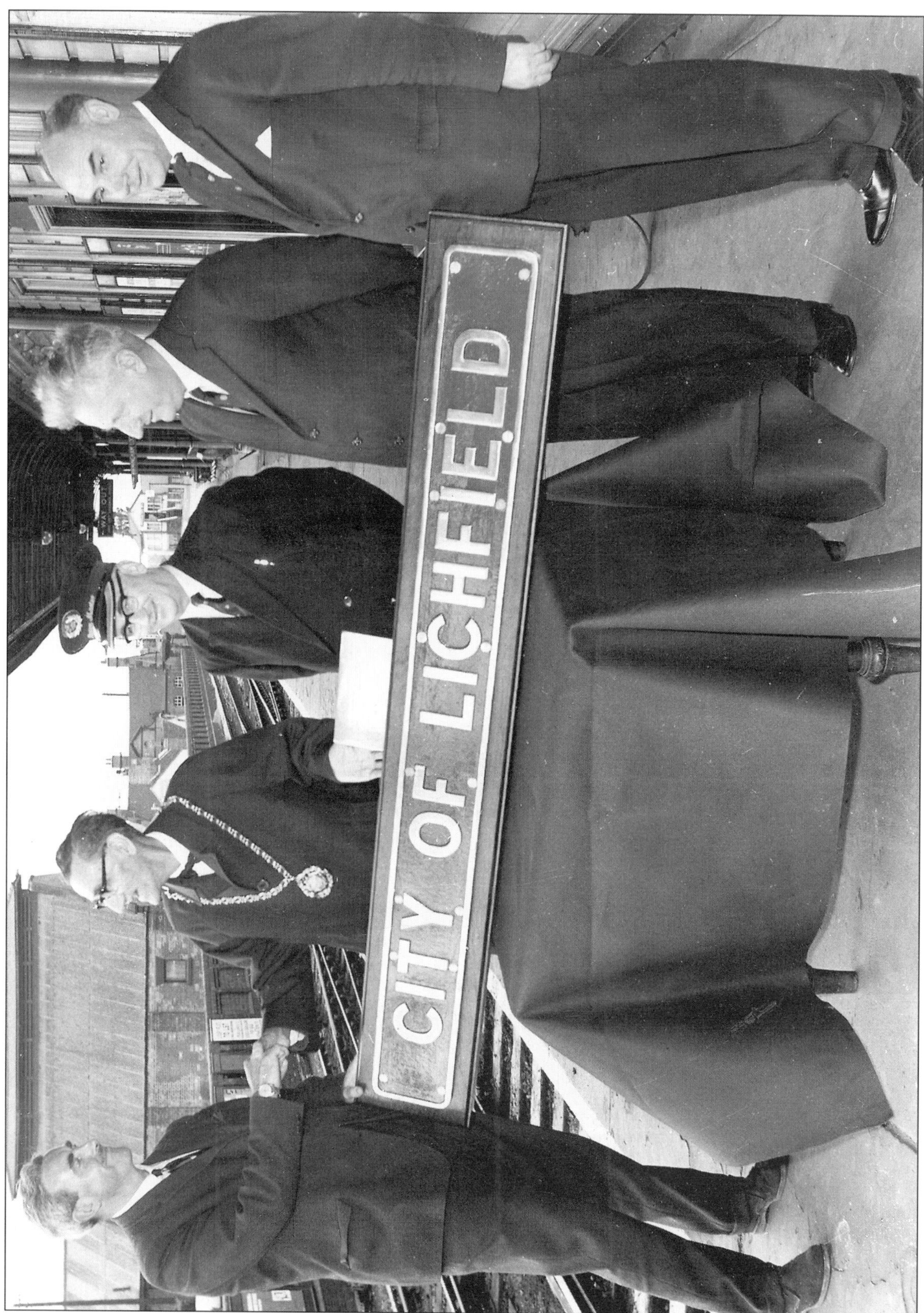
CITY OF LICHFIELD

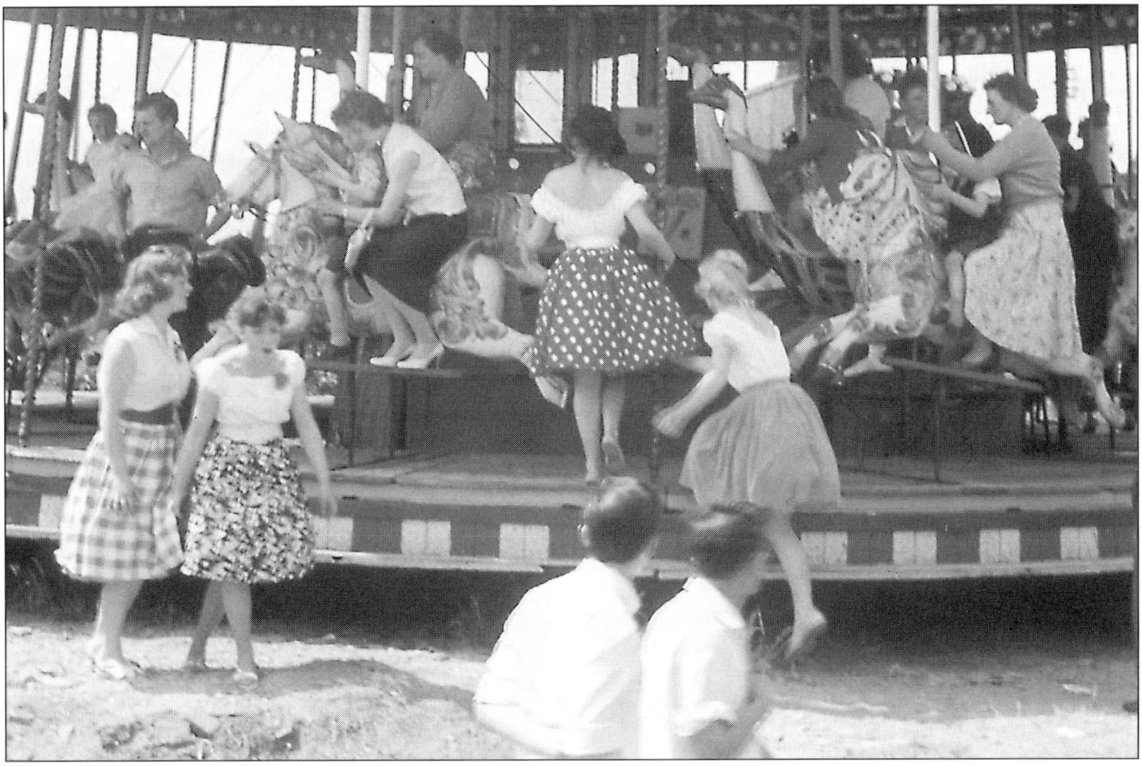

Girls on the carousel, sporting narrow waisted skirts with wide belts, full skirts and little flat shoes to bop the night away at the beginning of the sixties.

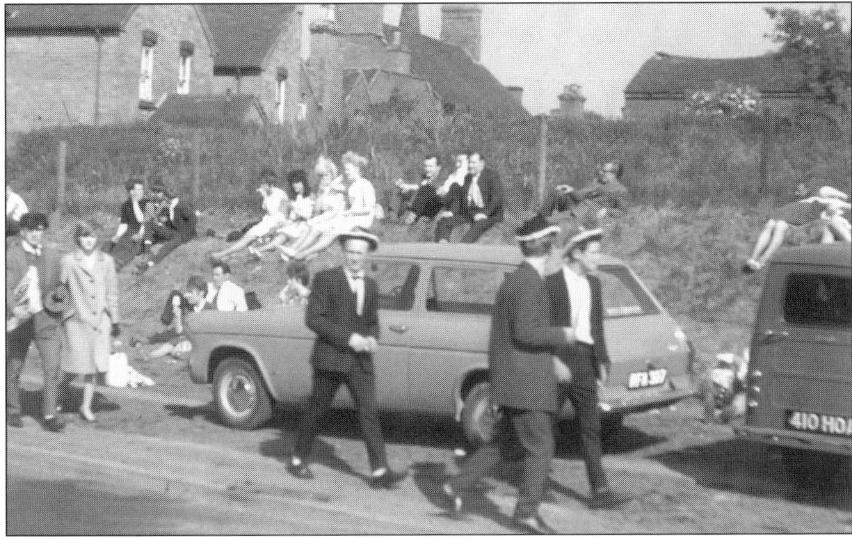

How quickly fashions change. The Bower 1963, when 'boys watch the girls, while the girls watch the boys on every street in town – they're making music to watch girls by'.

Opposite page: The end of the line. After twenty years and nearly two million miles, *City of Lichfield* is retired by British Rail and at a ceremony at Lichfield City Station one of the locomotive's nameplates is received by the Mayor Councillor Frank Halfpenny on behalf of the city. Beside the Mayor is Mr Ramm, Stationmaster of the City Station and Mr Callender, Town Clerk. The other two gentlemen are officials of British Rail. The nameplate can be seen today in St. Mary's Heritage Centre.

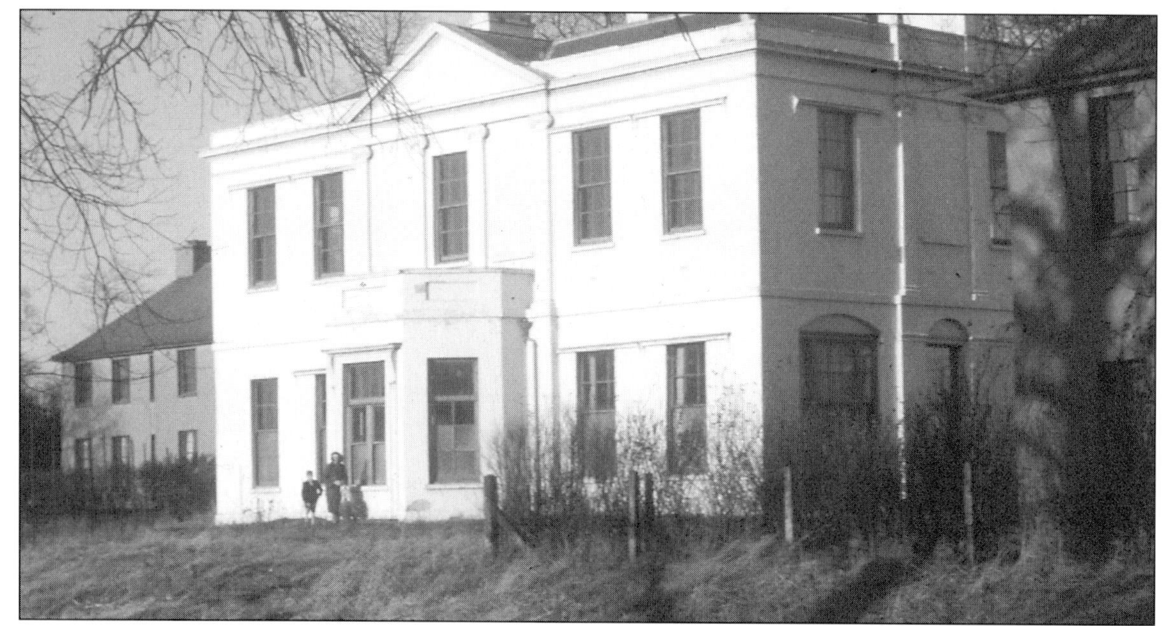

Beacon Place c 1960.

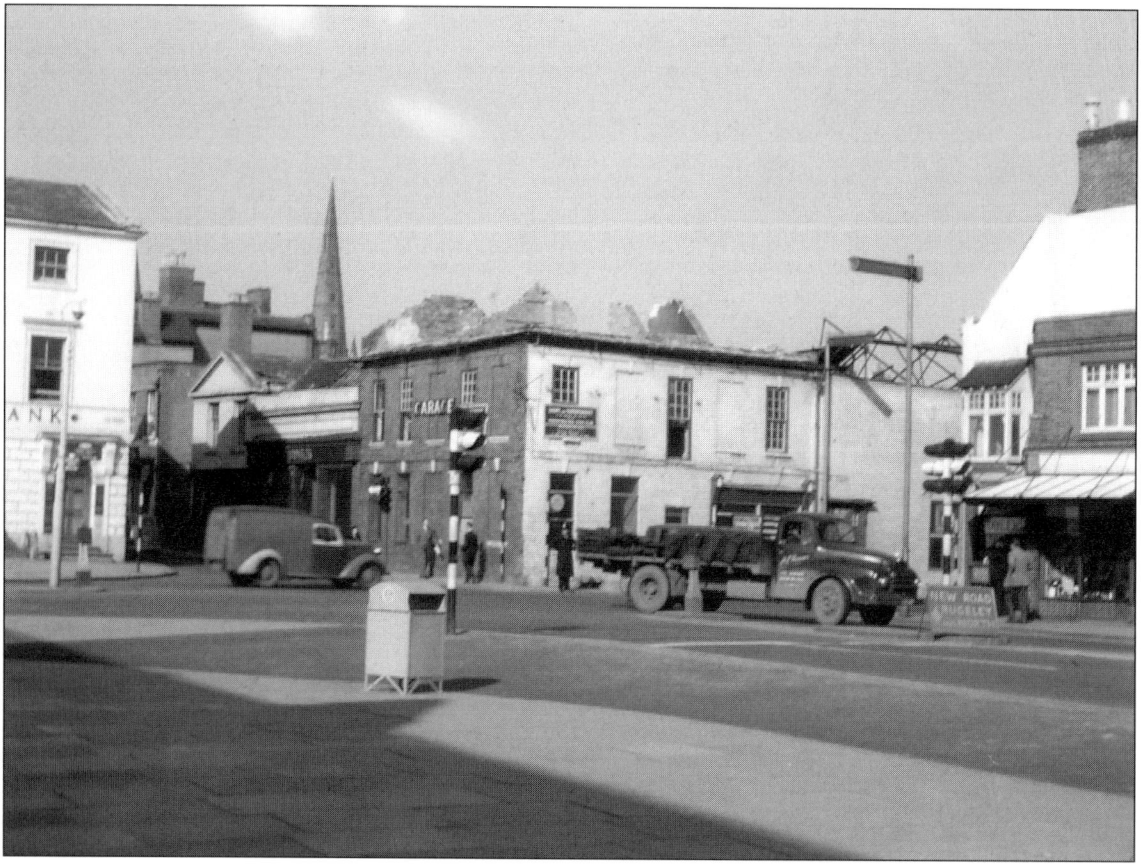

Goodbye to Jones's garage c 1960.

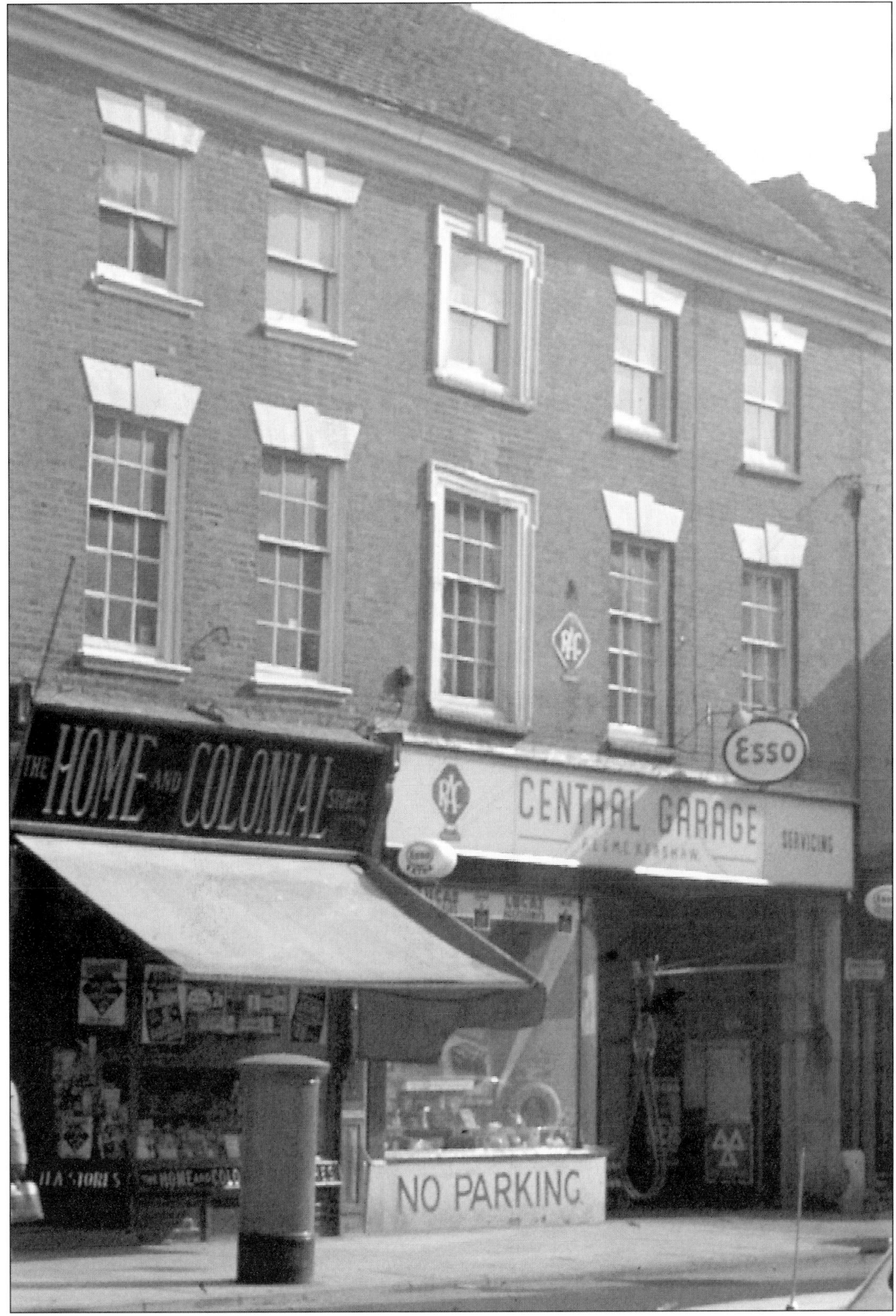

Home & Colonial and Central Garage in Conduit Street c 1960, where Macdonalds is today.

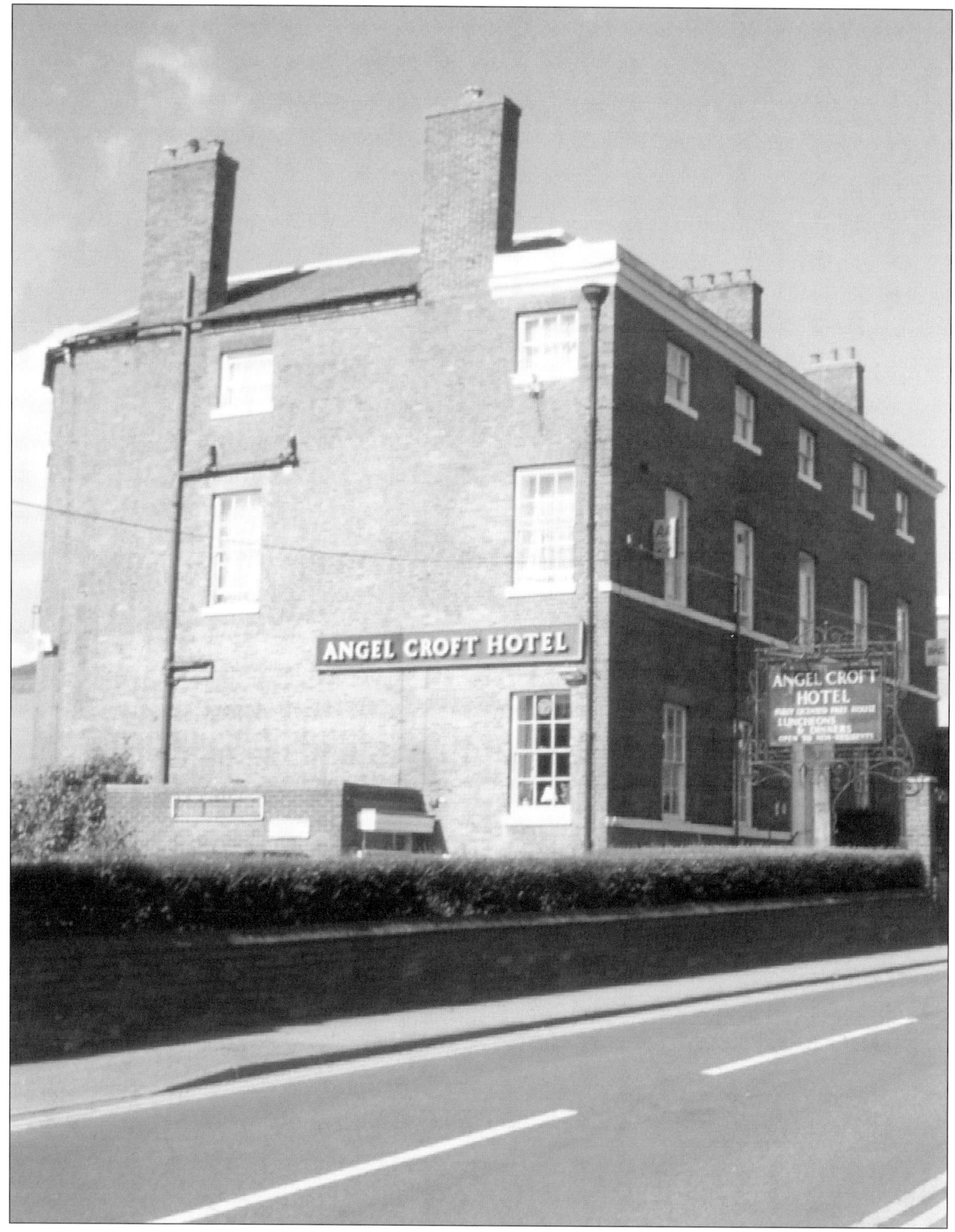

The Angel Croft Hotel, Beacon Street.

Chapter 8 – The Seventies

The decade of the Seventies was one of change for local government in England and Wales. The 1972 Local Government Act made sweeping changes all over the country and in Lichfield, it resulted in the abolition of the corporation which had been granted by the Charter of King Edward VI, nearly five hundred years ago. From March 1974, Lichfield would become part of a much larger District Council having 56 councillors of which only 15 would come from the City of Lichfield. Moreover, the city would now become a town.

The Act did permit the 15 members to form a group, within the new council, to be known as "The Charter Trustees" who would be able to elect a Mayor and to maintain the ancient customs and traditions of the city. They could not, however, raise a rate and had no decision making function.

Worst of all, Lichfield (but not the other parishes in the District) could not spend the money raised through the rates for matters of local community interest. Instead, it was spent by the District as a whole.

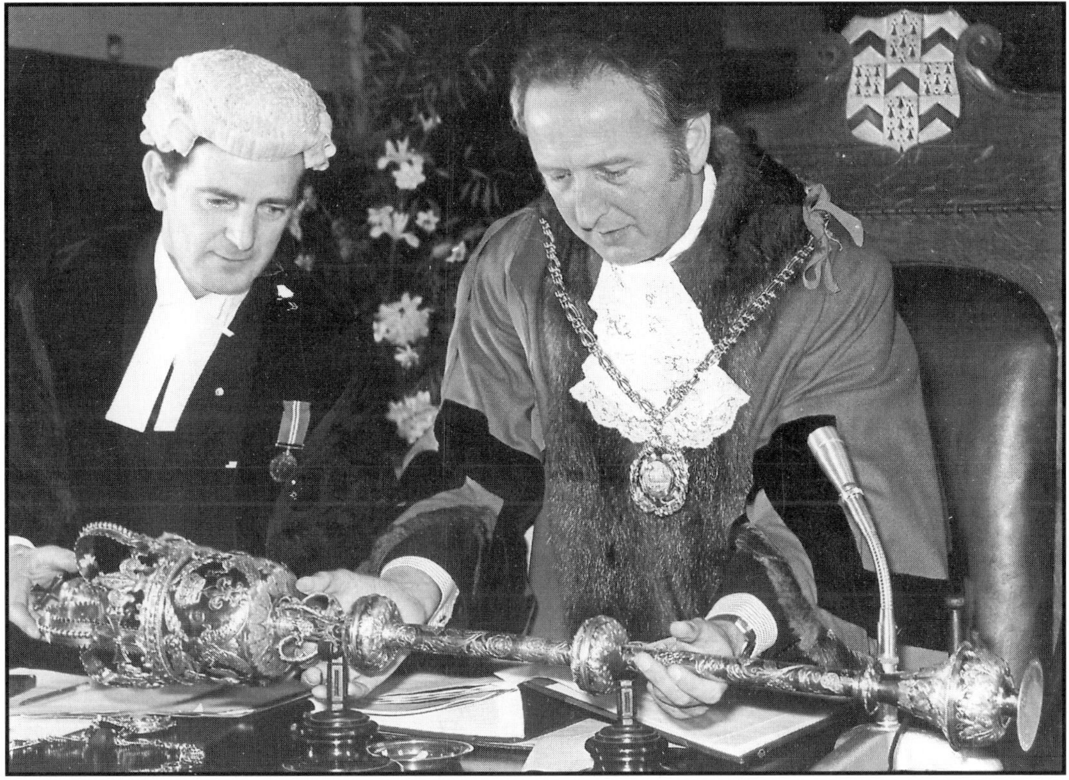

Above: The last Mayor of Lichfield under the provisions of the Charter of Edward VI was Councillor John Wilson, seen here at his inauguration in May 1973, together with Mr Kenneth Brownlow. Town Clerk. The 17th century silver-gilt mace, one of two which, with a fine Sword of State, symbolised the authority of the Mayor; the Mayor's chain and badge of office, (presented by a member of the Dyott family); and the arms of the city on the back of the chair all serve to recall a vanished period in Lichfield's history. While they remind us of the city's glory that was, they also indicate the power that has gone.

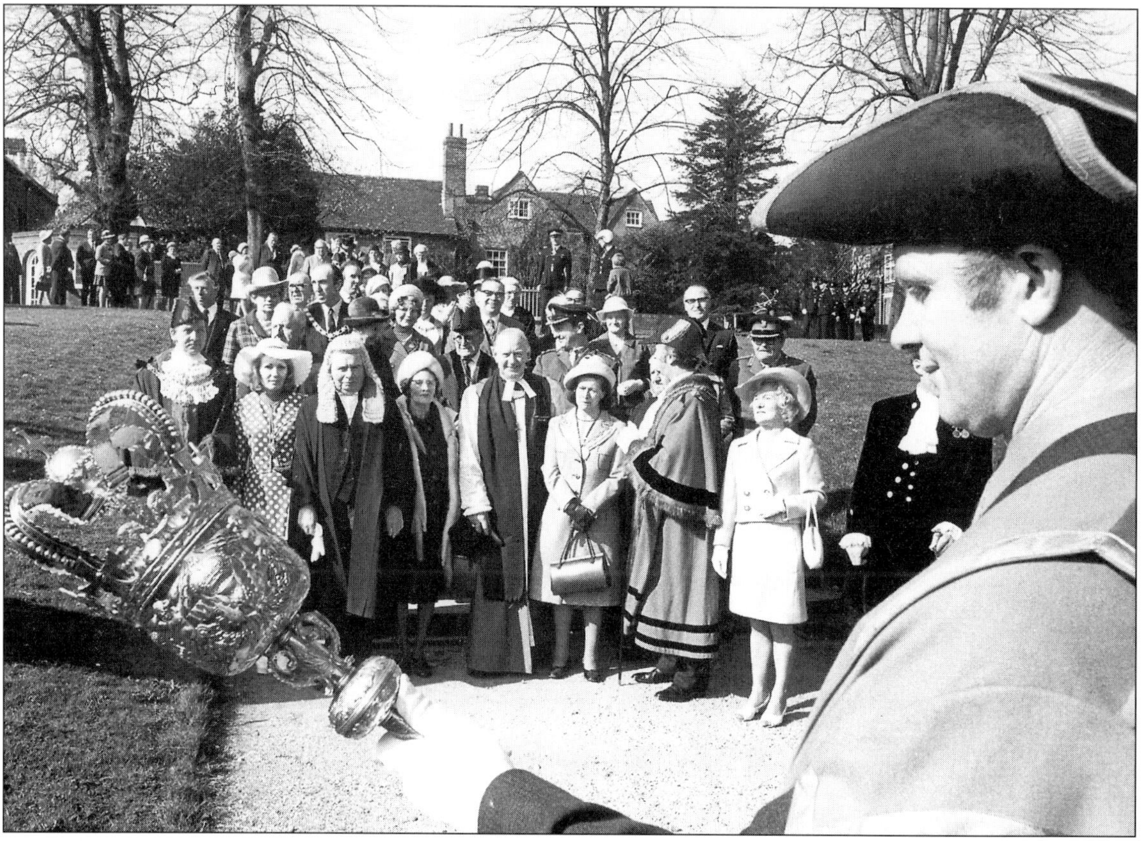

On the 31st of March, 1974, a service of thanksgiving was held in Lichfield Cathedral to which were invited representatives from all those local authorities which, like Lichfield, had come to the end of their respective roads. They are seen here entering the cathedral.

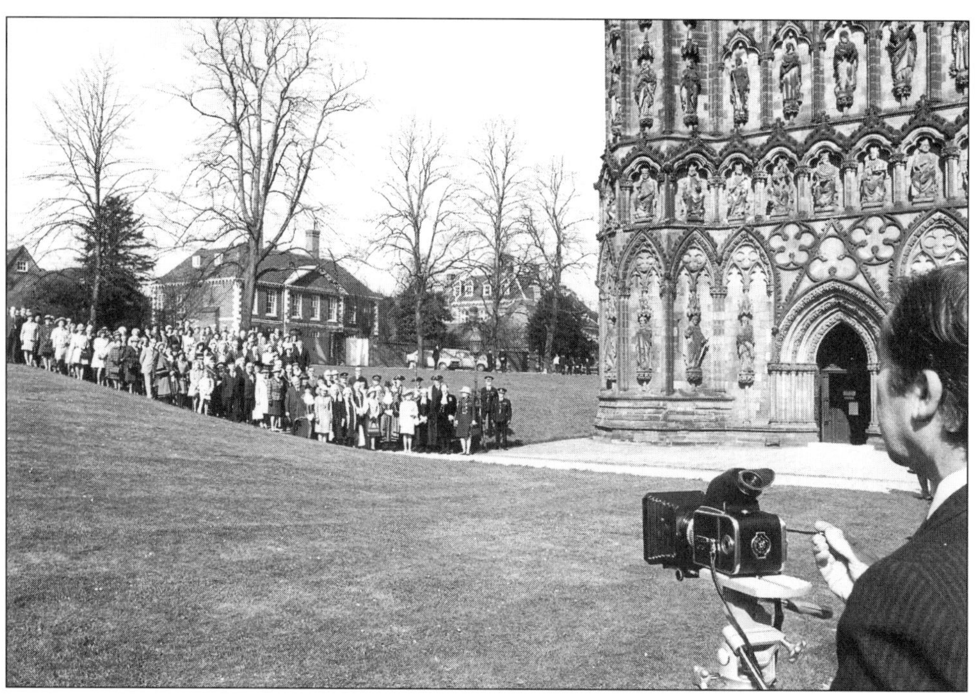

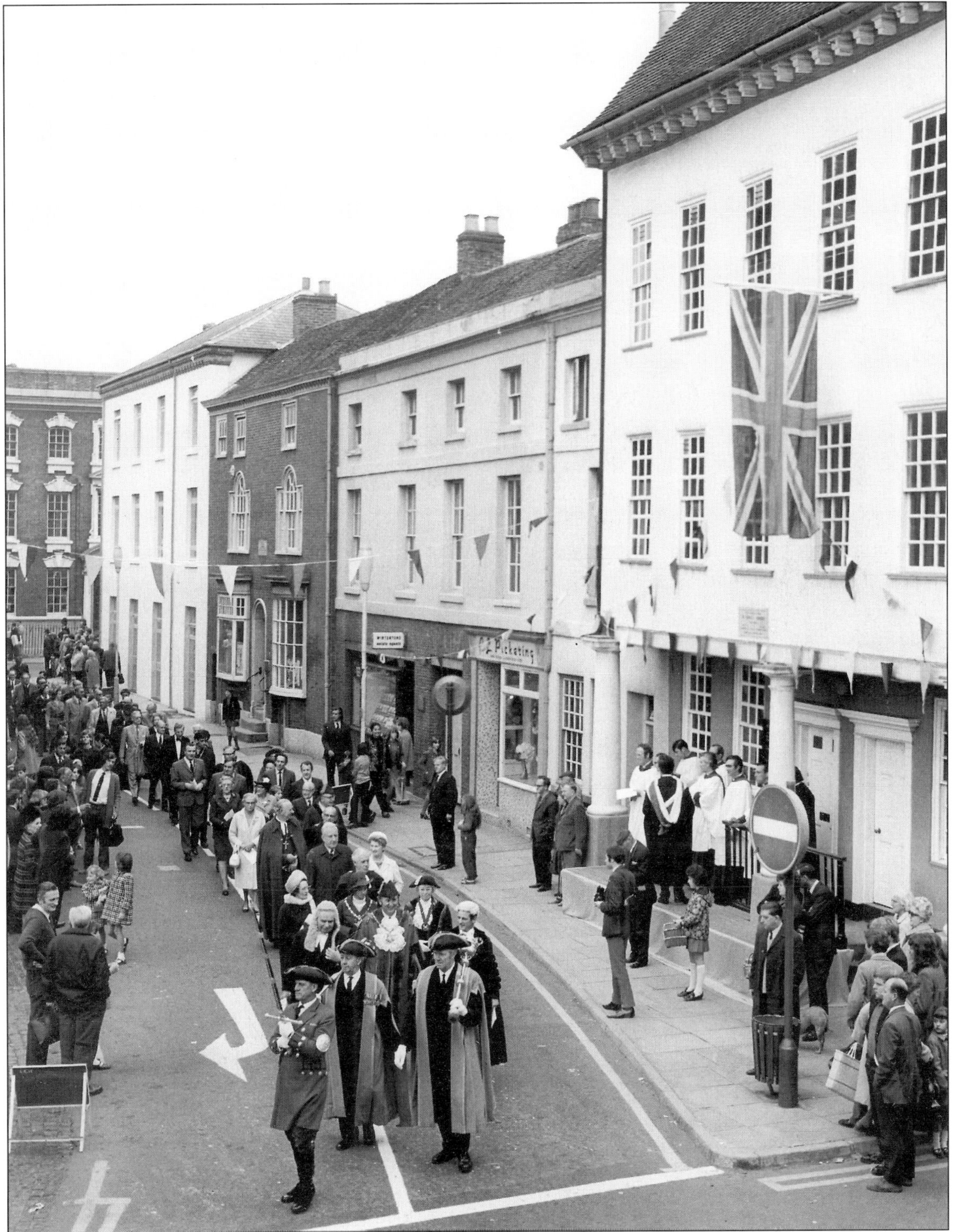

The Charter Trustees will carry on the traditional ceremonies of the City, and here we see one of these – the Dr. Johnson Birthday celebrations of 1973. Civic heads lead Councillors and members of the Johnson Society from the Guildhall to Johnson's statue. A Union Flag hangs from the Birthplace, and below, members of the cathedral choir prepare to play their part.

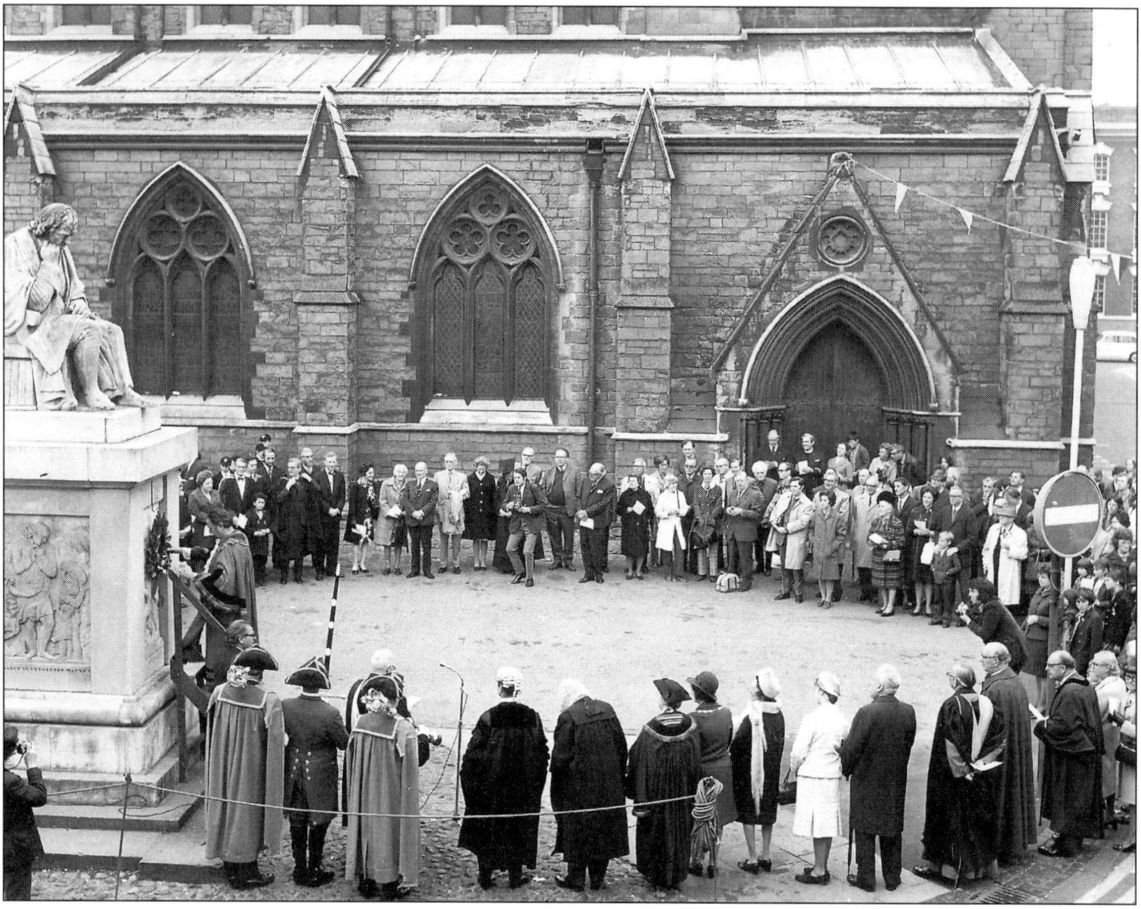

A service is held and the mayor lays a wreath after which the party returns to the Guildhall.

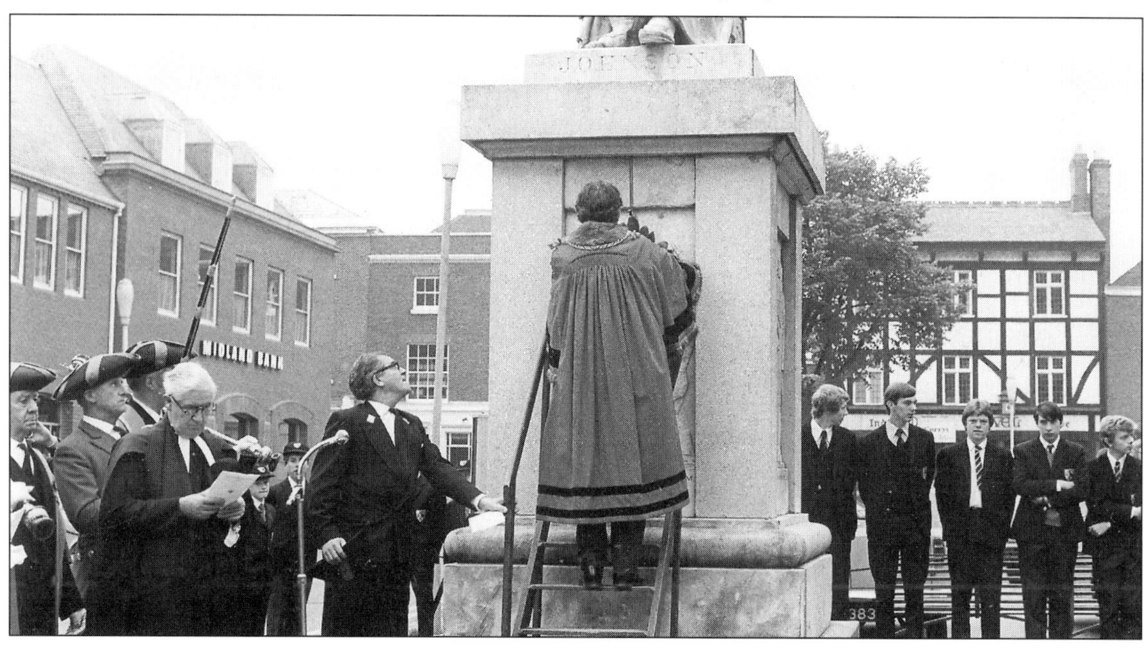

Behind the statue boys (no girls yet) of Johnson's old school watch with interest.

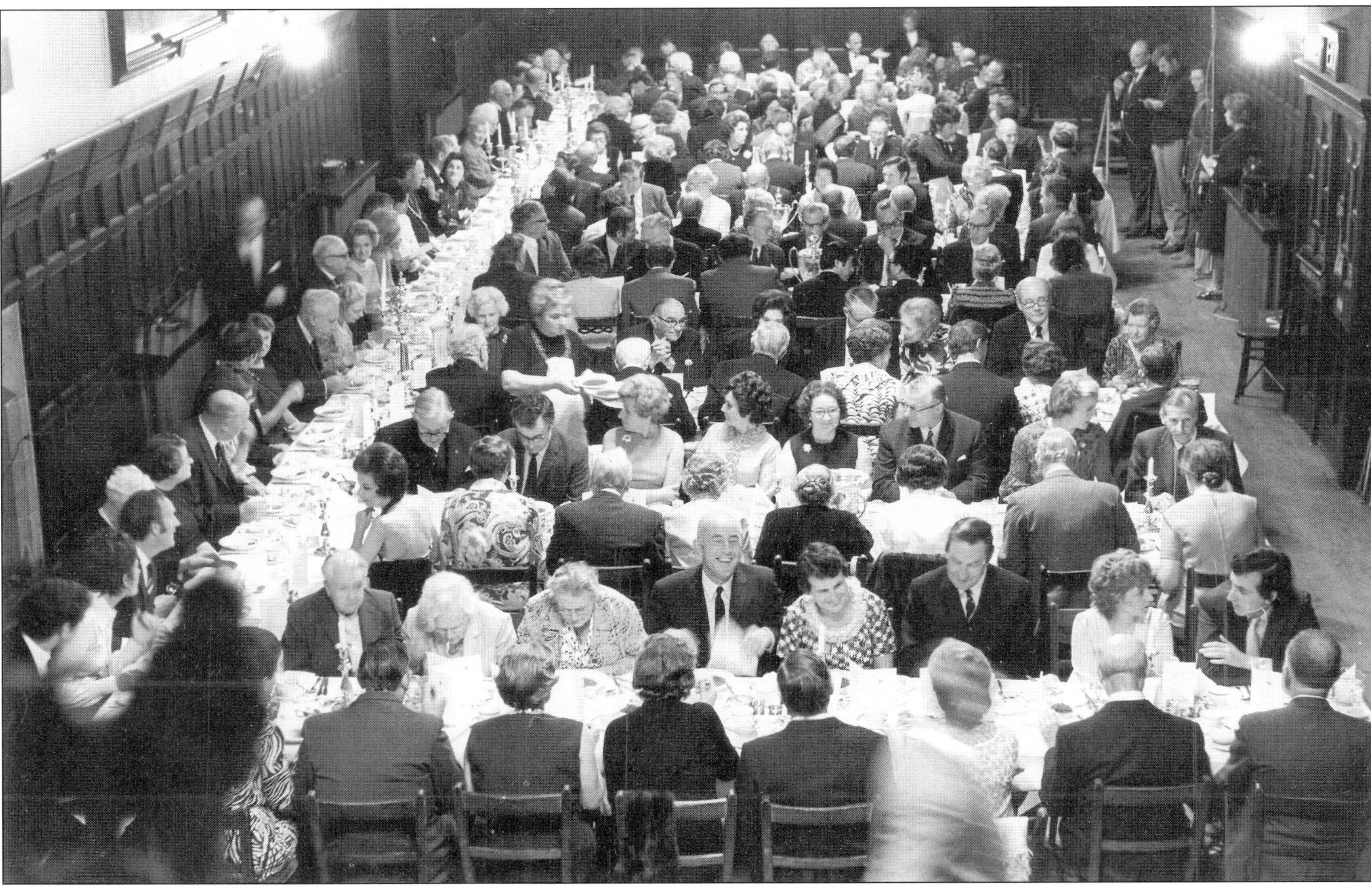

In the evening the Johnson Supper is held in the and now ladies are permitted to attend.

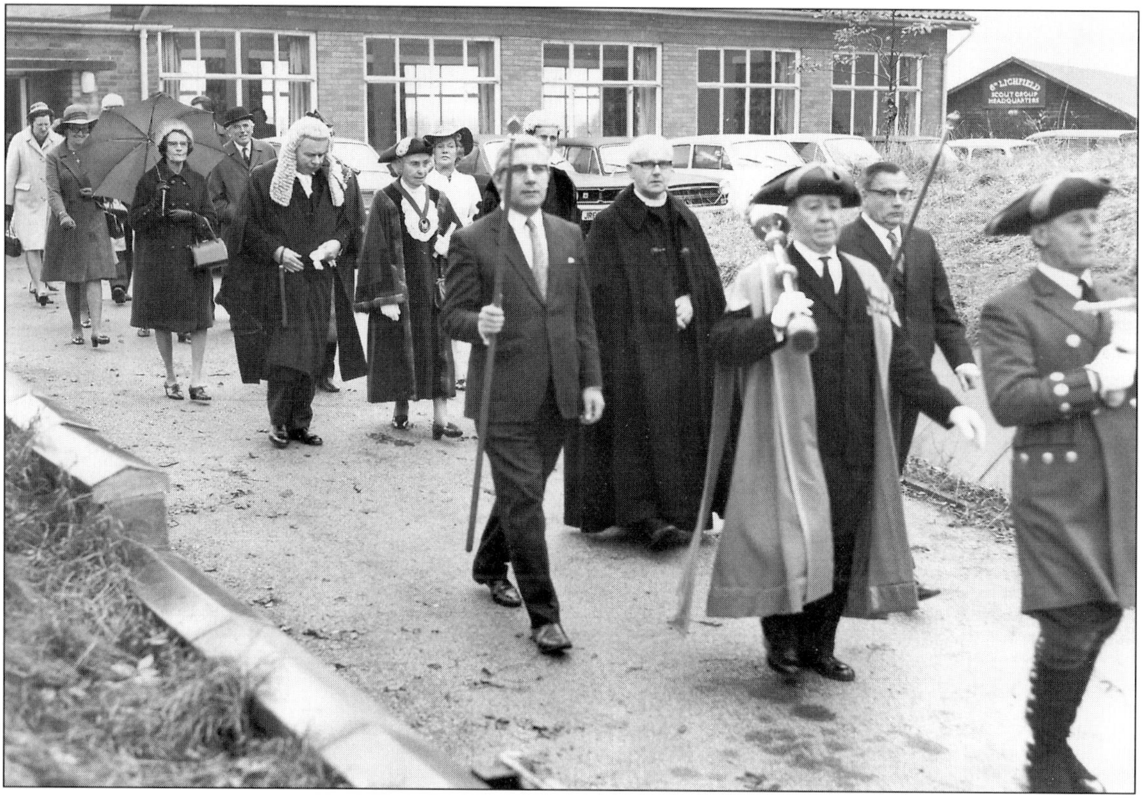

Councillors are expected to attend Divine Service at most of the Lichfield churches as a civic duty. Here they are in procession to Christ Church.

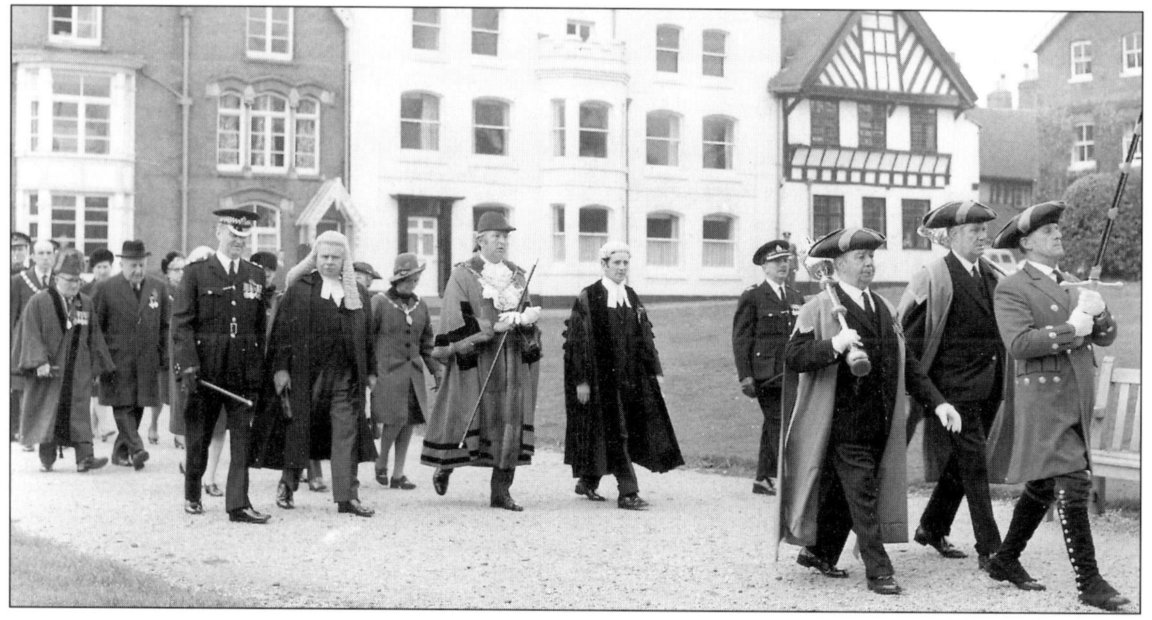

Here they attend the Cathedral, traditionally on Easter Day.

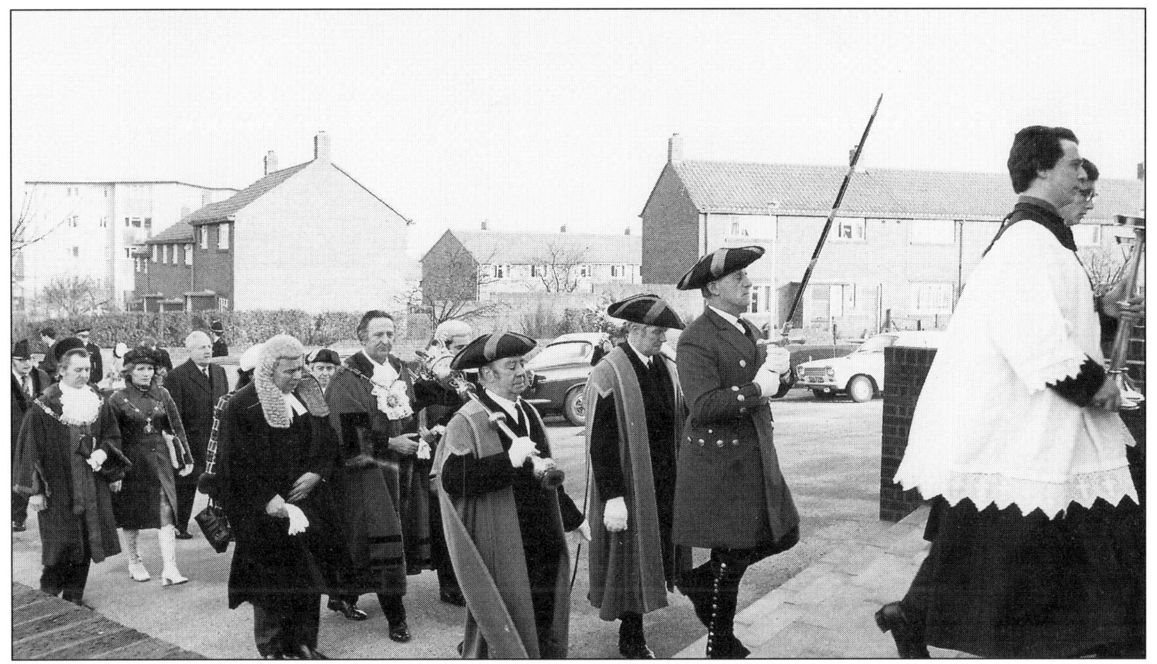

The Councillors also go to SS Peter and Paul Roman Catholic Church, the Dimbles and on Remembrance Sunday they go to the cathedral followed by wreath laying at the war memorial.

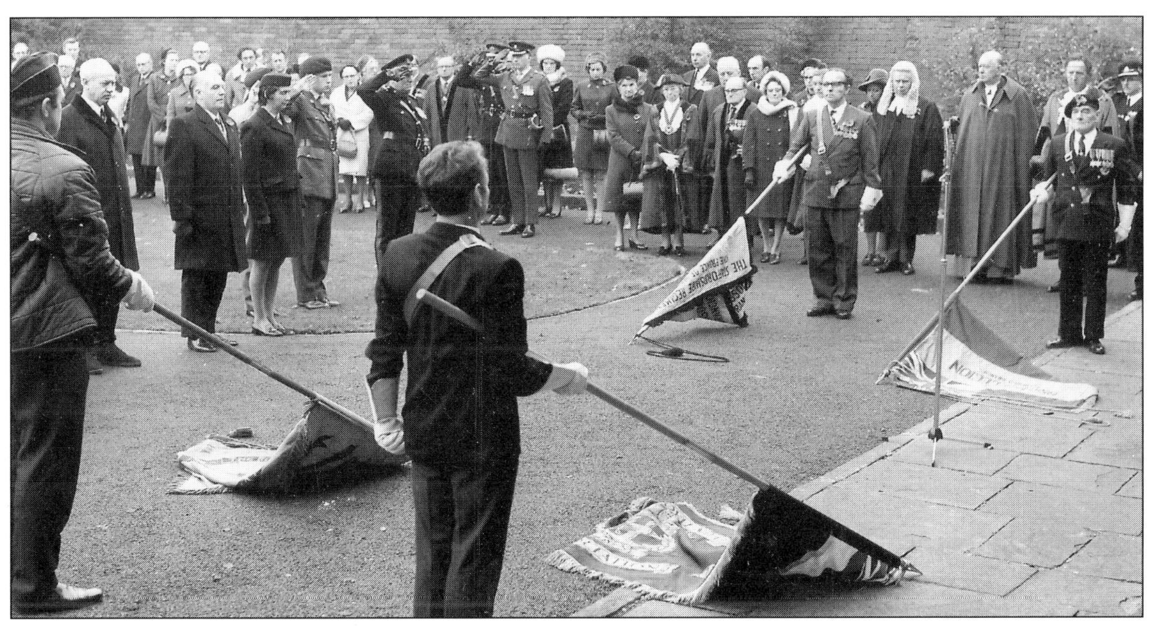

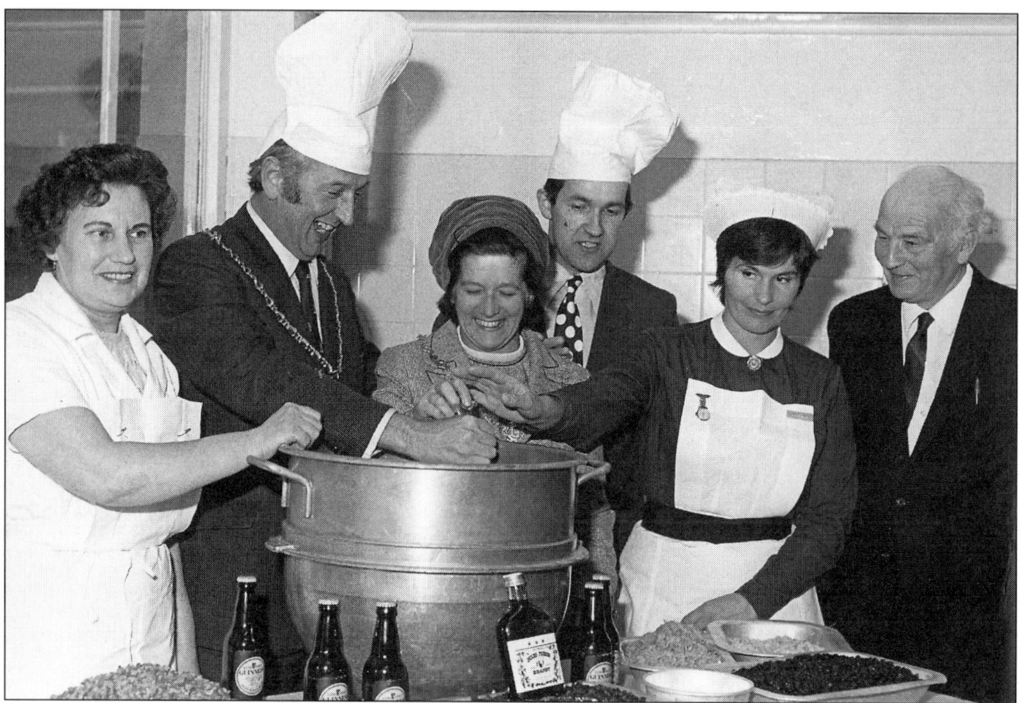

Another civic duty is often the stirring of Christmas puddings. At the Victoria Hospital the Mayor and Mayoress lend their hands to this good work.

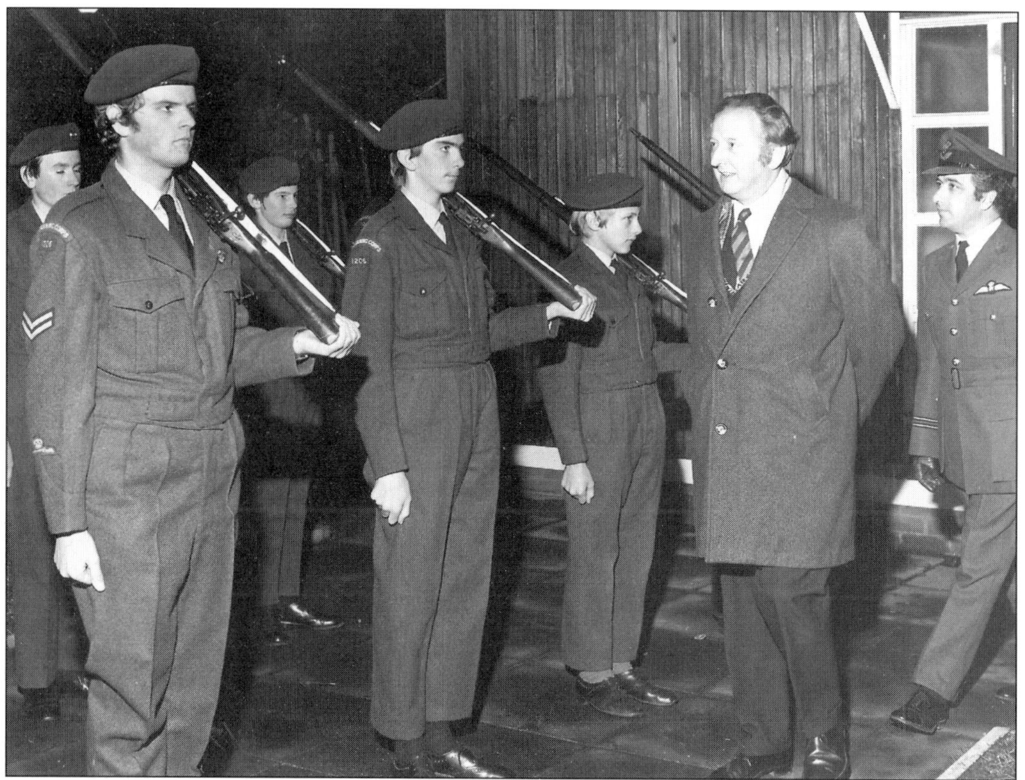

A visit by the Mayor to Lichfield's Air Training Corps Unit.

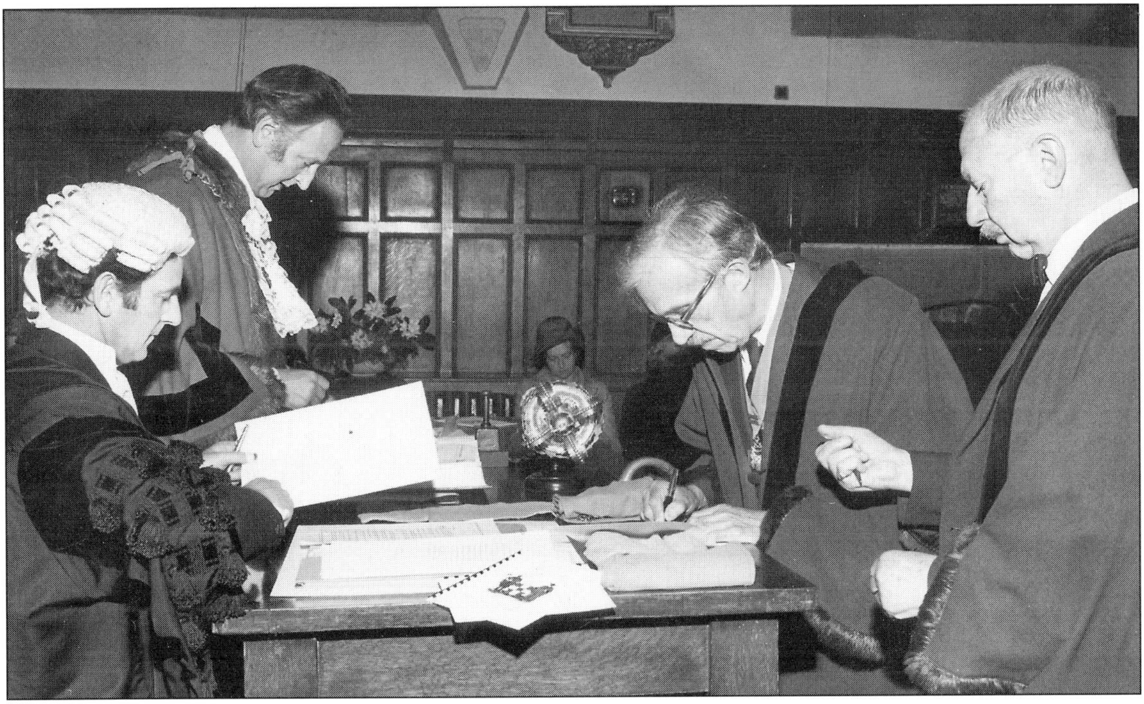

A Mayoral Court for the inauguration of a new Worshipful Master of the Company of Smiths, Lichfield's last remaining guild.

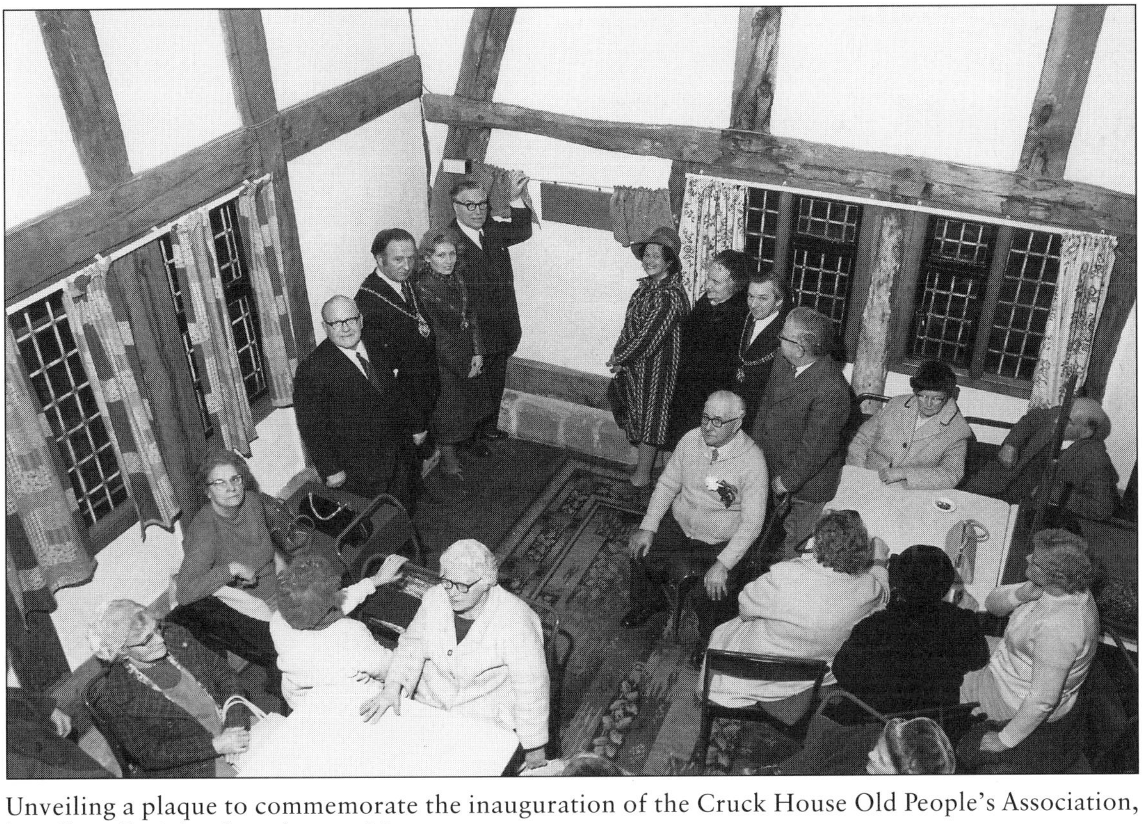

Unveiling a plaque to commemorate the inauguration of the Cruck House Old People's Association, by Cllr Bill Richards, a former Mayor.

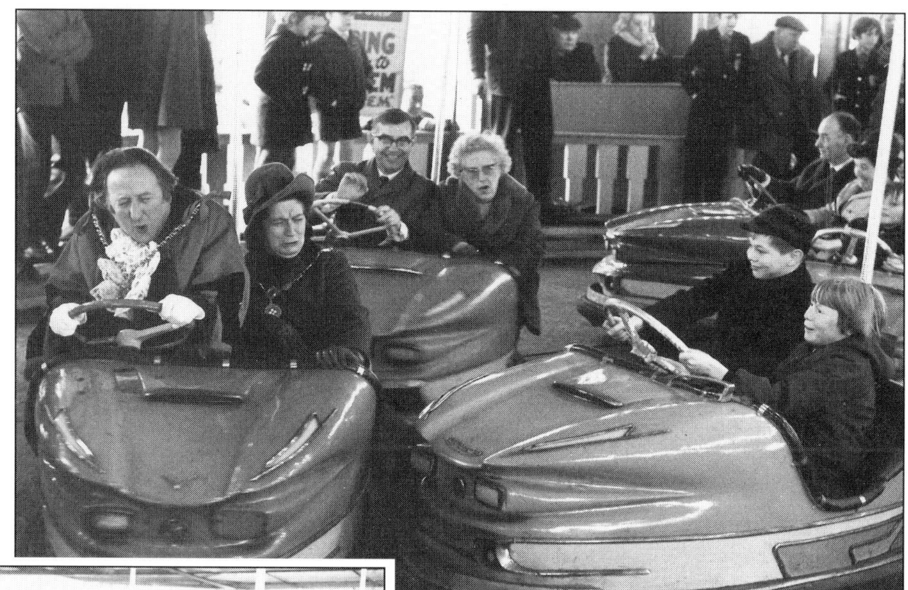

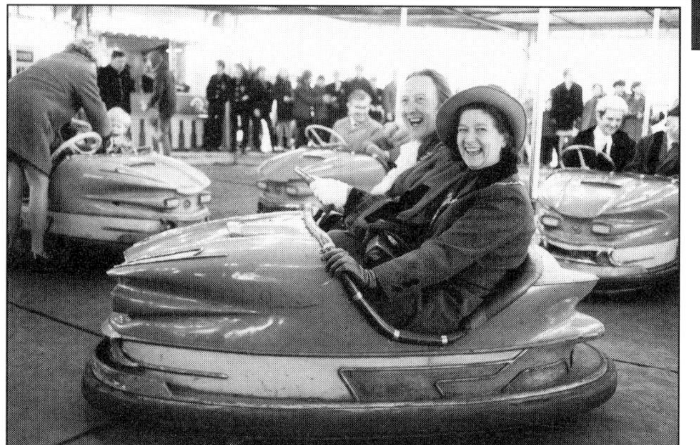

Above and left: Not all civic duties are pleasant. At the Shrovetide Fair the Mayor is expected to take a ride on the dodgems, in this case with dire results.

Below: At St Michael's Hospital someone is having an hundredth birthday, but sadly we don't know her name. She is visited on this important occasion by the Chairman's Lady of Lichfield District Council, Mrs Mary Ward and the Mayoress of Lichfield, Mrs Janet Wilson.

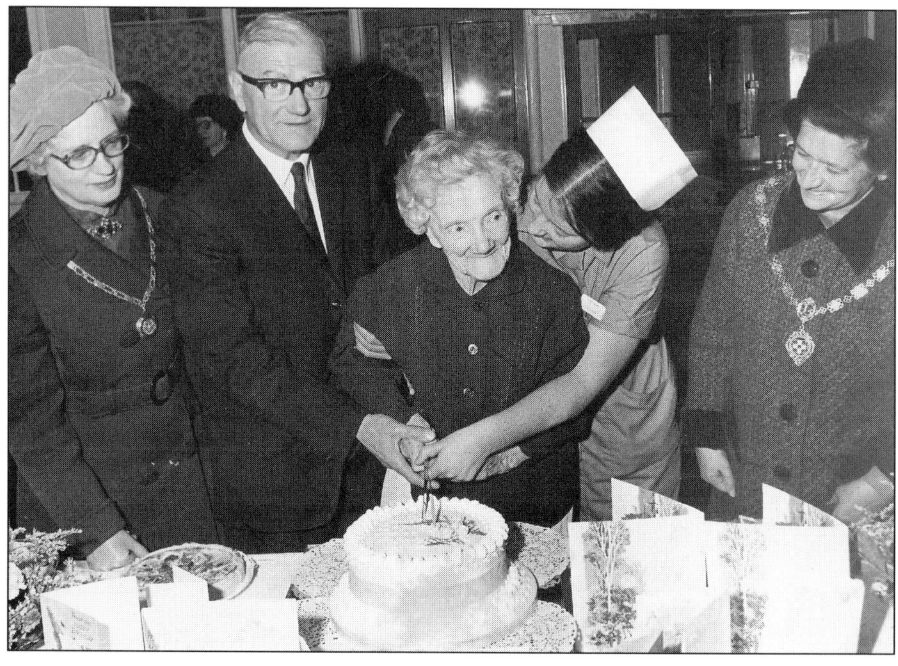

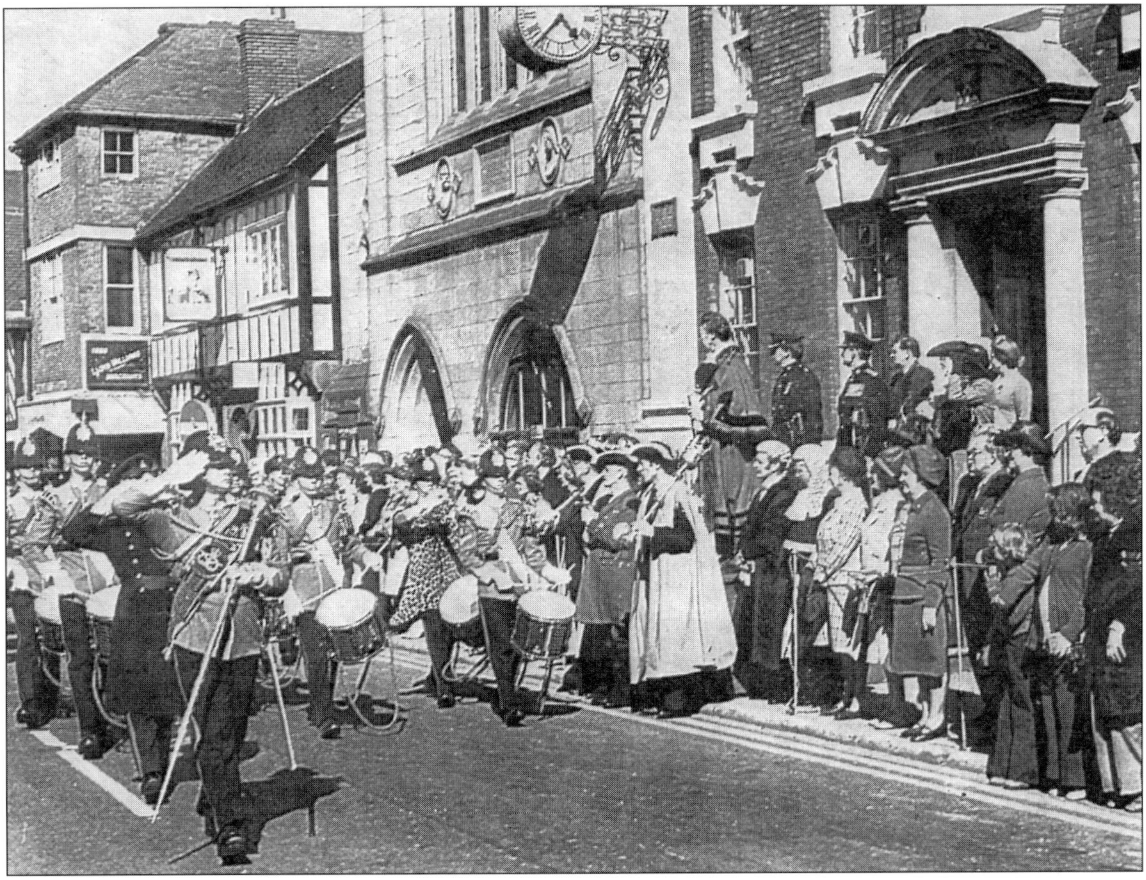

Lichfield has always had a close connection with its county regiments which it has signified by granting the freedom of the city to them. Here the Corps of Drums of a Battalion of the South Staffordshire Regiment lead a march past at which the Mayor takes the salute.

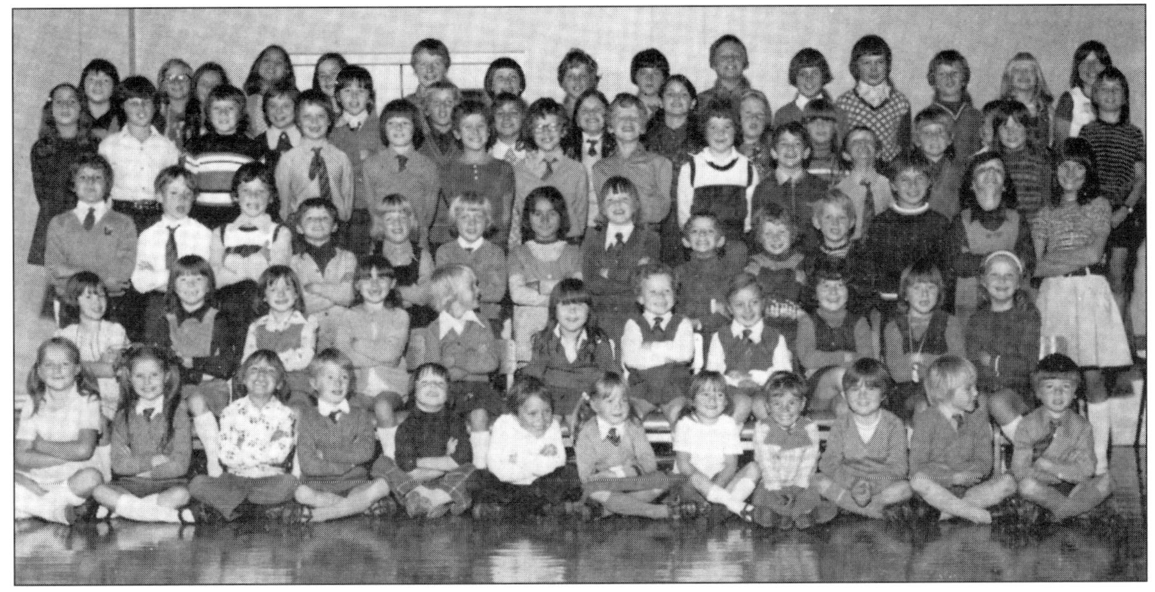

In 1975 St Joseph's Roman Catholic Primary School celebrated its centenary. Here they all are.

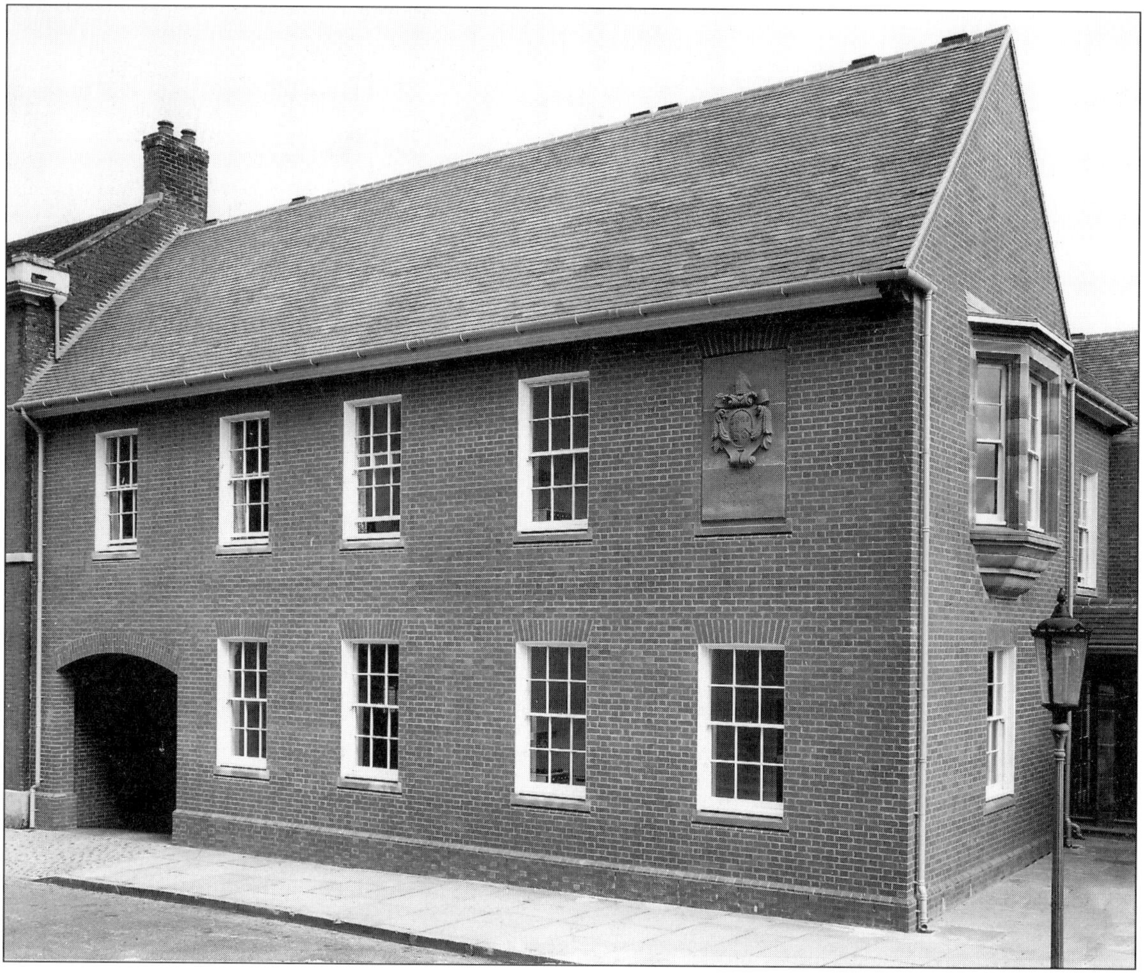

St John's Hospital extension in the Close, on the site of the former Theological College. It opened in 1976.

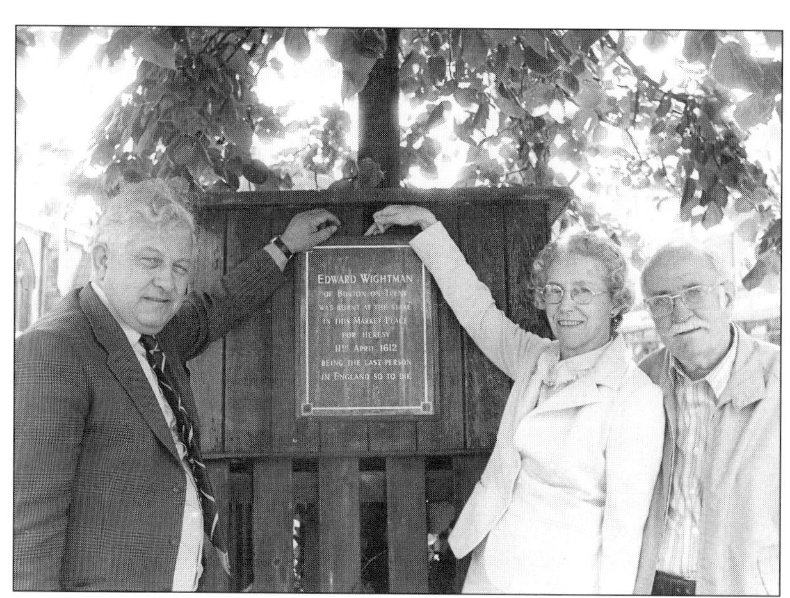

In 1978 Mr and Mrs Wightman from the U.S.A. visited Lichfield to find out about their ancestor who was burnt at the stake in Lichfield Marketplace for "heresy". Councillor Howard Clayton, the at that time, shows them round the city.

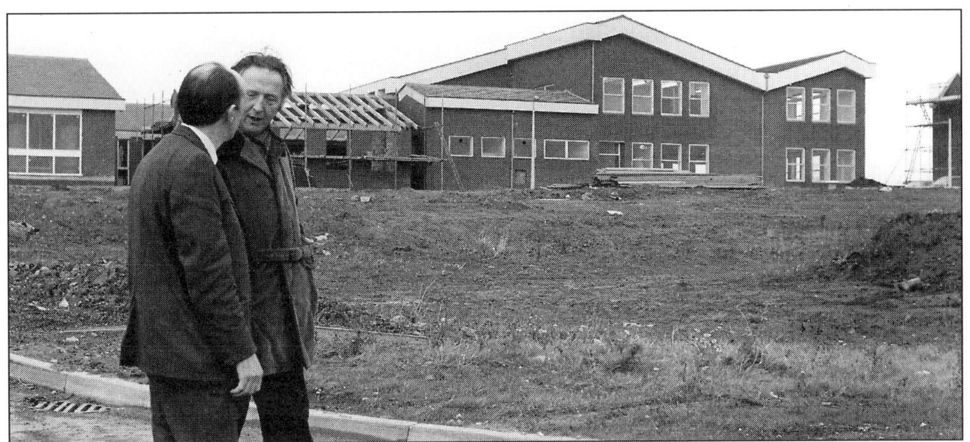

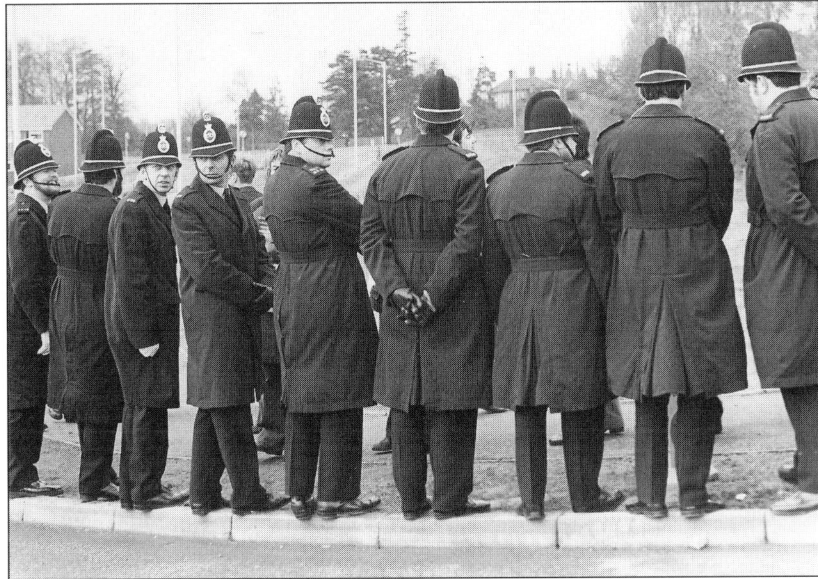

Above: The replacement building for the Friary School under construction in 1972. It would be named Friary Grange School. (A grange was a farm serving a Friary and the name was therefore most appropriate).

Left: Friary Grange School. Somebody important must be coming.

Below: The offical opening by the Prime Minister, the Right Honourable Edward Heath January 14th 1964.

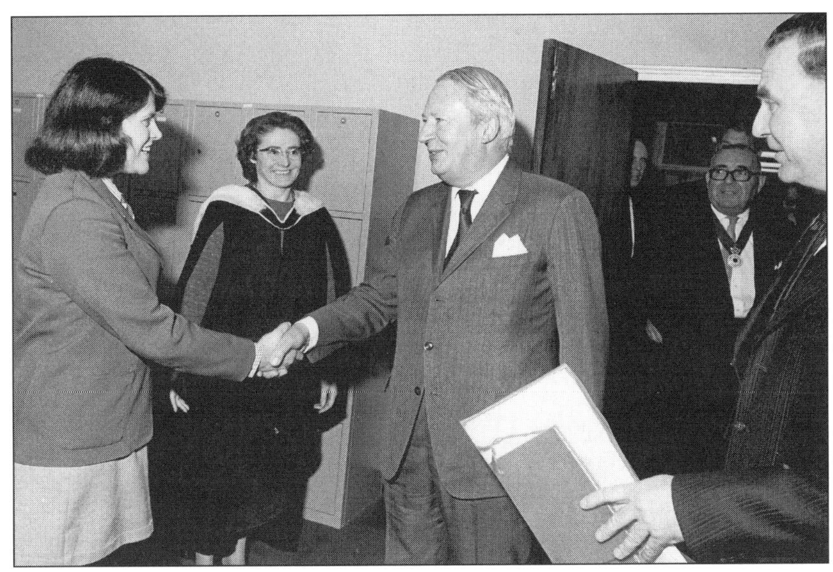

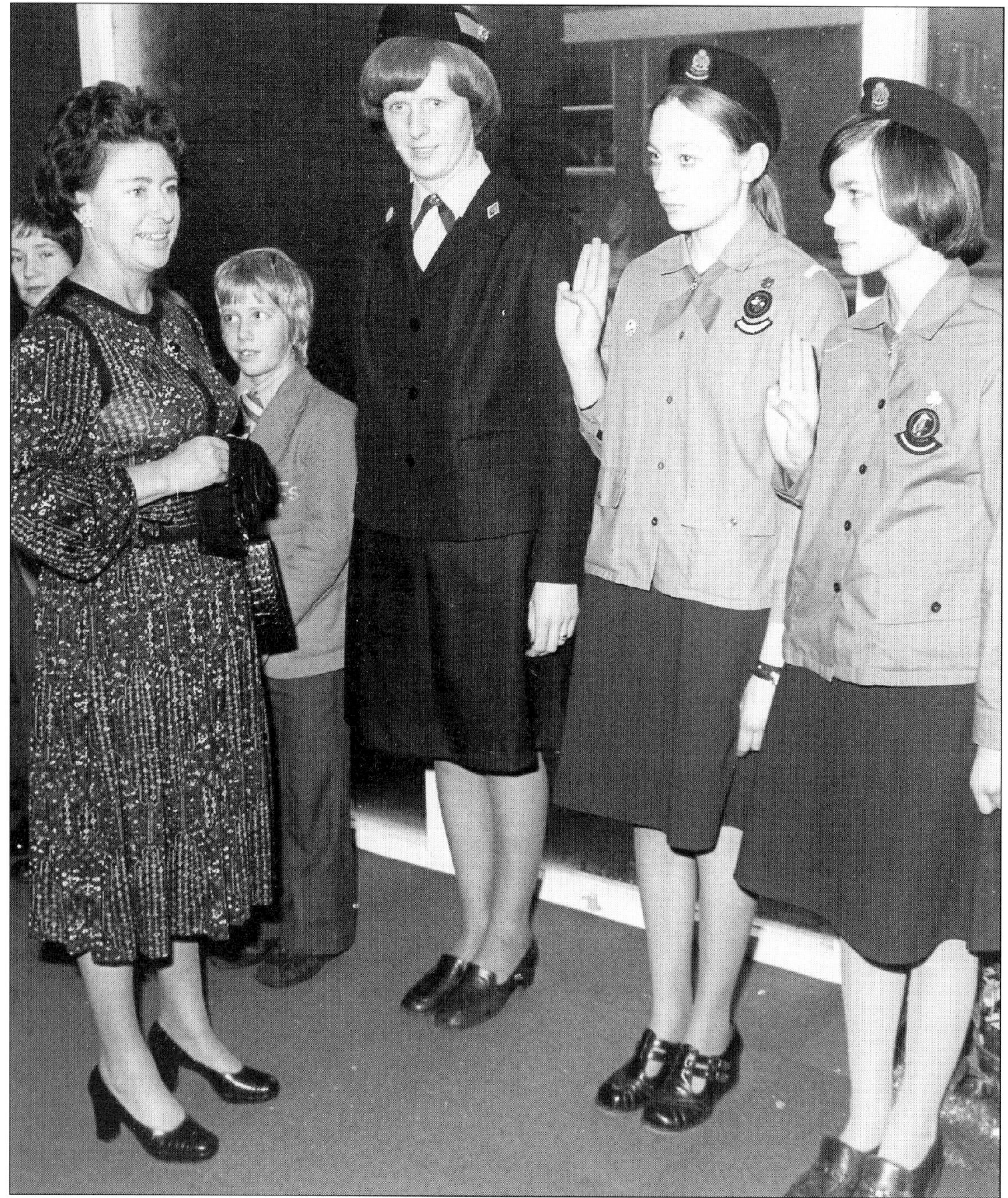

As a joint project between Staffordshire County Council and Lichfield District Council, a sports complex, including a swimming pool, was planned on the Friary Grange site. This was opened on March 14th, 1977 by H.R.H Princess Margaret, seen here with Mrs Pauline Cox and members of the Guides present.

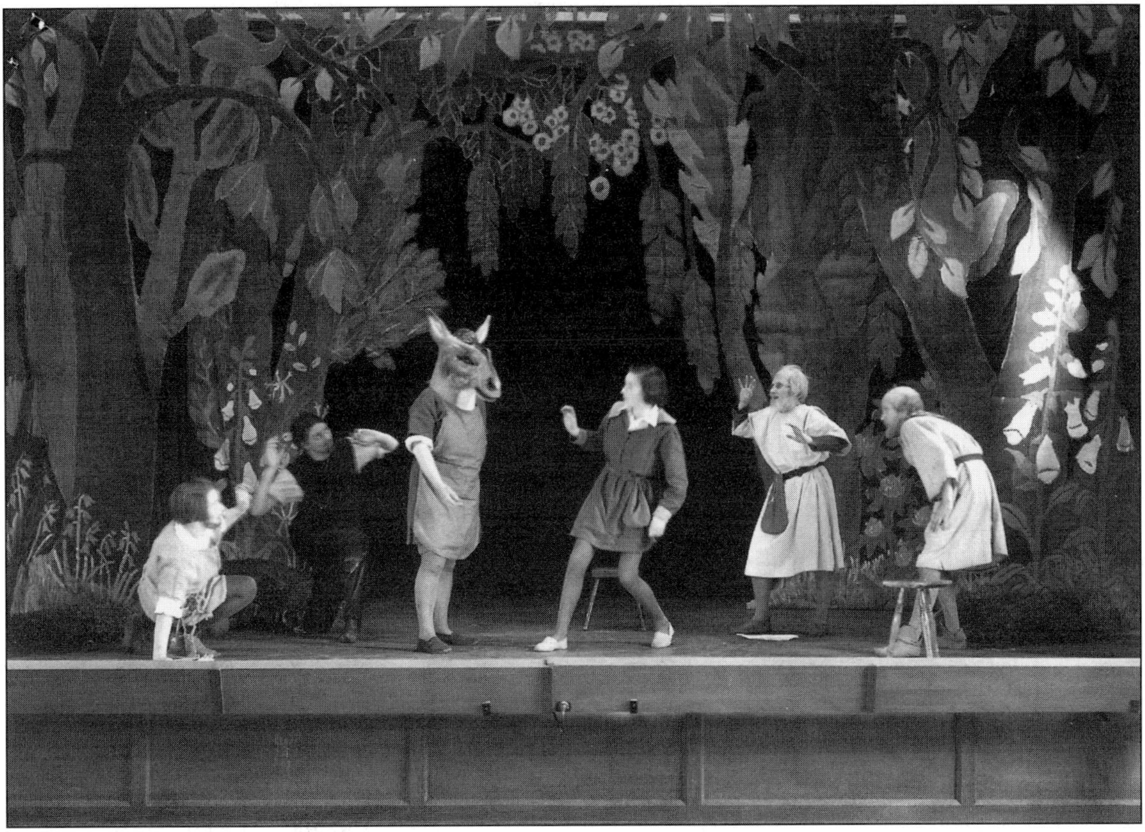

A Midsummer Night's Dream at the Friary School.

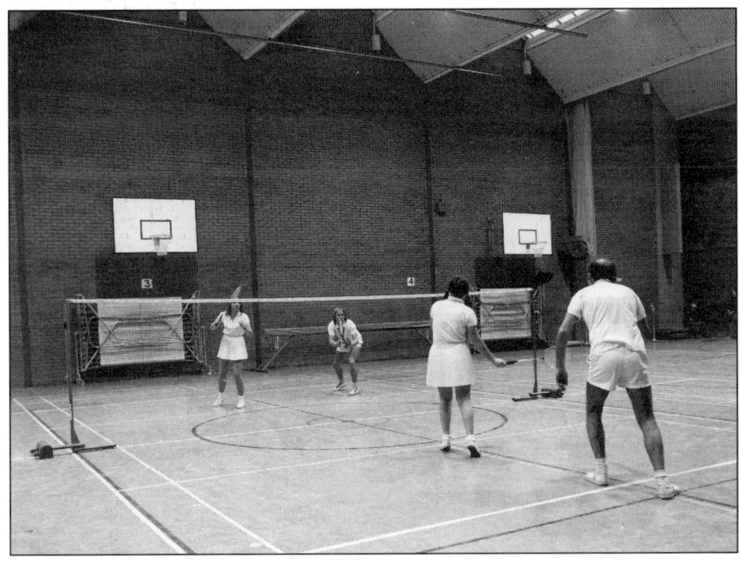

The new Friary Grange Sports Centre in use

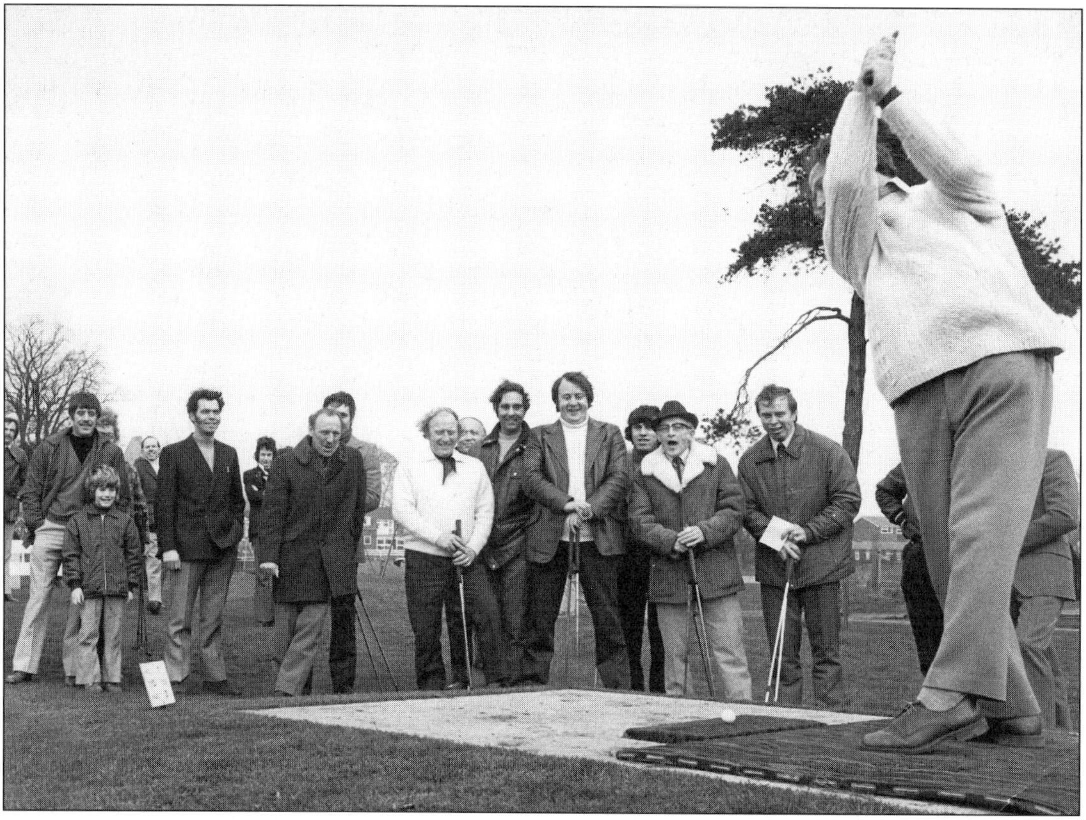

In 1973 a nine-hole golf course was opened in Beacon Park. The Mayor drives off.

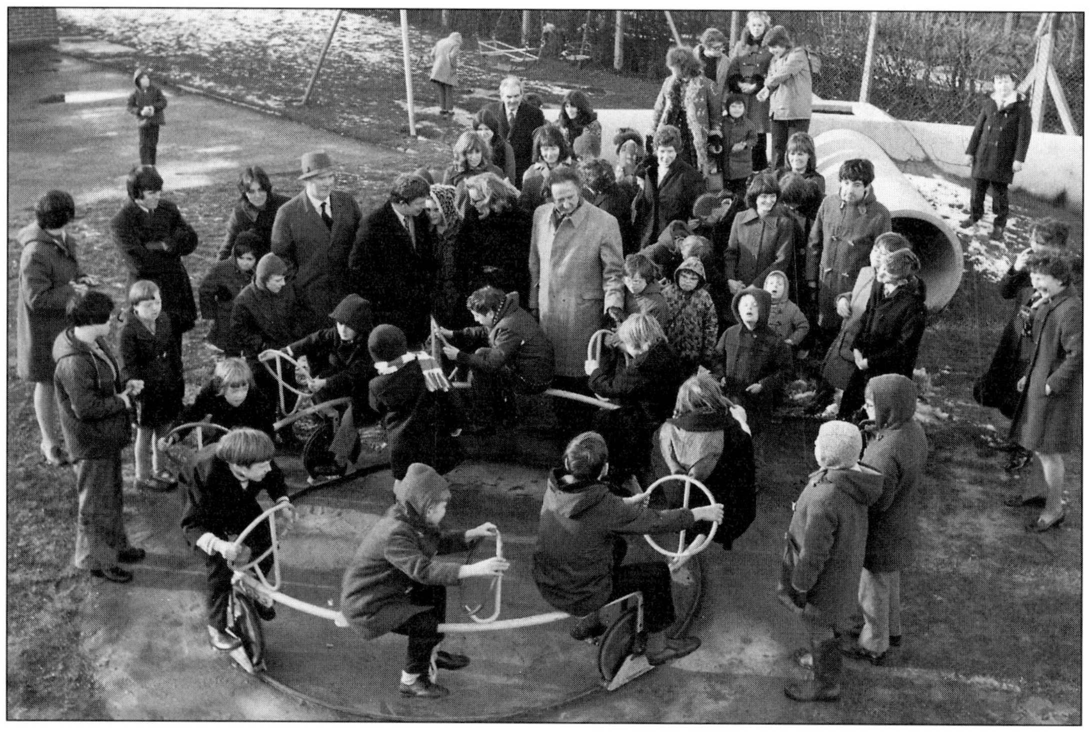

And the children are not forgotten.

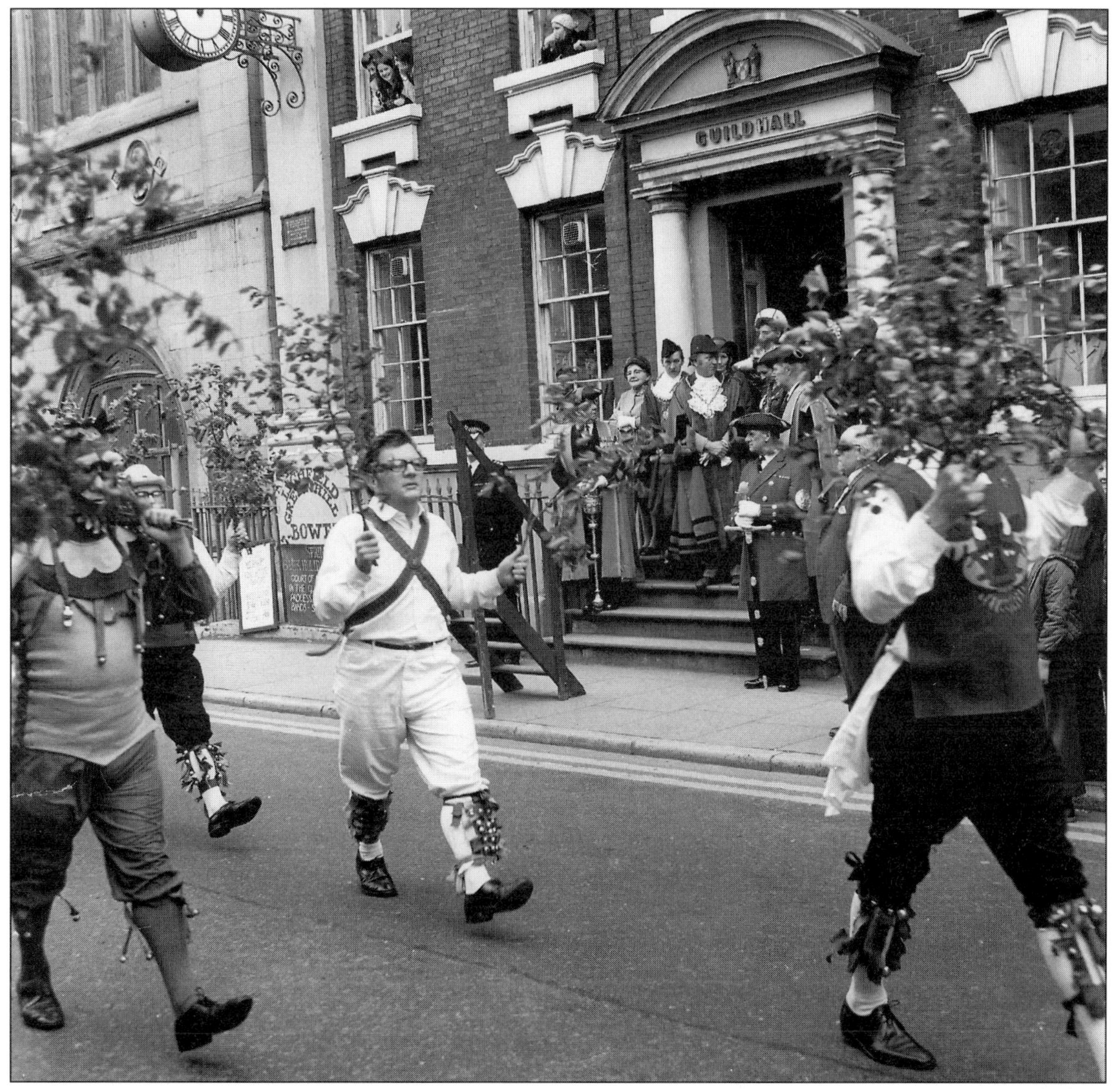

Leading the Bower Procession is one of the duties of the Morris dancers. The branches they carry represent the laurel and lilac, traditional decorations of the Bower.

Right: In 1972 Lichfield celebrated the 1,300 anniversary of the death of St Chad. One day was given over to a pageant which turned Lichfield once again into a mediaeval city. Typical of the costumed participants were John Wilson and his wife Janet and Nicky their faithful hound. Behind them is the first St. Chad's Church.

Below: Another group of pageanteers. The one nearest the camera is John Sanders, Principal of Lichfield School of Art, whose idea the Pageant was and who organised it. A small figure from the 20th century seems to have muscled in.

Opposite page: The Pageant ended with a mediaeval banquet in the Guildhall.

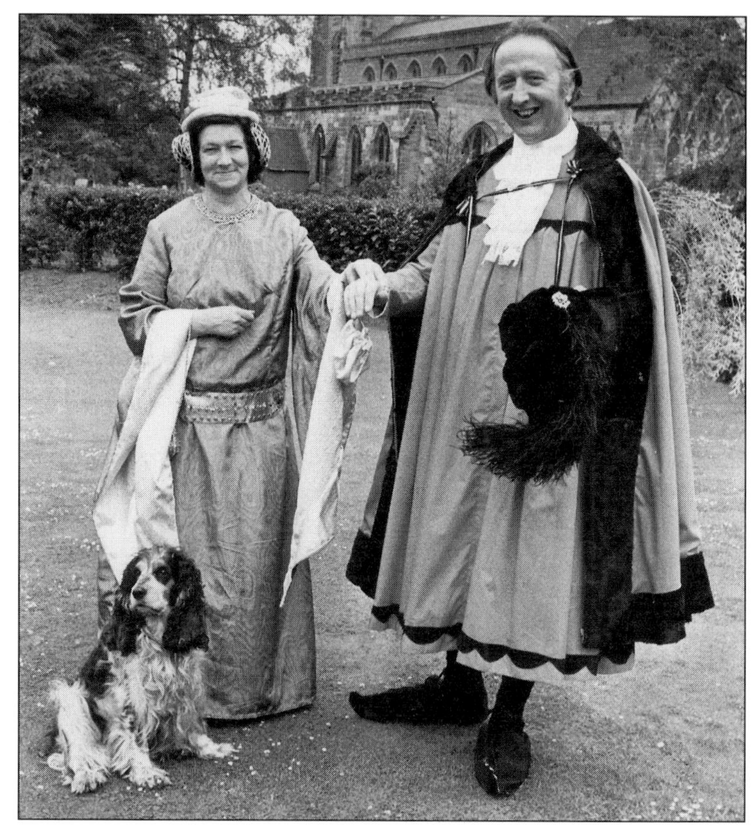

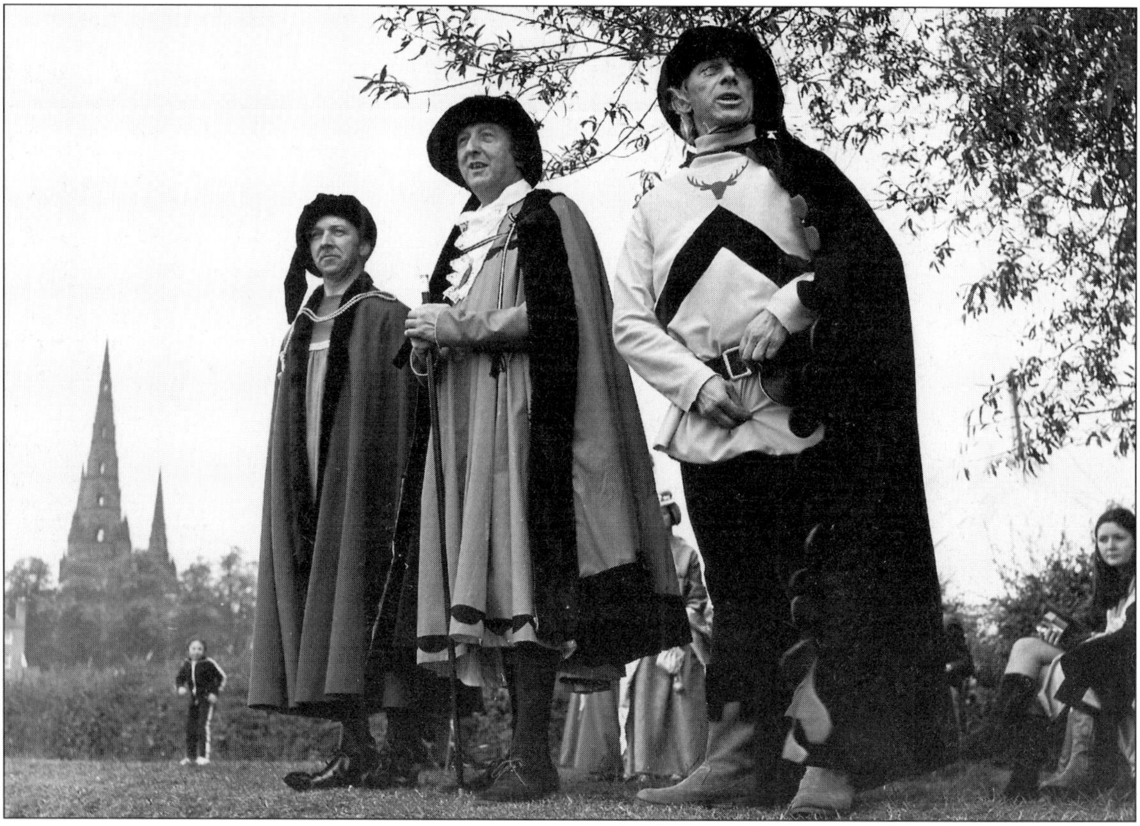

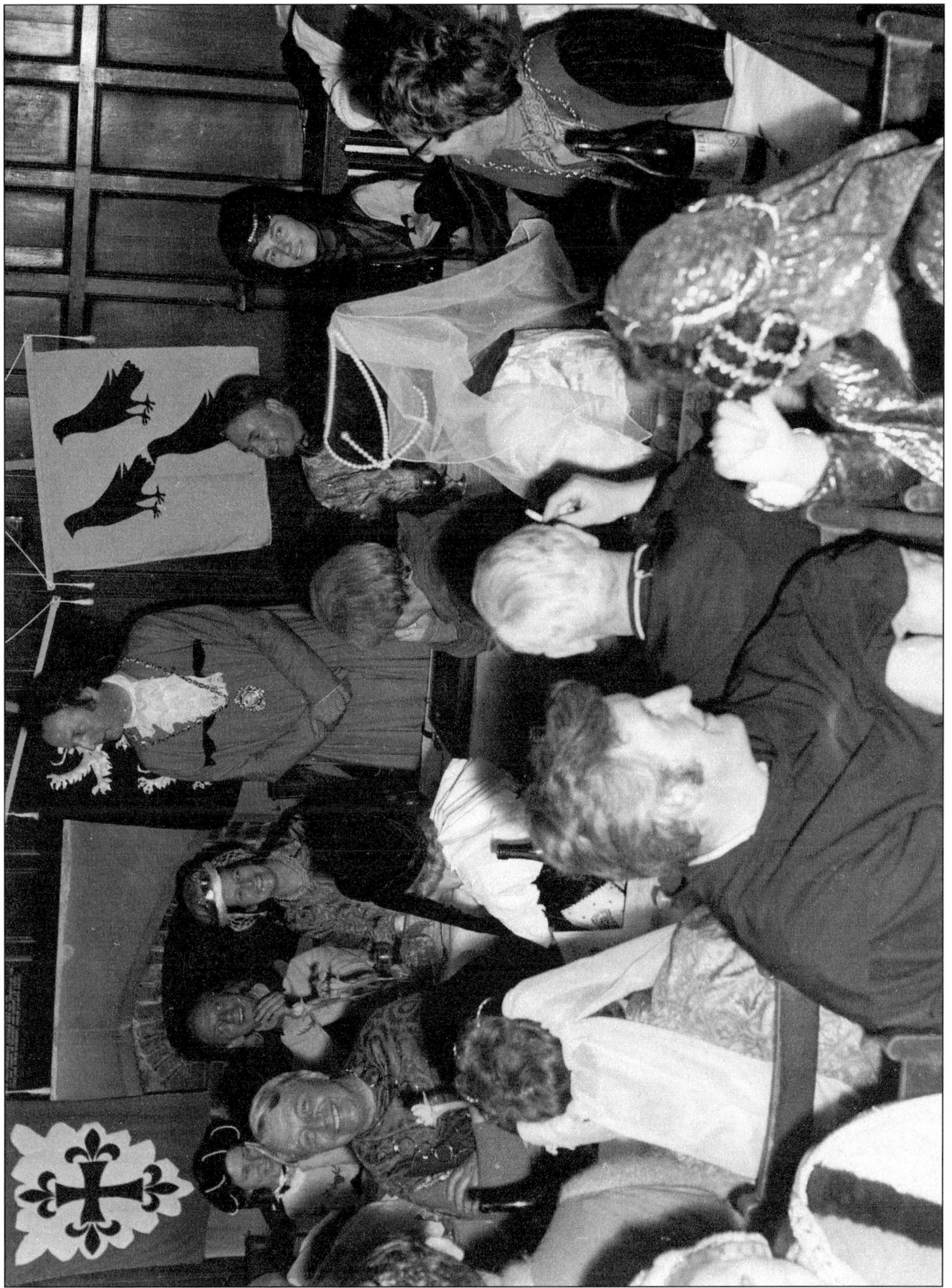

CITY OF

Lichfield.

THE MARQUIS OF ANGLESEY having signified his intention of passing through this **CITY**, on ***FRIDAY NEXT***, all Persons intending to form the Procession to attend his Lordship, are requested to meet precisely at **TEN** o'Clock, at the **GUILD-HALL**.

The Carriages to draw up in line in Boar-street, with the Horses heads towards St. John's-street.

Persons on Horseback to assemble in the Market-place, and Market-street, and to follow the Carriages

The Procession not to move 'till a signal is given.

The Carriages and Horsemen to form in line behind *The Marquis of Anglesey's Carriage*, and to return to the Guild-Hall in the same order in which they set out, after which they are to go through Butcher-Row, and up Market-street, and to return down Boar-street to the Guild-Hall, and from thence up Market-street, Bird-street, and Bacon-street, to the end of the County of Lichfield.

LICHFIELD, August 9th. 1815.

W. MORGAN, PRINTER, LICHFIELD.

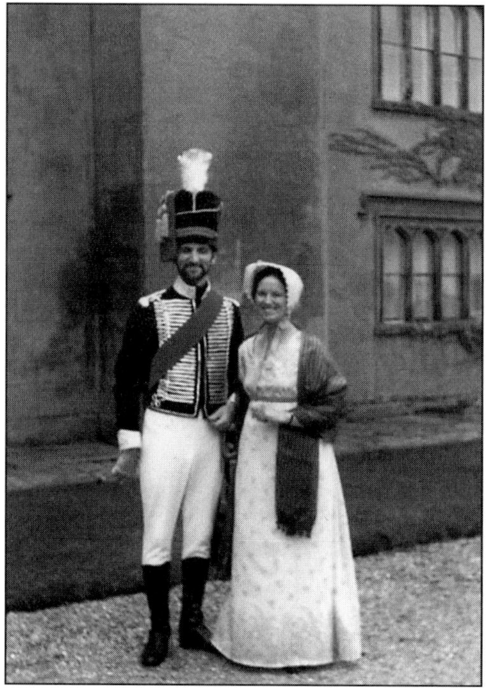

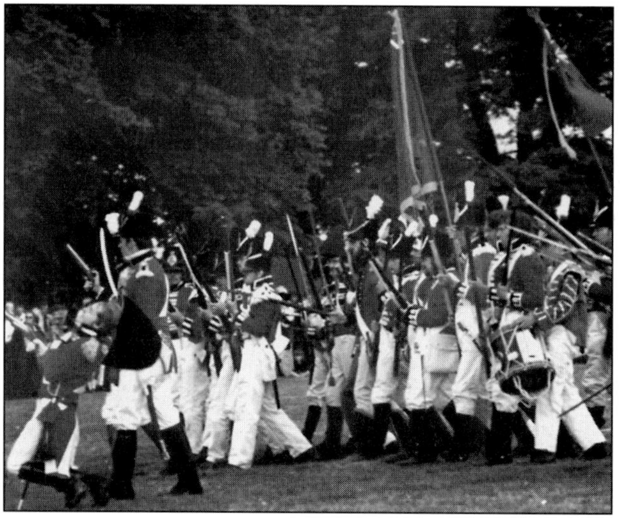

Above left: So successful was the 1972 Pageant that it was decided to hold another one in 1975. Much hard work went into the preparation, including fundraising, for this was before grants were available on the scale they are today. This time the subject was to be the return to Lichfield of the 1st Marquis of Anglesey after the Battle of Waterloo.

Above right: Many of those taking part in the Pageant made their own costumes, as did Brian and Shirley Field.

Left: In the afternoon, there was an enactment of the Battle of Waterloo, complete with artillery, in Beacon Park. The British won, of course.

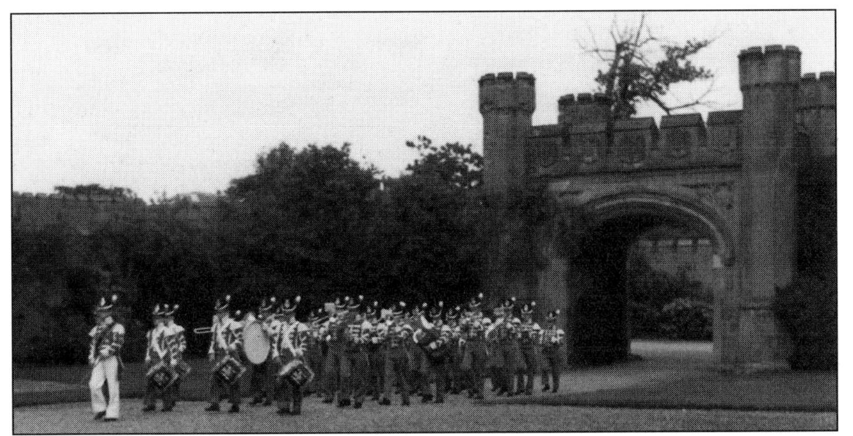

For the occasion a whole Regular Army band (from Whittington Barracks) which took part in the procession were outfitted with correct uniforms for the period, made by students of the Lichfield School of Art.

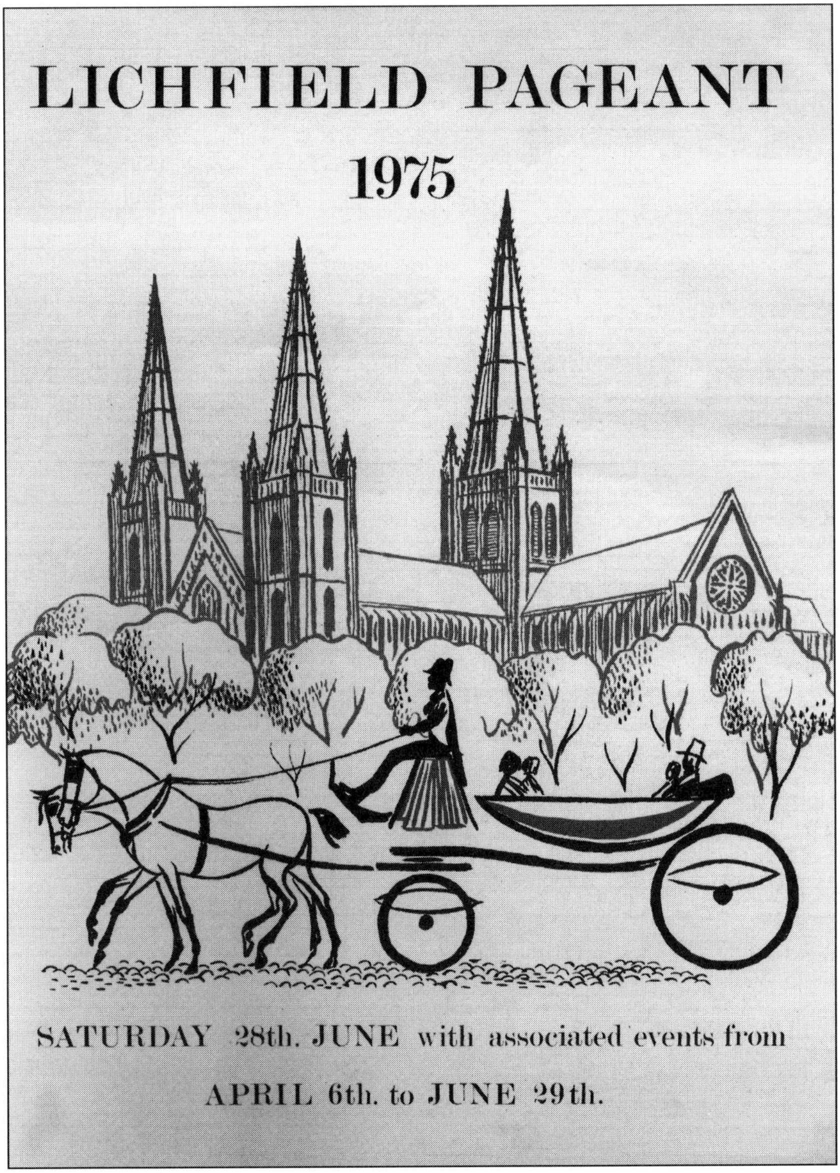

LICHFIELD PAGEANT

1975

SATURDAY 28th. JUNE with associated events from

APRIL 6th. to JUNE 29th.

The Marquis had commanded the British Cavalry in that engagement and during the battle had been wounded and lost a leg. On his return the City of Lichfield had presented him with a sword of honour.

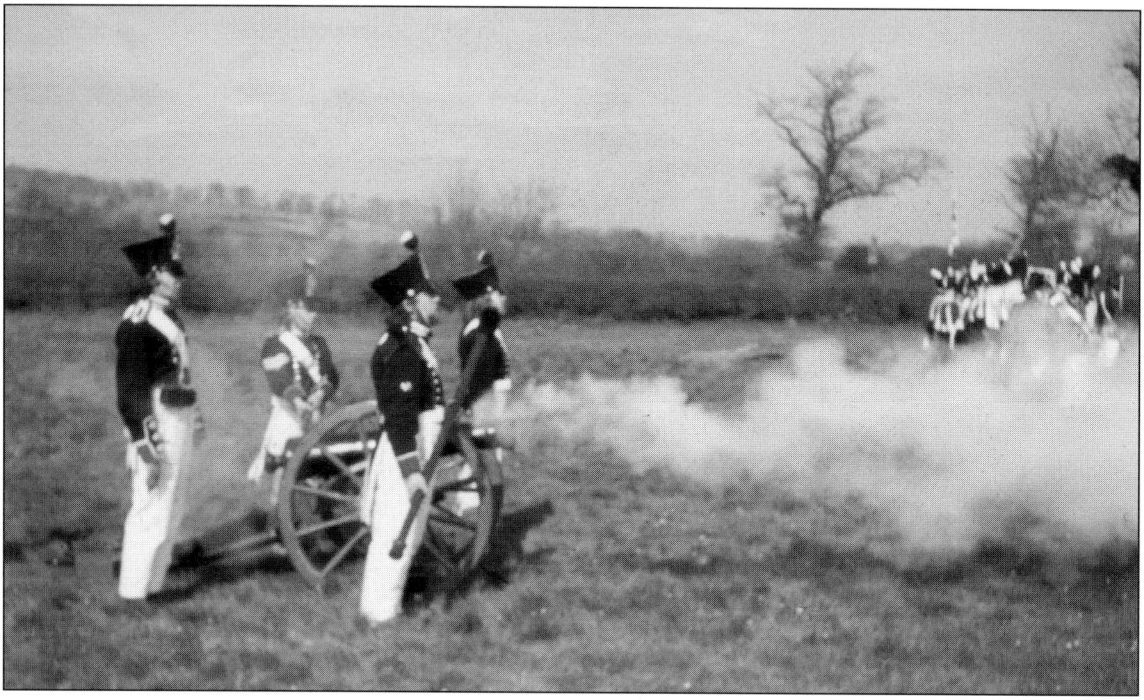

Gunners of a re-enactment society practising for the Battle of Waterloo at the 1975 Pageant.

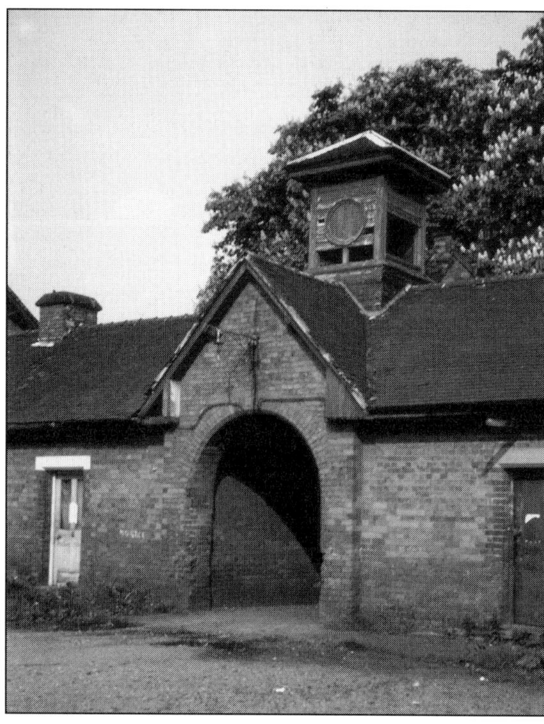

Entrance to Militia Barracks, Birmingham Road, Lichfield vacated by the military in 1890 and used for civilian housing until demolished c 1970.

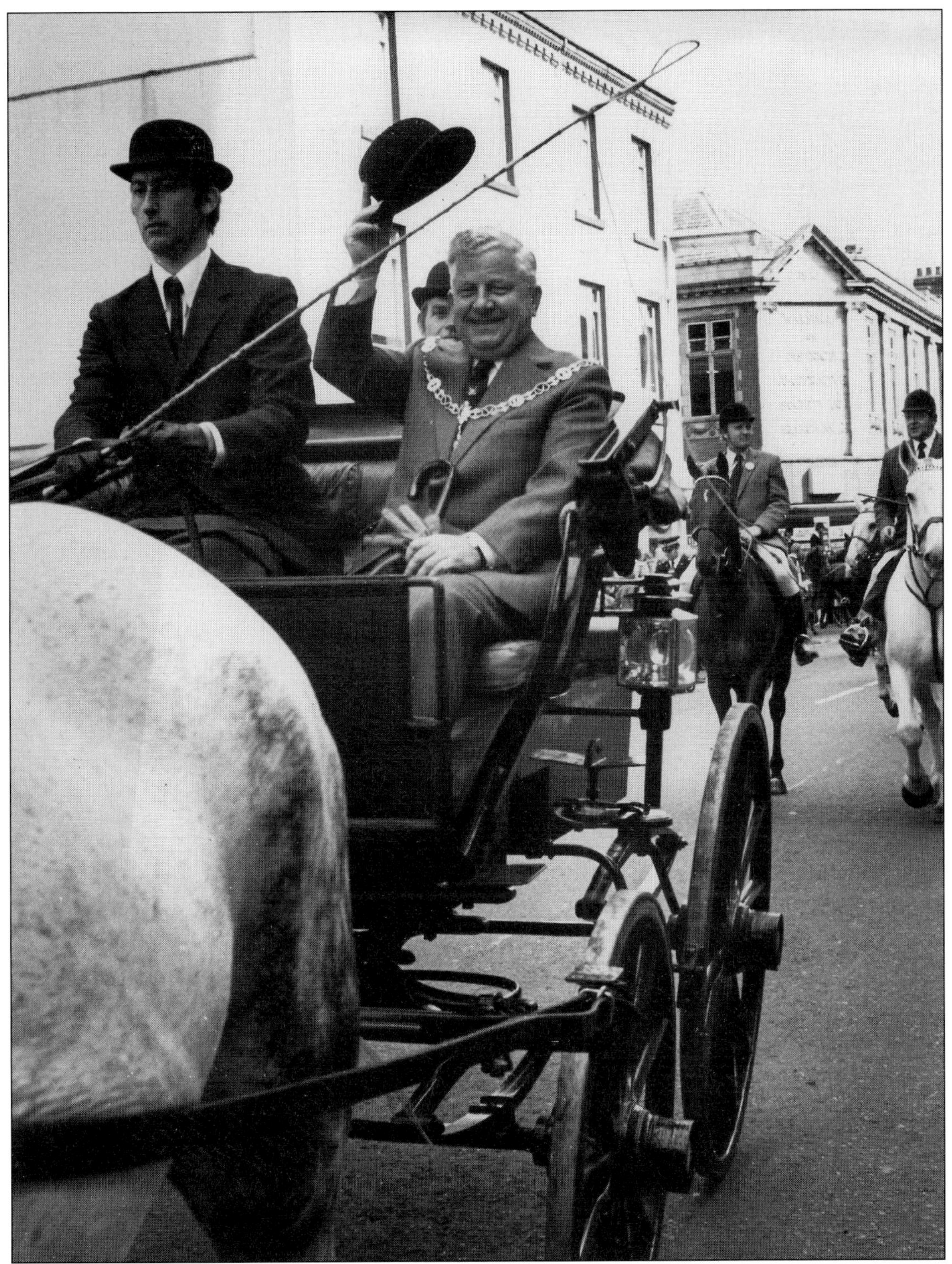

Most Sheriffs lead their Ride on horseback if they can, even though it may mean lessons in an hitherto unaccustomed activity. Others, through disability, may have to use other forms of transport. In 1978, Sheriff Howard Clayton travelled in a two-horse phaeton.

More to pay for the precinct super loo?

IT SEEMS ANOTHER CONTRACTOR MAY HAVE TO FINISH THE JOB

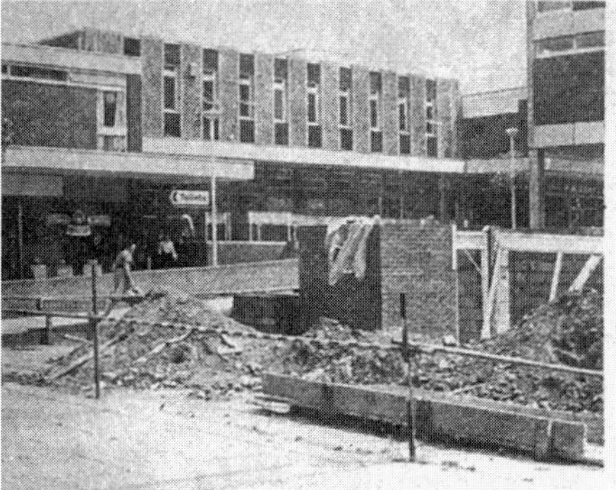

Above, the site of the toilet block in Lichfield's shopping precinct. Work has ground to a halt because of a dispute. Below, the site at Sankeys Corner. Work there is also affected.

LICHFIELD'S £12,000 "super-loo," already under fire because of its siting, may cost more and take longer to complete.

Work on the project at Levetts Square has ground to a halt because of a dispute with contractors.

Now public health planners are to consider terminating the contract, due for completion in August, and ask another company to finish the work.

A second toilet block, being built by the same contractor at a cost of £8,000 at Sankey's Corner, Chase Terrace, is also affected.

NOT MAKING PROGRESS

Mr. John Bradshaw, the district council's deputy planning director, said yesterday: "It sems obvious we are not going to make progress on the scheme under the present circumstances."

If the council's Public Health Committee decides at its meeting next Thursday to seek new tenders for completion of the two blocks, it is likely it could face an additional bill.

Mr. Bradshaw said: "It is quite likely that the cost will be more than when we first started and it will hold up work for a month or so. But what increased cost is involved is difficult to say."

Newspaper report of the contractor's failure to complete the superloo.

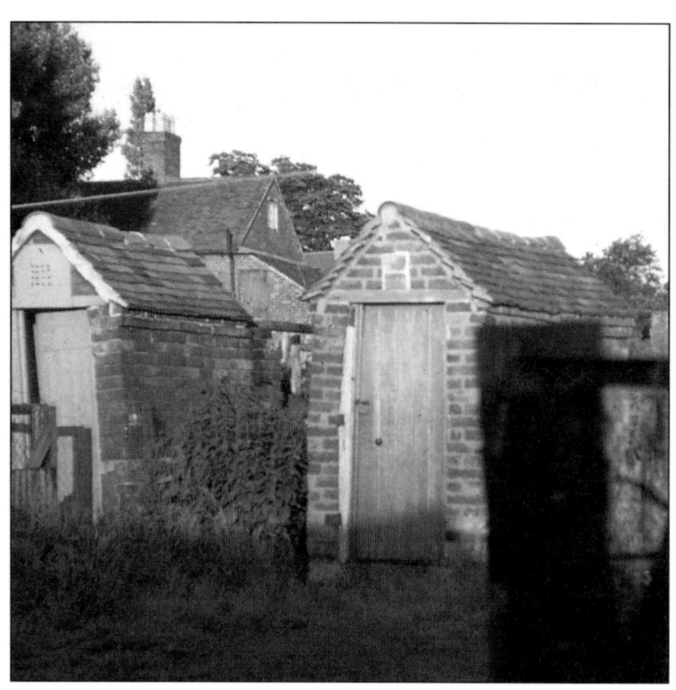

Still on the subject of loos, these two fine examples of 19th Century private, free-standing loos came to light during demolitions in Stowe Street.

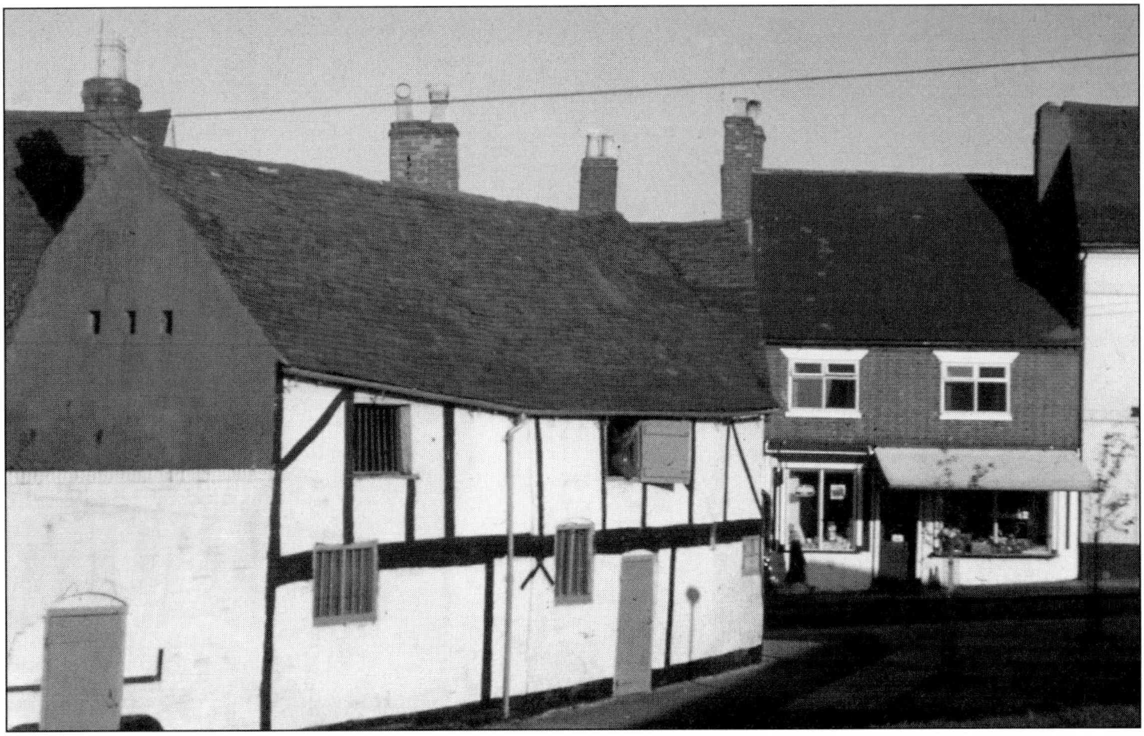

Fellow's Butchers Shop, Greenhill (now Thrale's Restaurant). For many years the cow's head was seen poking out of an upstairs window until it was stolen by a visiting rugby football team.

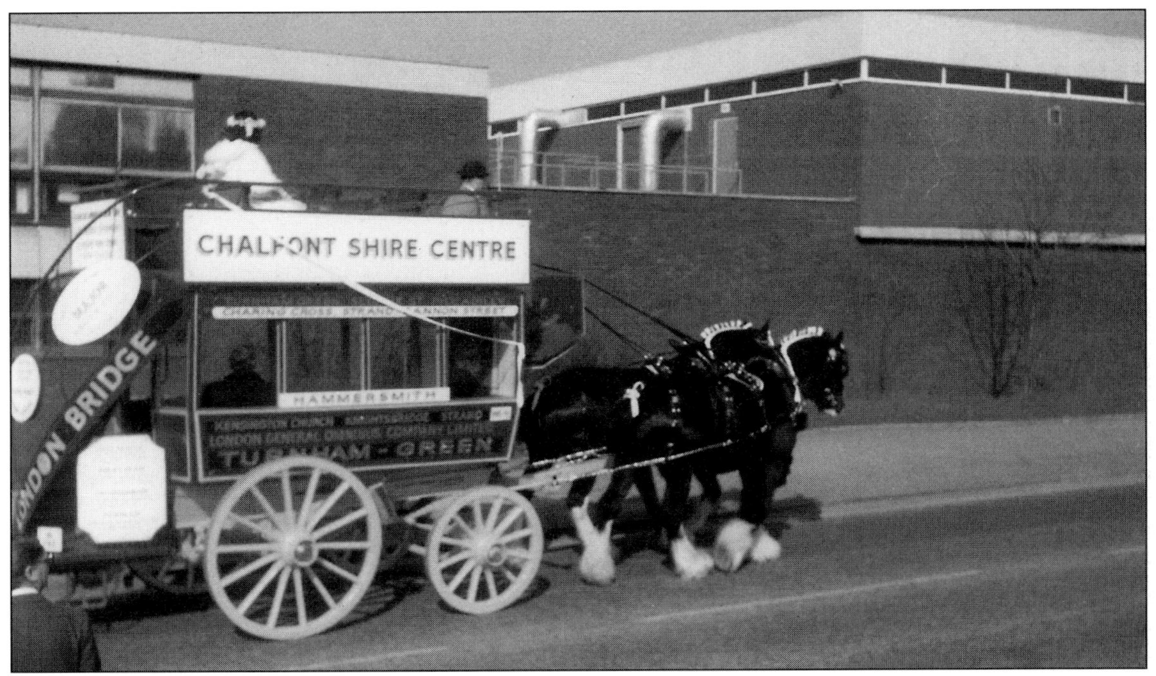

A visiting horse bus passes Tesco stores in 1976. Buses like this ran between the Swan and the George and the two railway stations up to the First World War.

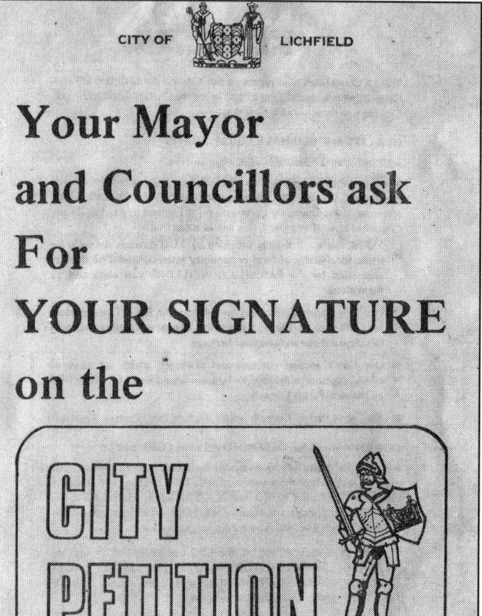

The decade ended with the resolving of a problem that had troubled the charter trustees – the lack of parish council status for the City of Lichfield. A petition organised by the Mayor and Councillors was presented to the District Council as a result of which an application was made to the Boundary Commission for Parish status and this was duly granted. The Charter Trustees ceased to exist and Lichfield had a Town Council with all the rights of an elected parish council. A final step was a petition to Her Majesty Queen Elizabeth II for a new charter restoring the title of "City". This was granted and Lichfield became once more "The City Of Lichfield", with a City Council.

CITY OF LICHFIELD

The 15 Councillors who represent our City on the Lichfield District Council (which totals 56 members) being the Charter Trustees of this City are unanimous in the view that:–

OUR CITY SHOULD HAVE EQUAL RIGHTS

with the other 27 parishes in Lichfield District.

The City is the only part of Lichfield District without an administrative parish and we have therefore applied to the District Council to recommend the Boundary Commission for England to grant us Parish Council status. If approved, this would mean that:–

- **YOUR money – already provided by YOU through the rates for items specifically of local community interest, would be directly controlled by the PARISH COUNCILLORS you elect and by them alone.**
- **Our new Parish Councillors would have the RIGHT to vet plans for OUR City, and act as a watch-dog over new planning proposals to safeguard our architectural heritage.**
- **Our City's ancient customs and privileges, which we value so highly, together with our City Treasure would be SAFEGUARDED by the new Parish Council.**
- **This new Parish Council would replace the 'Charter Trustees'.**

OUR CITY MUST BE DEFENDED AS ONE COMMUNITY

We must fight any proposals by the Boundary Commission to split our City into two or more communities. The Commission could split communities of over 20,000 people – Lichfield is 25,000 (1976) – unless such proposals are opposed by **YOU** as a citizen and by the District Council who will have regard to your views.

The History and Tradition of the City has developed around its people as an **ESTABLISHED COMMUNITY.** We believe any division of the City **WOULD BE DISASTROUS** and would destroy the very fabric on which communities are founded.

Chapter 9 – A New Century

At the beginning of May 1980, the newly-elected Town Council of Lichfield held their first meeting. The Mayor, Councillor Dr. Neville Brown, was in the chair. In the accompanying photograph, the Deputy Mayor, Councillor Mrs Anne Hall sits on the Mayor's left and the Town Clerk, Mr Harold Coton, on his right. On the Town Clerk's right is the Sheriff, Councillor Dick Wingrove. It is still only a Town Council as the Charter of Queen Elizabeth II restoring the title of City Council has not yet been received.

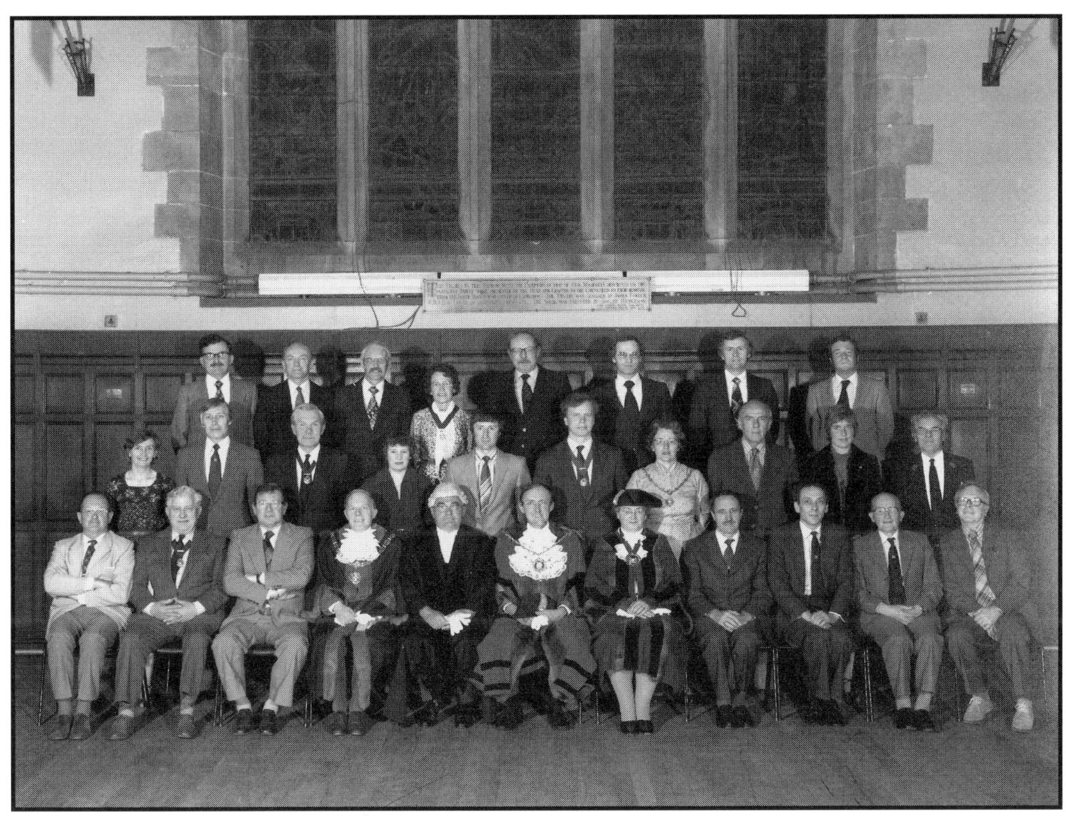

TO ALL ELECTORS

OF

LICHFIELD

TOWN

MEETING

You are invited to take part

It will be held at

GUILDHALL, BORE STREET, LICHFIELD, ON THURSDAY, 29TH MAY, 1980 AT 6.30 P.M. UNDER THE CHAIRMANSHIP OF COUNCILLOR DR. E.N. BROWN, THE TOWN MAYOR.

This is the first Town Meeting for the newly created township of Lichfield and is a good opportunity for you, as an elector, to express your views. The recently elected Lichfield Town Council will welcome your views, which could be very useful in relation to the many important matters to be decided in the period ahead.

There is no formal agenda but the Town Meeting may by law discuss all Town affairs and pass resolutions about them. The Town Mayor will make a statement on behalf of the Town Council and for the remainder of the meeting comments, recommendations or questions will be received from electors present.

COME ALONG AND EXERCISE YOUR RIGHT TO PLAY A POSITIVE PART IN THE AFFAIRS OF YOUR COMMUNITY.

District Council House,
Lichfield.
Tel: 54181

20th May, 1980

N. BARTON
Designated Officer

As part of the business of the meeting a date is fixed for the first Town Meeting.

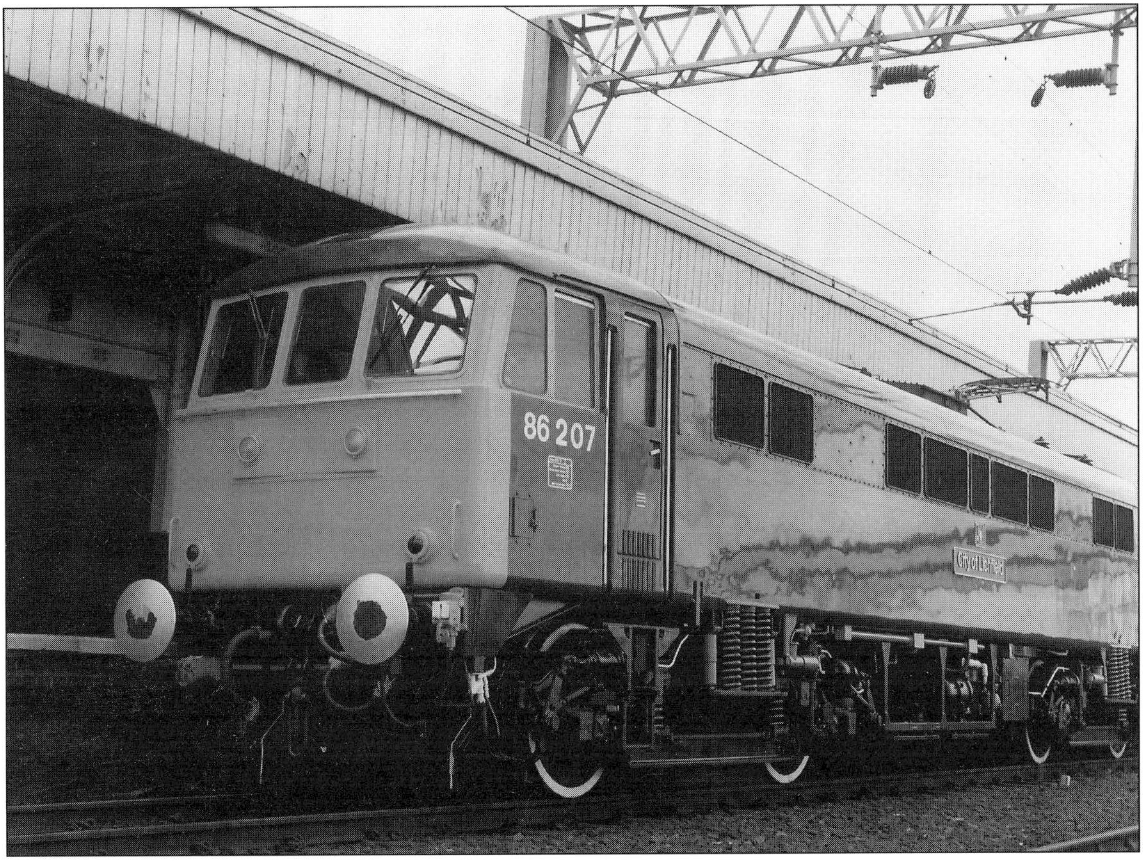

Another matter on the agenda is a request from British Rail to name one of their electric locomotives "*City of Lichfield*". In doing so they are following a long established tradition, for this will be the fourth railway engine so named.

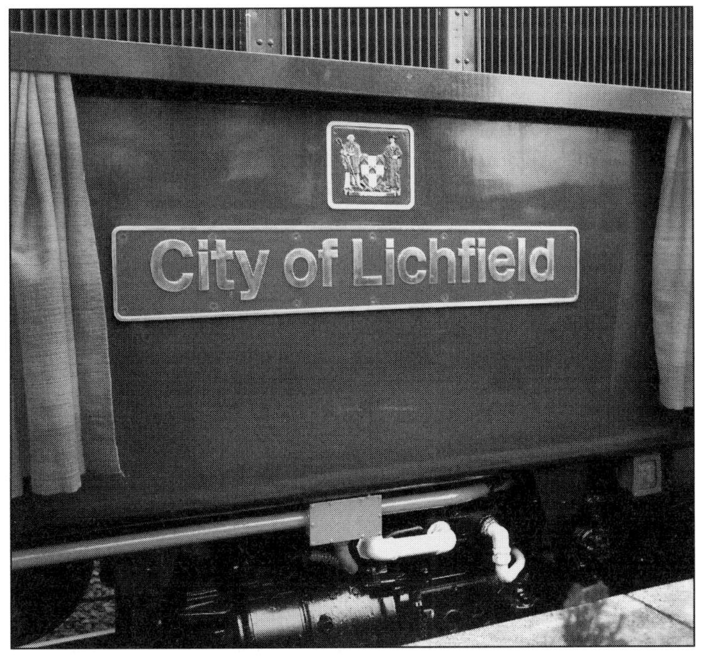

Permission having been granted, it was discovered that according to protocol the Chairman of Lichfield District Council, and not the Mayor would be the proper person formally to name the locomotive. This was done and produced the curious situation of the Chairman of the District Council, Councillor Dennis Stubbs unveiling a nameplate with the City of Lichfield coat of arms above it.

An interesting detail of the photograph of the locomotive is that it stands at a platform of Lichfield Trent Valley Station with a roof over it. No such amenity for passengers exists today; indeed, for London passengers a bus shelter has to suffice.

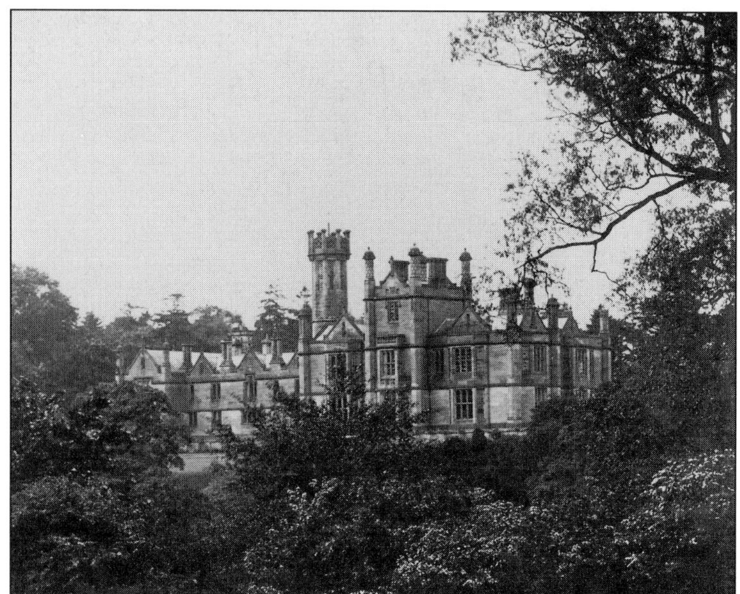

Left: Manley Hall was demolished in c 1980. It was situated off the A38 trunkroad near Weeford and was approached via the lane leading to the Holly Bush Restaurant and the South Staffordshire Waterworks Company at Little Hay. The lodge to the hall is still there on the right. At the opening of Manley Hall in the nineteenth century the guests were said to have danced all night.

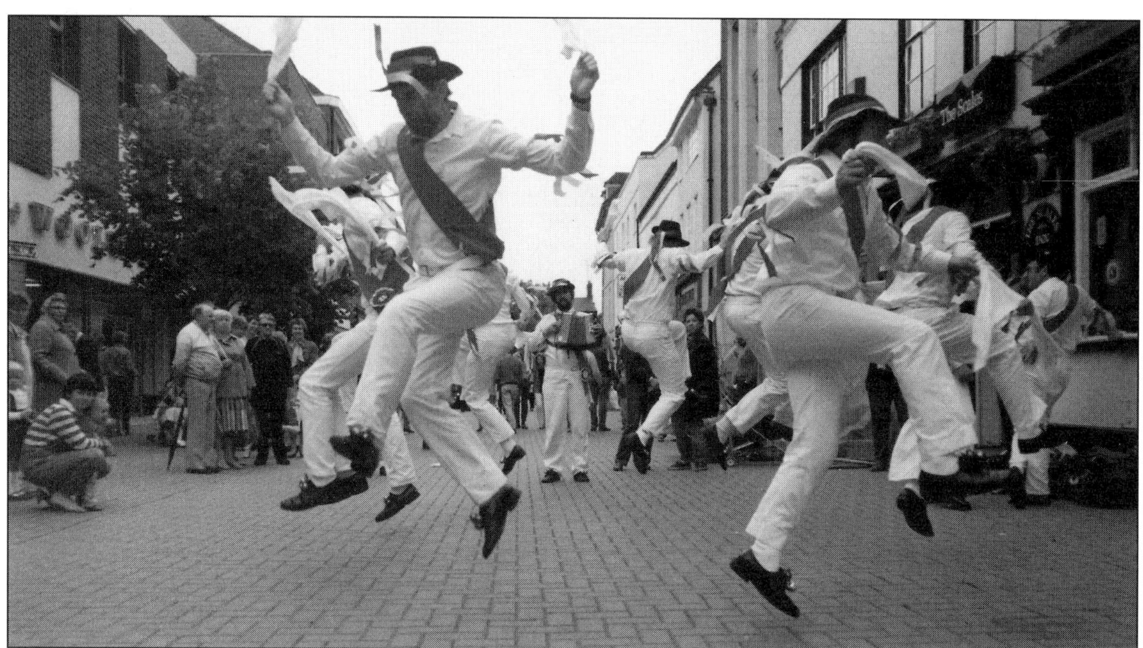

Above: The Lichfield Morris Men high-flying outside the Scales Public House in Market Street

Opposite page: After four long years of hard work and great expense, St Mary's Heritage Centre was completed and opened its doors in December 1980. The official opening by the Earl of Lichfield took place on 30th May 1981. Never before had there been such a project which would comprise the different aspects of worship, community involvement, educational facilities and entertainment concentrated in just one building. It also provided a once in a lifetime opportunity to add a little extra, both worthwhile and beneficial for the community and visitors to Lichfield alike.

The firm of W Archer of Birmingham took on this huge task.

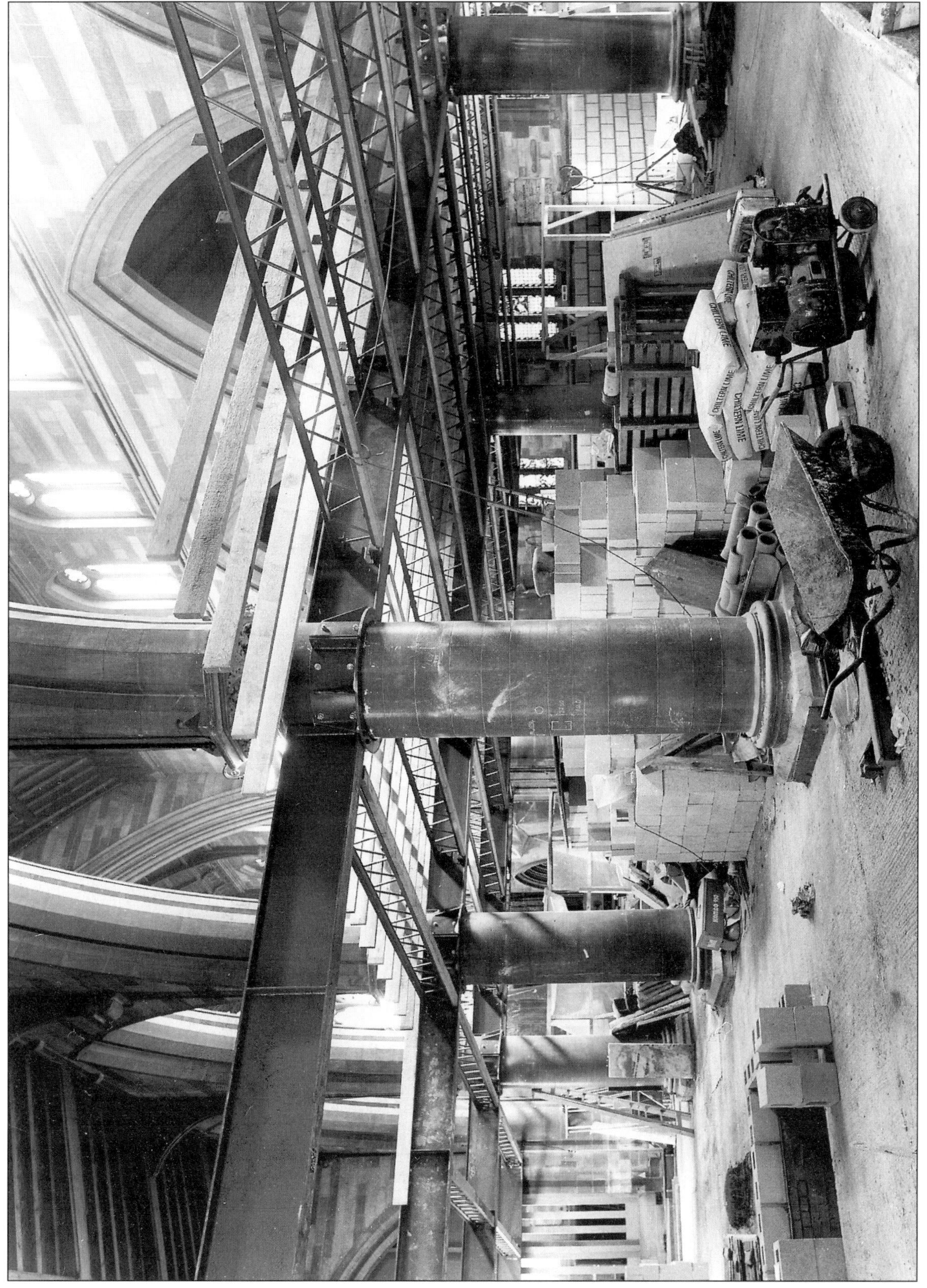
CHILTERN LIME

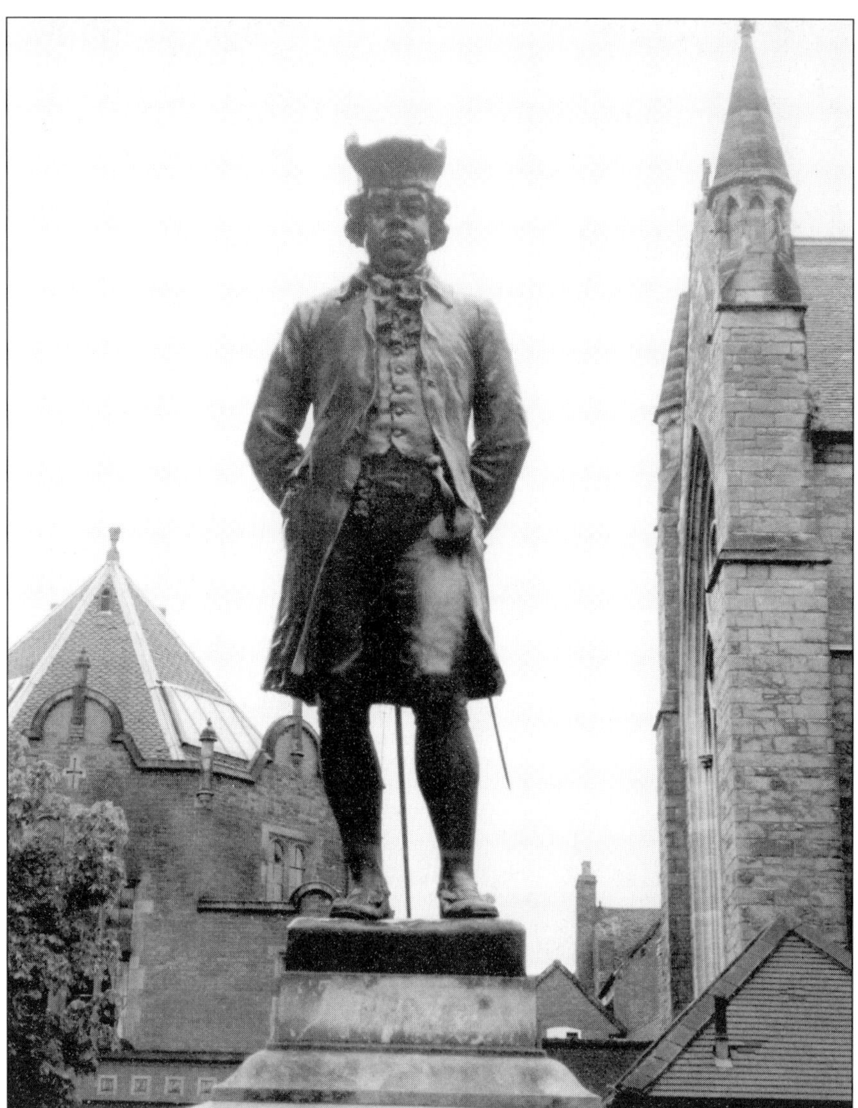

And the figure of James Boswell, biographer, friend and travelling companion of Dr Samuel Johnson, which also resides in the Market Square was refurbished and reinstated.

Opposite page: During the Lichfield Festival of 1983, on a glorious day in July, the Patrick Lichfield XI, which included members of the Lichfield Cricket Team, whose club had been founded in 1869, challenged the Lords Tavener's to a friendly match to be played at Lichfield Cricket Club Grounds in Chesterfield Road. Fred Rumsey, who played for England, had organised the competition through the Chairman of the Cricket Club, Terry Finn. There were 6,000 spectators who watched the play under blue skies. The Lords Tavener's won by a 'Gentleman's Agreement'!

A 'who's who' from Debretts – People of Today!

Before reading the names of the celebrities listed, look to see how many faces you recognise.

From left to right:

Bill Tidy cartoonist, Robert Powell, actor; Bill Frindall, author and cricket scorer; Barry Norman, film critic; Robin Asquith, actor; Ted Moult, broadcaster; Billy Wright, captain of England's Football Team; Patrick, Earl of Lichfield, photographer; R T Simpson of Notts County, who played for the England cricket team twenty seven times; Fred Rumsey (tallest at the back), the organiser and ex-England cricketer; Butch White; Marquis of Stafford, in front of Lichfield Cricket Club Chairman Terry Finn, and members of the L.C.C.

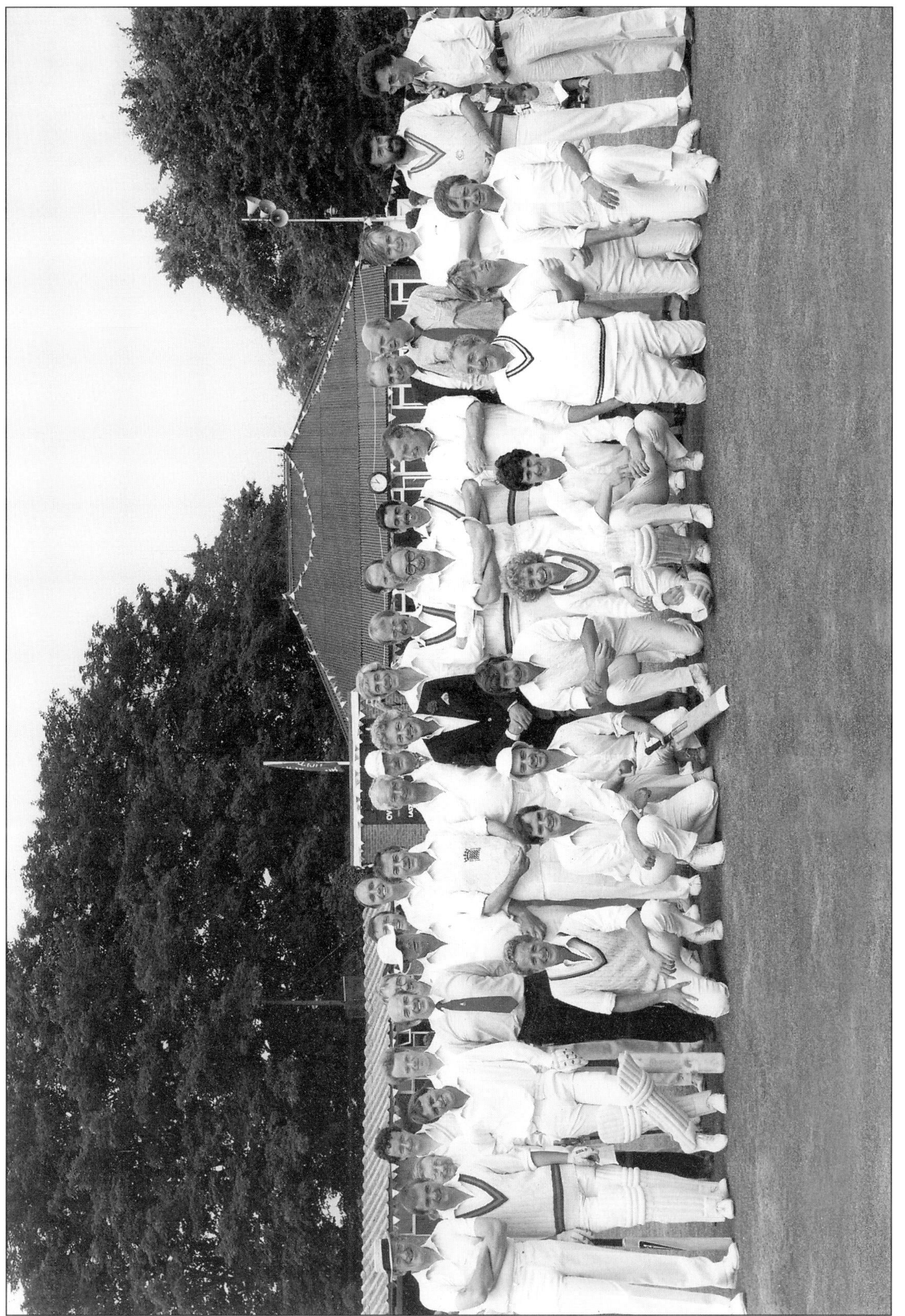

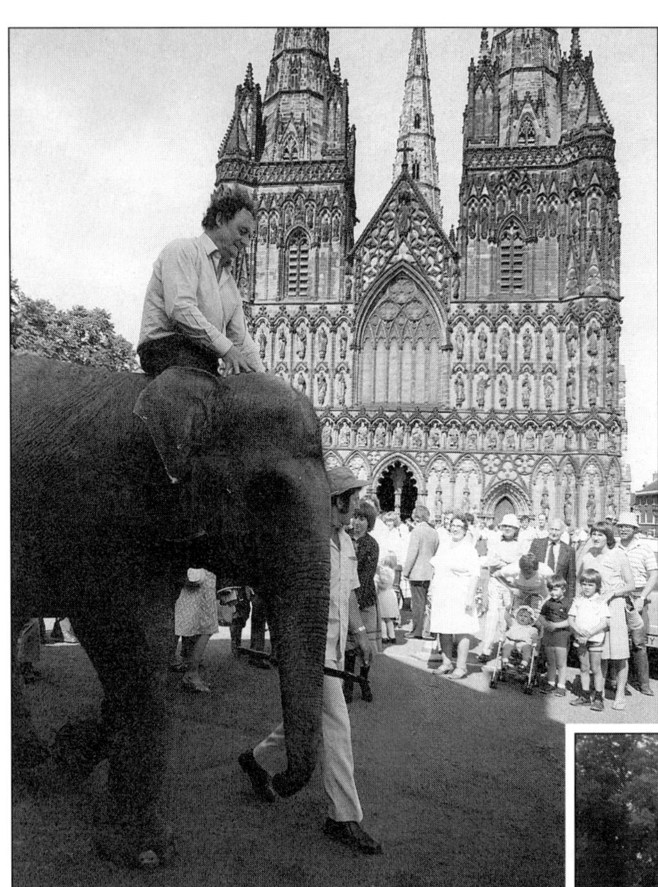

There was also an elephant in the 1983 festival.

The Director of the Festival, Gordon Clarke, had decided to have 100 double basses played by the music students of Staffordshire and leading the procession would be an elephant! They had great difficulty finding one until they hit on the idea to telephone Harrods of Knightsbridge to enquire about the possibility. They were only asked two questions by the dour voice at the other end – 'dead or alive?' and 'African or Indian?' The elephant's visit was duly arranged and the picture shows Rani, an Indian elephant, outside Lichfield Cathedral. A miracle perhaps!

One month later in August 1983, torrential rain produced a flash flood and the Museum Gardens, which in medieval times had been the Bishop's Fish Pool, was brought to life again and marooned Captain Edward Smith, commander of the ill-fated S.S.*Titanic*, once more in water.

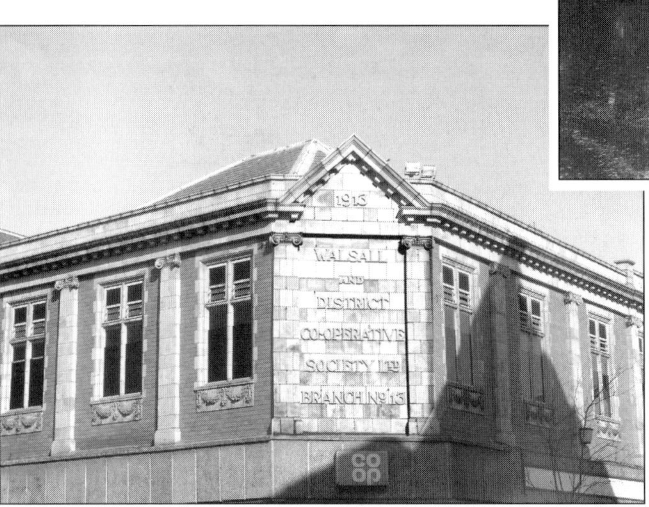

The West Midlands & Walsall Co-operative branch no 13 was built in 1913. It is situated on the corner of Breadmarket Street and Bore Street and is now Burton's Tailoring.

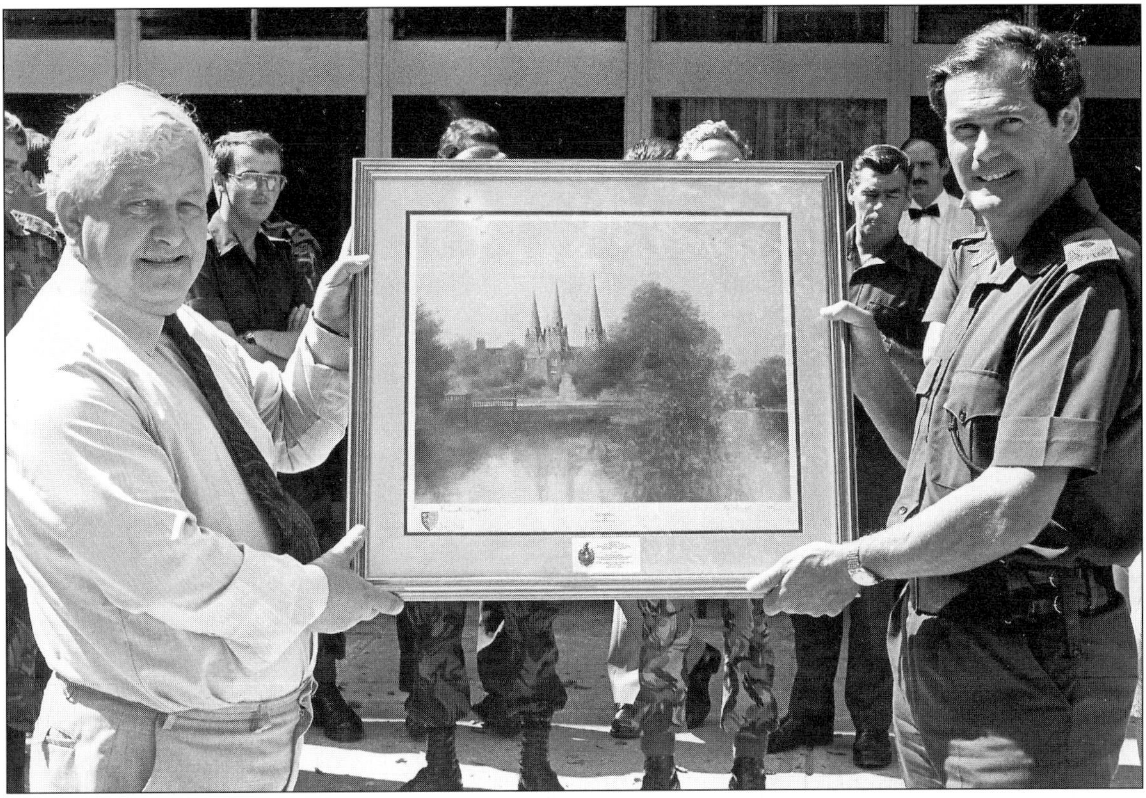

Part of the duties of the Chairman of Lichfield District Council in 1984 was to visit the 1st Battalion of the Staffordshire Regiment in Gibralter. Cllr Howard Clayton presenting a fine print of Lichfield Cathedral to the Commanding Officer.

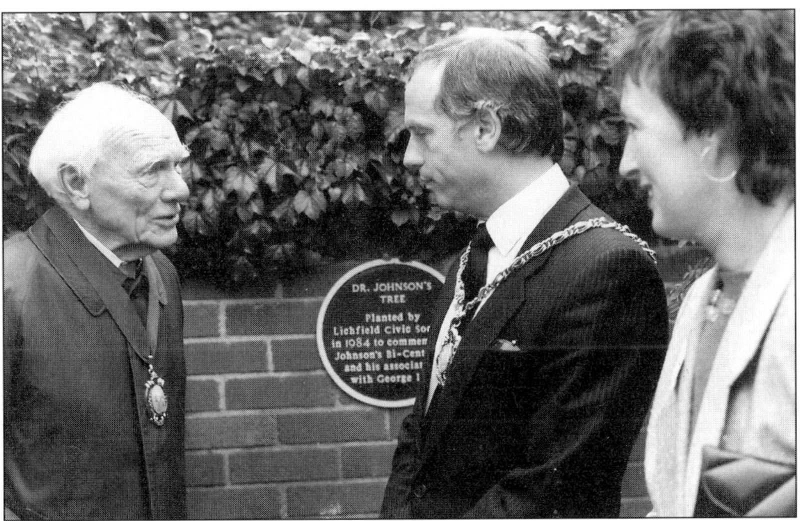

This year also marked the Bi-Centenary of Dr Samuel Johnson's death and his association with George III. A tree was planted by the Lichfield Civic Society to commemorate the anniversary and a Jasper Wedgwood plaque approximately six inches high was produced as a keepsake.

Malcolm Muggeridge, the President of the Johnson Society in 1984, is seen talking to the Mayor of Lichfield, Cllr John Russell.

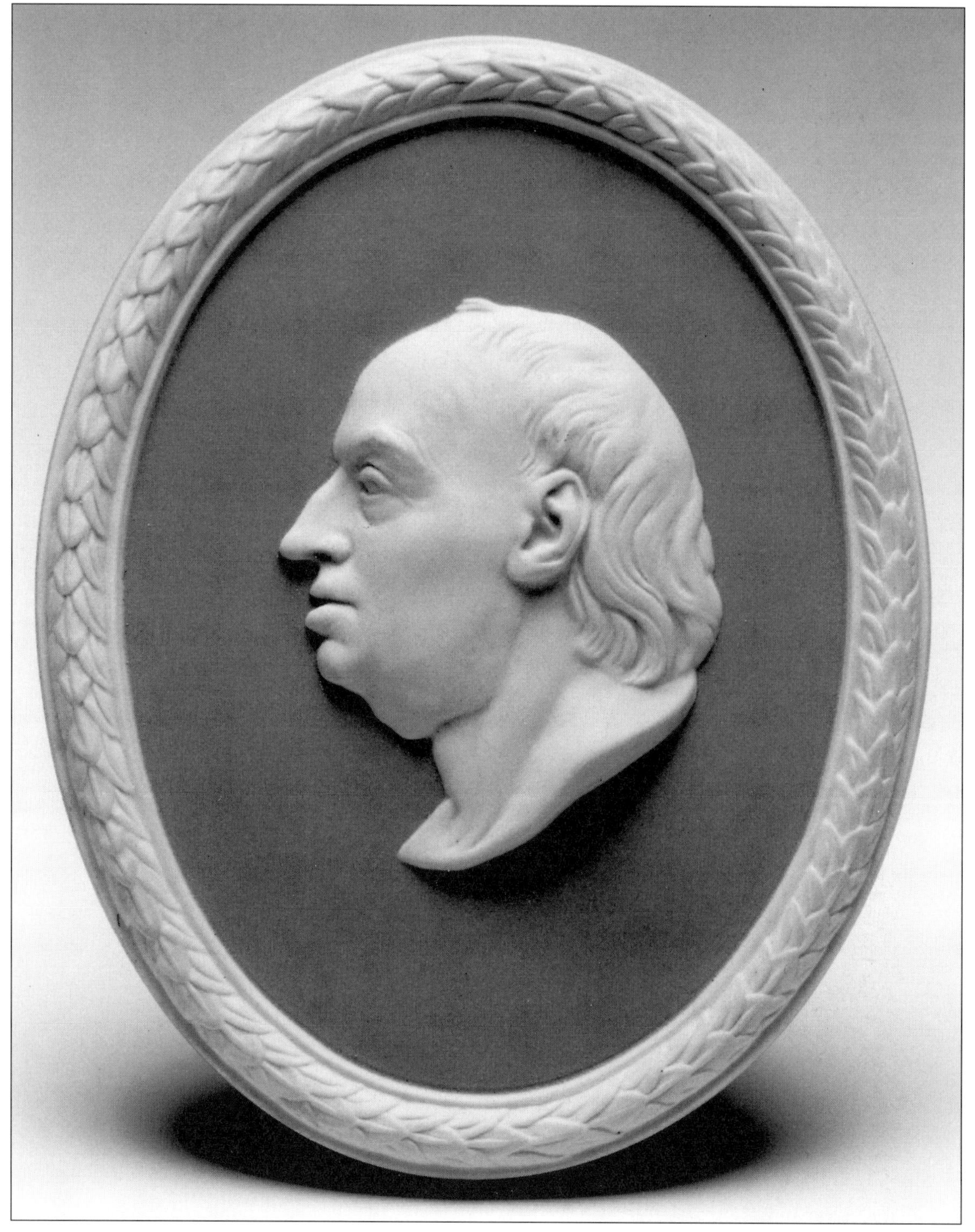

The Wedgwood Plaque produced to mark the Bi-Centenary of Dr Samuel Johnson's death.

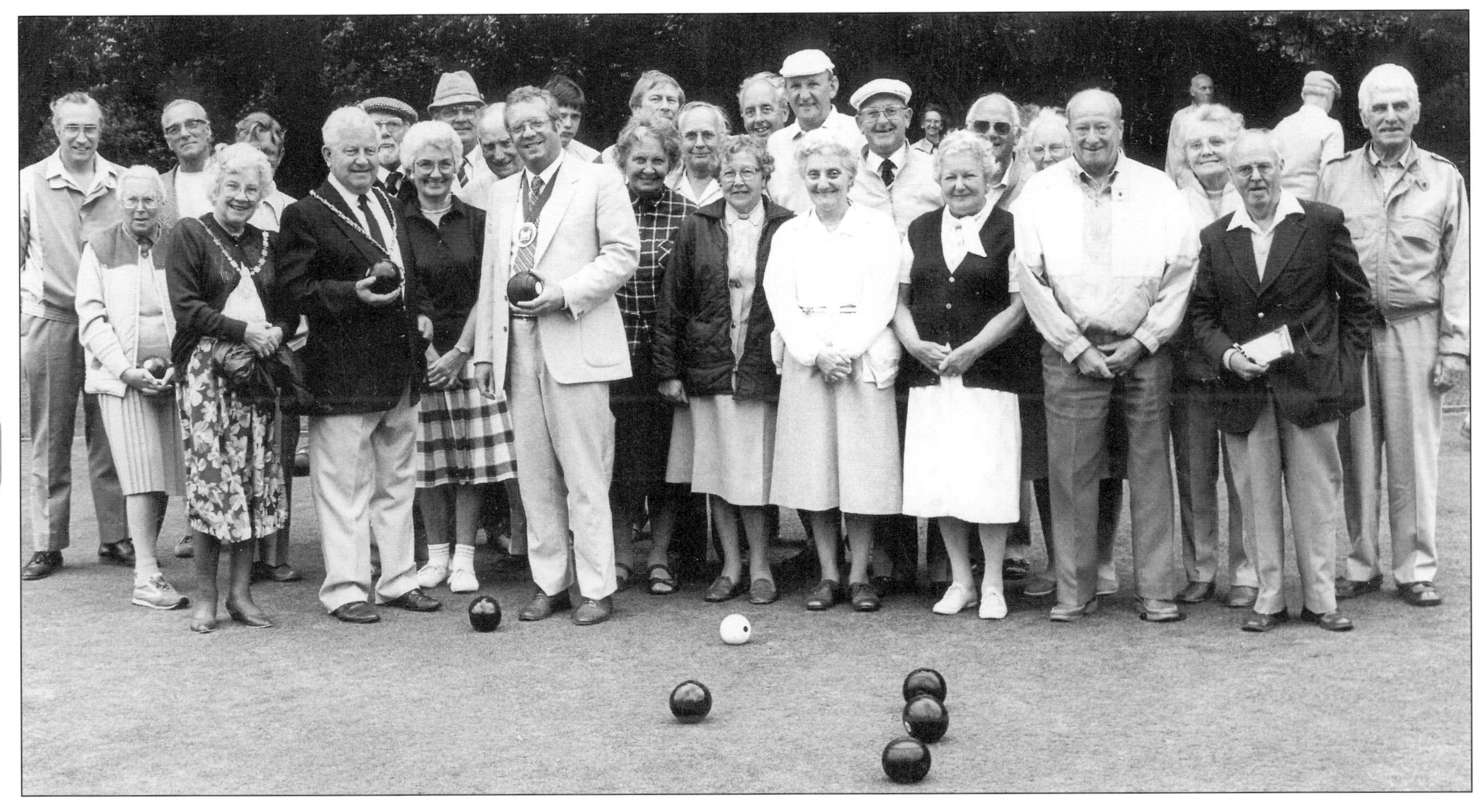

This is what the Museum Gardens Crown Green should really be used for – very different to 1983 when it was flooded. The Mayor, Cllr Howard Clayton and Mayoress Helen are seen here with the Mayor's deputy Cllr Jim Hopping and members of the bowls club. Each year the Lichfield City Councillors play against the club and except for one memorable wartime year the city have lost each time.

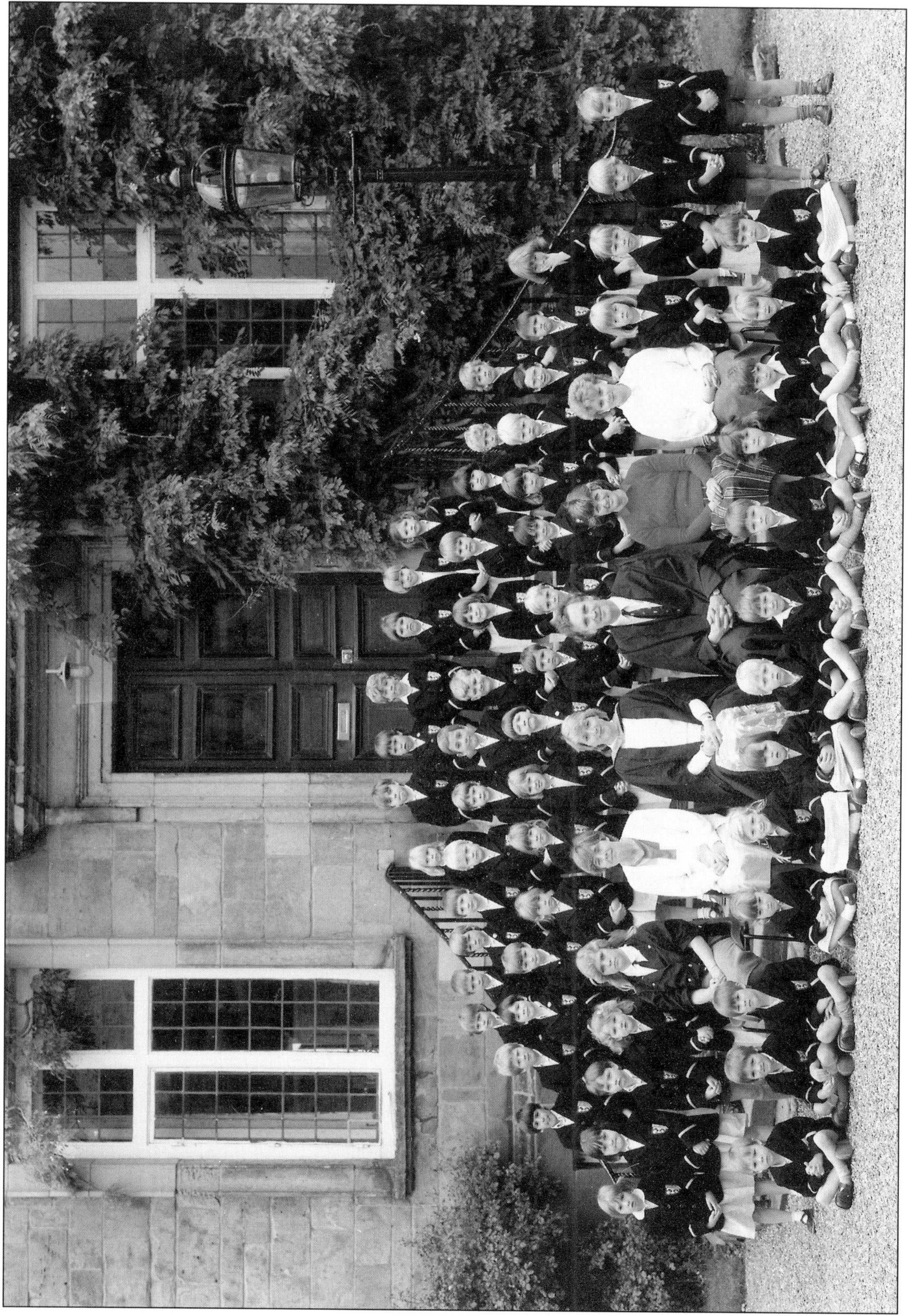

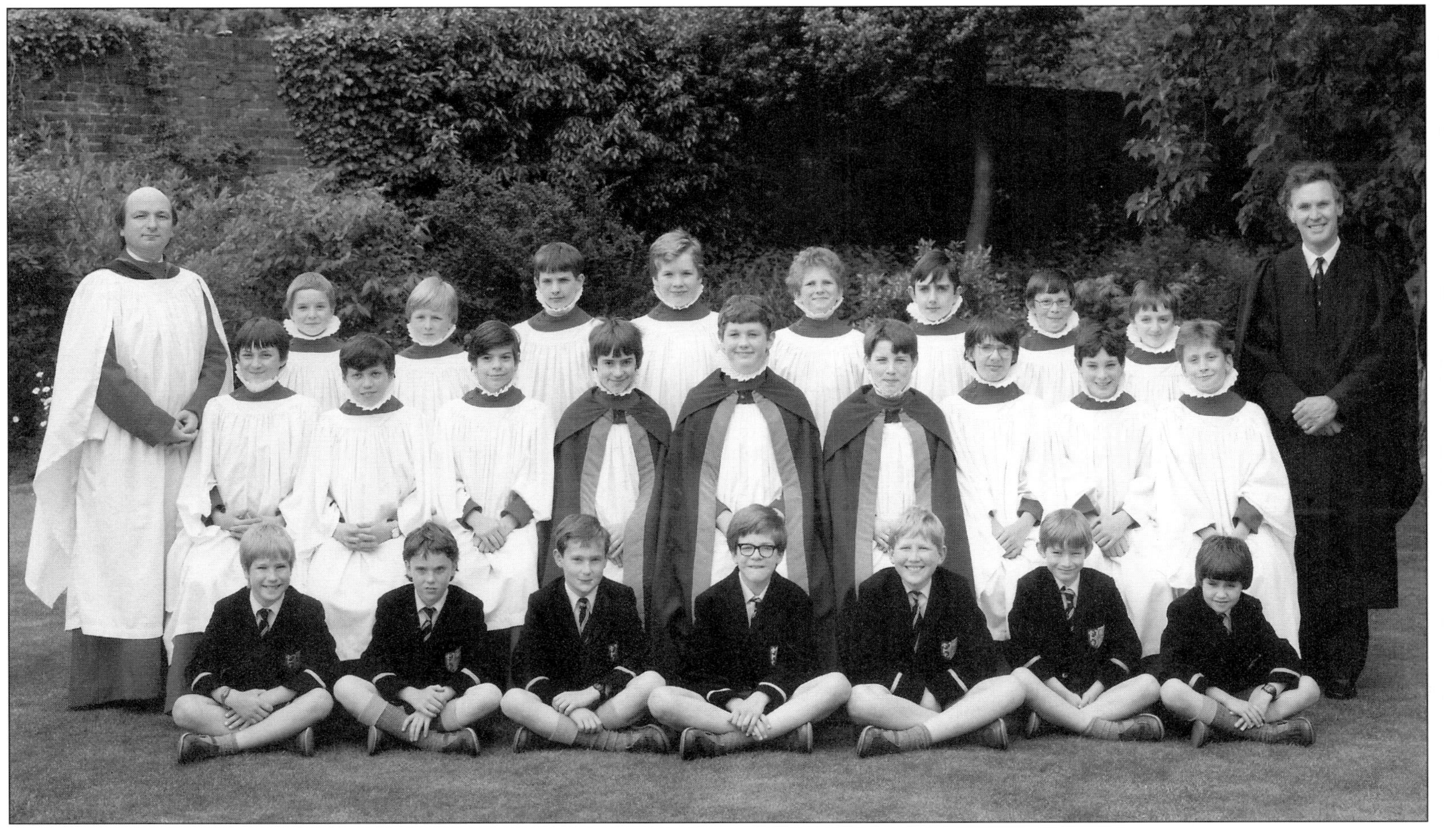

Above: Lichfield Cathedral Choristers with organist and choir master Jonathon Rees Williams and Headmaster Ian Wren taken in the same year.

Opposite page: Lichfield Cathedral School c.1985 with Headmaster Ian Wren, teachers and pupils on the steps of the Bishop's Palace in Cathedral Close. Notice the preparatory group who seem far too young to be in school uniform.

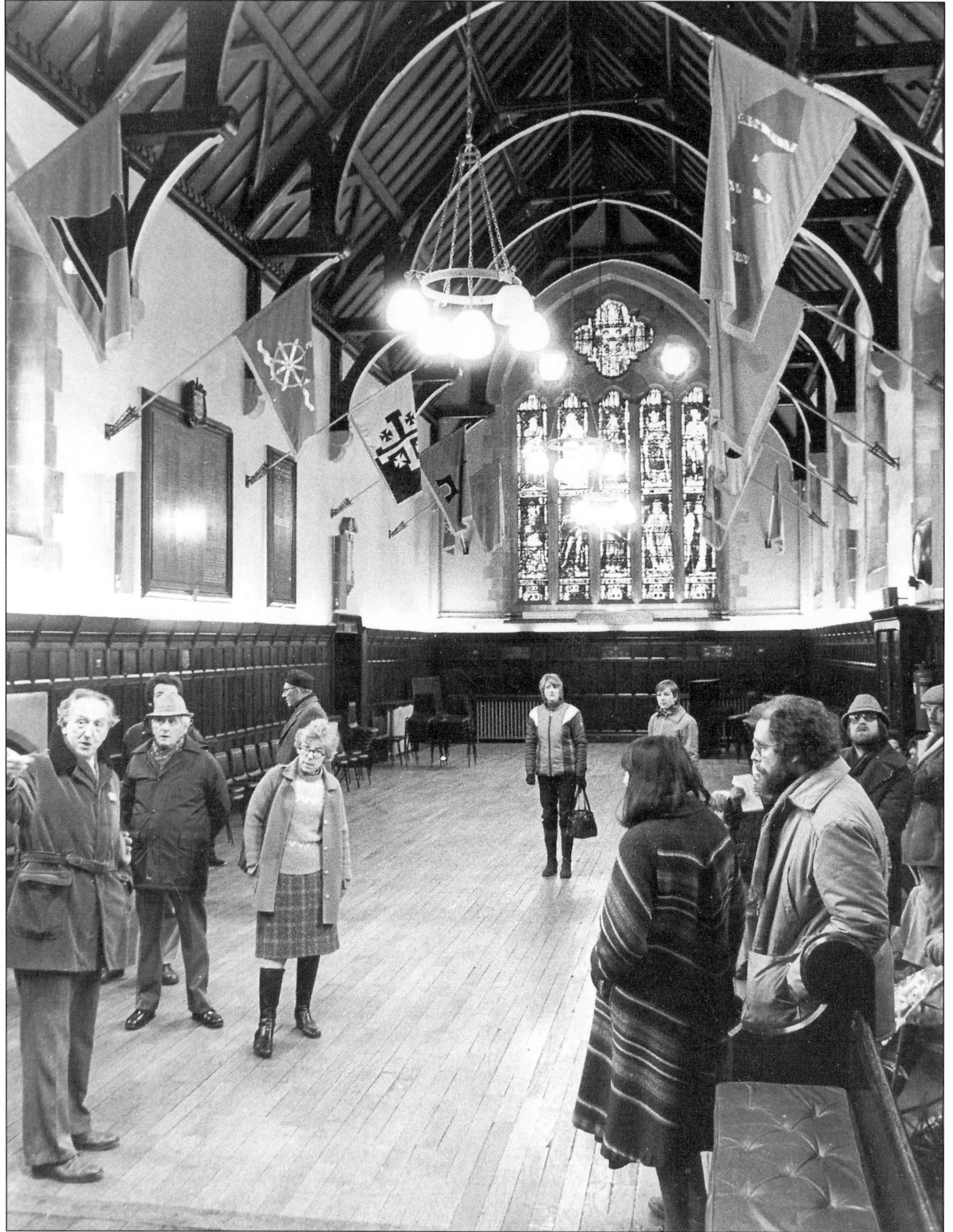

Later in the year John Wilson acted as town guide, pointing out the famous figures depicted below the Minstrel's Gallery. The front of the Guildhall faces Bore Street.

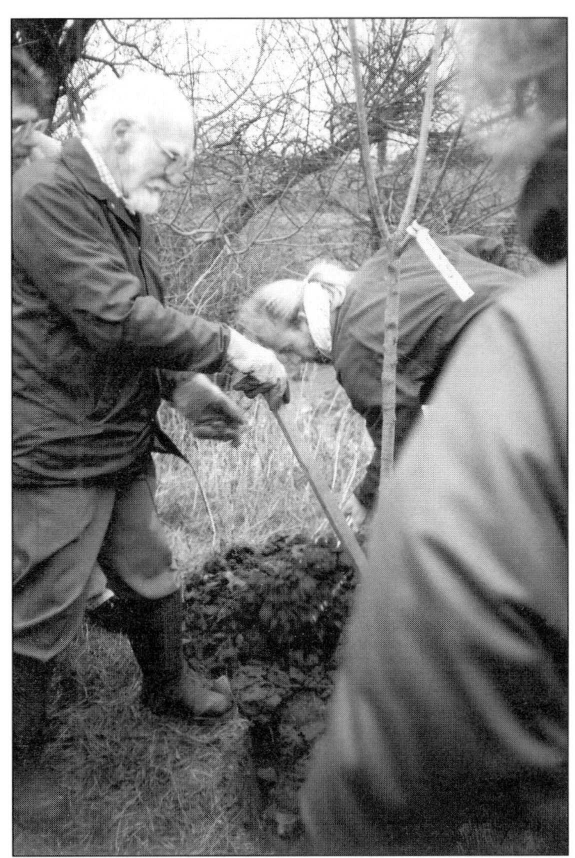

The Darwin Walk was founded in 1986 by John Sanders MBE, artist and retired principal of Lichfield College (formerly the School of Art). It was the first project to be funded by the New Horizons Trust and was to be an effective and inexpensive way of commemorate a great man who had been historically neglected both in Lichfield and nationwide. It was proposed that a ten mile route, 90% of which would be along public rights of way and approval obtained for the rest from the landowners, would form a 'green necklace' around the city.

Left: The newly planted orchard near Apsley House with 'Nick' Nicholls staking the young fruit trees.

Below: Grandparent's Day tree planting in November 1986 when each family who participated received a certificate.

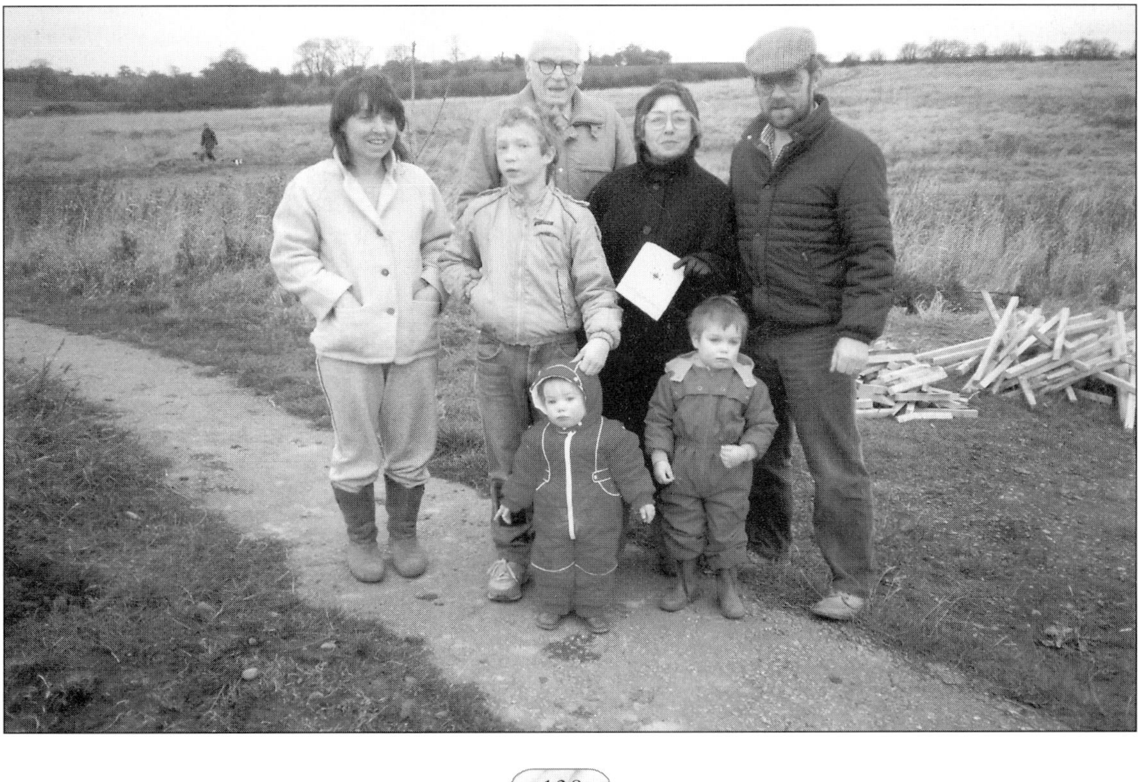

Assembly point with John Sanders on the summer walk which begins from Maxstoke Grange Farm on a summer afternoon in July.

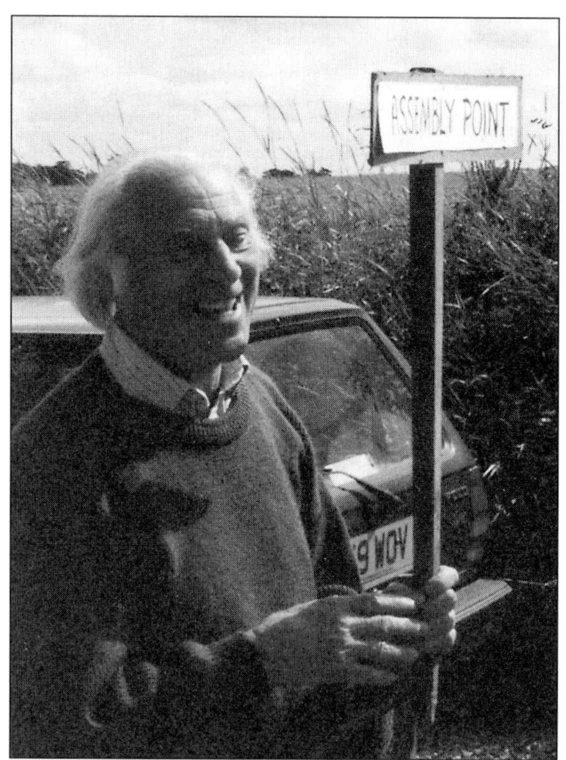

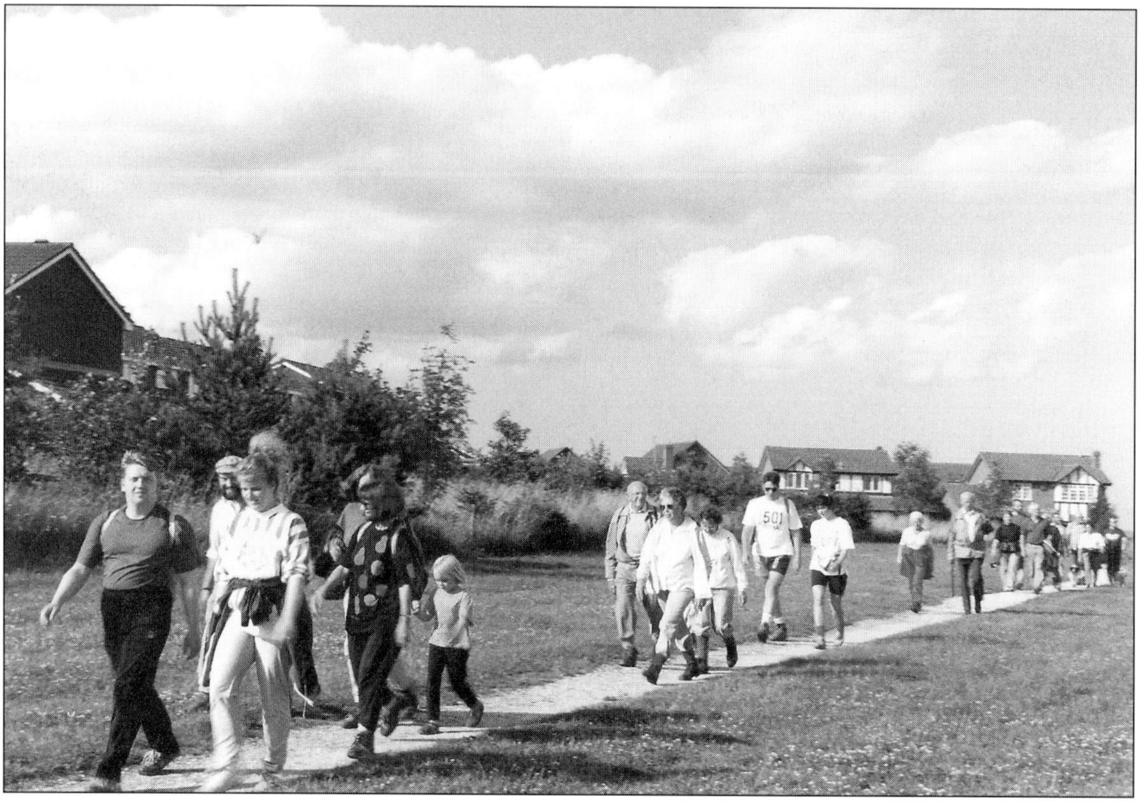

A happy band along the Darnford Park footpath towards Mallet's Corner and the Ryknild Street traffic lights

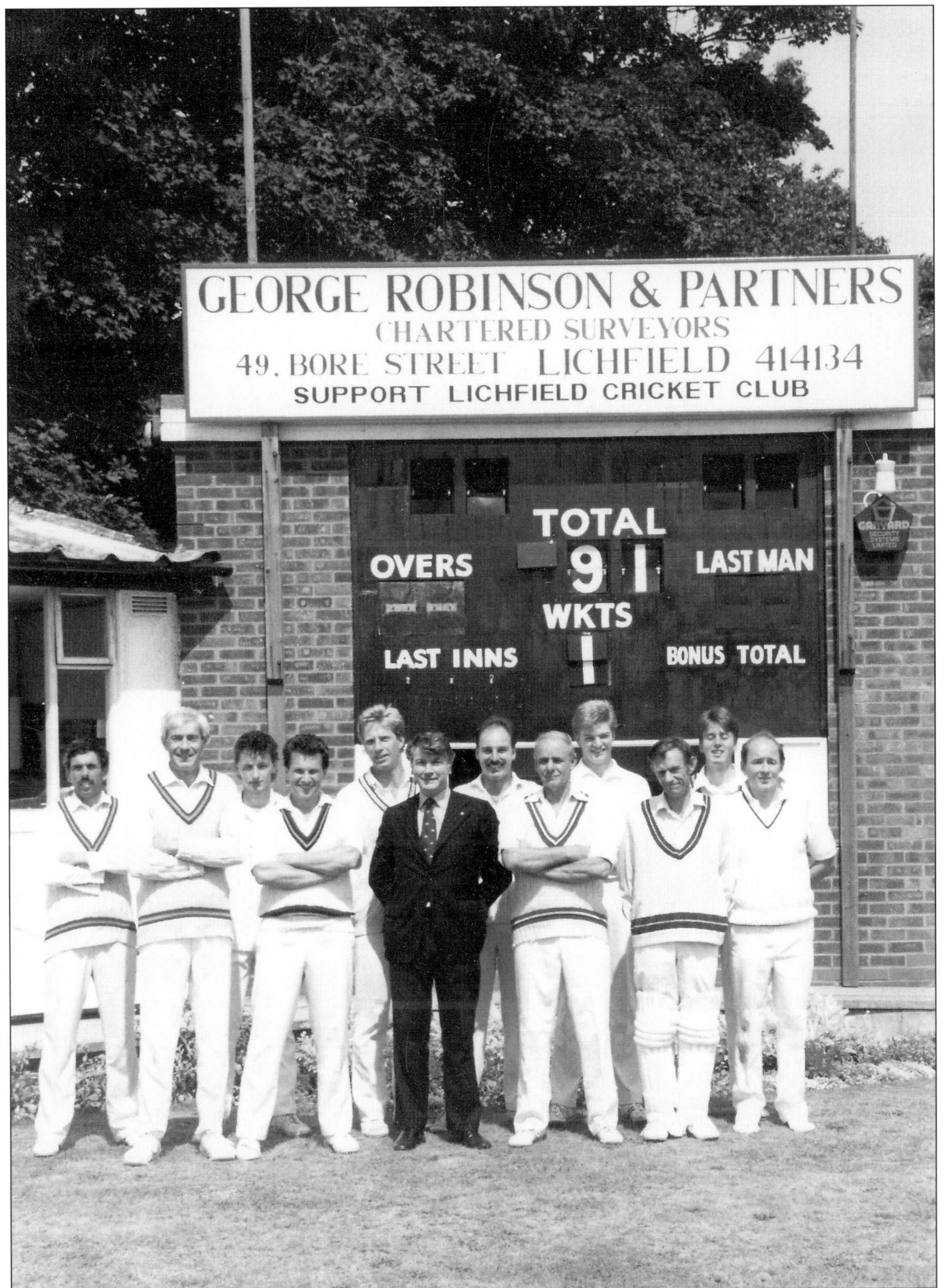

The Lichfield Cricket Club was sponsored by George Robinson & Partners in 1987. Peter Robinson is seen here with Captain Bernard Wootton on his right.

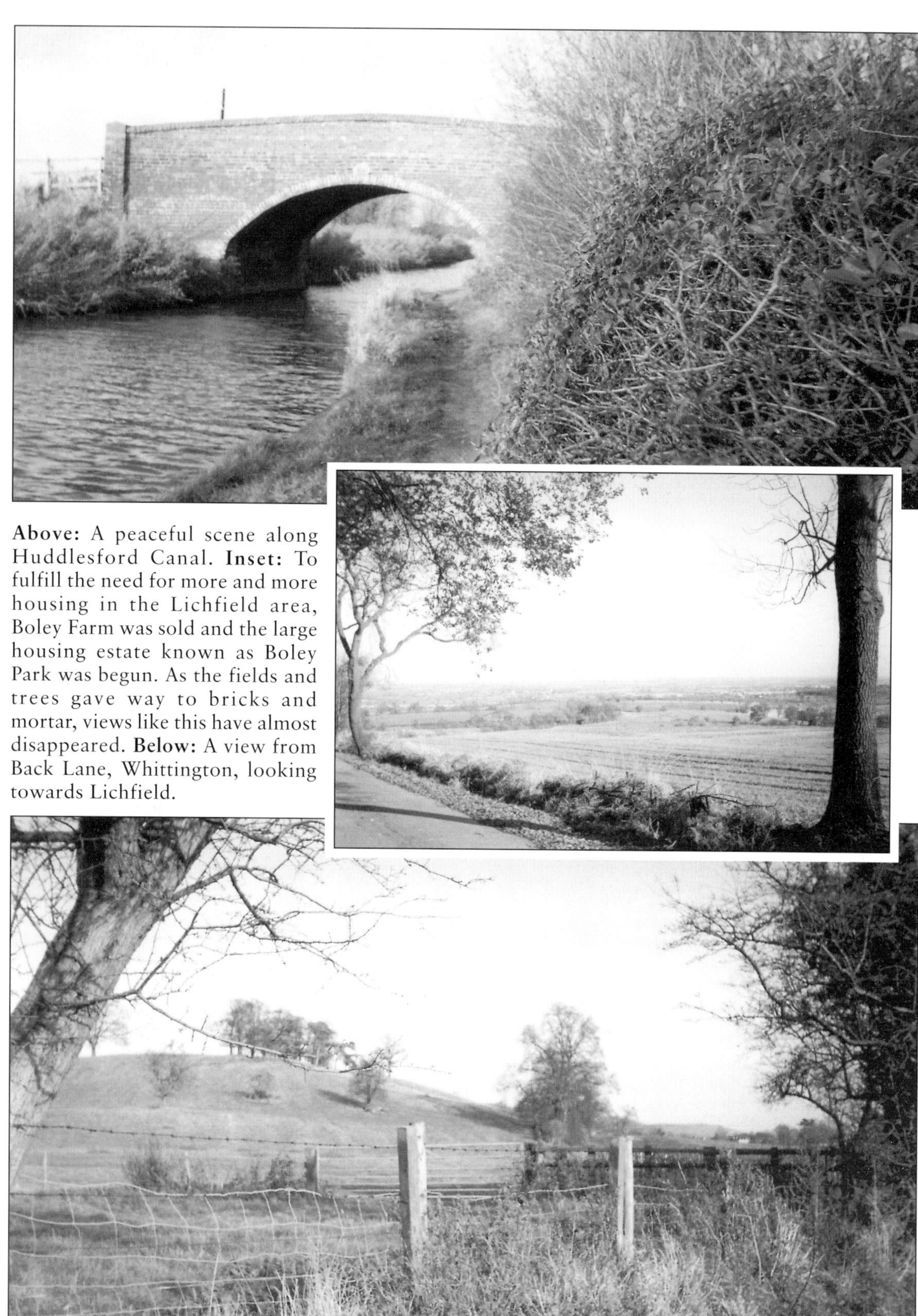

Above: A peaceful scene along Huddlesford Canal. **Inset:** To fulfill the need for more and more housing in the Lichfield area, Boley Farm was sold and the large housing estate known as Boley Park was begun. As the fields and trees gave way to bricks and mortar, views like this have almost disappeared. **Below:** A view from Back Lane, Whittington, looking towards Lichfield.

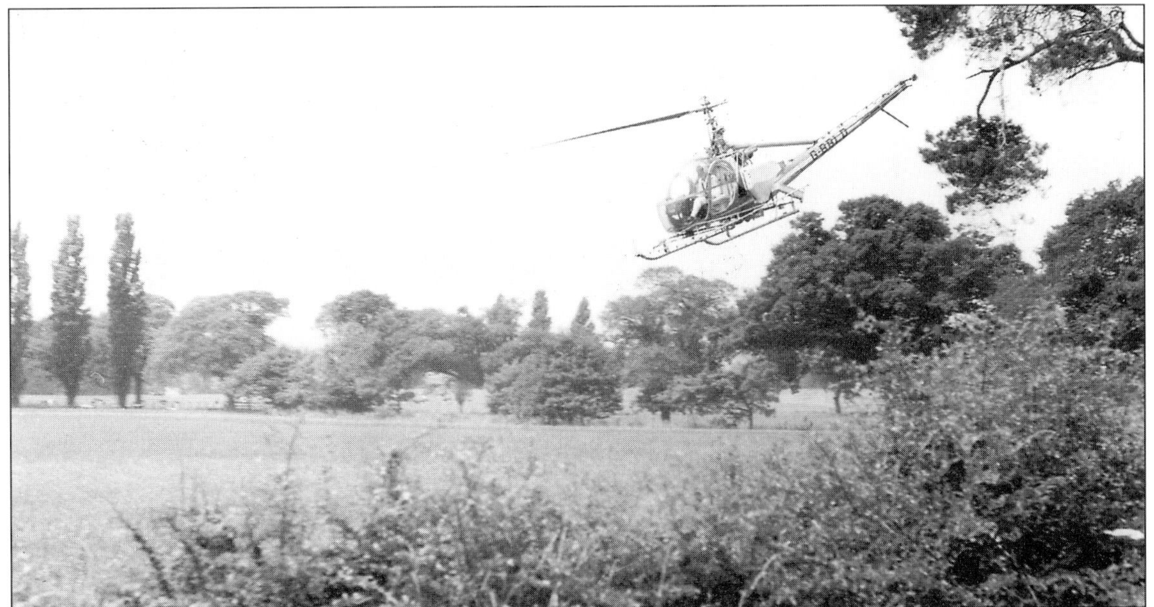

Some of the beautiful meadowland to the south of Lichfield stretching out towards Hopwas woods, with the Barratt helicopter swooping like an angry gadfly over the scene. Residents of Lichfield were to hear it many times over the next few years as the meadowland gradually became what is now known as Boley Park.

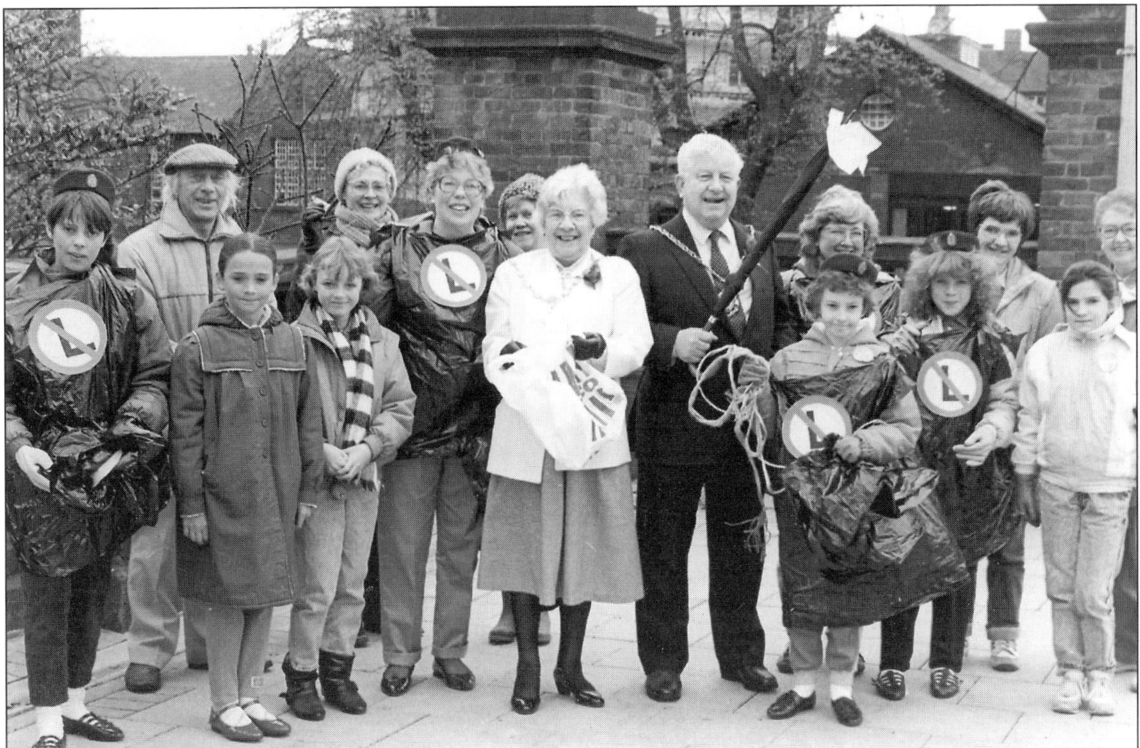

A 'Litter Pick' was organised by the Lichfield Guide Association and the Lichfield City Council in 1984. The Mayor Cllr Howard Clayton and his wife Helen were there to assist, ably encouraged by John Sanders.

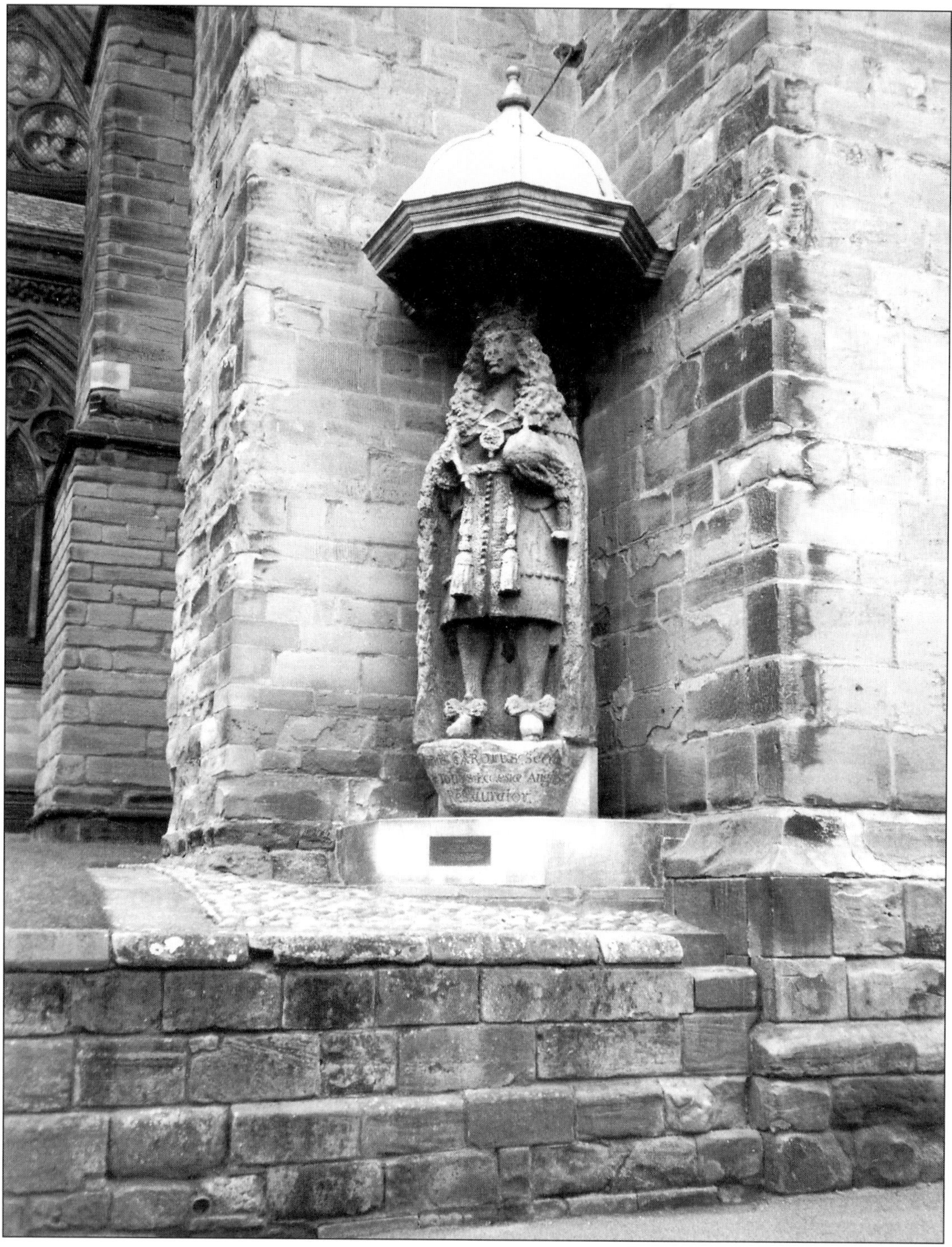

Today King Charles II stands just round the corner from the south door of Lichfield Cathedral, but once he stood in a niche at the top of the gable of the west front. He was carved by Sir Andrew Wilson and placed there in 1680 at the restoration of the cathedral after the Civil War. After two centuries of weathering, he was removed and placed in one of the towers at the request, it is said, of Queen Victoria who objected to having her statue near his. After a spell 'in the tower' he was allowed out on parole in 1986 and placed in his present, sheltered position.

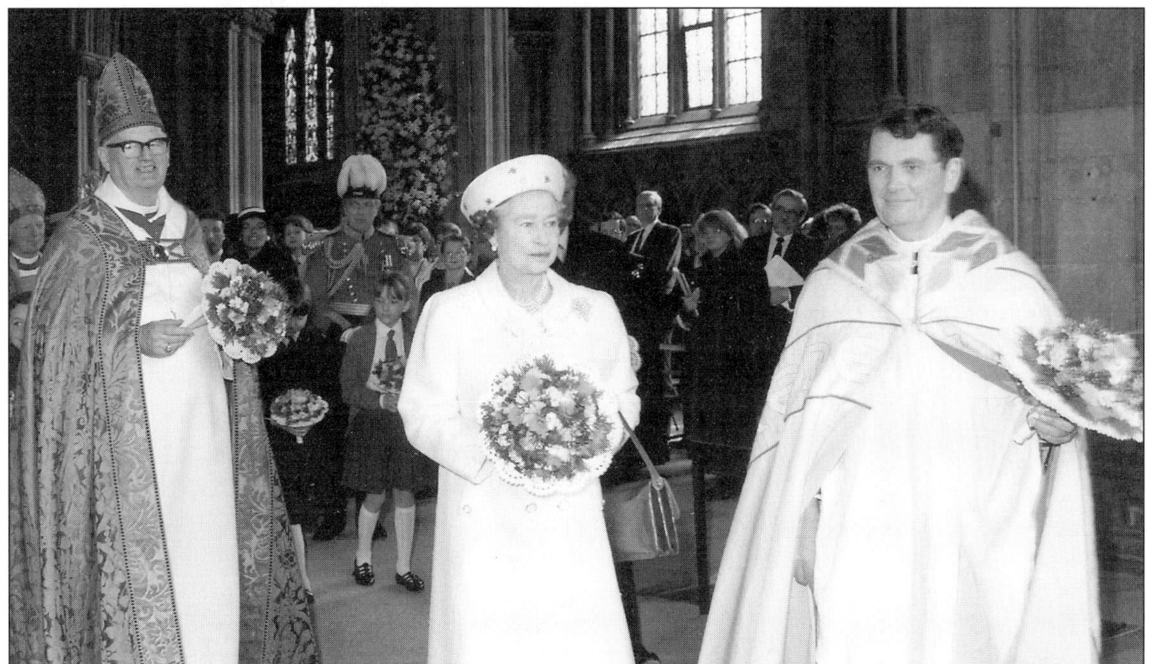

In 1988 the Royal Train arrived at Lichfield City Station bringing the Queen and the Duke of Edinburgh to attend the Maundy Service in Lichfield Cathedral at l0am. After the service, Queen Elizabeth distributed the Maundy Money (special silver pennies given to worthy citizens) which is produced by the Royal Mint especially for the occasion.

Inside the cathedral with the Dean Rev John Lang (right). Notice the nosegays.

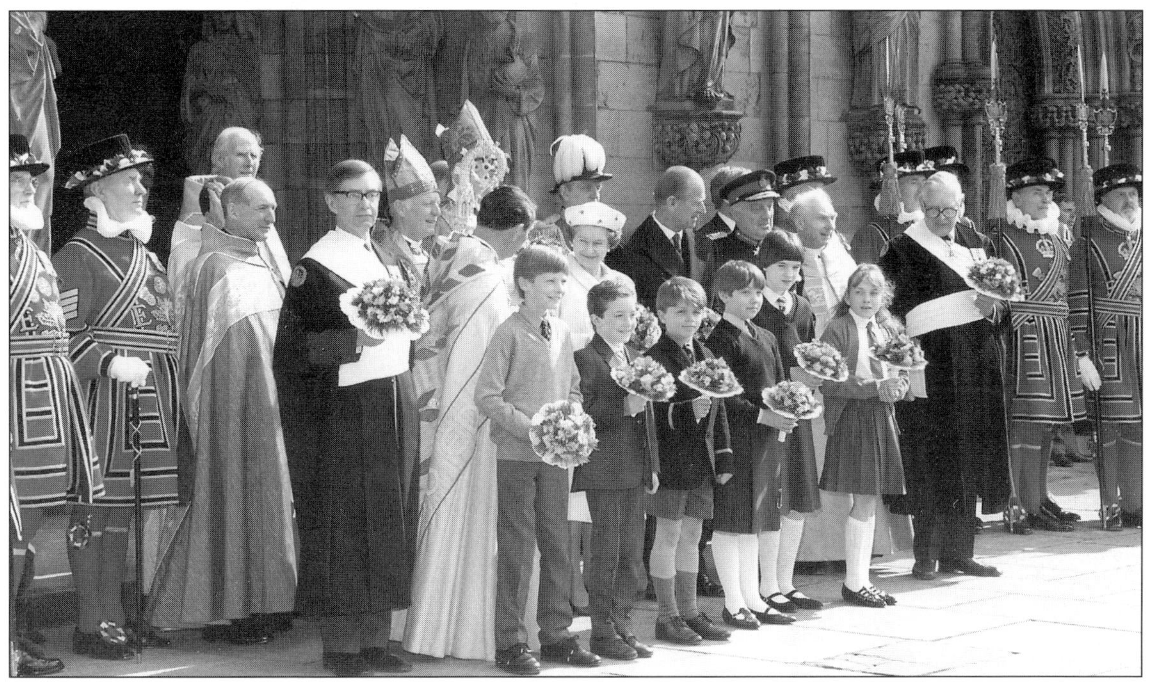

Outside the west front with Bishop Keith Sutton of Lichfield, Canon John Turner, Dean John Lang and other notables. The spectacle was richly embroidered by the Queen's Yeoman of the Guard – the famous Beefeaters. After a walkabout to meet the people of Lichfield Queen Elizabeth and the Duke of Edinburgh went to the Civic Hall for lunch.

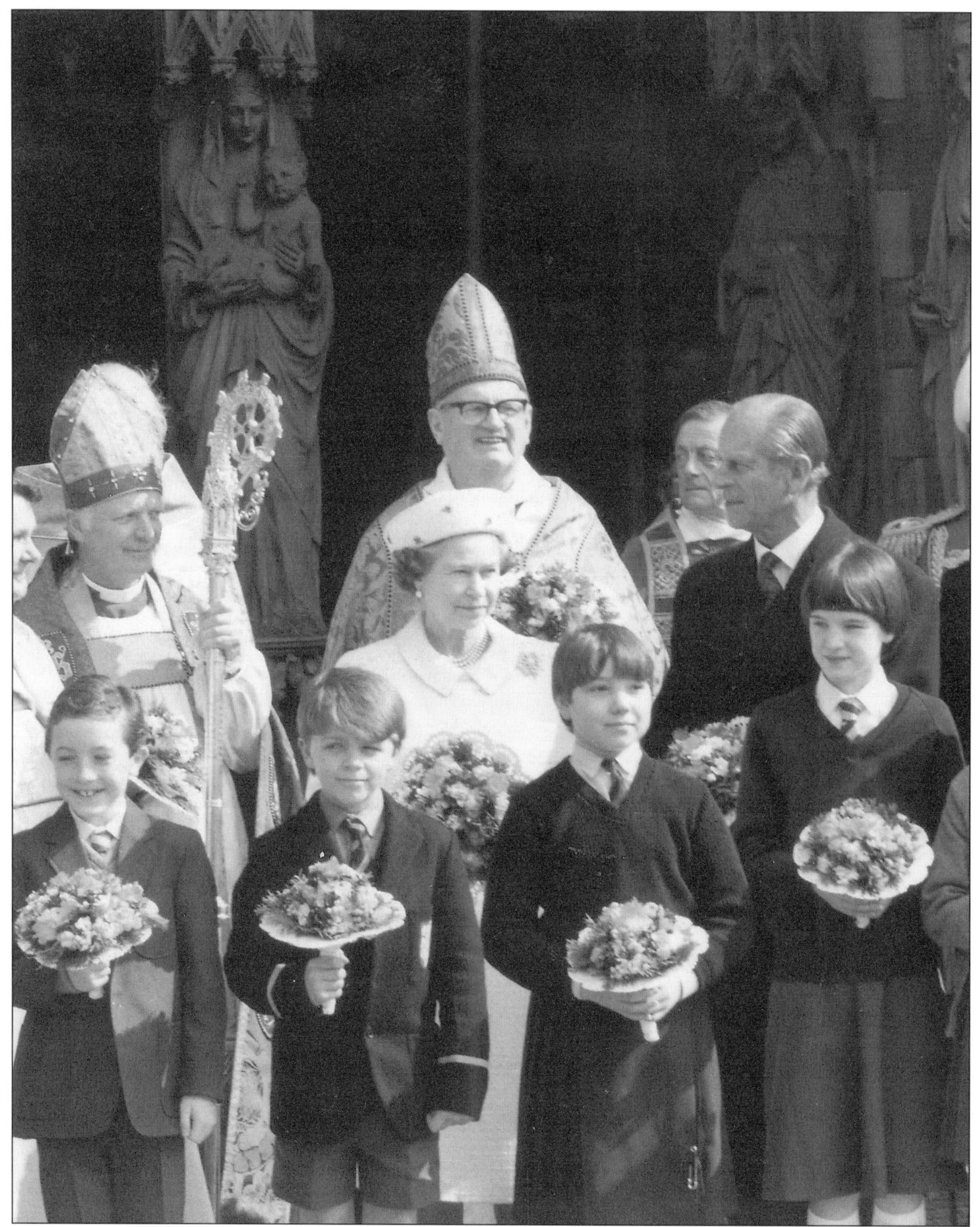

A close-up of the Queen on the Cathedral steps.

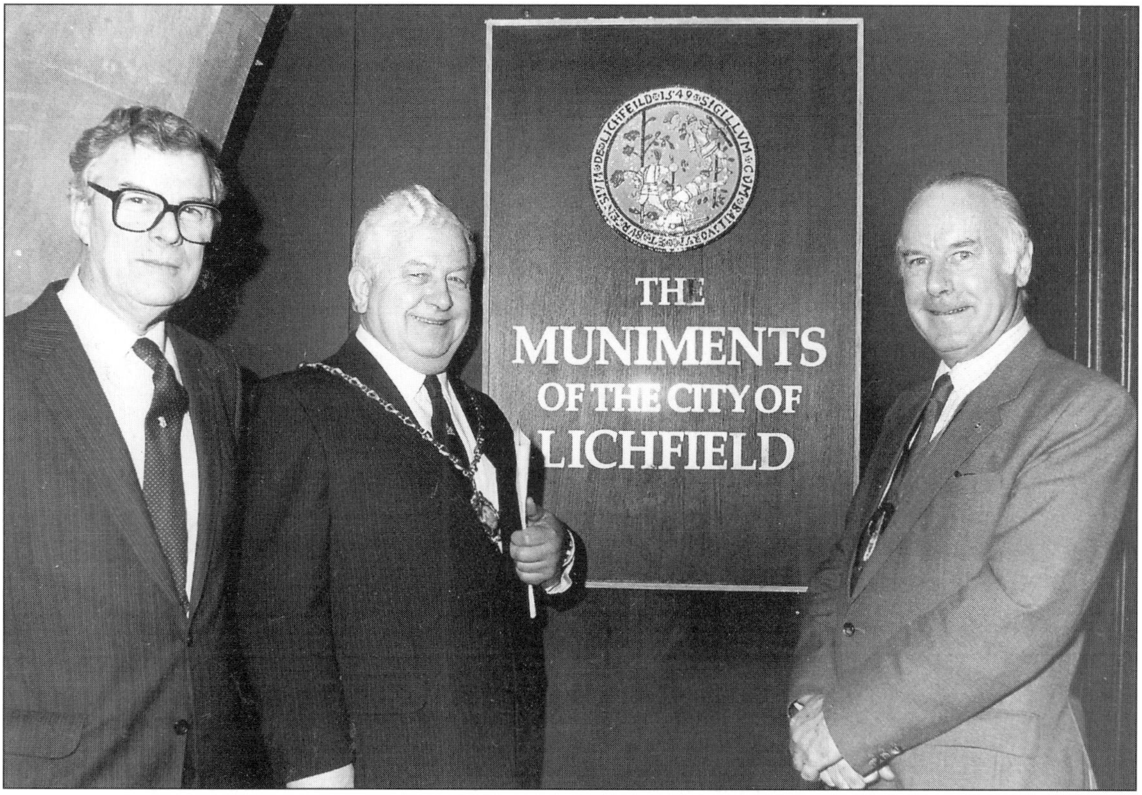

The opening of an exhibition of the Charters of the City of Lichfield by the Mayor, Cllr Howard Clayton seen here with John Salloway, Curator of the Treasury in St Mary's Heritage Centre, on his left. Co-incidentally, Stafford Record Office had found a very early copy of the City Seal c.1549 from the reign of Edward VI and a cast had been made of it for the city.

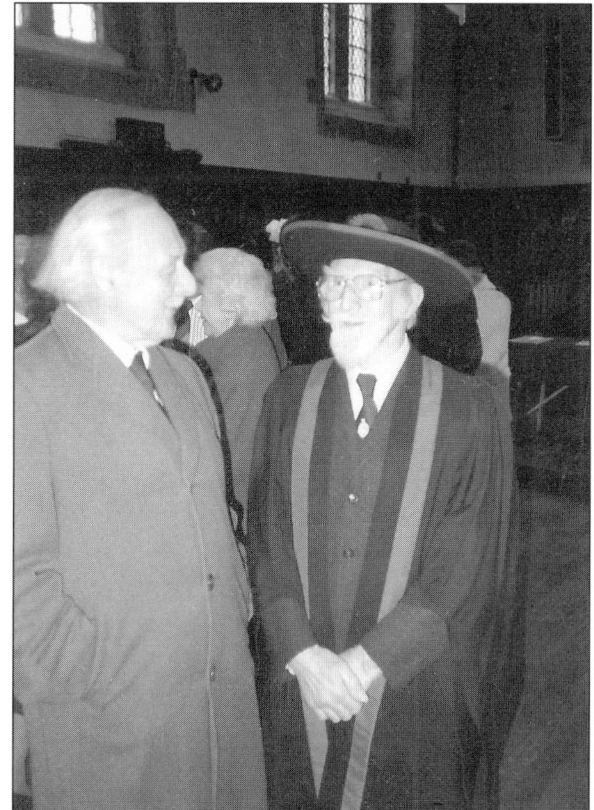

The Master of the Worshipful Company of Smith's for this year was Norman Nicholls seen here with Jack Ballinger.

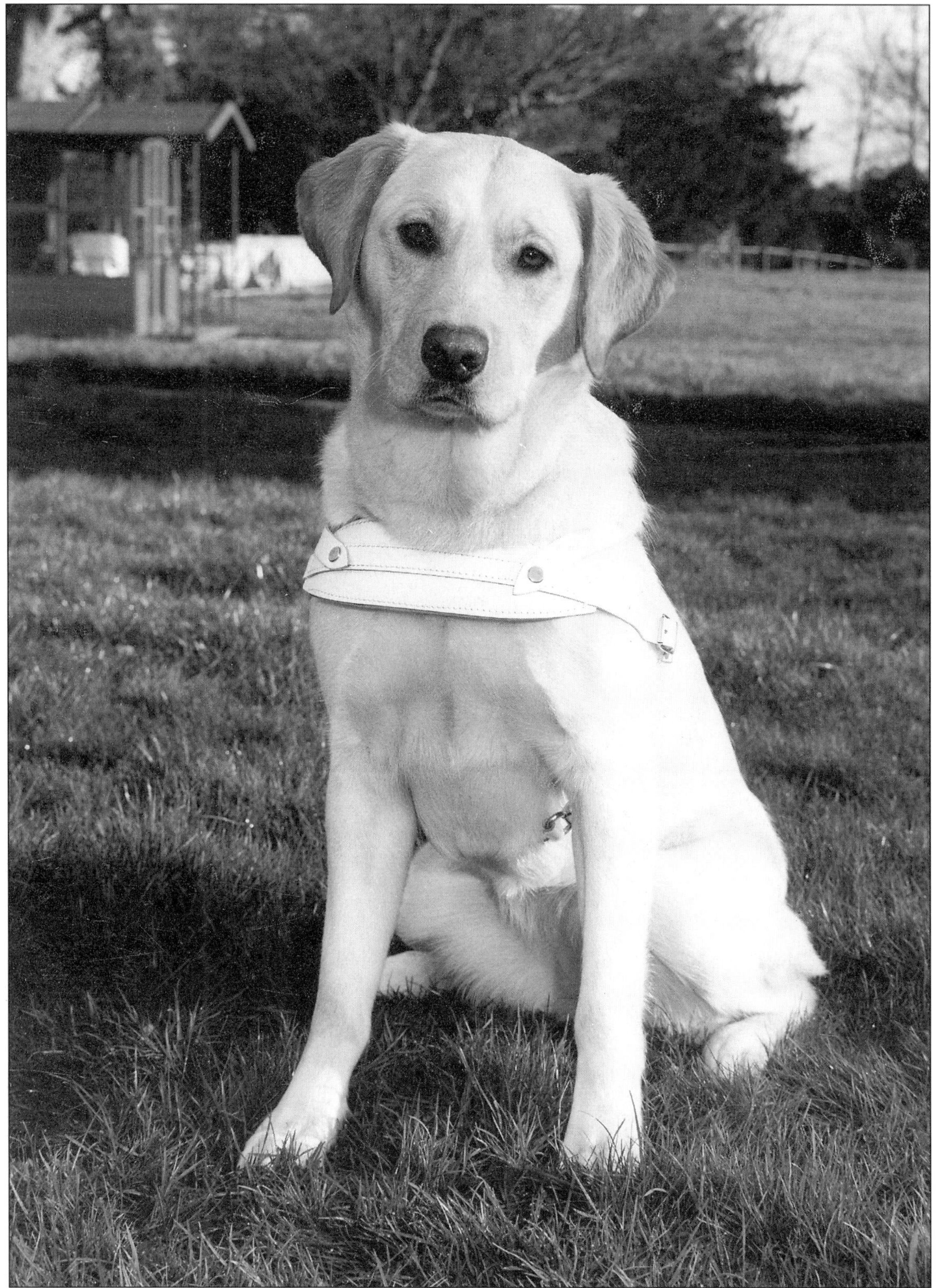

Tosca, a Guide Dog for the Blind, was purchased through the efforts of the Lichfield Friary School and her photograph was sent to them to be put in pride of place for their achievement.

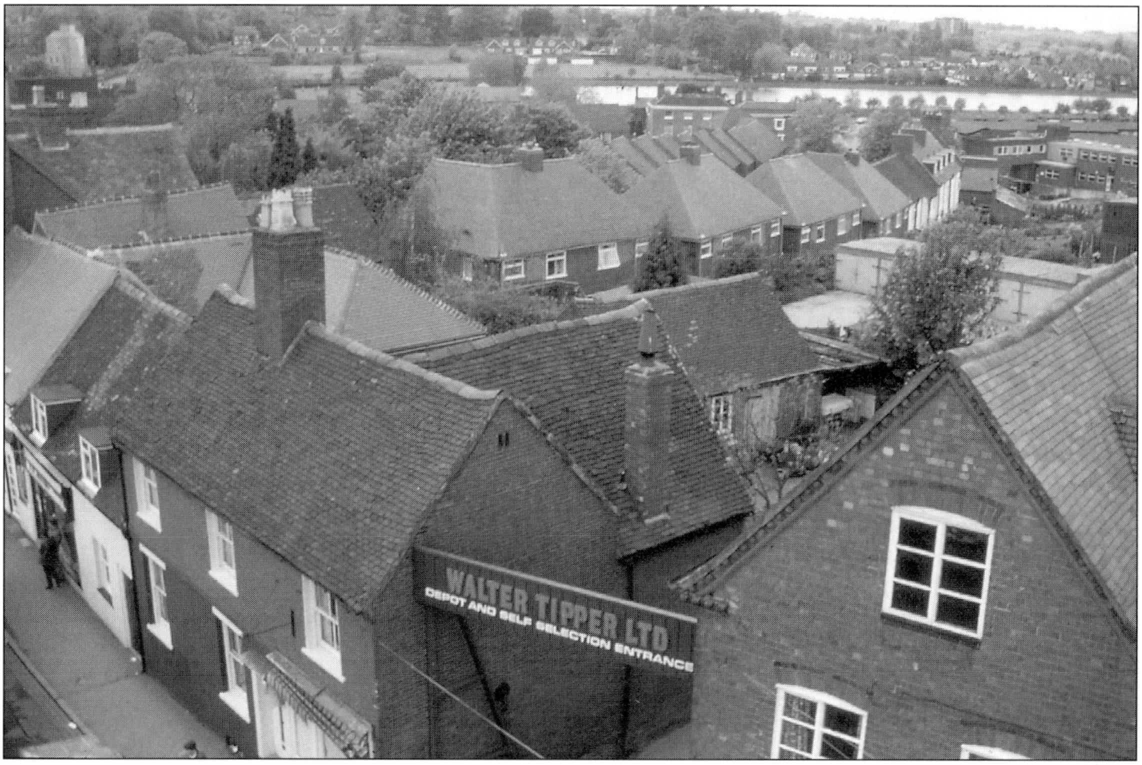

Remember Walter Tipper Ltd of George Lane before it moved premises to Britannia Way Industrial Park?

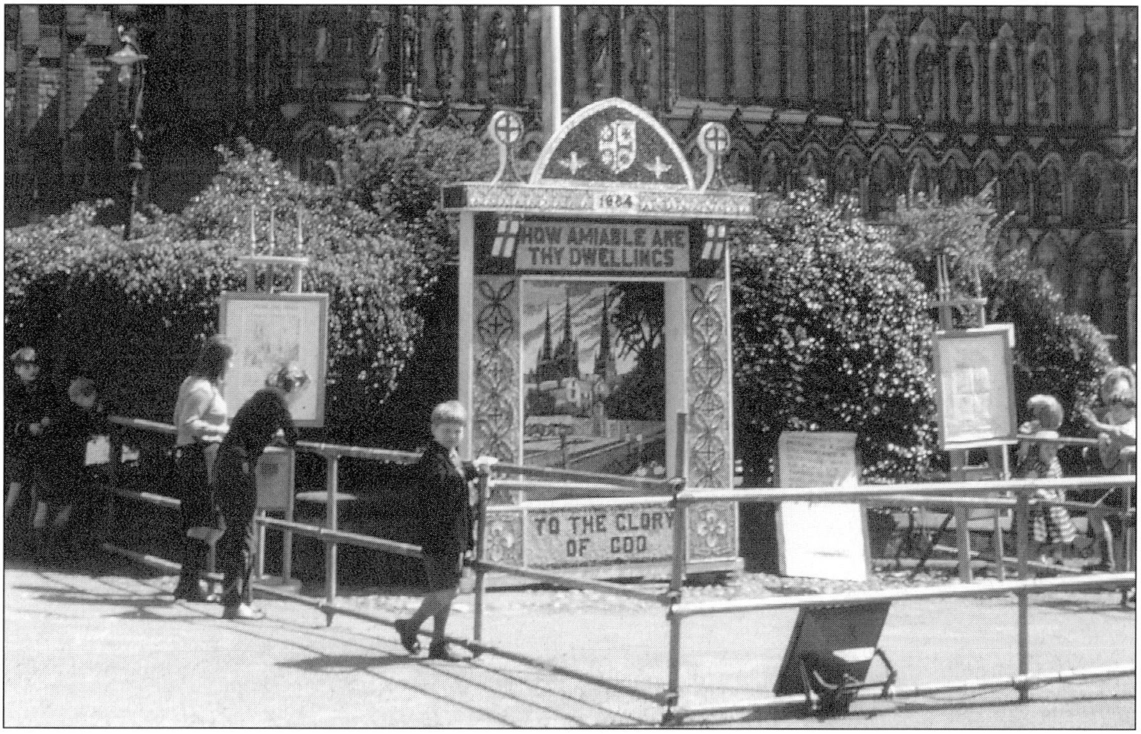

A Well Dressing at the site of the old conduit which was the water supply for the Close in medieval times. The water was carried by lead pipe from Maple Hayes.

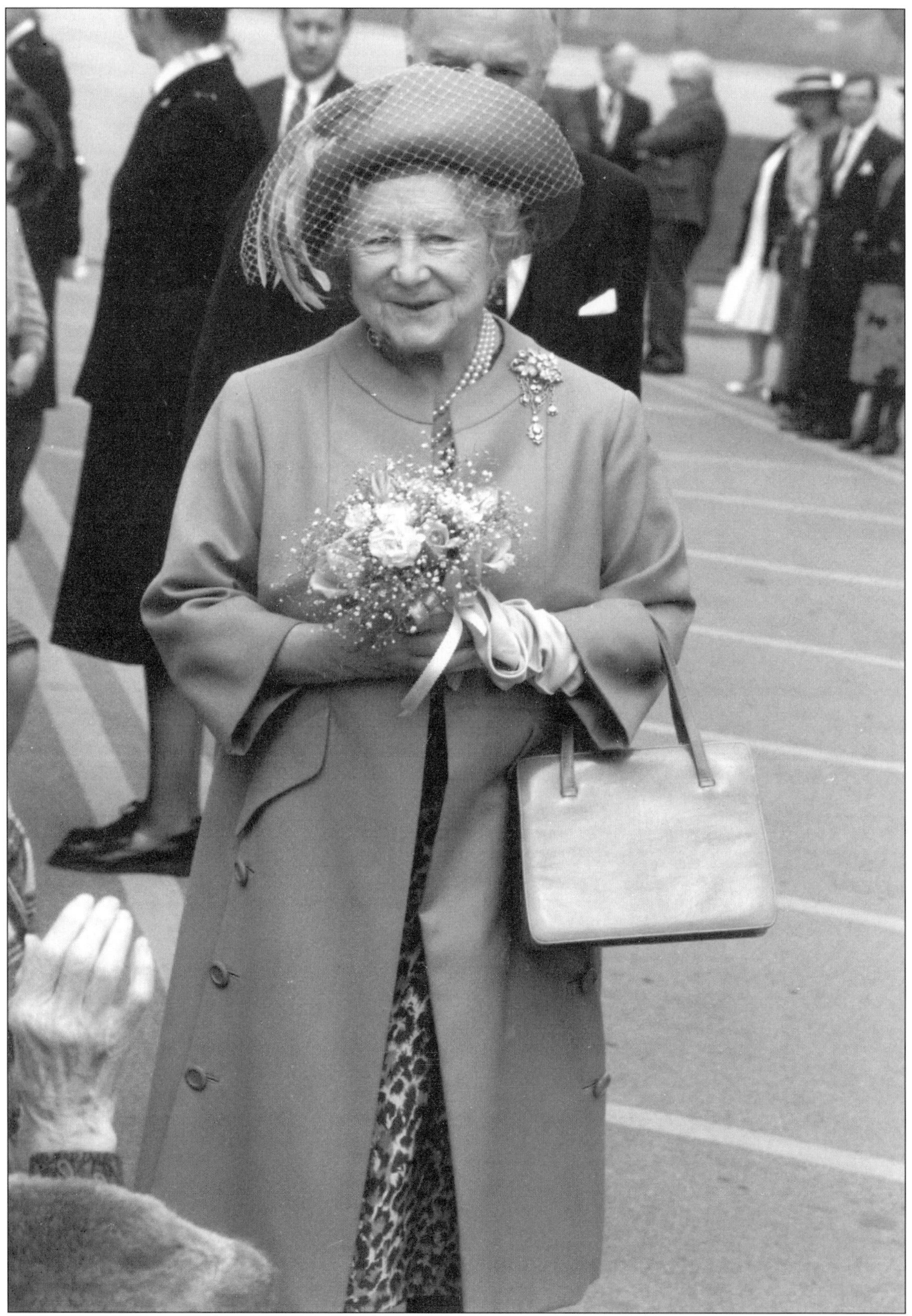

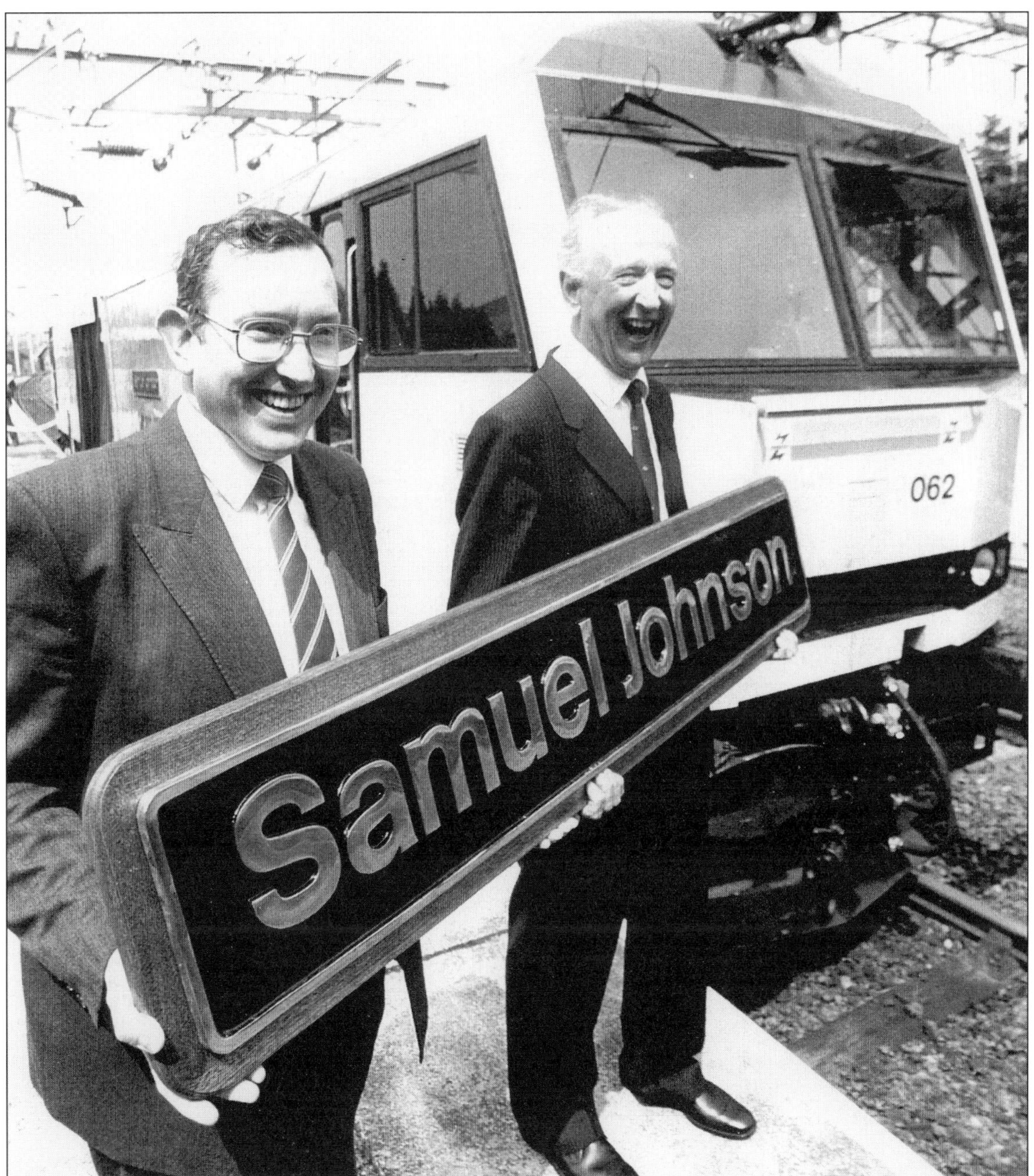

Above: In the eighties British Rail introduced a class of heavy goods diesel locomotive. They were known collectively as *Bescot Castles* and they were given names, mostly of people with Midland connections (*Sister Dora* for example). There was also a *Samuel Johnson* and in 1989 at a ceremony at Lichfield Trent Valley Station the new locomotive received the nameplate in the presence of the Chairman John Wilson and members of the Johnson Society and a member of the staff of British Rail.

Opposite page: On 18 April 1989, Queen Elizabeth the Queen Mother visited Lichfield to unveil a bronze bust of Bishop Woods by Sir Jacob Epstein in the cloisters of the cathedral. She had last visited Lichfield in July 1942 when as Queen, she and King George VI had stayed with Bishop Woods, an old friend, at the Bishop's Palace. Her equerry Sir Morton Gillist is following closely behind her.

Chapter 10 – The Nineties

The nineties began tragically, shattering the tranquility of Lichfield when two young soldiers from Whittington Barracks were gunned down at Lichfield City Station on 1st June 1990. Private W.R.Davies lost his life and the Royal British Legion commemorate each anniversary by laying a poppy wreath below the plaque.

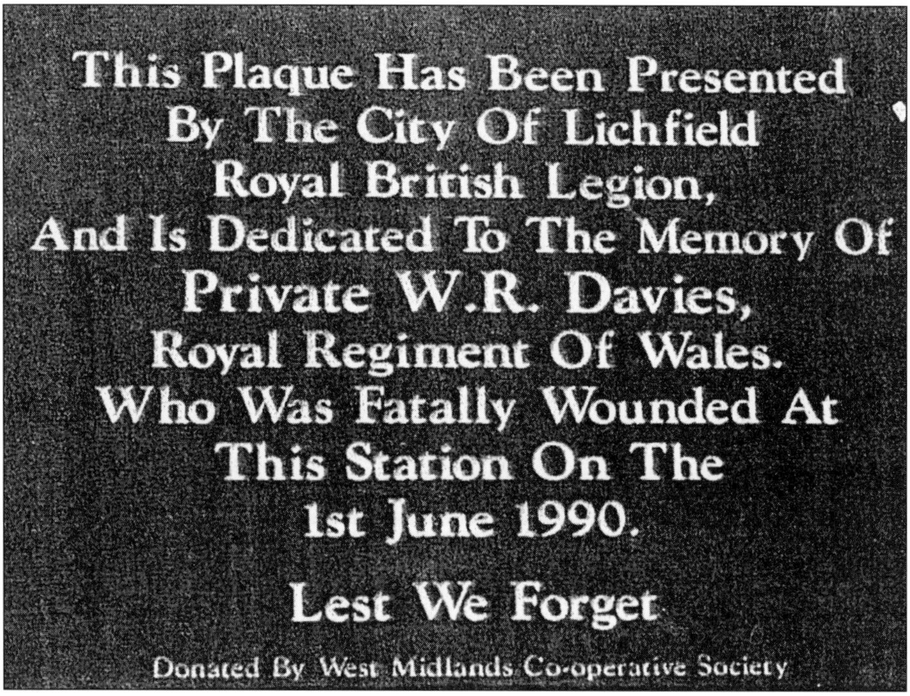

Opposite page top left: In St Michael's Chapel, inside the south transept of Lichfield Cathedral hang the colours of the Staffordshire Infantry Regiments including the 1st and 2nd battalion, South Staffordshire, formerly the 38th and 80th Foot.

Opposite page top right: Another inside view of the cathedral taken from the choir stalls looking toward the high altar and the Lady Chapel to the east. The Cathedral has Belgium sixteenth century Herkenrode glass and stunning vaulted architecture.

Opposite page bottom: The 'Ladies of the Vale' at dusk taken from the water's edge of Stowe Pool. Lichfield Cathedral, unique with its three spires, was given this name of endearment by the poetess Anna Seward in the eighteenth century. She and her family lived at the Bishop's Palace and received many distinguished visitors including Sir Walter Scott.

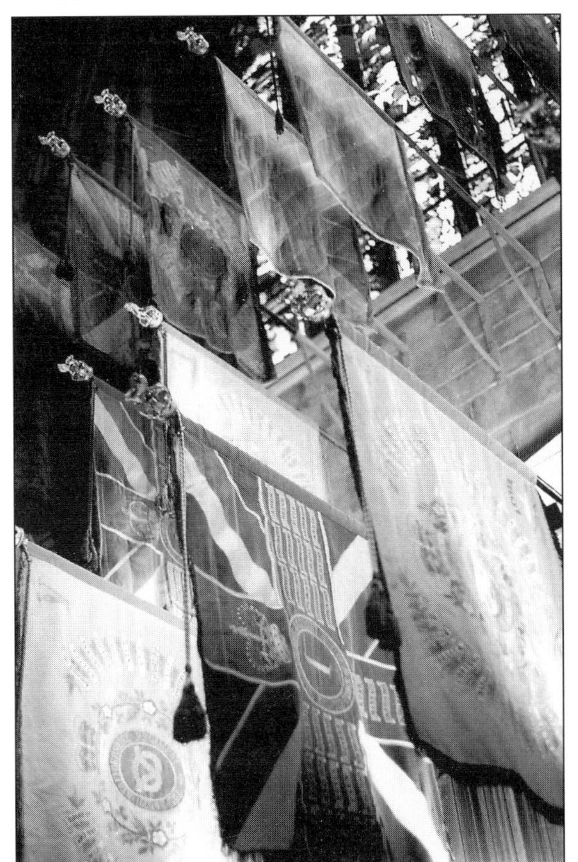

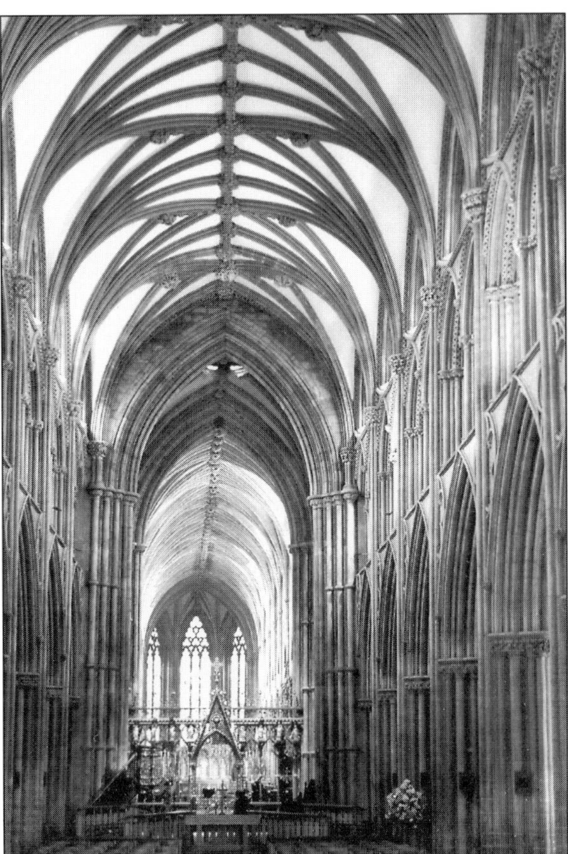

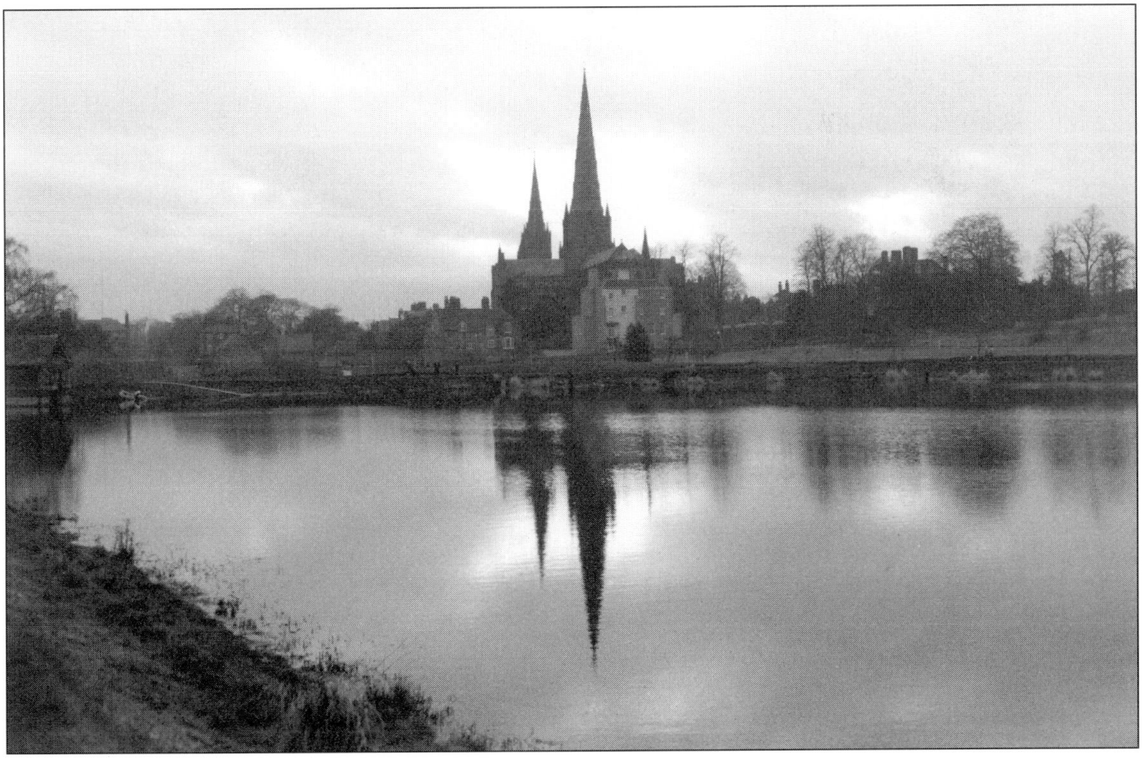

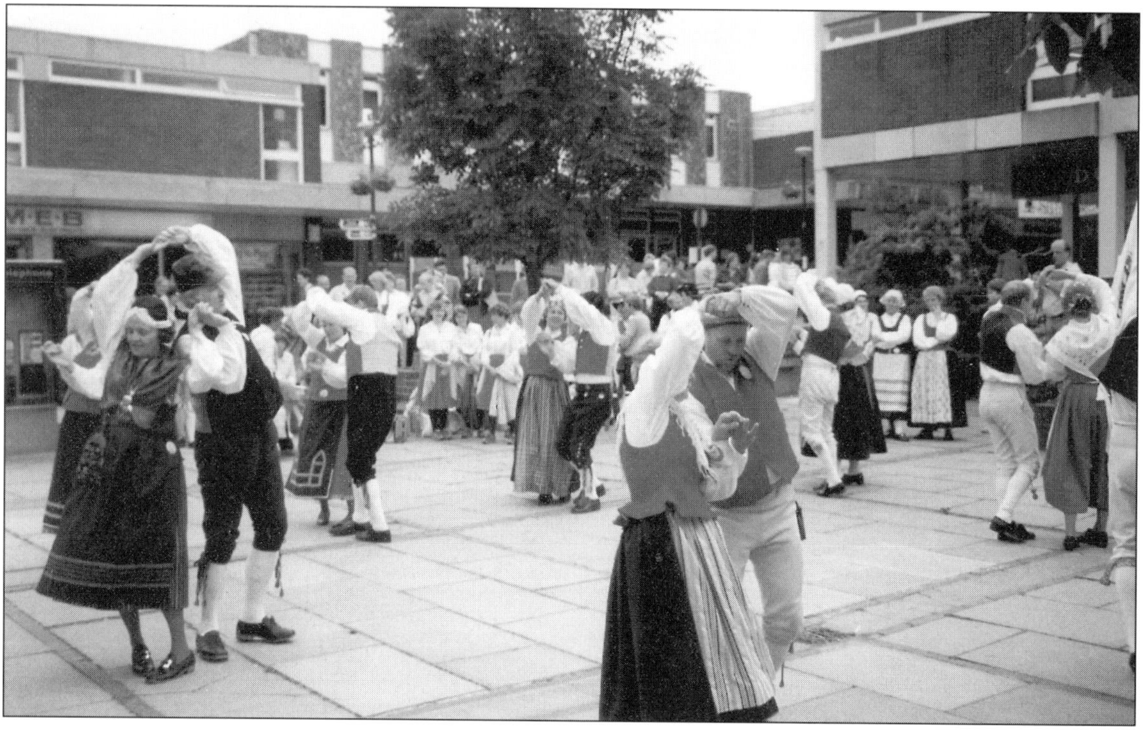

Morris dancing is often seen around the city. This visiting group from Scandinavia are seen performing in Levetts Square. The Three Spires Morris Group are in the centre of the scene.

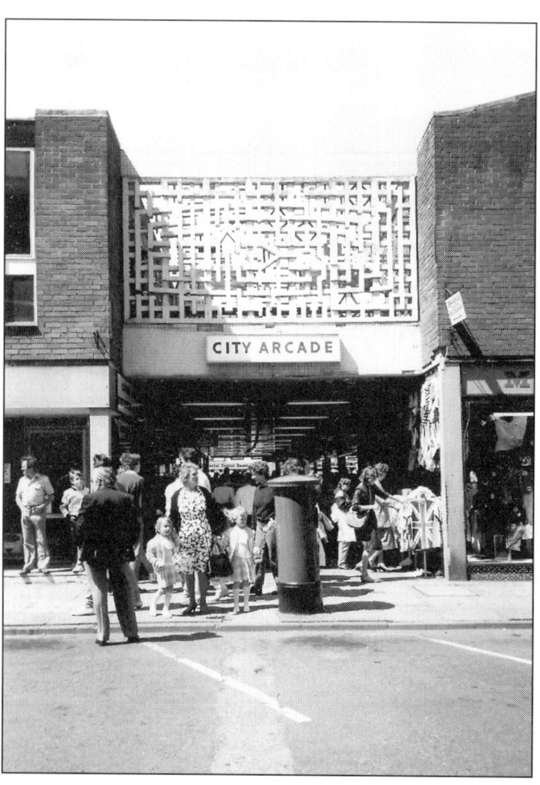

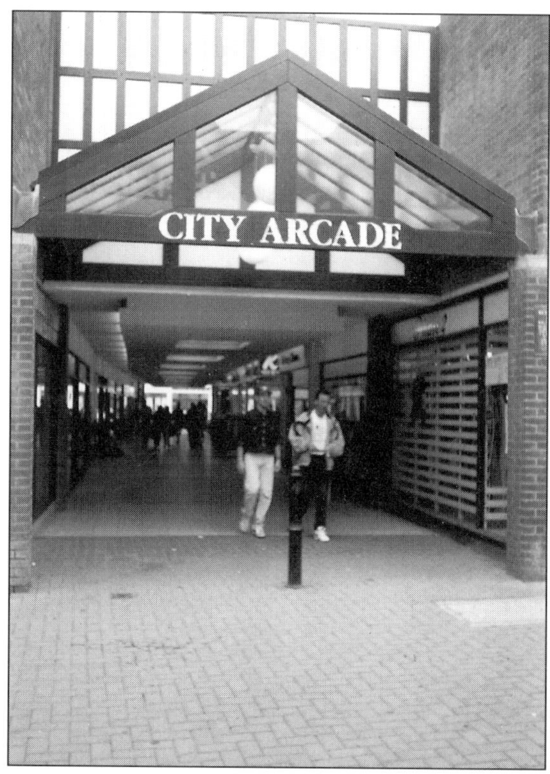

The city arcade in Bore Street, underwent some much needed improvements in 1992. It was originally built to replace Garretts Bakery which was pulled down c 1960.

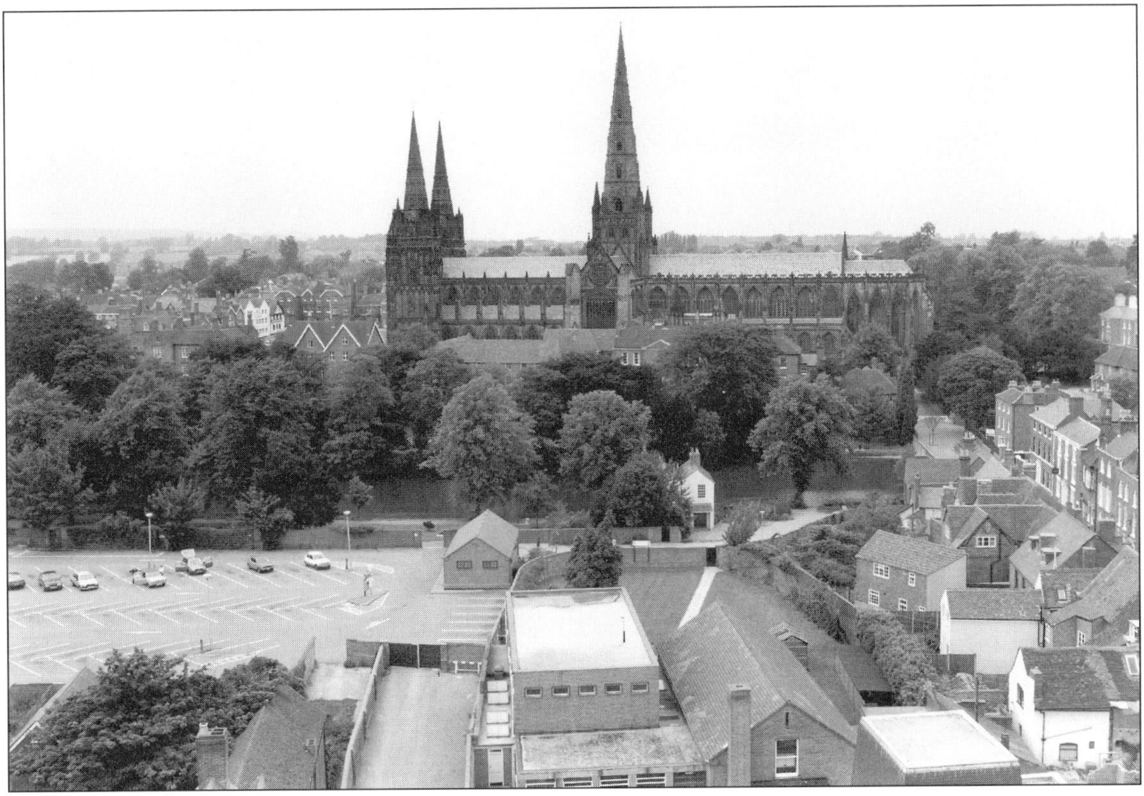

In 1992, St Mary's Guild Church in Market Square, which had opened in May 1981 as a Heritage Centre after the threat of closure in the 1970s, constructed a viewing platform from its west front and 192ft spire. The view of the cathedral is looking north toward Stafford whereas the other view following Bore Street and the Friary looks westward towards Burntwood.

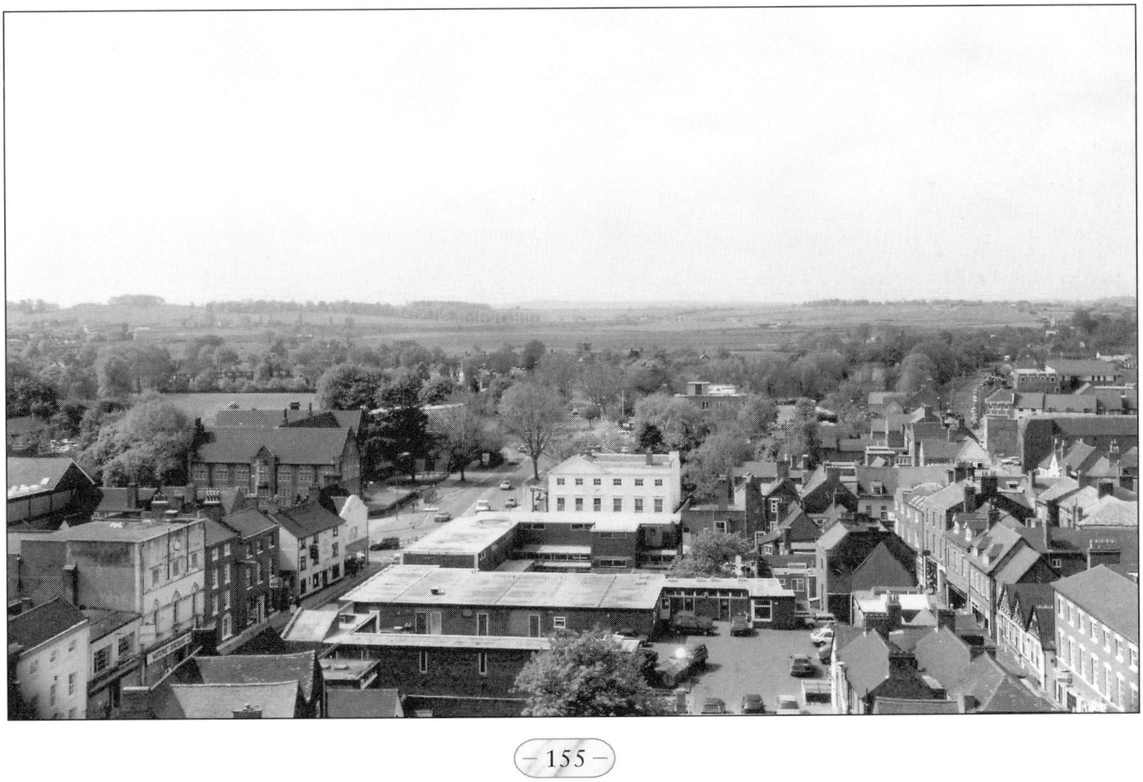

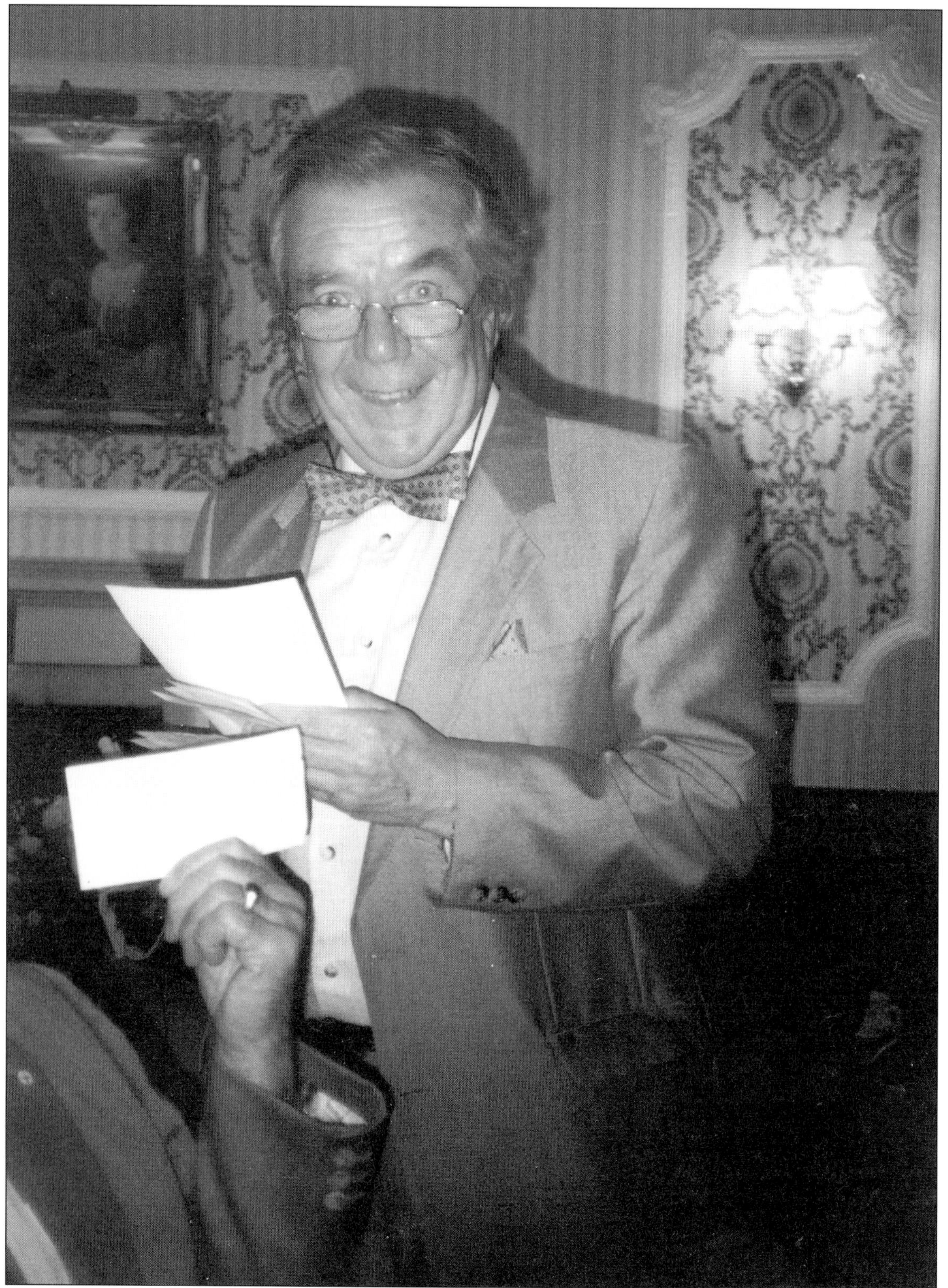

John Rackham, President of St Mary's Heritage Centre since 1994 looking happy and elated – every inch a Mister Pickwick.

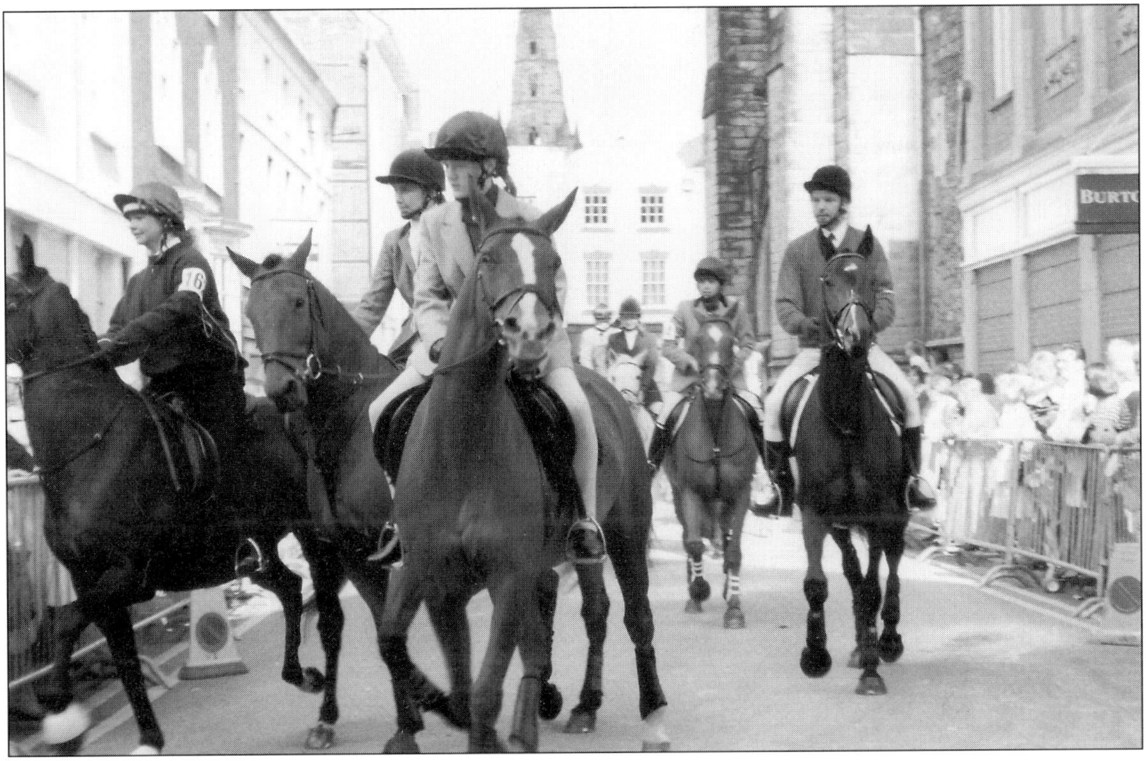

In 1994, the Sheriff was Cllr David Bailey. The Sheriff's Ride, an annual event which takes place every September, begins with the horses and riders gathering on the Market Place outside St Mary's and cantering up Breadmarket Street into Bore Street, to follow the mounted Sheriff and police riders. They are joined by jeeps and 4x4 vehicles to 'beat the bounds' of the 16 miles of the city boundary.

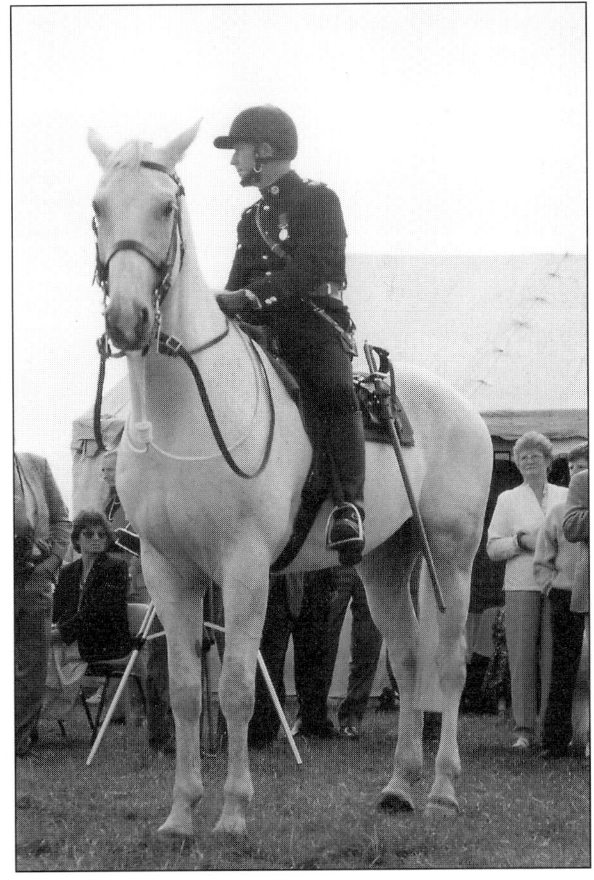

The presence of the calming influence of the police horses is always welcome.

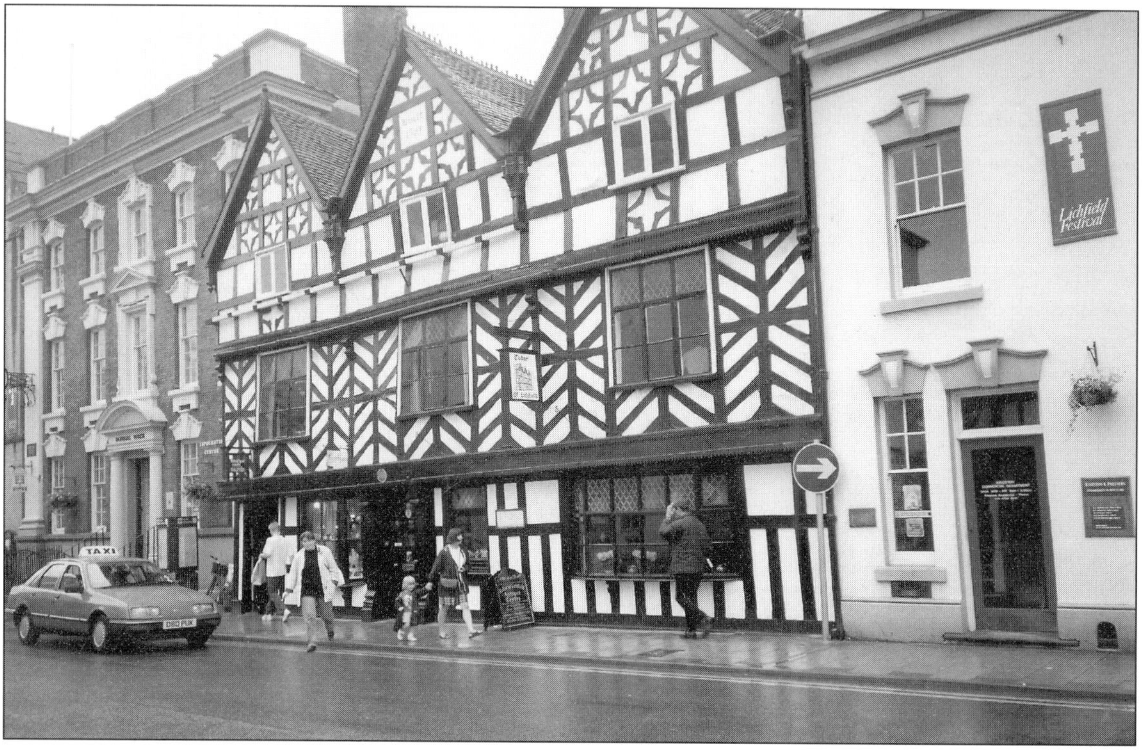

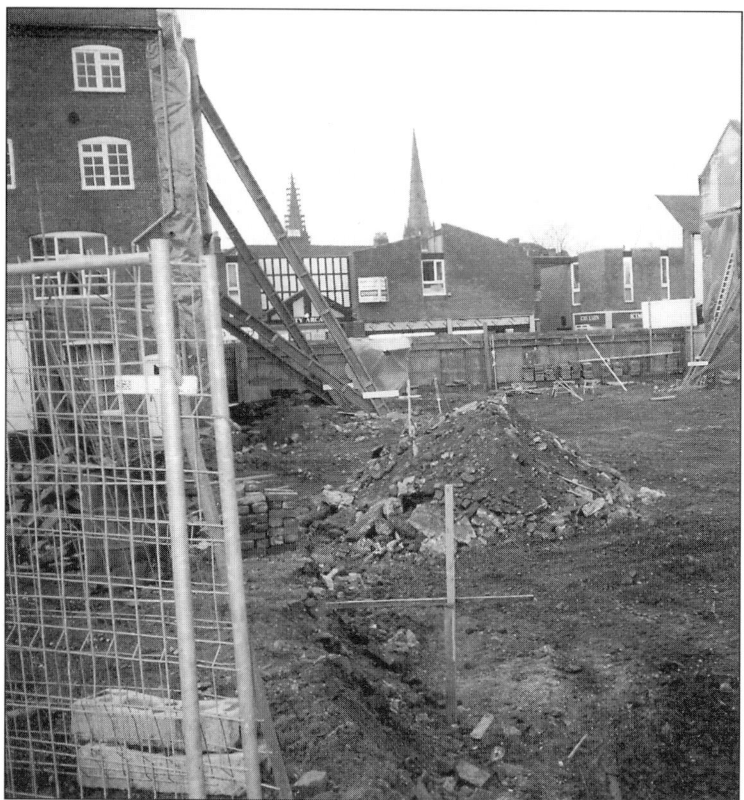

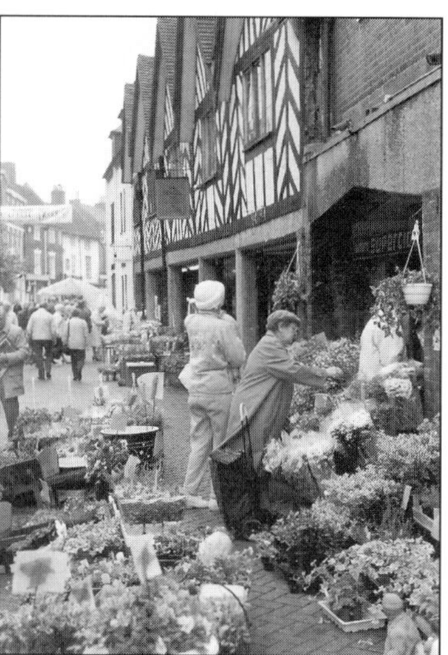

The Tudor buildings of the Five Gables and Tudor Café and the site of the old theatre cleared and ready for the new Wilkinsons store in Bore Street, 1993.

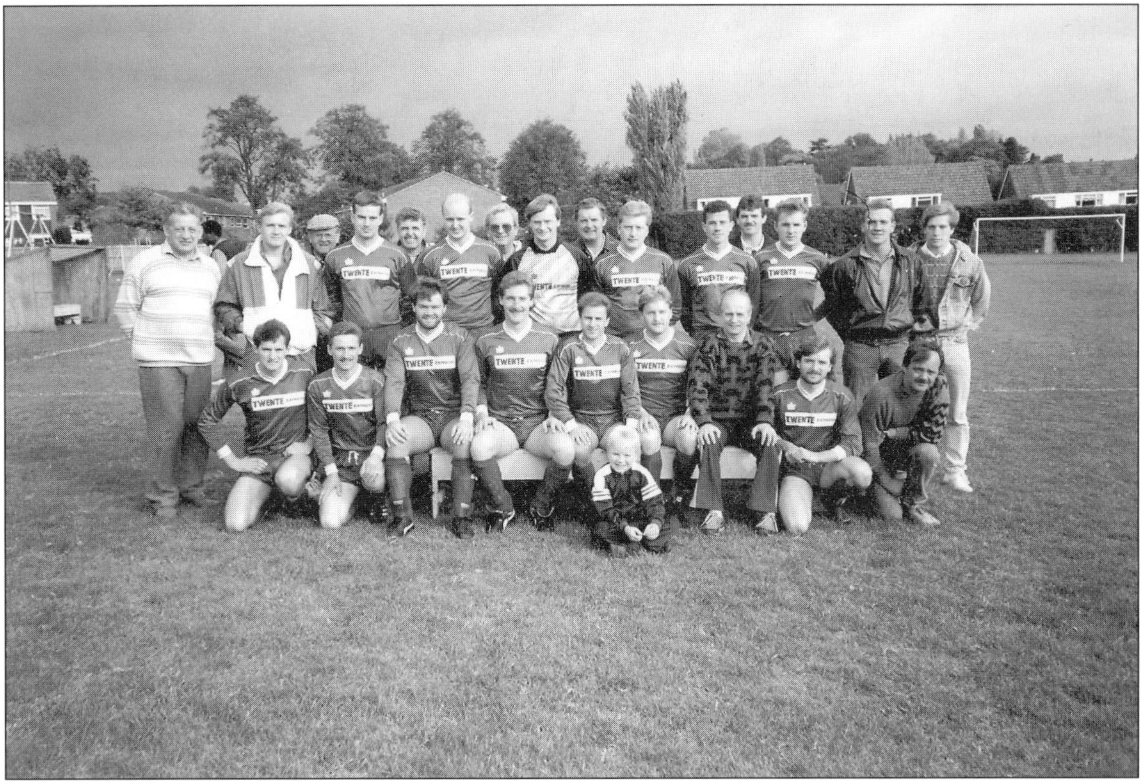

The sportsmen of Lichfield. Lichfield Soccer Team and Lichfield Cricket Club, Chesterfield Road.

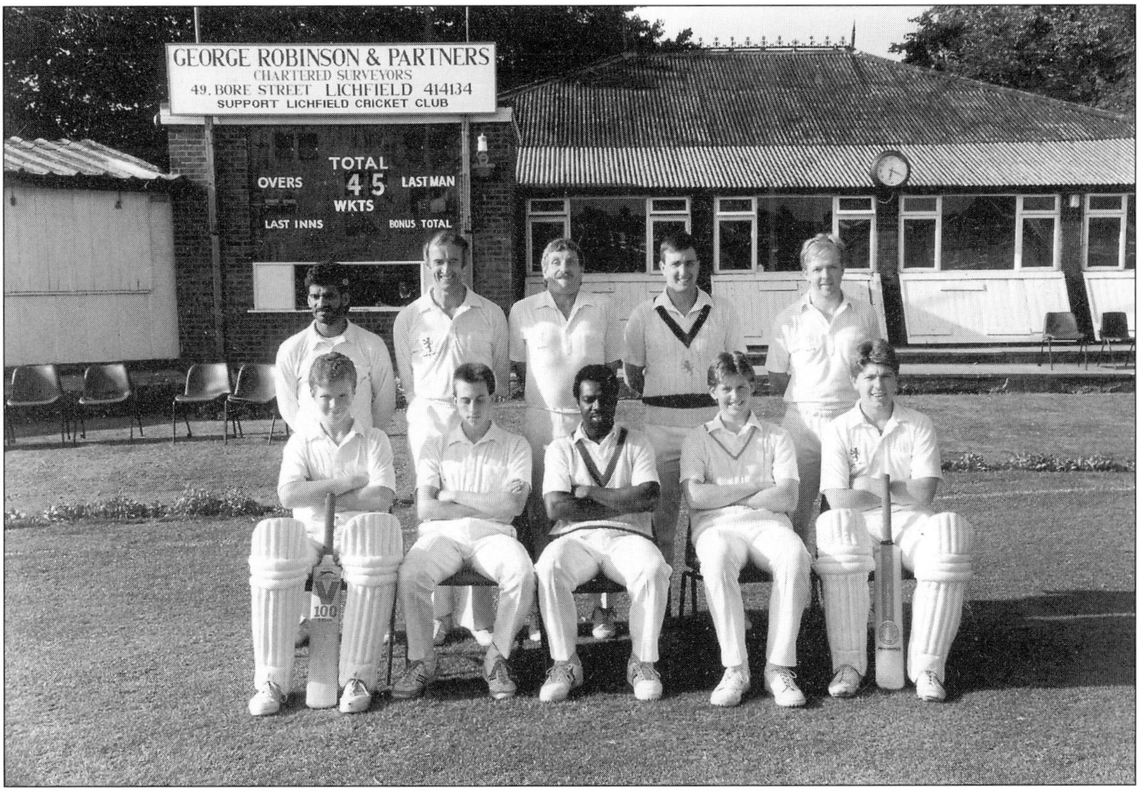

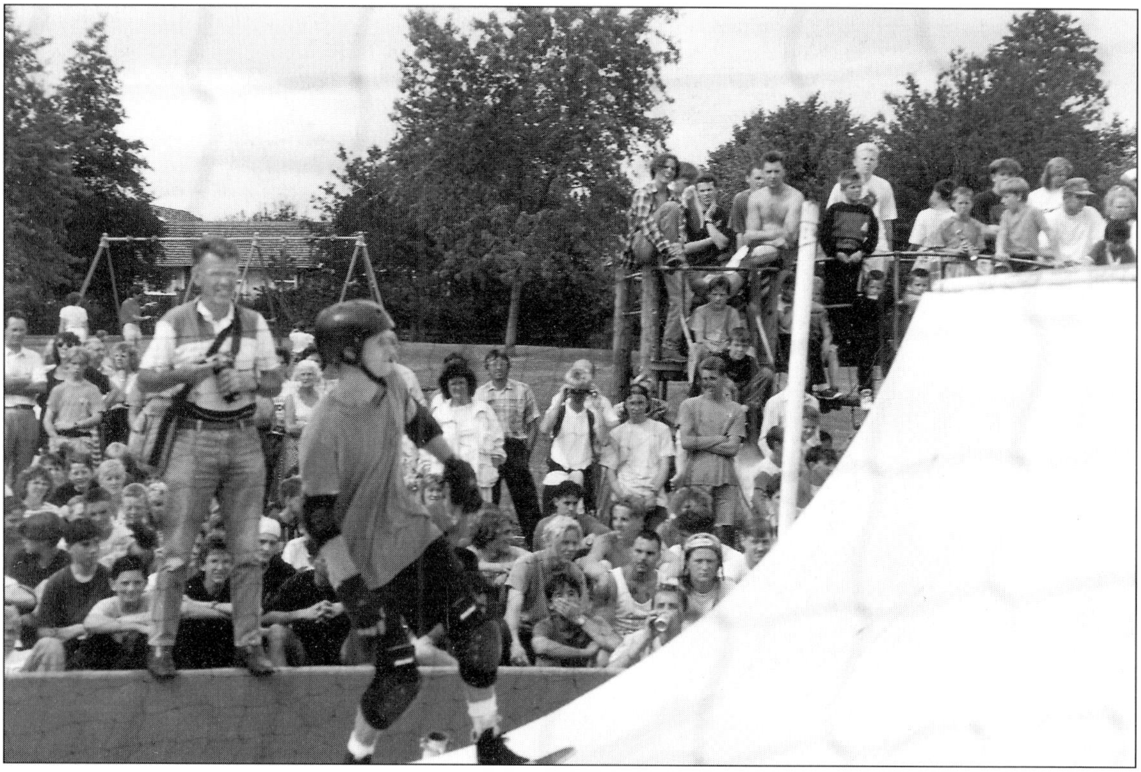

A skateboarding competition at Beacon Park, a newer form of sport for the high-flyers.

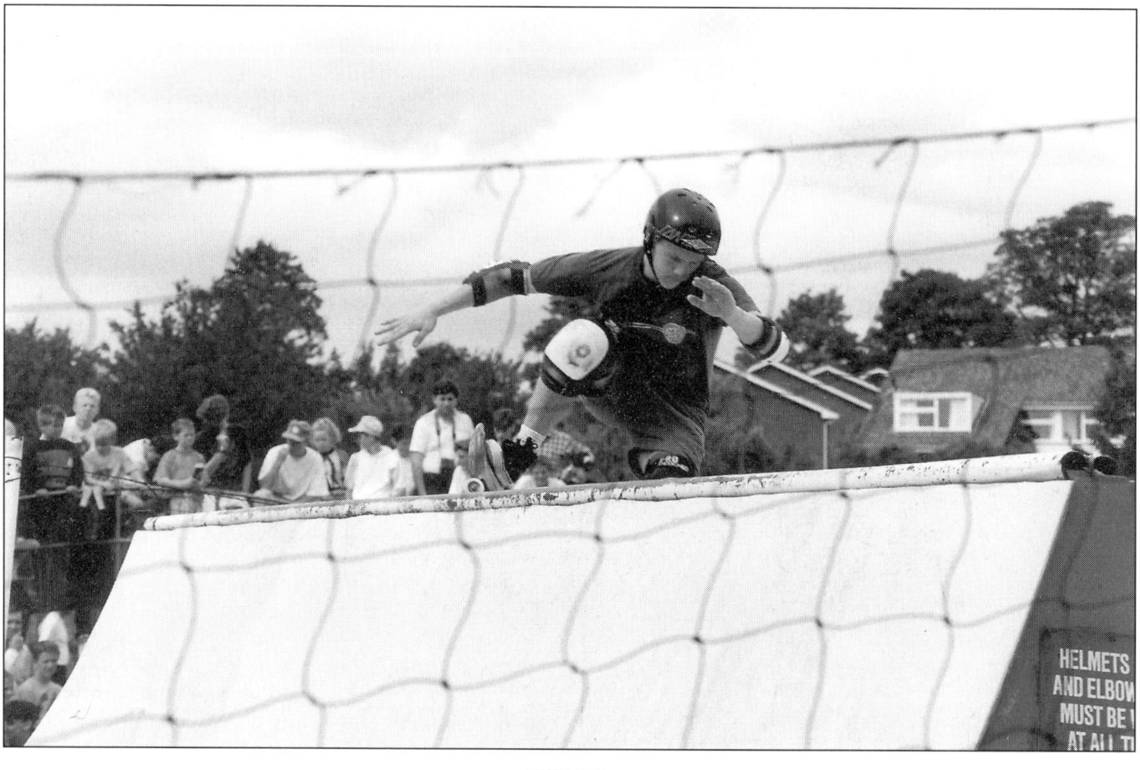

Right: Crowds making their way through the medieval market in Dam Street.

In 1994 the *Lichfield Mysteries*, twenty four plays depicting familiar tales from the old and new testaments, were performed for the first time as a community arts project. They were so popular with visitors and local people alike that they have become a triennial event in the city.

Below: *Exodus* being performed in Stowe Fields.

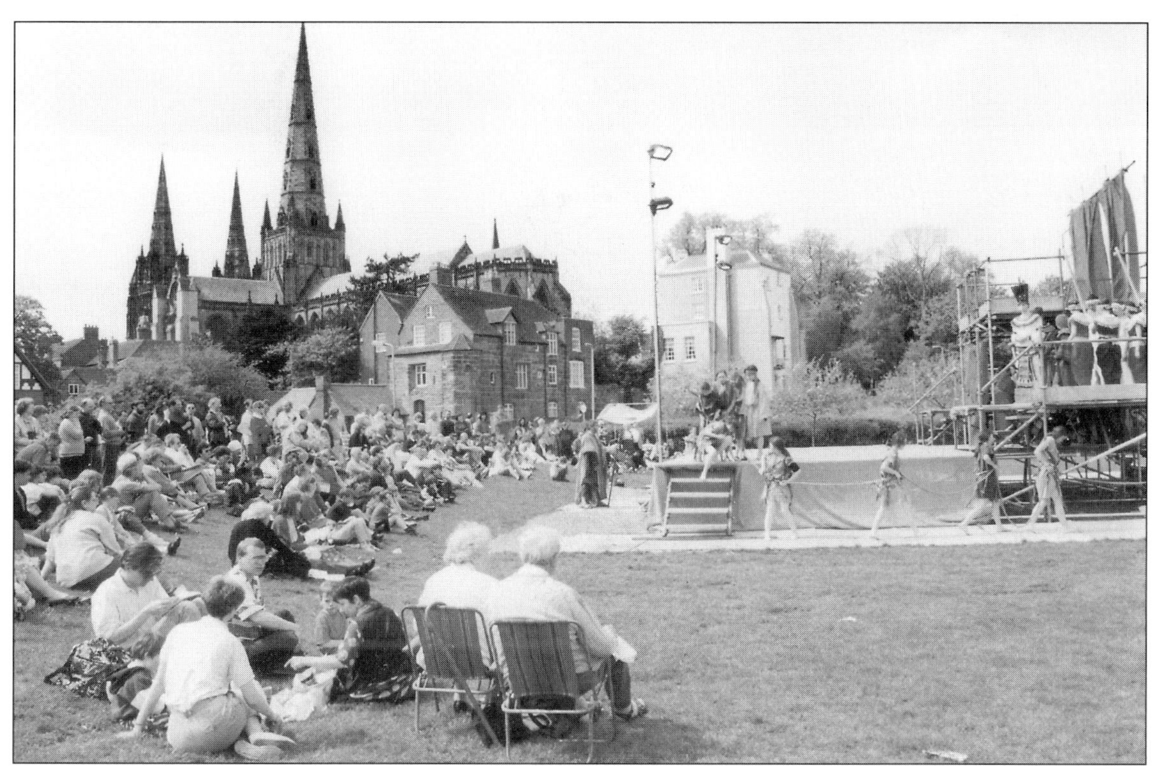

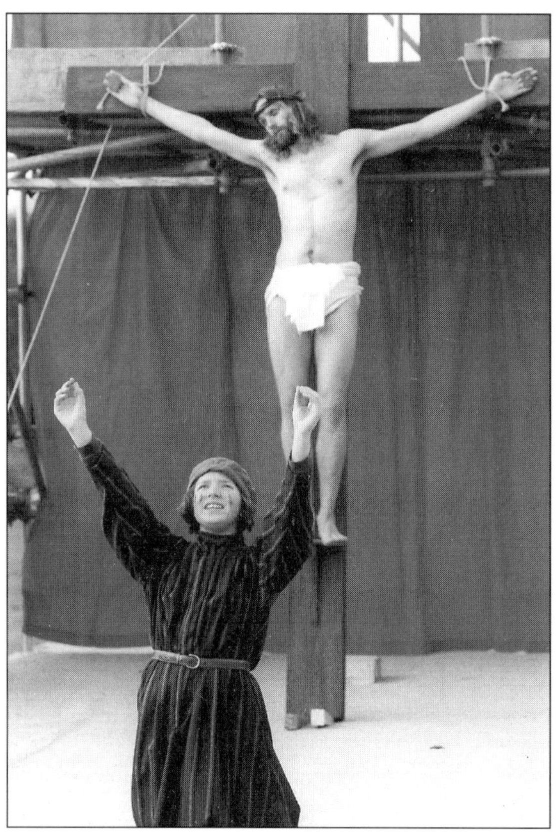

The crucifixion with Rev Ian Hayter as Jesus.

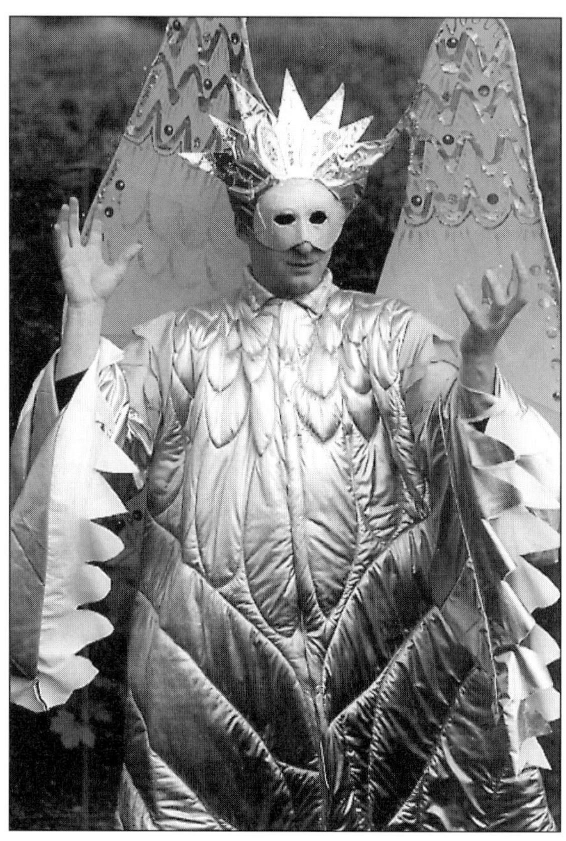

Angelic intervention by the angel Gabriel.

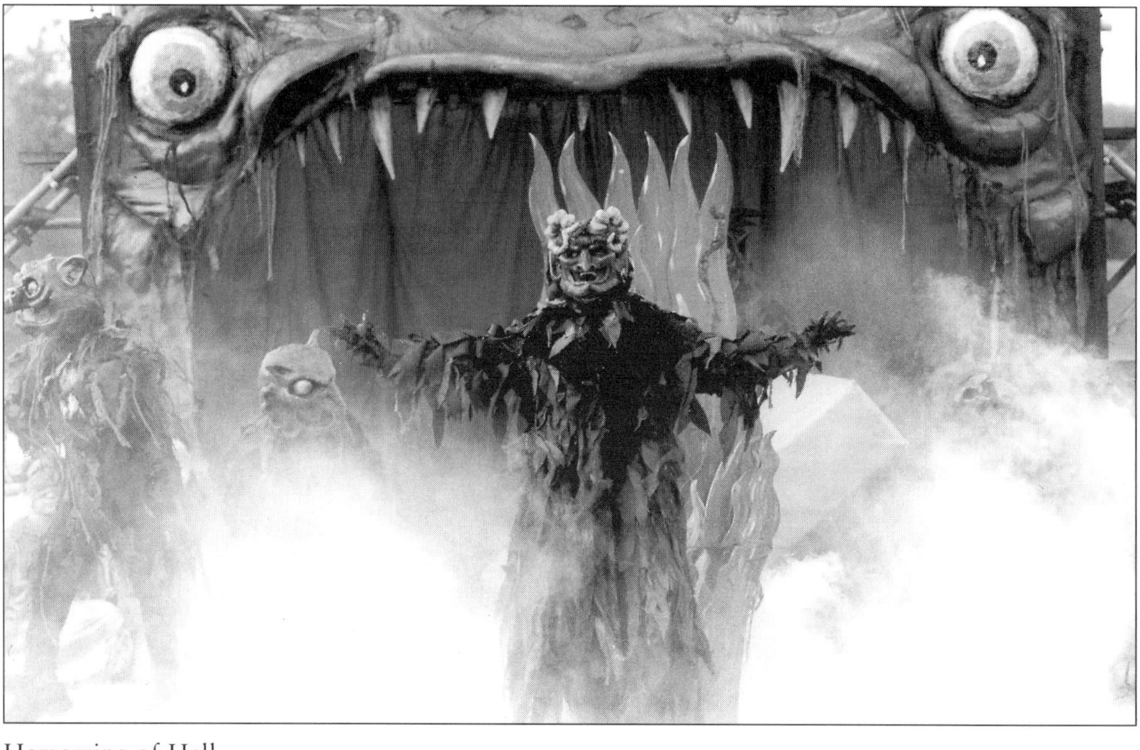

Harrowing of Hell.

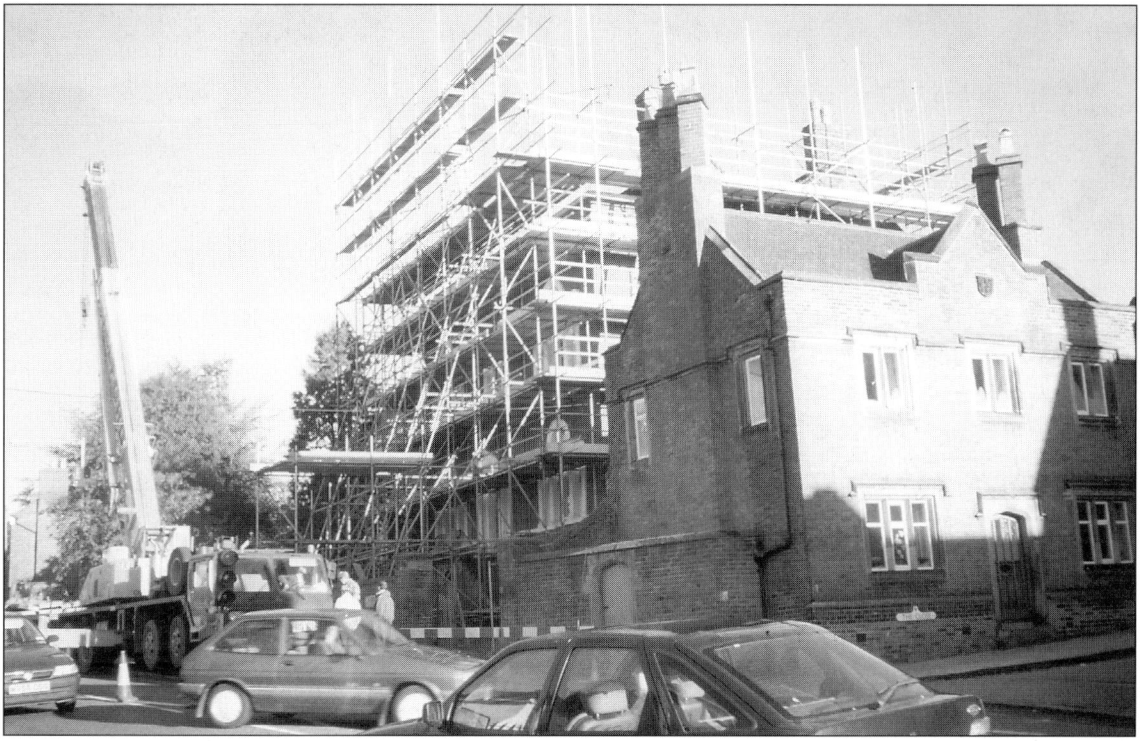

Above: Darwin House festooned in scaffolding – were you one of the unlucky drivers caught up in the traffic jam in 1997?

In 1994, the Royal Society of Medicine's History Section met in Lichfield at the visitor's study centre. Part of the programme was a talk about Erasmus Darwin the noted eighteenth century physician, botanist, inventor, poet and philosopher, indeed, a polymath and grandfather of evolution. He had lived and worked in Lichfield for twenty three years, from 1758-1781. The talk was followed by a visit to his house in Beacon Street which had stood empty and neglected for a considerable time. Extensive work was needed to restore this fine Georgian house to its former glory. The seeds of an idea were sown and a plan formulated to achieve the ultimate goal of a fitting memorial to a great man, which would be open to the public and would develop educational resources in the multiple fields in which he was eminent.

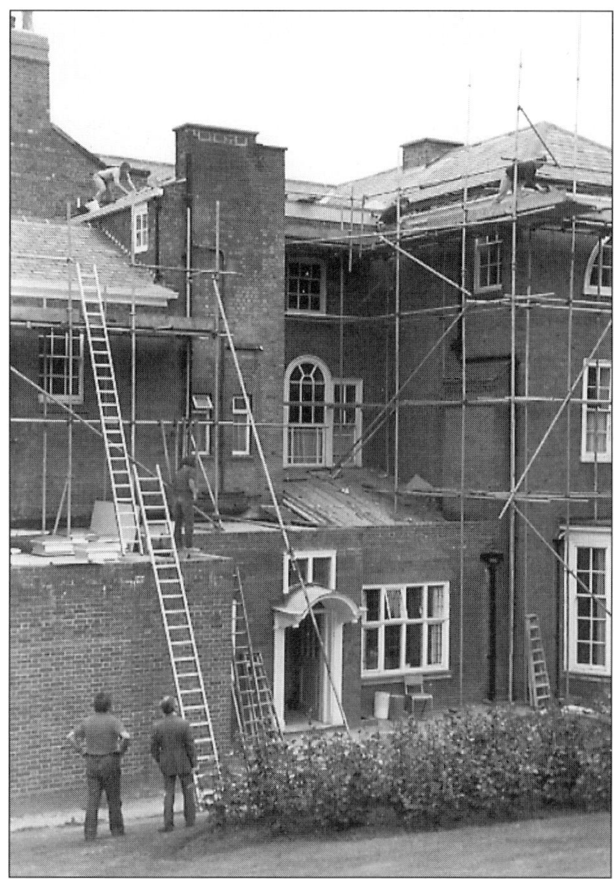

Right: At work on the rear of Darwin House.

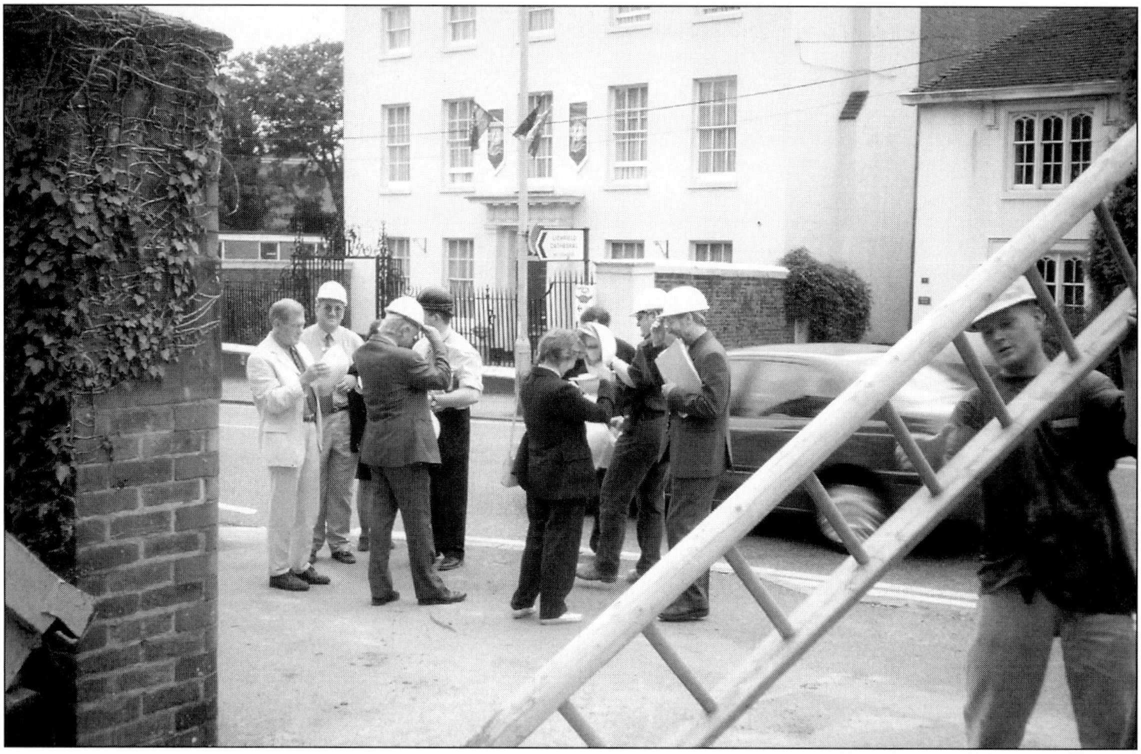

Hard hats must be worn on a building site.

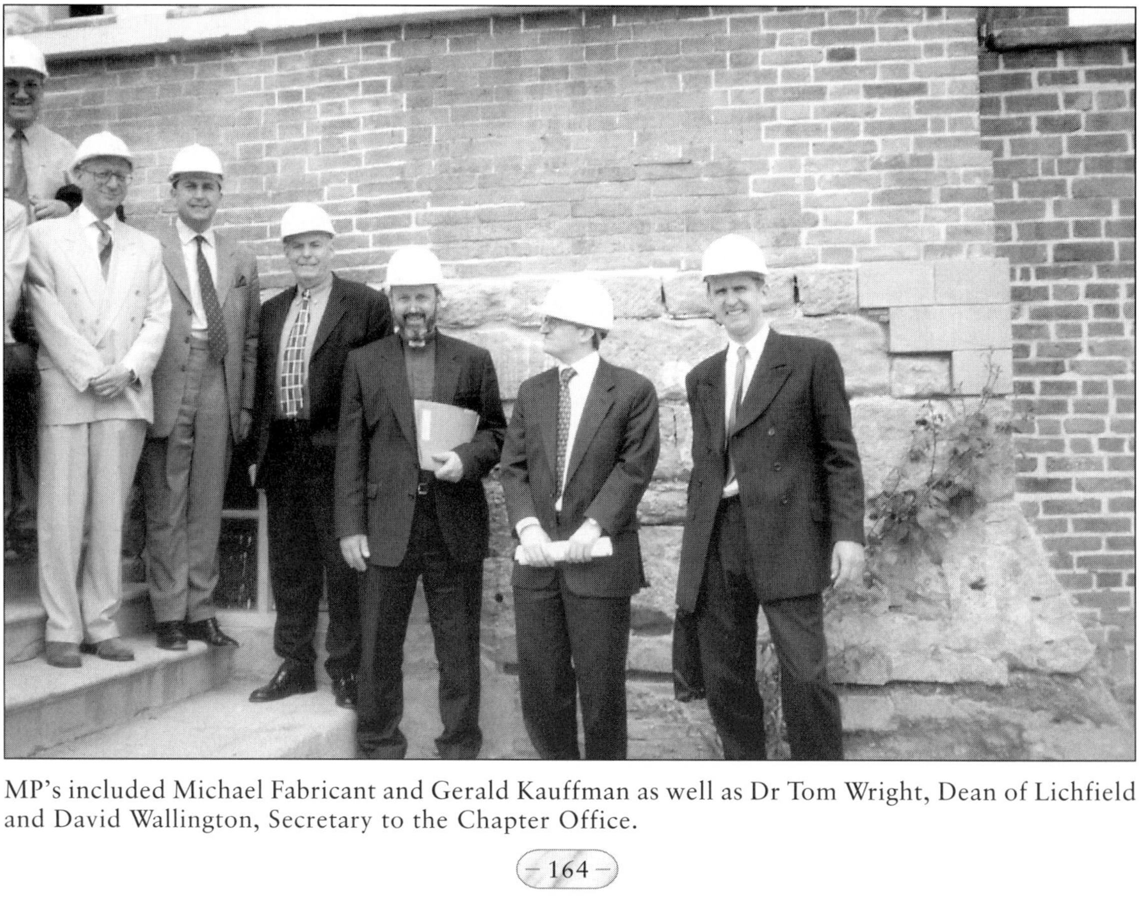

MP's included Michael Fabricant and Gerald Kauffman as well as Dr Tom Wright, Dean of Lichfield and David Wallington, Secretary to the Chapter Office.

Darwin House gardens before restoration.

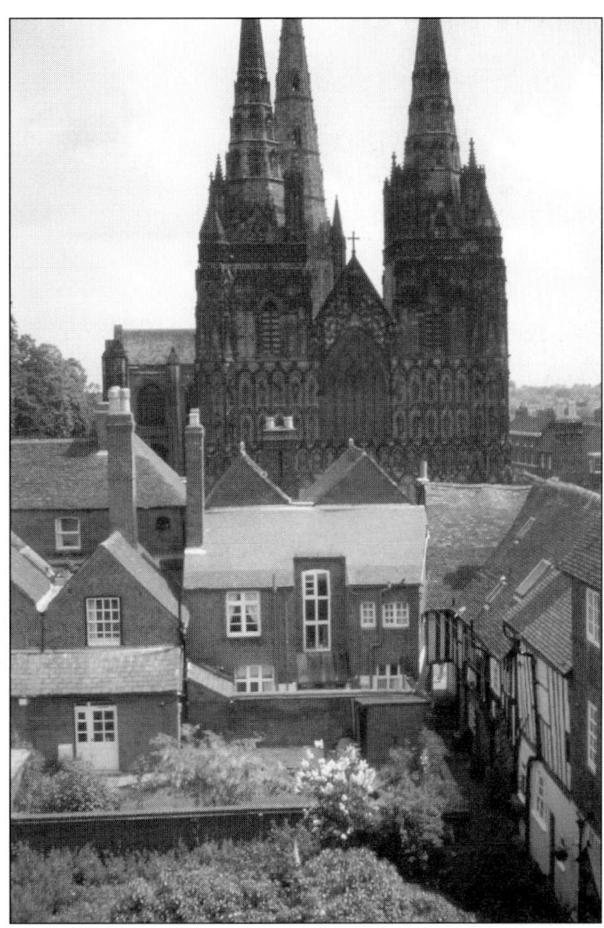

Many plants of special interest are included in the restored and tranquil gardens.

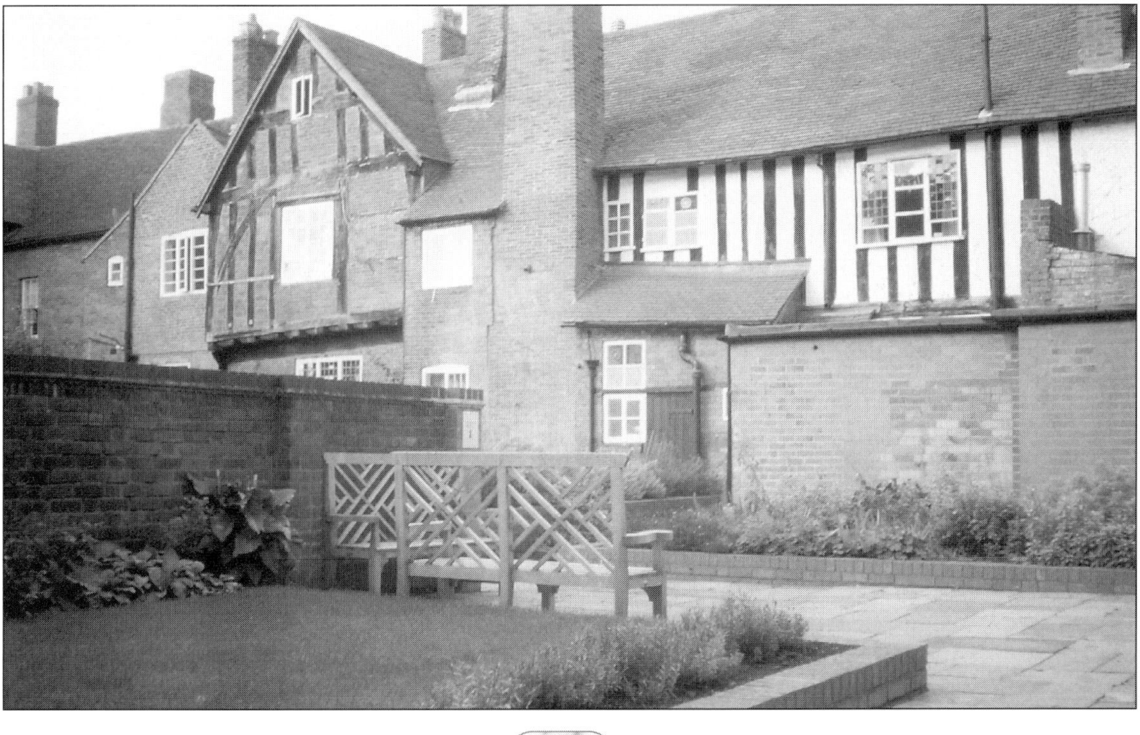

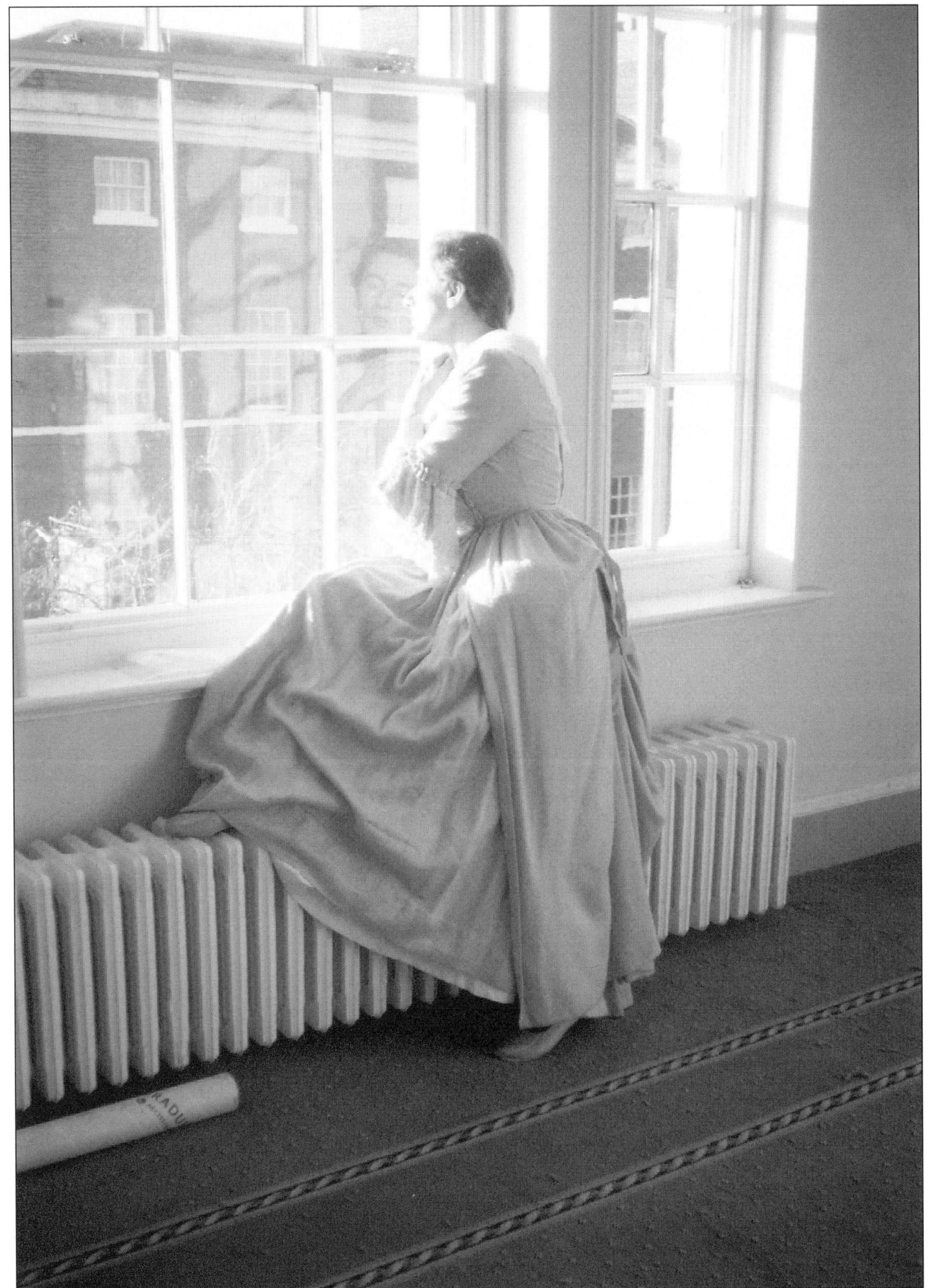

Lorna Bushell in period costume.

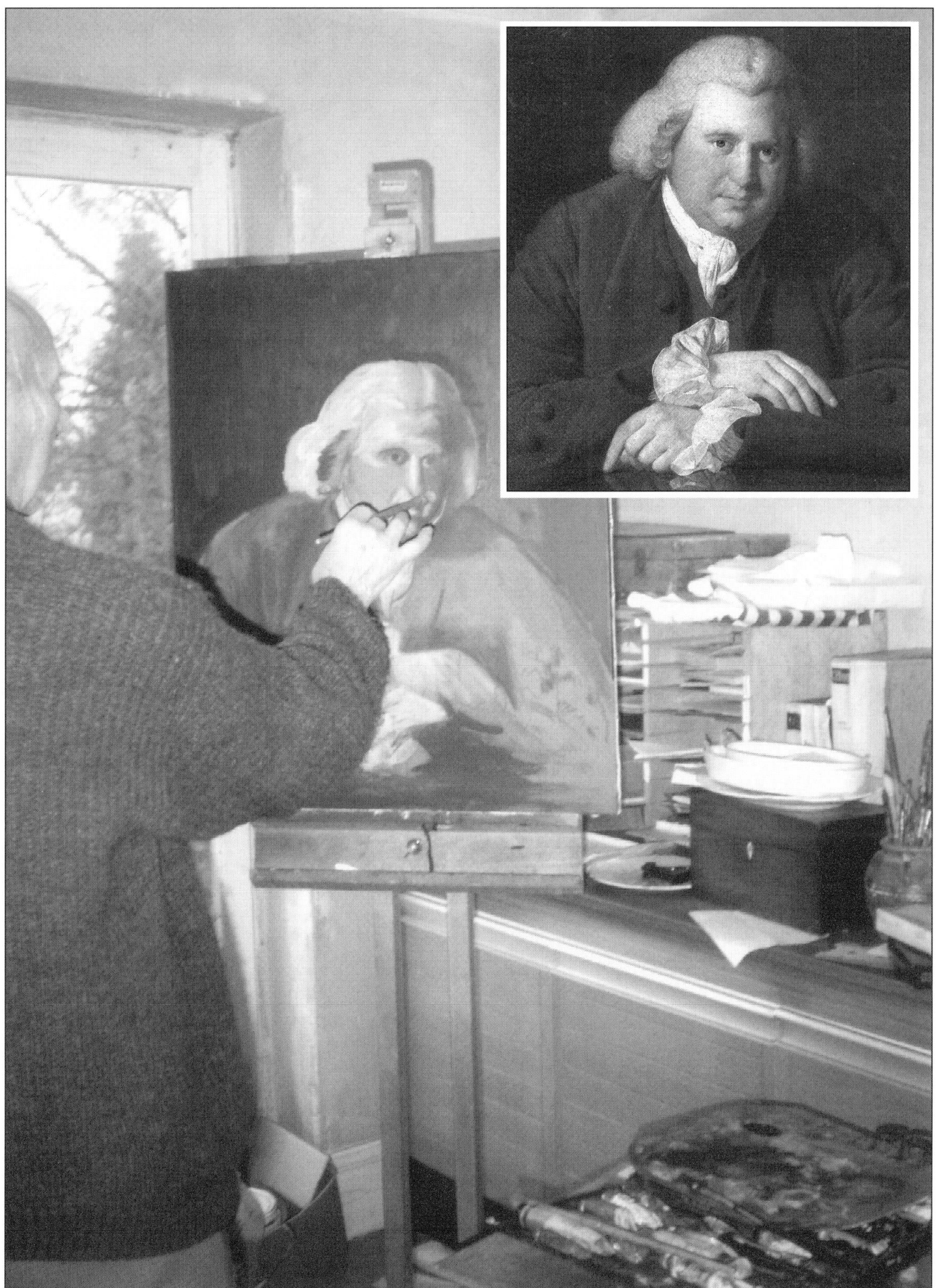

John Sanders MBE, co-founder of the Erasmus Darwin Foundation at work in his studio on a portrait of the great man. **Inset:** Erasmus Darwin.

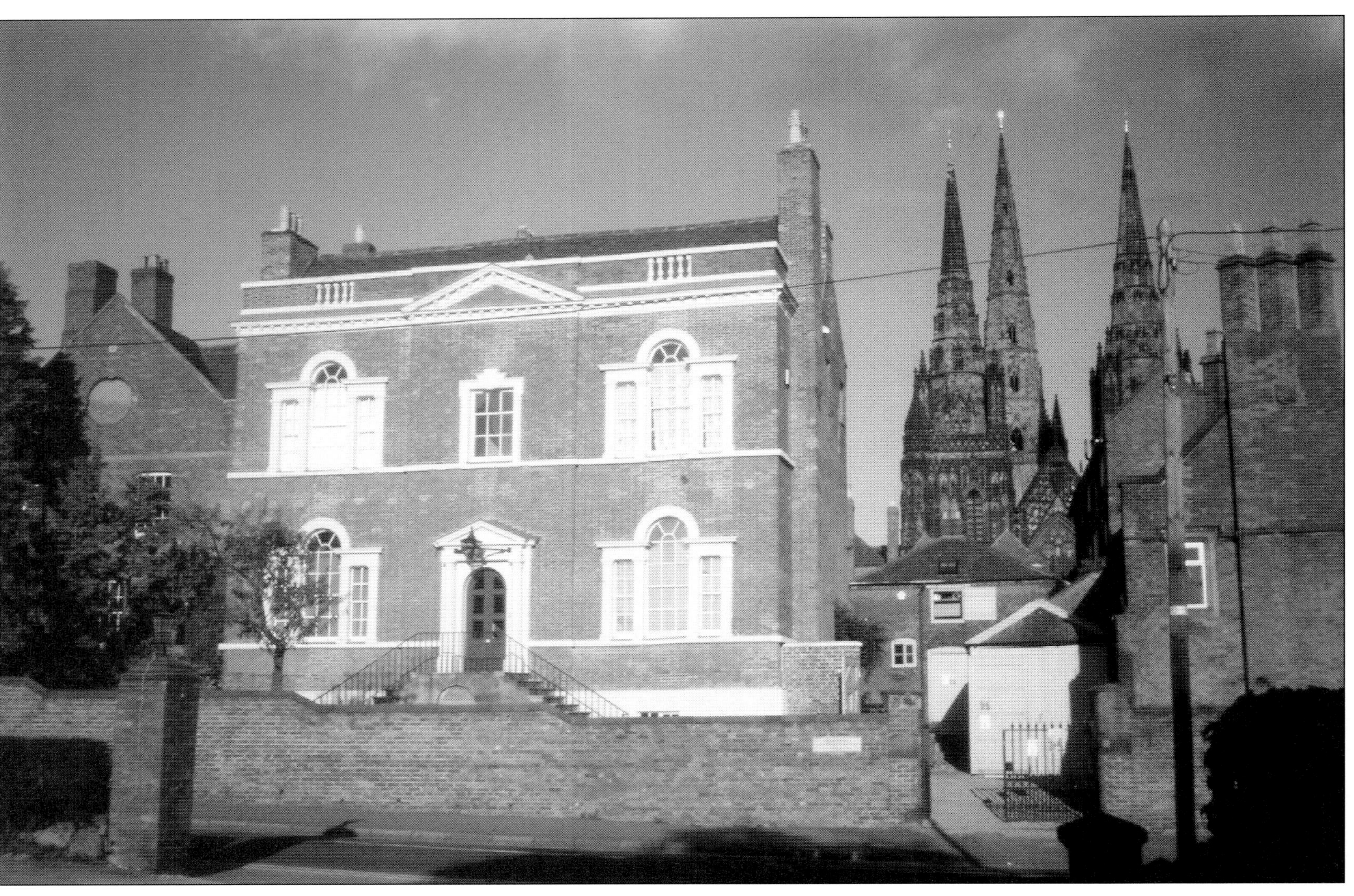

Darwin House, completed in August 1998 and officially opened on Easter Monday 1999, as it would have looked when it was the family home two centuries ago.

Sue Smith, Head of Leisure Services, Lichfield Distrct Council with the statue which symbolises Time compelling a reluctant Youth to go with him.

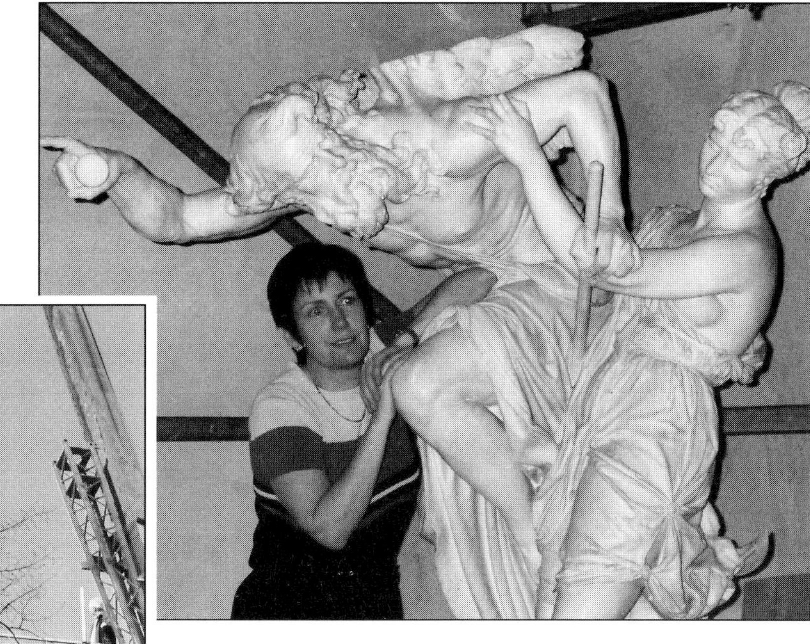

In March 1999, the magnificent marble statue affectionately known as *Old Father Time*, which had been bequeathed to the people of Lichfield by Colonel Swinfen Broun and housed in the museum above the library in Beacon Street, was removed through the roof of the building and taken to be restored prior to it becoming part of the site dedicated to Lichfield at the National Arboretum, Alrewas.

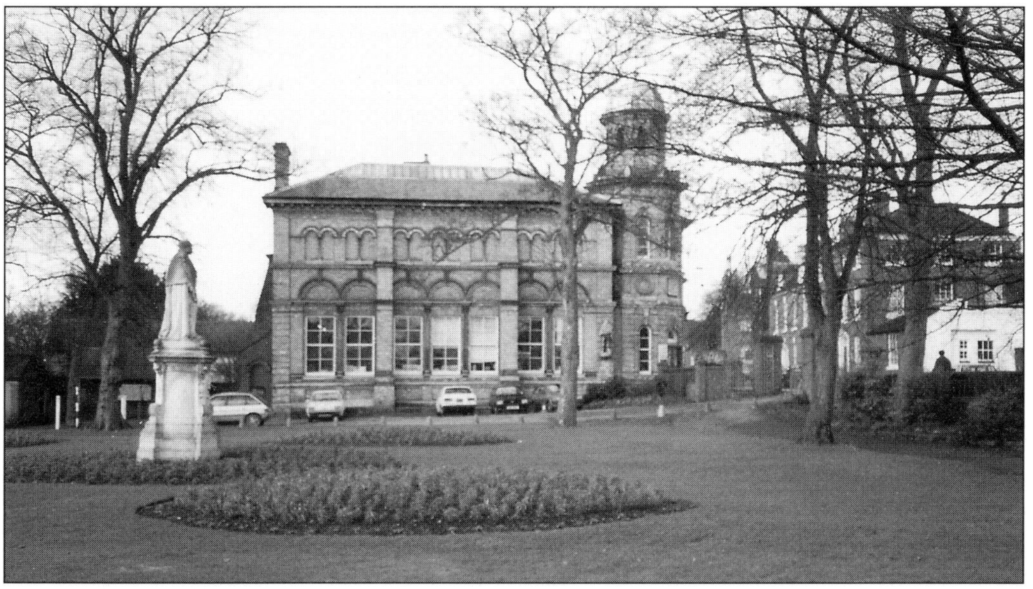

The old Public Library, museum and art gallery viewed from Museum Gardens, Beacon Street watched over by a statue of King Edward VII.

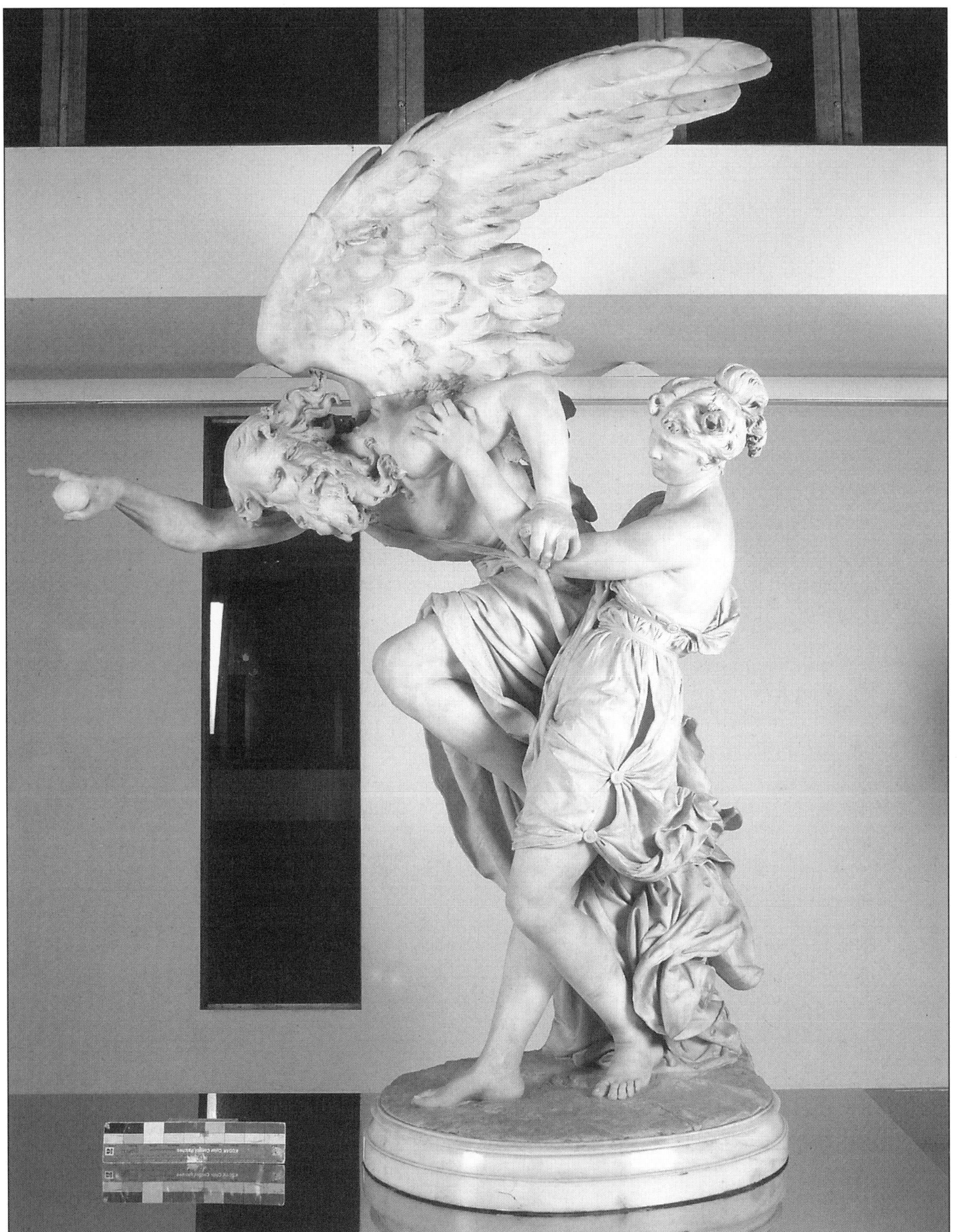

Old Father Time seen here in all his glory.

Opposite page: Thomas Rowley's Drinking Fountain originally attached to the old Library, Beacon Street on the south side of the building and removed by the council within living memory. Where is it now?

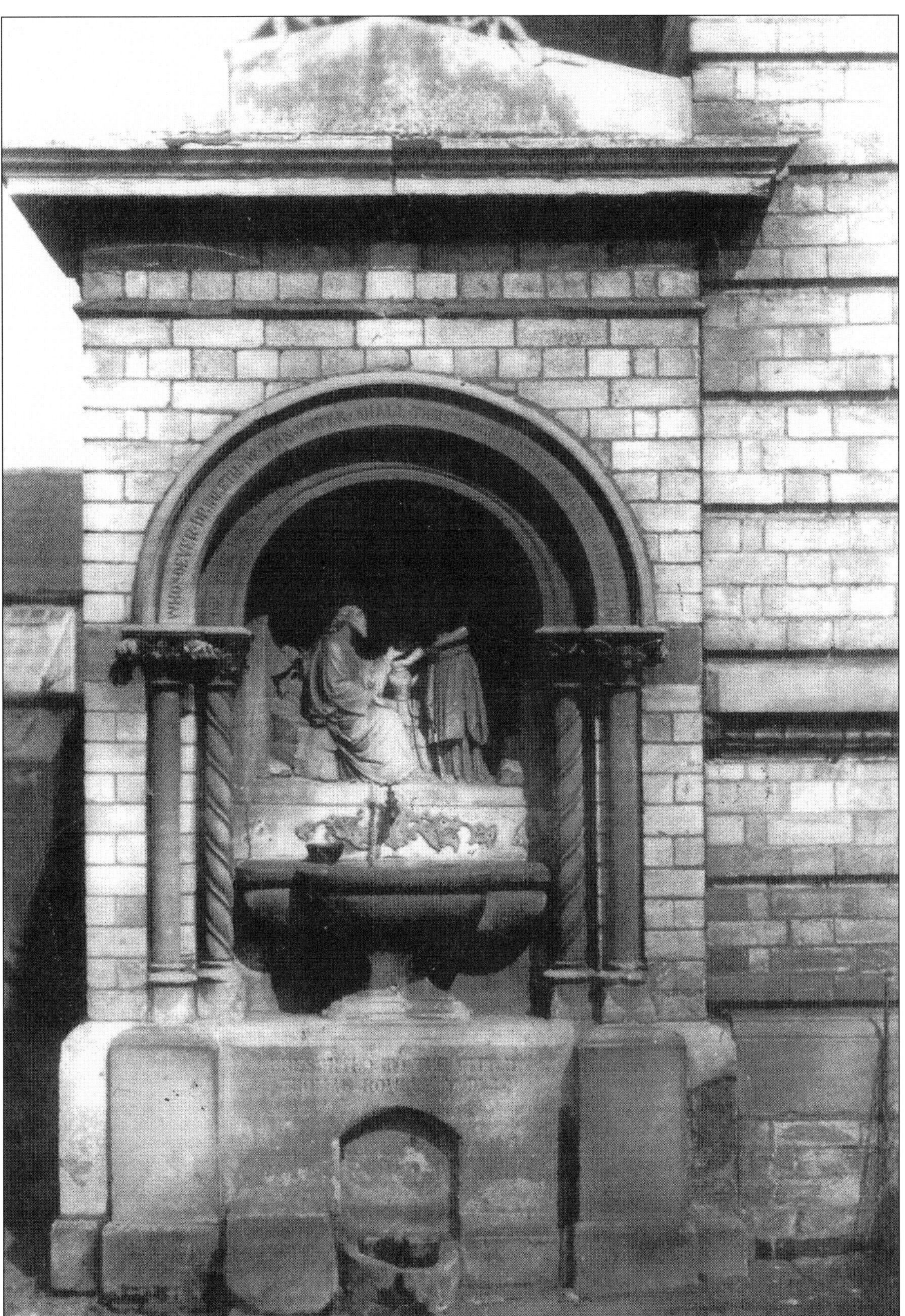

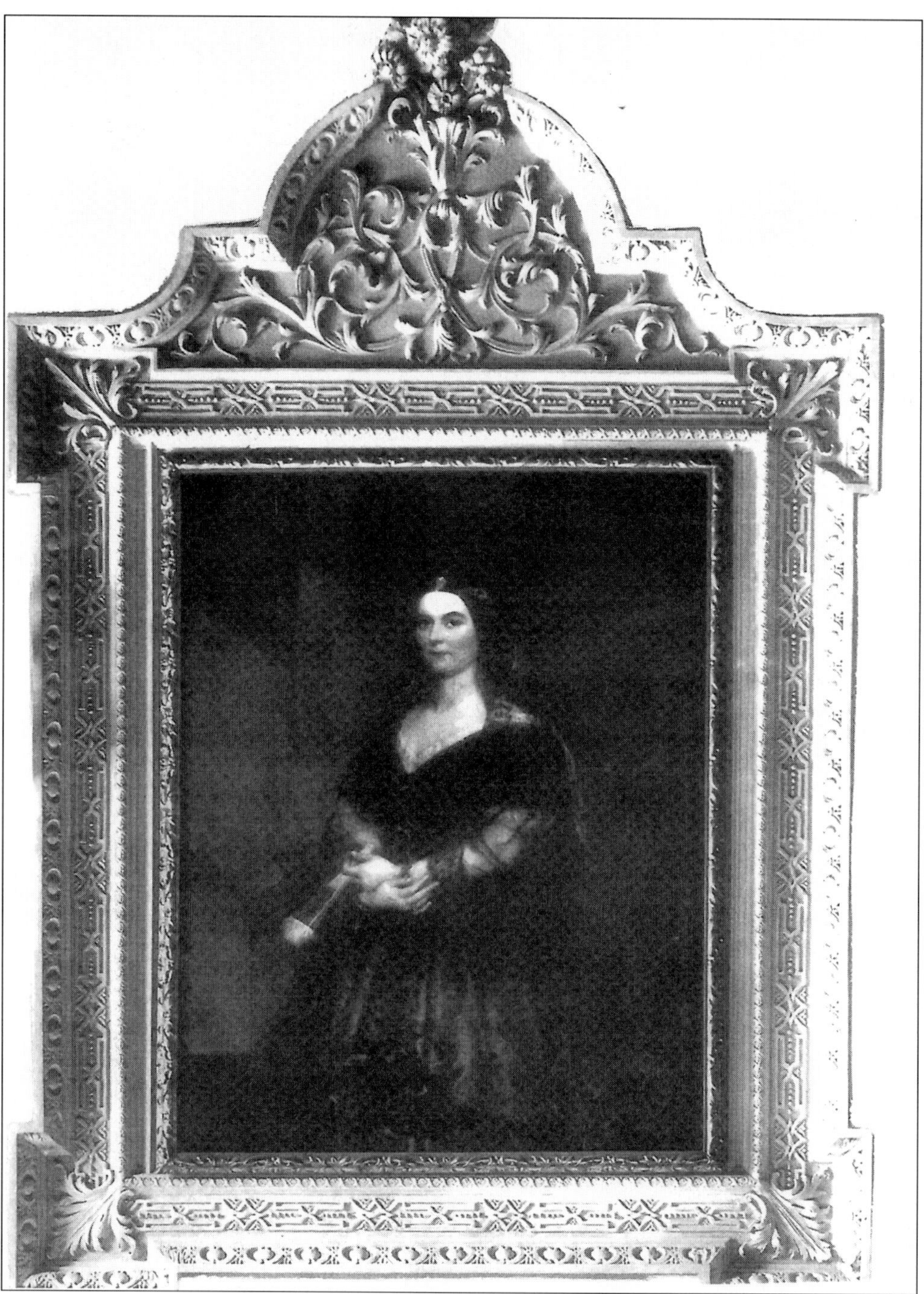

Dr Thomas Rowley was a physician in Lichfield in the nineteenth century. He was a friend of Patience Swinfen of Swinfen Hall and had been called upon to witness the will and later to sign the death certificate of Samuel Swinfen her father-in-law. With his death on 26th July 1854, the Swinfen estate passed to her at his bequest, as his son Henry had pre-deceased him. The stage was thus set for the biggest legal battle that Lichfield had known, reaching as high as the Lord Chancellor of England. It became a *cause celèbre* with Patience Swinfen the heroine.

The painting of Patience Swinfen by Samuel West hung in the left hand panel of the entrance hall at Swinfen was sold at auction in 1948. If anyone knows of its whereabouts, the authors would like to hear from you as its location has become their Millennium Quest.

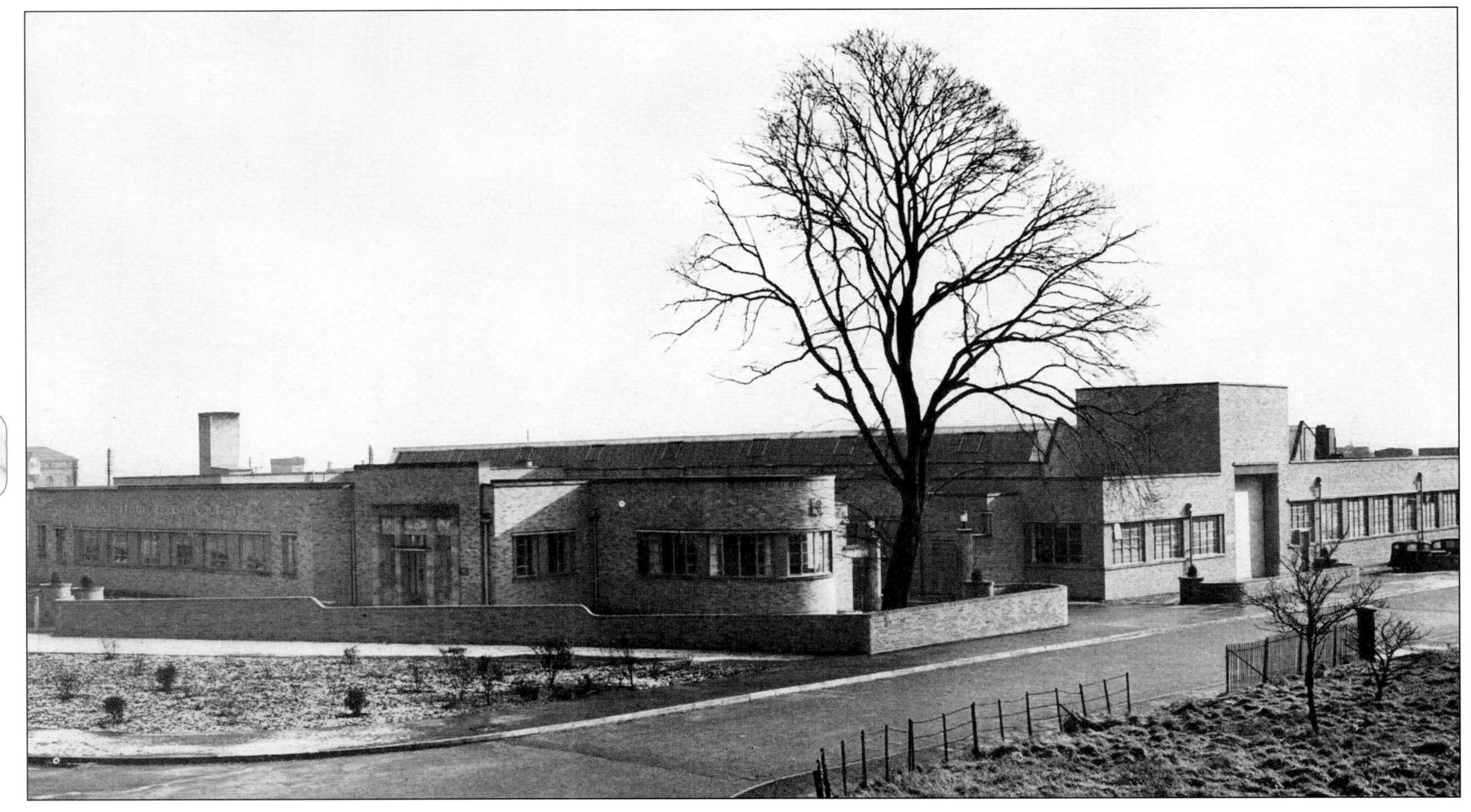

GKN Sinter Metals in Trent Valley Road celebrated its 50th anniversary in June 1999 and underwent major refurbishment in preparation for GKN's new image for the Millennium. The factory, which manufactures car components, first opened its gates in the city in 1949 and was formerly known as GKN Bound Brook.

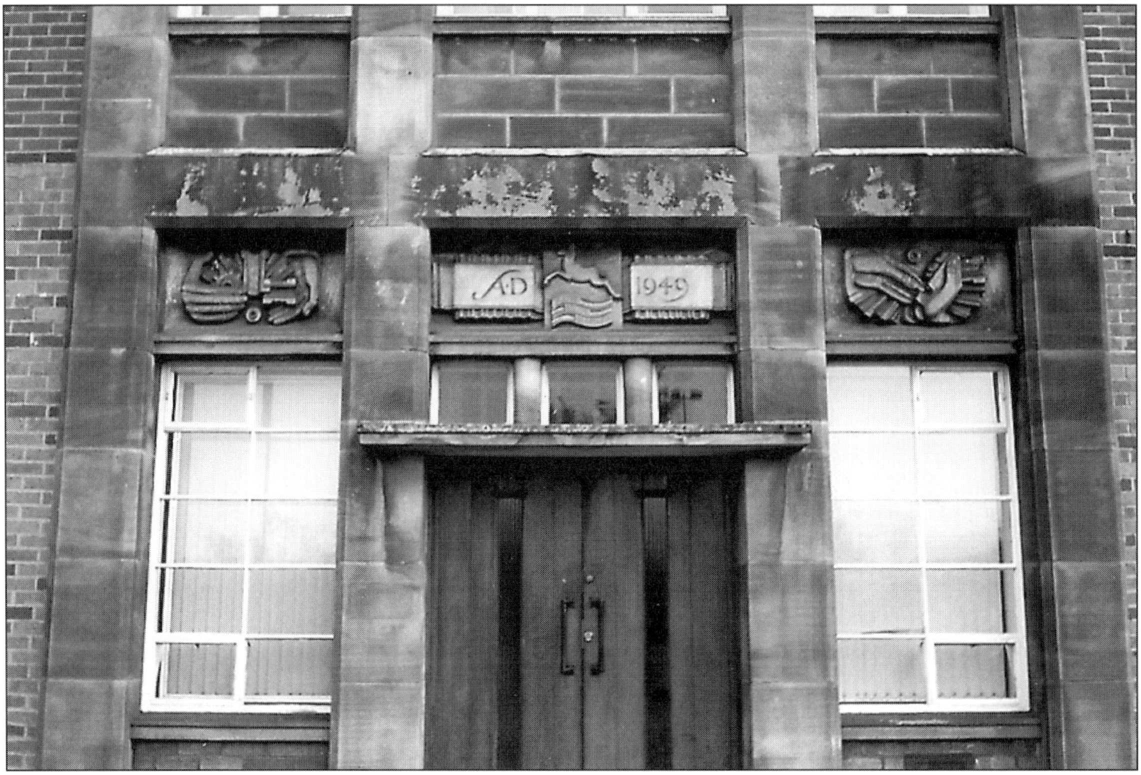

The relief panel above the original entrance doorway, depicting the Bound Brook emblem of a leaping deer and AD1949 in the centre panel, and stylised hands holding machine parts or measuring in the side panels. It is now restored and set in a free standing panel within an architectural feature, garden and paved area fronting Trent Valley Road.

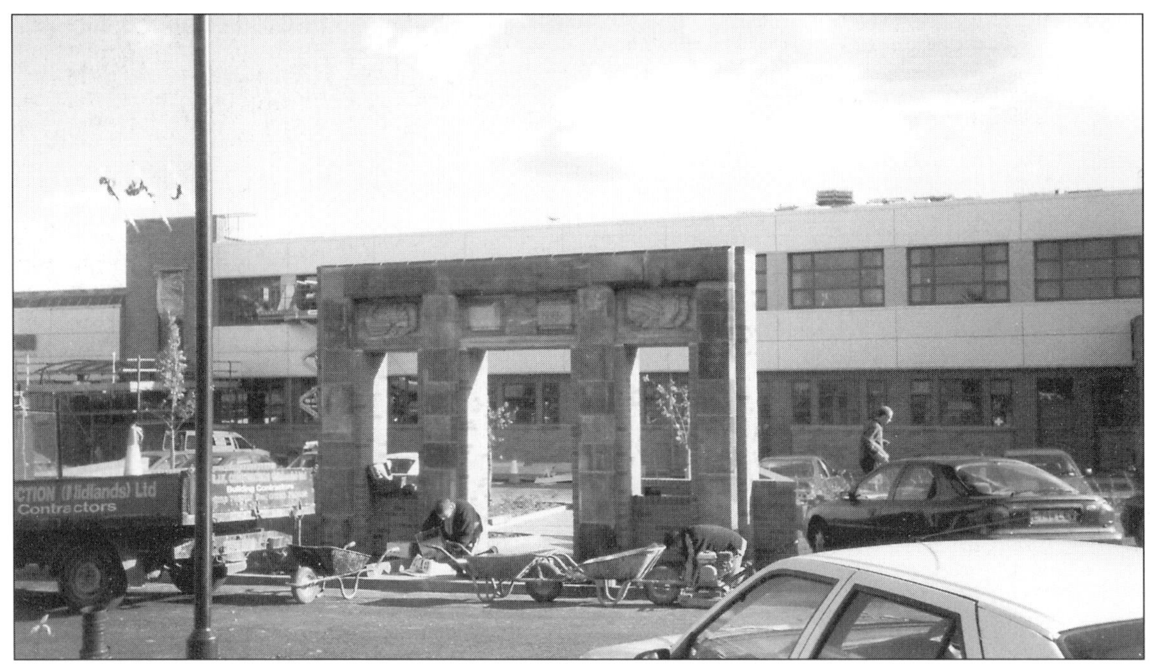

At work on the free standing panel in front of the new look GKN Sinter Metals.

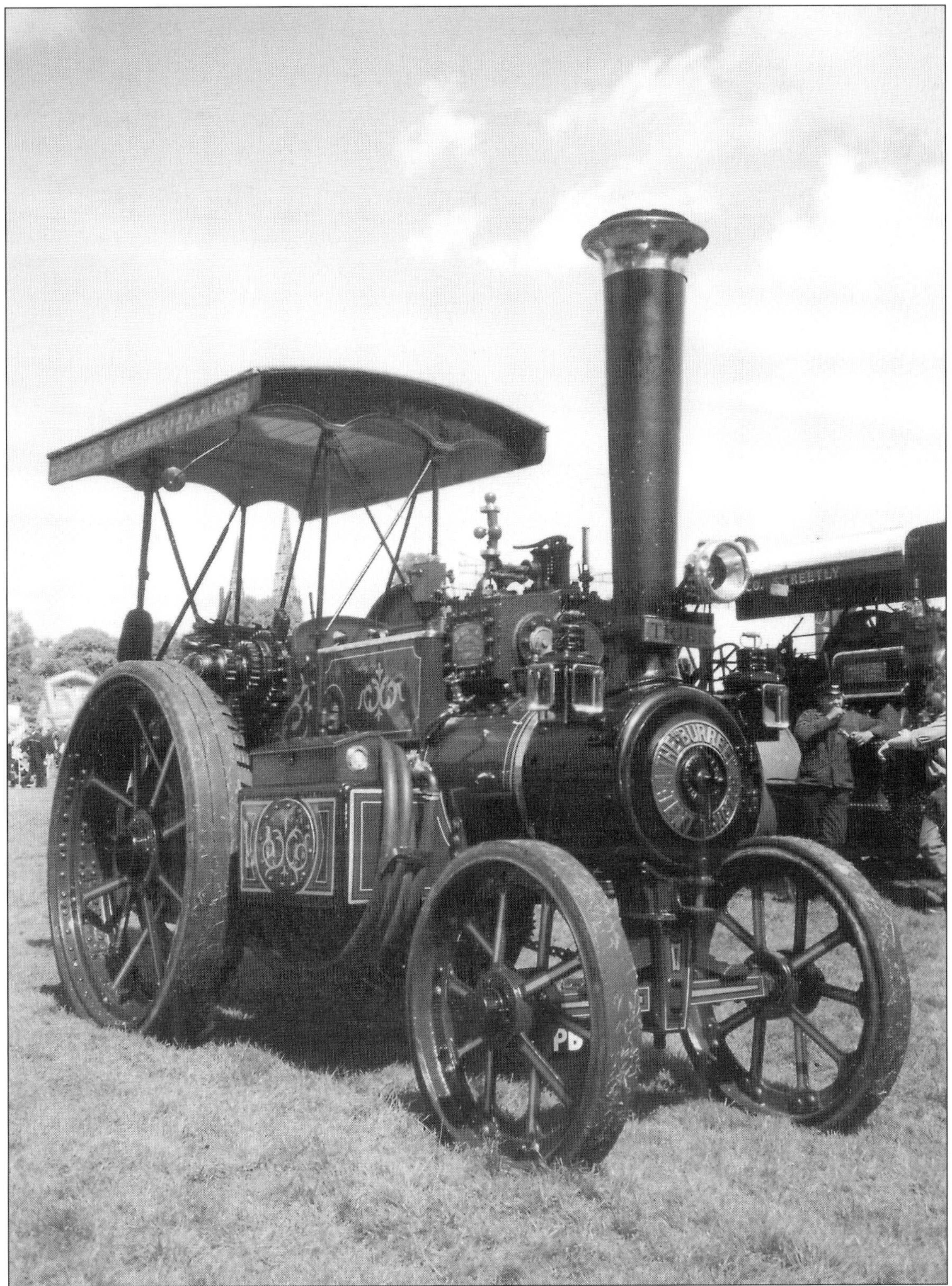

Lichfield Bower which takes place annually on Spring Bank Holiday Monday when the whole city comes out to play. Always a great favourite is the steam traction engine on display in Beacon Park.

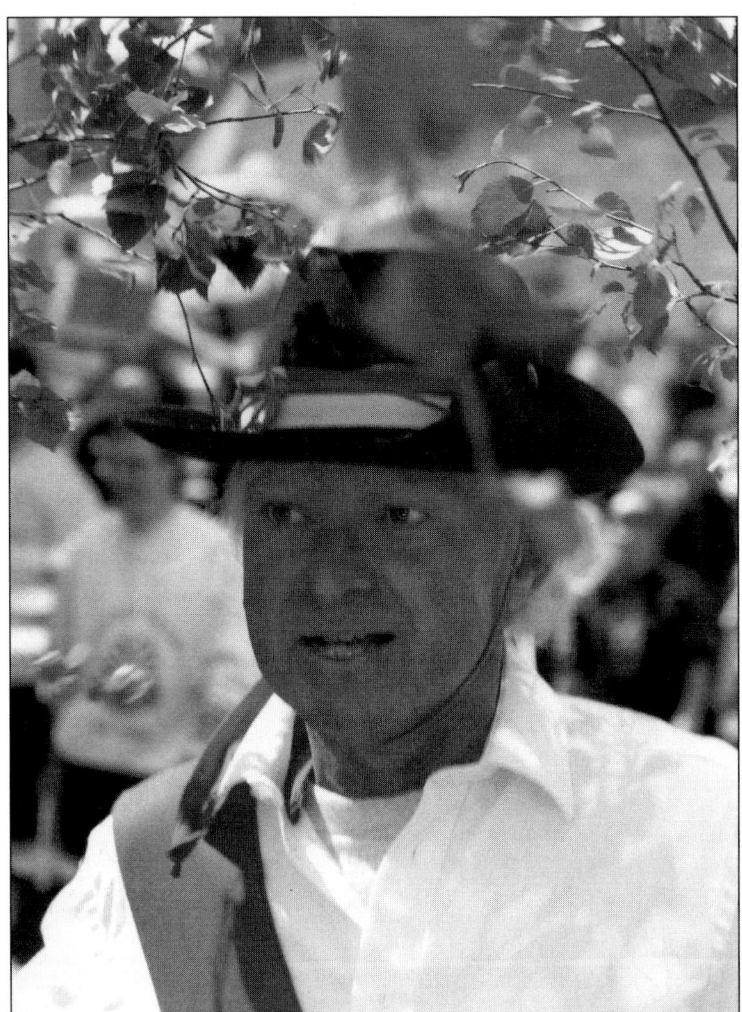

Our own Michael Fabricant MP joins the Lichfield Morris Men on their dance through the city.

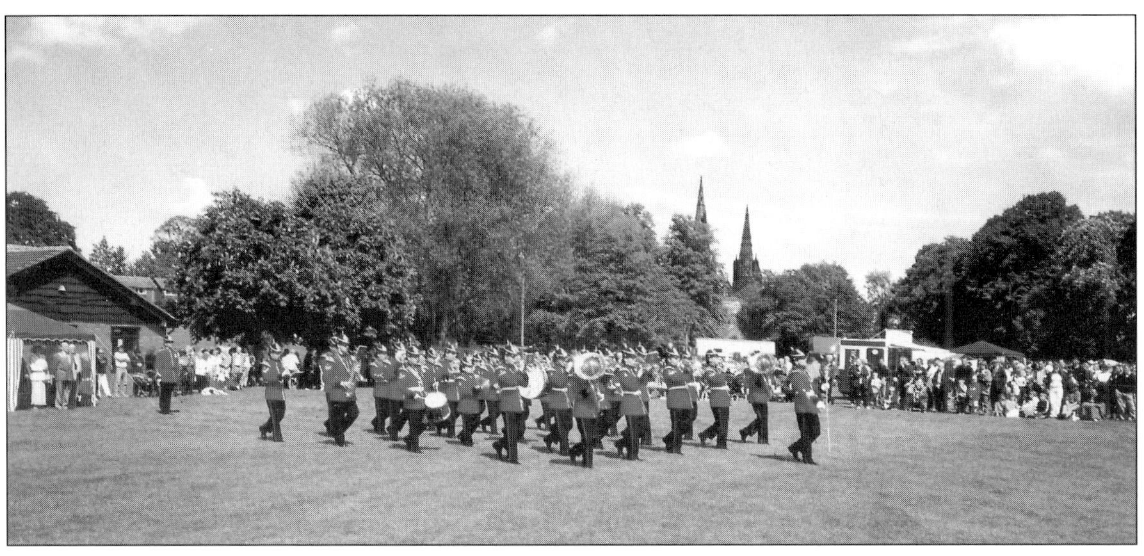

A brassband performing in the sunshine in Beacon Park

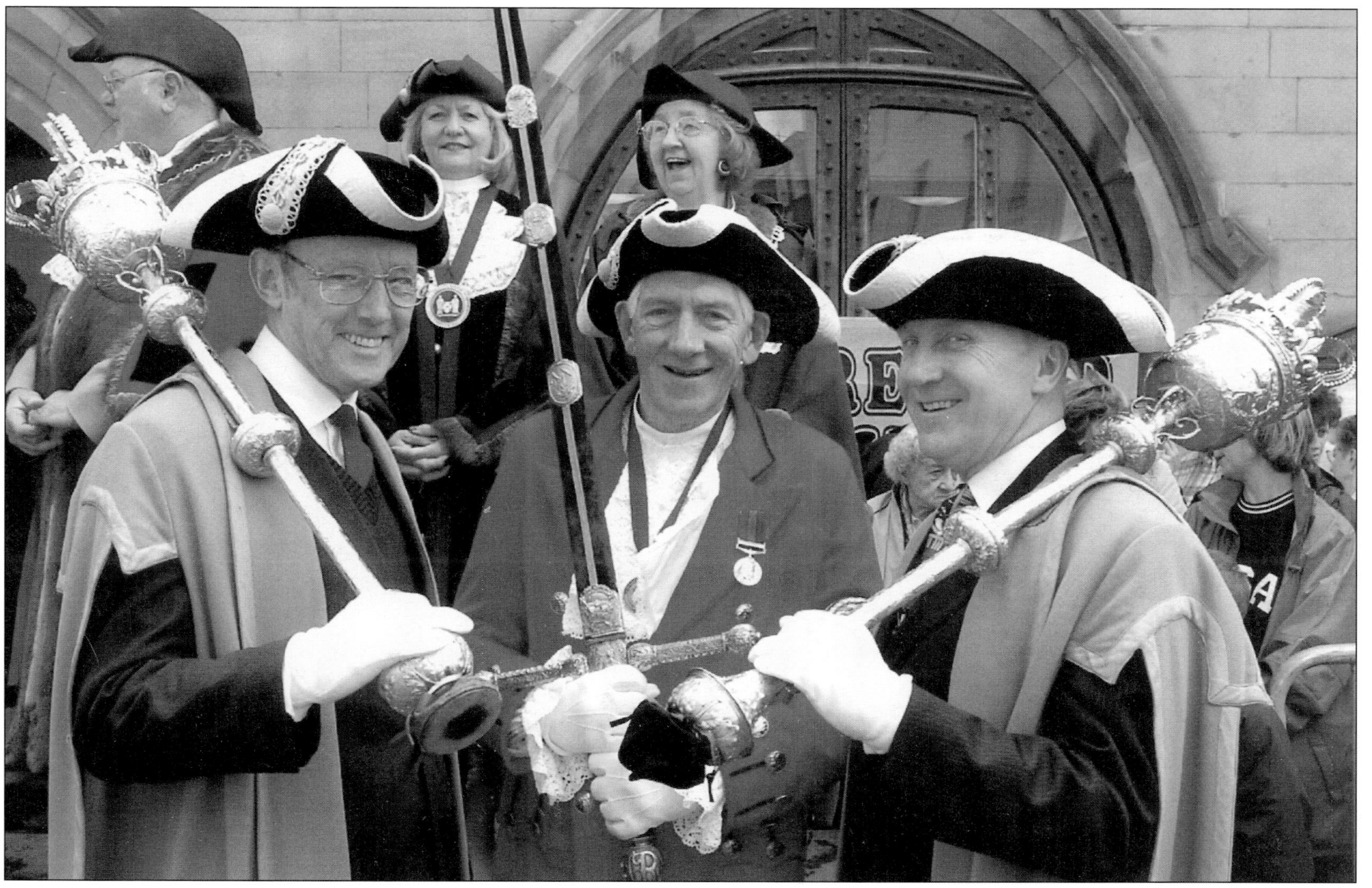

Seen outside the Lichfield Guildhall on Bower Day are Swordbearer Lonza Atkins flanked by Macebearer Mike Williamson on the left and Graham Woodall on the right. The Mayor Cllr Barry Diggle, his deputy Cllr Janet Eagland and Sheriff Cllr Doris English watch over the proceedings.

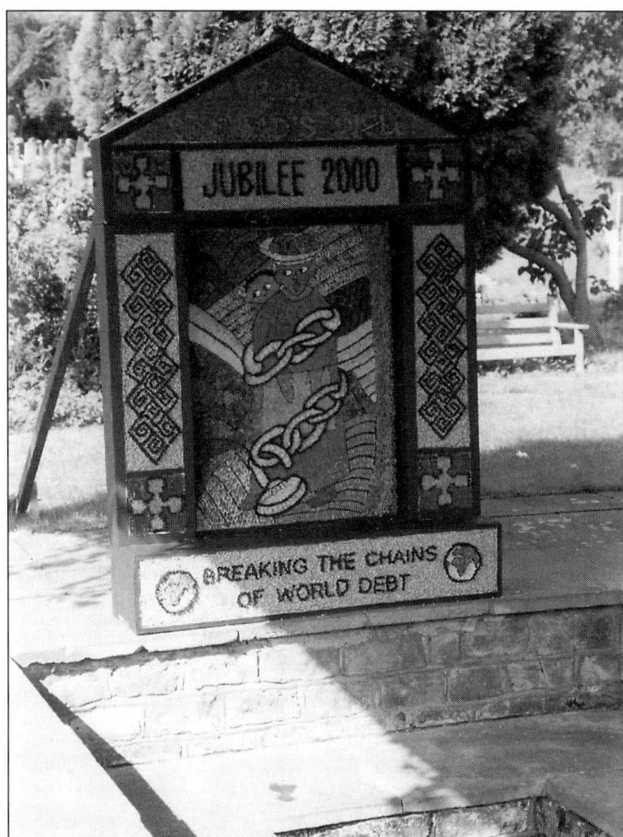

Summer is a wonderful time for festivities and Lichfield is no exception. The ancient art of well dressing was used in 1999 by St Chad's Church to support the Jubilee 2000 attempt to persuade wealthy governments of the Western world to cancel the world debt of the poorer nations which culminated in the G8 Summit in Rio. This work of art made of flower petals was displayed at St Chad's Well, ancient pilgrimage site of the early Christians.

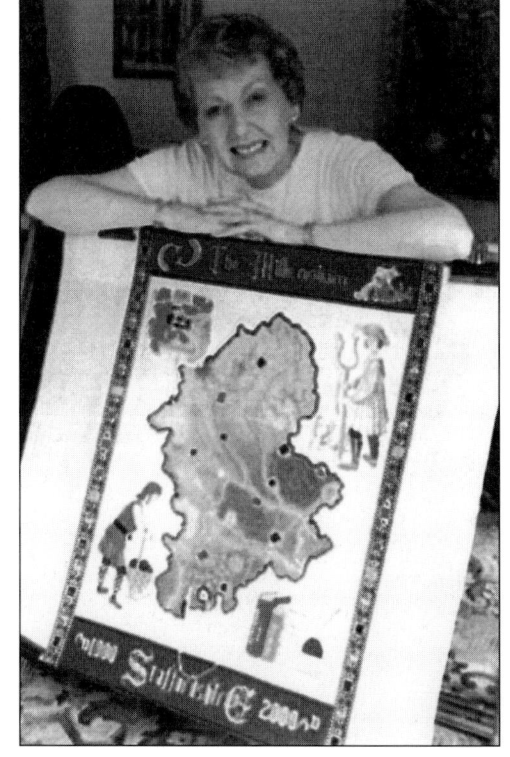

Right: Sylvia M.Everitt with the Tudor map of Staffordshire.

Opposite page: In May 1999, Sylvia M.Everitt, a very gifted lady, completed the Staffordshire Millennium Embroideries which had taken her five long years to produce from the initial idea, in the Spring of 1994. It was to be a 'sort of mini Bayeaux tapestry incorporating a thousand years of Staffordshire's history', when people all over the country were being asked to think of ideas to celebrate the new Millennium. There are eleven separate panels, each one representing a century and one depicting the main towns and roads of Staffordshire in Tudor times. The embroideries were to be her gift to the county but with such a costly enterprise she sought and found willing sponsors. A permanent home for these incredibly beautiful historical records has been offered by St Mary's Heritage Centre, Lichfield when the Millennium Tour finishes later in 2001. Do go and see them! Who knows, perhaps these priceless embroideries will become as important to Staffordshire as the sumptuous, illuminated Lichfield Gospels are to the city.

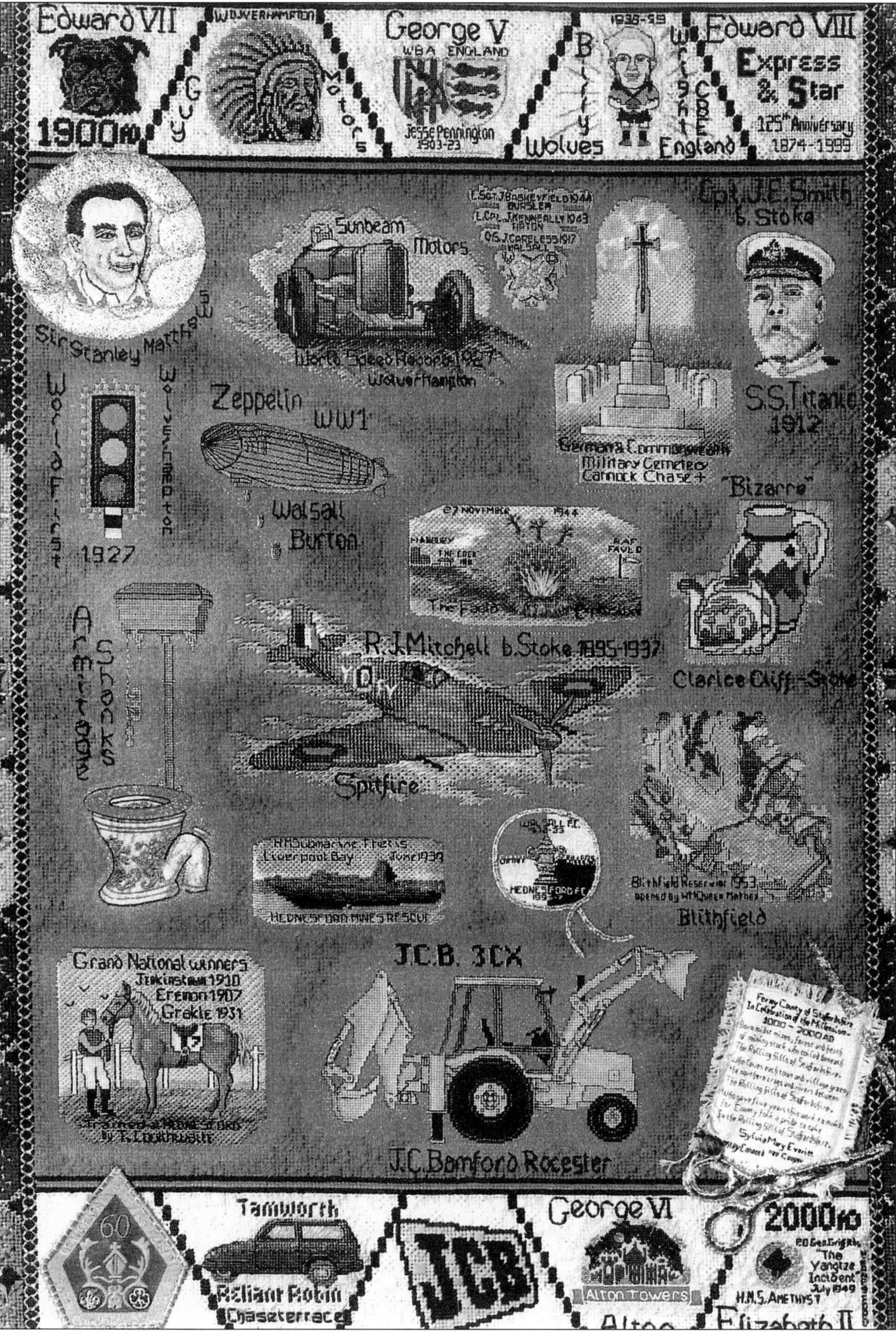
Edward VII
1900AD
Guy Motors
Wolverhampton
George V
WBA England
Jesse Pennington
1903-23
Billy Wright CBE
1938-59
Wolves
England
Edward VIII
Express & Star
125th Anniversary
1874-1999
Sir Stanley Matthews
Sunbeam Motors
World Speed Record 1927
Wolverhampton
Cpl. J.E. Smith
b. Stoke
S.S. Titanic
1912
German & Commonwealth
Military Cemetery
Cannock Chase
World First
Wolverhampton
1927
Zeppelin
WW1
Walsall
Burton
"Bizarre"
The Fauld
Armitage Shanks
R.J. Mitchell b. Stoke 1895-1937
Clarice Cliff - Stoke
Spitfire
H.M. Submarine Thetis
Liverpool Bay
June 1939
Hednesford Mines Rescue
Walsall F.C.
Hednesford F.C.
Blithfield Reservoir 1953
opened by H.M. Queen Mother
Blithfield
J.C.B. 3CX
Grand National winners
Jenkinstown 1910
Eremon 1907
Grakle 1931
J.C. Bamford Rocester
1000 – 2000 AD
Sylvia Mary Everitt
Tamworth
Reliant Robin
Chasetown
JCB
George VI
Alton Towers
Elizabeth II
2000AD
"The Yangtze Incident"
July 1949
H.M.S. Amethyst

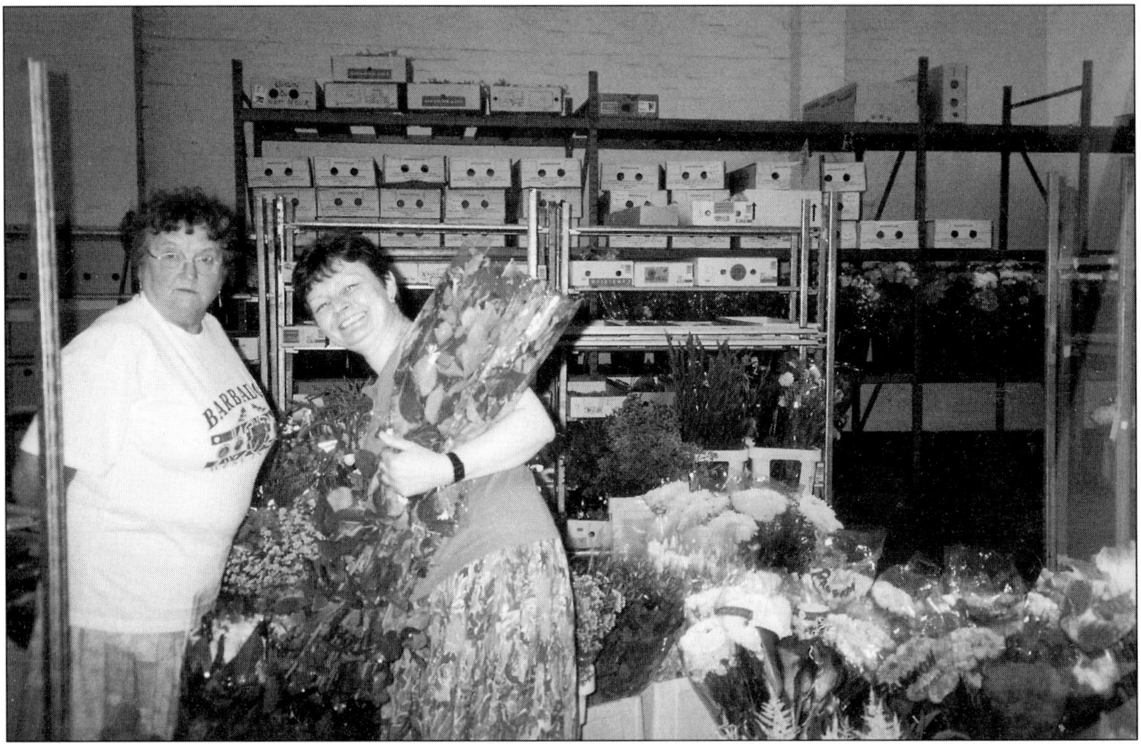

Molly Haynes and Ann Morrison at the flower wholesaler's G & M Hale of Tipton – it took a box van and three cars a total of five hours to collect all the flowers.

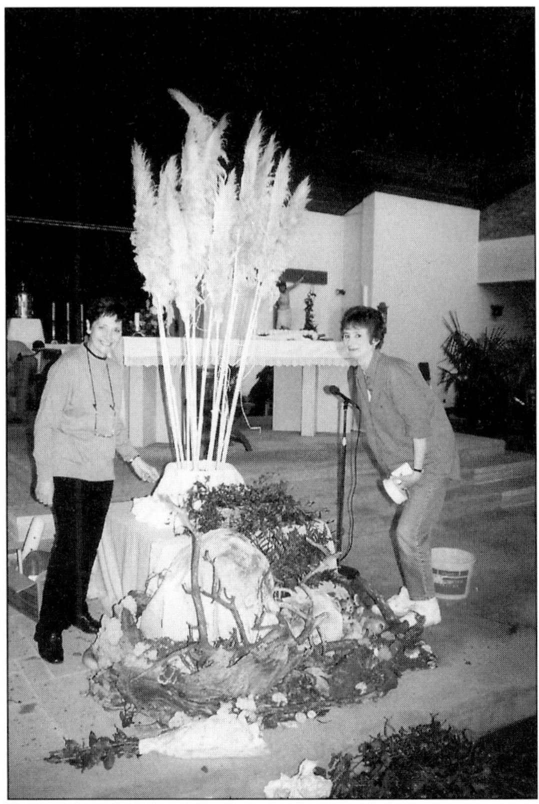

The Rosary was the theme of the Jubilee 2000 Festival of Flowers at St Peter and Paul's Roman Catholic Church. Pauline May and Mo Llewellyn work on the Resurrection

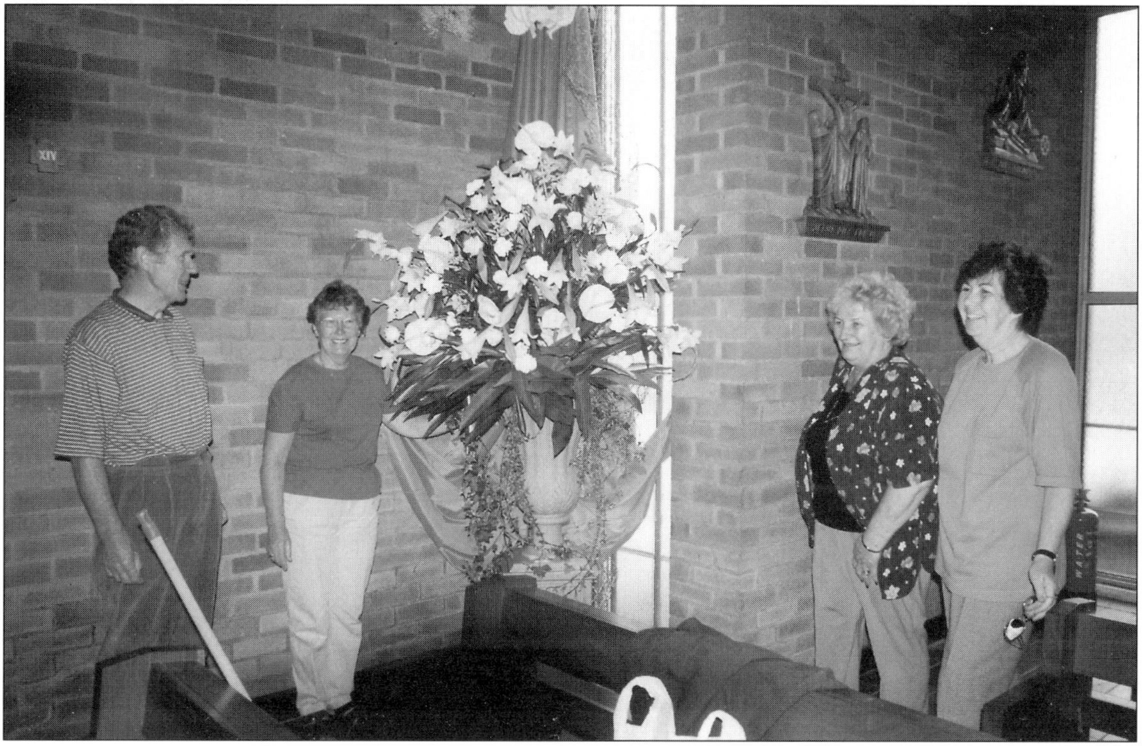

Festival of Flowers Ascension Team – Ian & Jane Dick, Mavis Thompson and Collette Thorne, Committee Chairman.

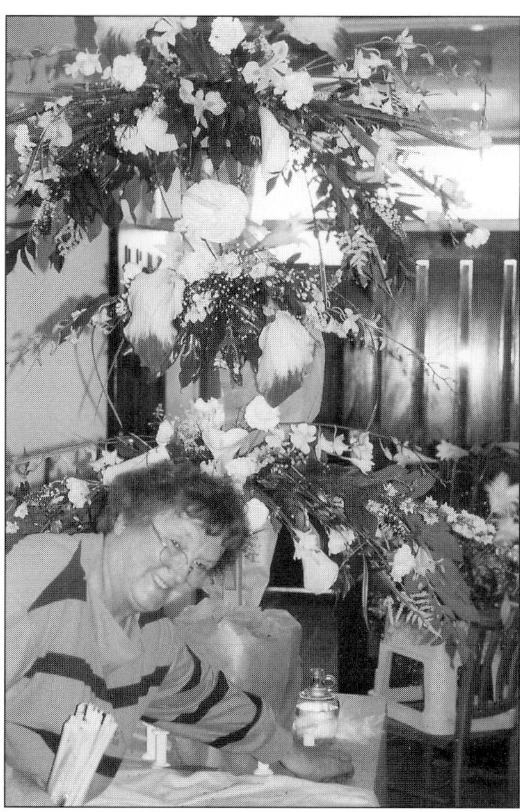

Molly Haynes, Festival co-ordinator working on the Annunciation. The end is in sight.

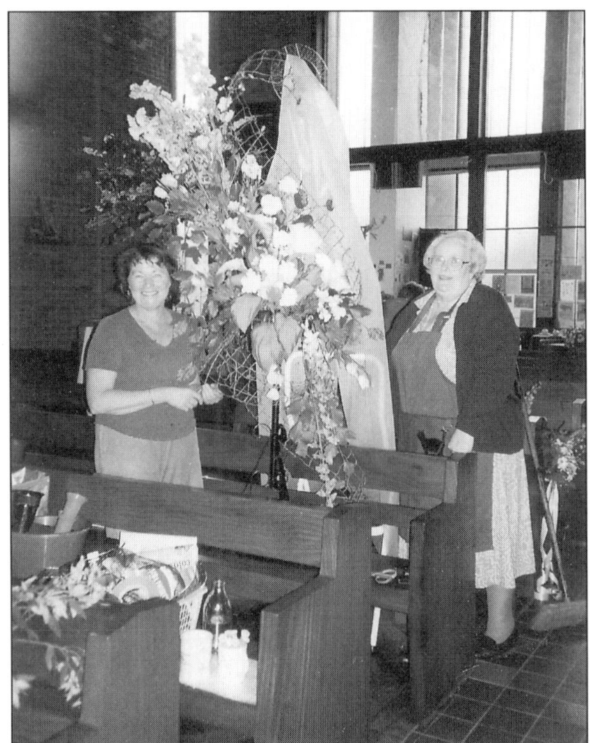

The Assumption and Coronation of the Blessed Virgin Mary team, Kathy Simmons and Barbara Maddox

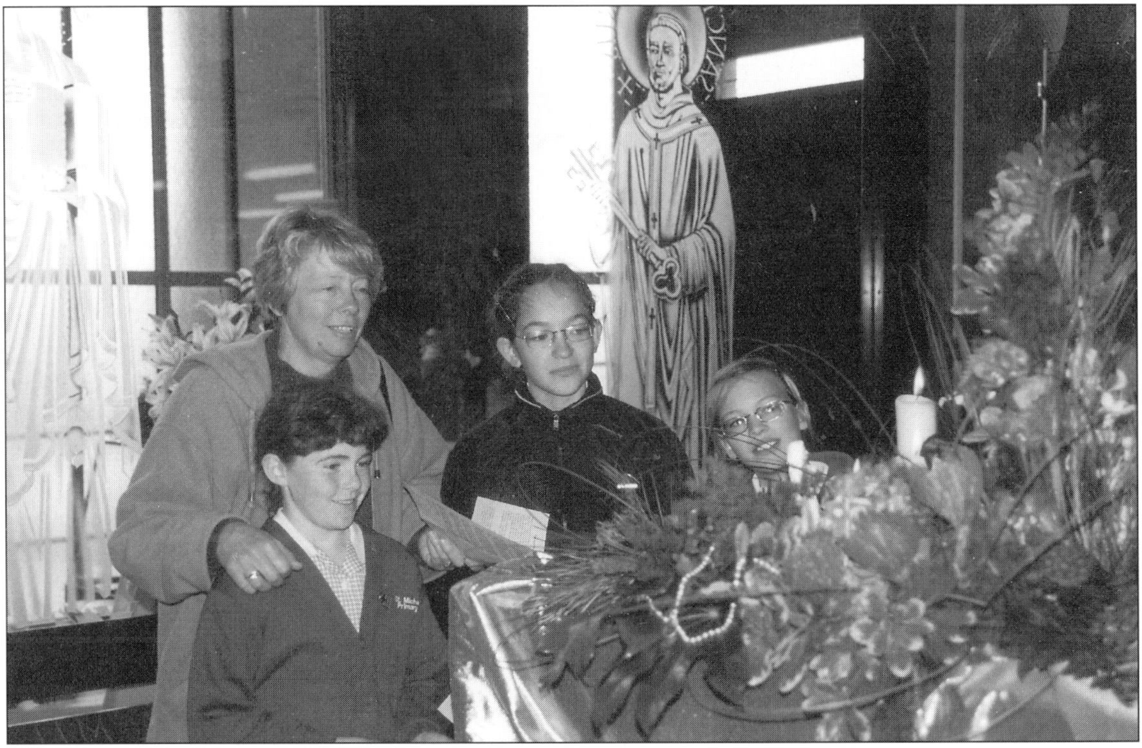

When all the floral artwork was done, St Peter and Paul's Roman Catholic Church was opened for the Festival of Flowers to begin. St Michael's Church of England Primary School sent 4 classes (approx.140 pupils)! Teacher Glynis Russell is seen here with Laura Slater and her own children.

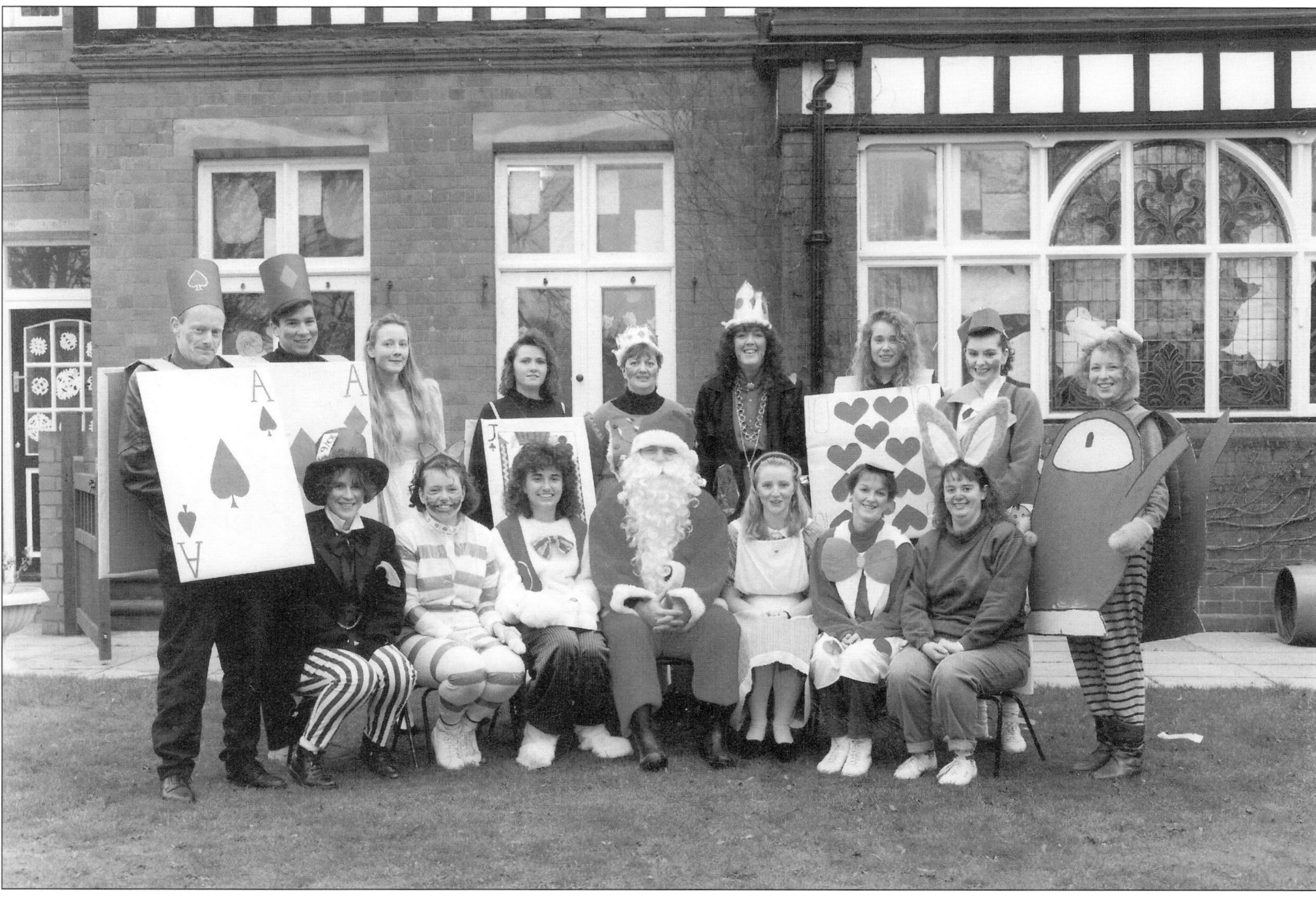

Alice in Wonderland at Christmas featuring the staff of Busy Bees Children's Day Nursery, Rocklands.

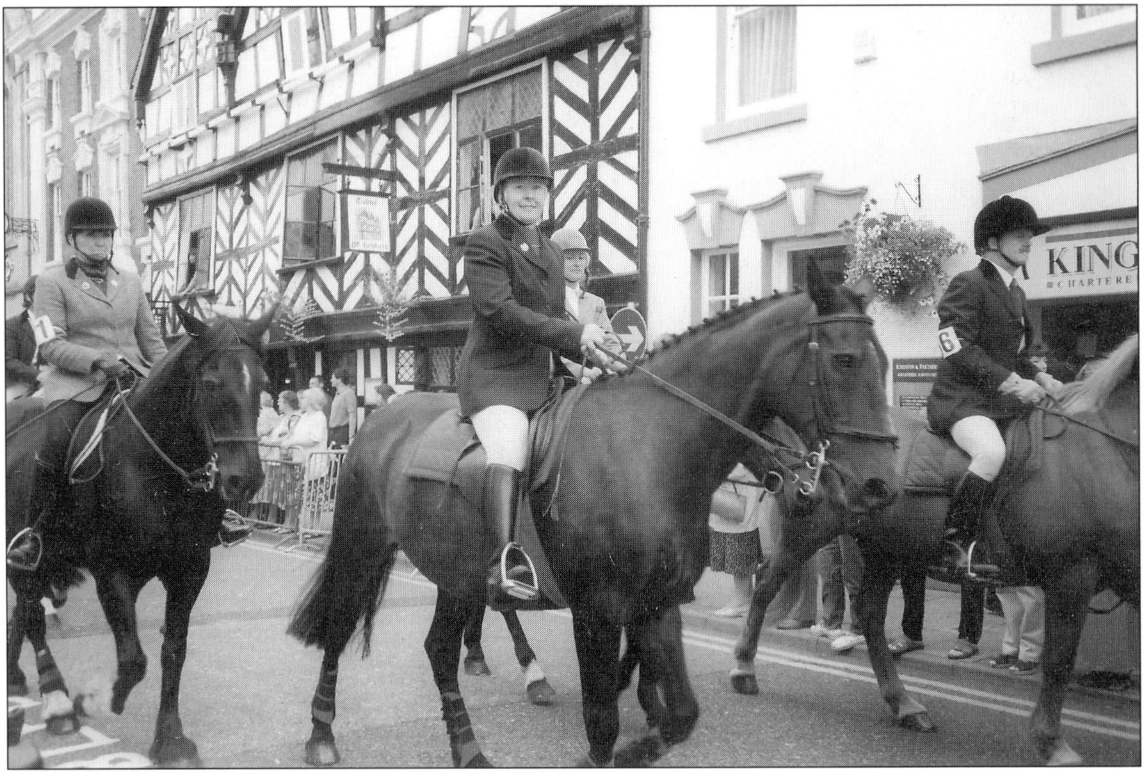

The 1999 Sheriff's Ride.

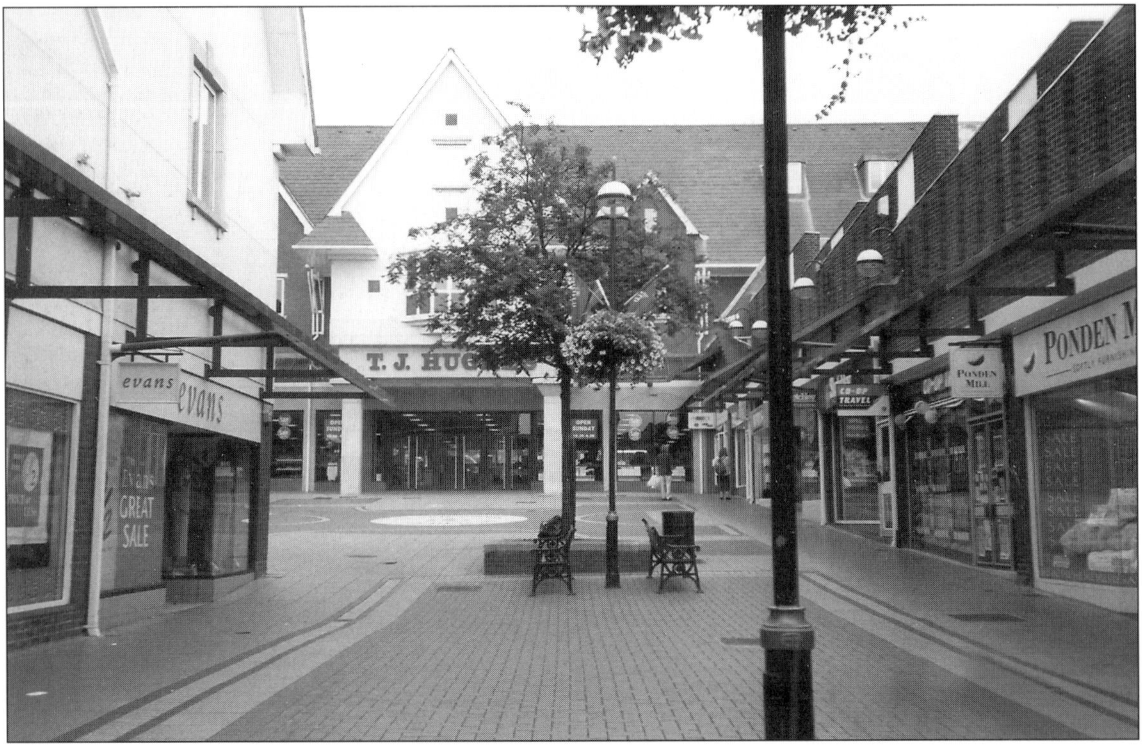

The old Baker's Lane precinct at festival time looking towards TJ Hughes Ltd. The precinct is now known as the Three Spires Shopping Centre.

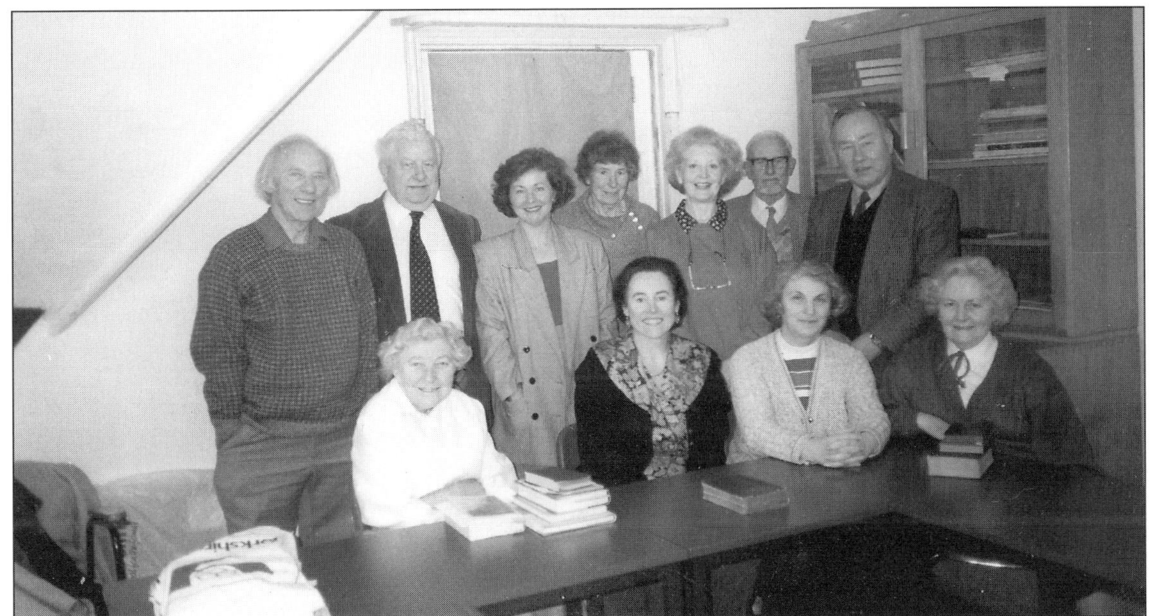

In 1992 a group of dedicated poetry enthusiasts enrolled at Lichfield College for the Poetry for Pleasure class led by tutor Catherine Spencer. Under her guiding hand the students grew in knowledge and appreciation of poetic language. Following a trip to the Cheltenham Literary Festival in October 1994 to hear the finalists of a Speak a Poem Competition founded by Betty Mulcahy, Catherine suggested that we might hold a similar competition for schools in the annual Lichfield International Arts Festival. As a result, in 1995 the Lichfield Poetry Speaking Competition was born, with just seventy entrants from the five high schools of Lichfield and District.

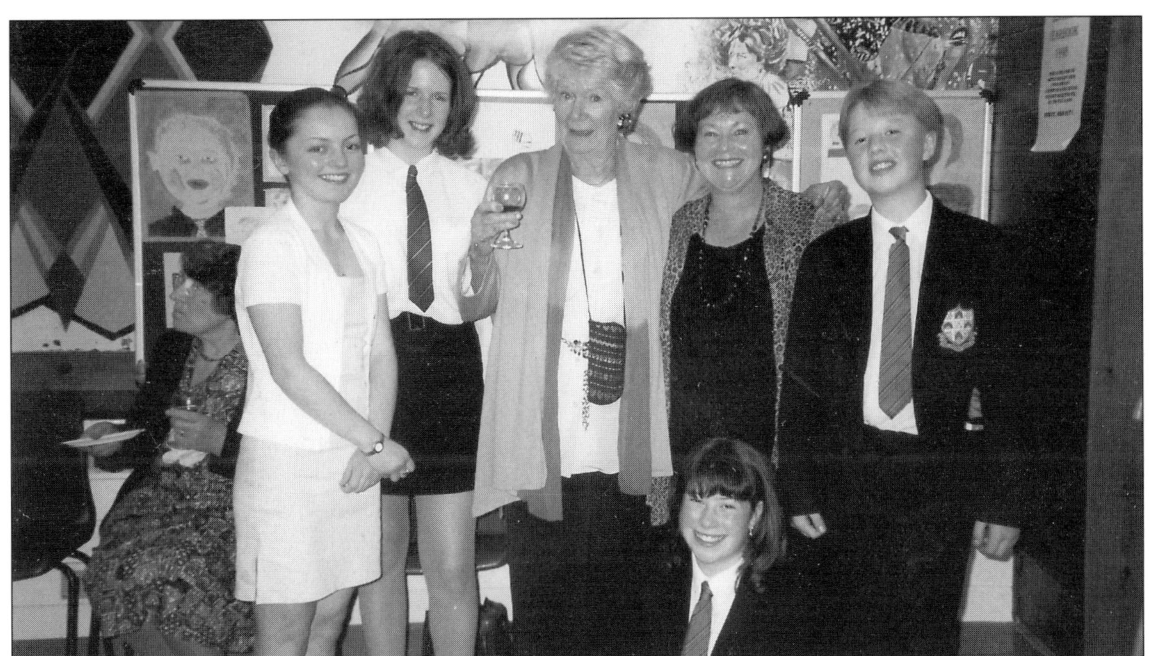

Adjudicator Betty Mulcahy with Chairman of the fourth Poetry Competition, Kathy Simmons and winners of the 1998 competition, Paul Talbot, Laura Wood from King Edward VI 11-13 group, Joanna Keith from Chasetown High 14-15 group and Samantha Tipper King Edward VI 16-18 group.

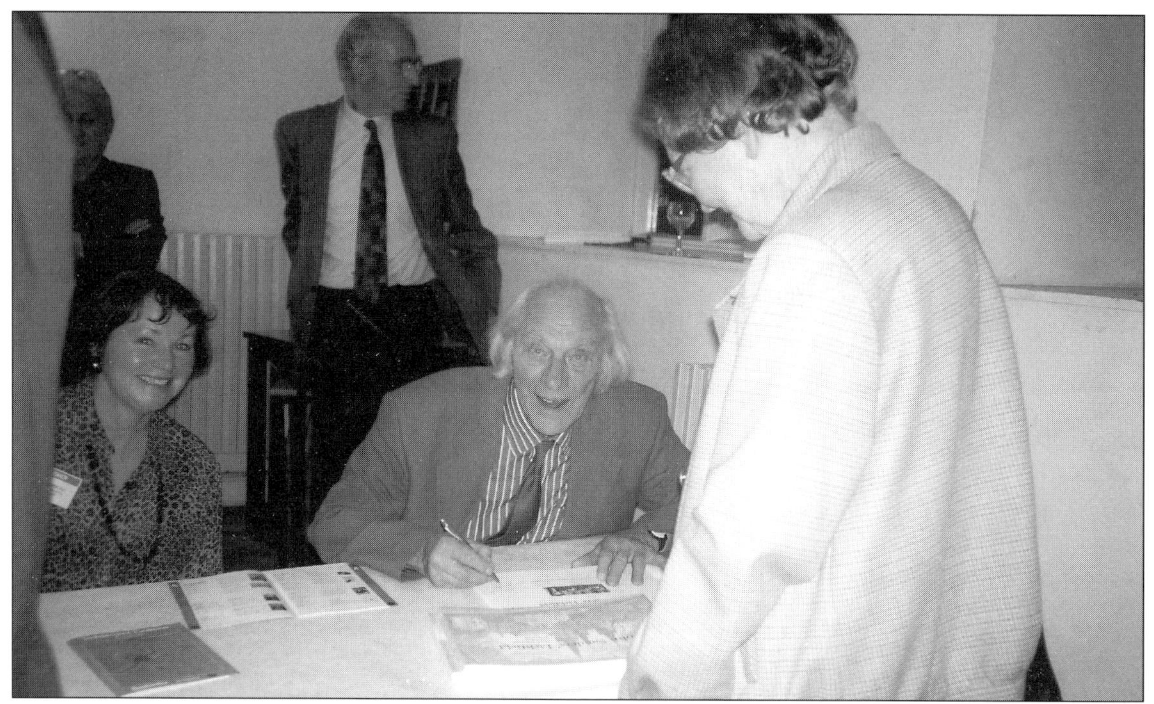

John Sander's book launch at the Guildhall in October 1998, seen here with publisher Kathy Simmons.

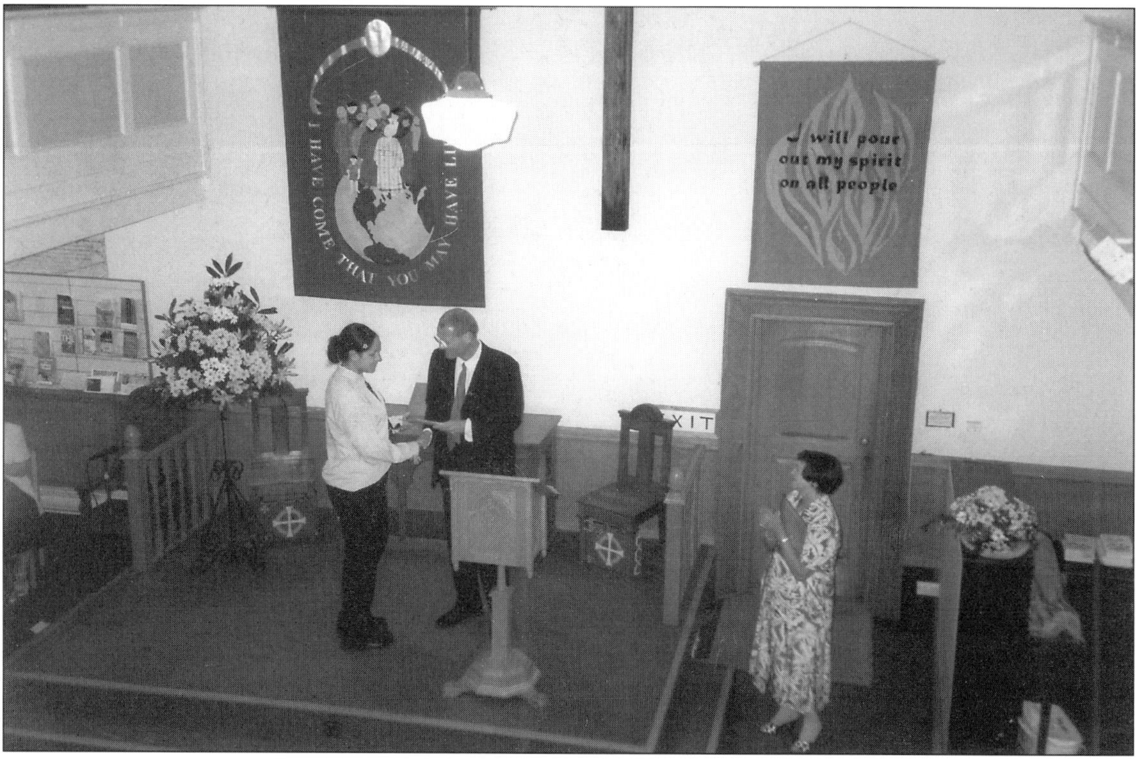

Eleni Trattos, finalist in the 14-15 group receiving her prize of a certificate, book plate and book token from the Poet Laureate. Master of Ceremonies for the evening was Kathy Simmons, Chairman of the Poetry Speaking Competition.

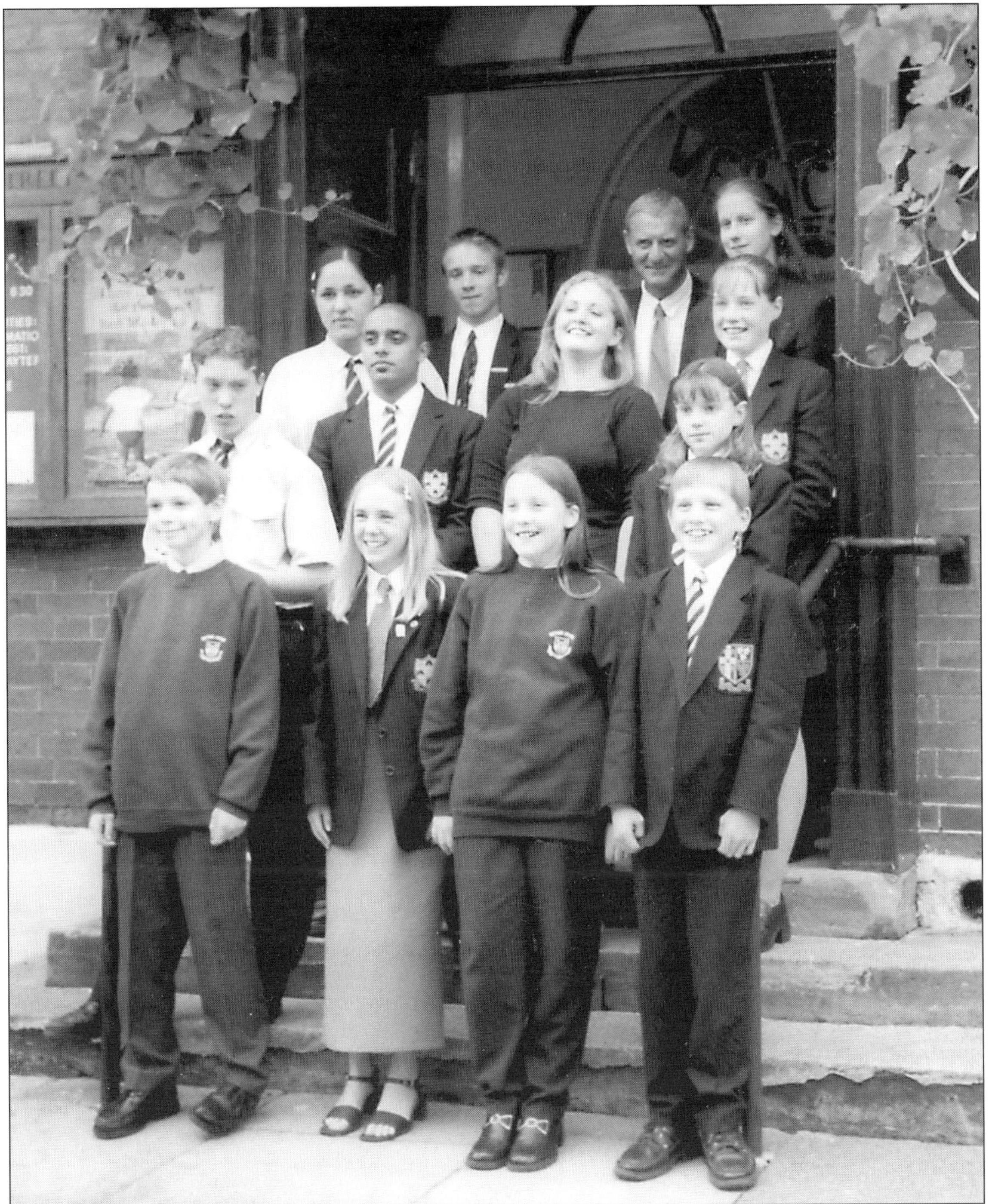

The Millennium competition in our sixth year was the largest with almost three hundred competitors from the Lichfield and District High Schools. We were honoured to have the Poet Laureate, Andrew Motion as our adjudicator for the event, a treasured memory for all those taking part.

Andrew Motion, centre back, with the twelve finalists on the steps of the fine late-Georgian Chapel of the United Reformed Church.

Linsie Donegan and Daniel Hopkins from Friary High. Alan Tindal, Anna Coley, Simon Deeley and Eleni Trattos from Nether Stowe High. Kirsty Langdell, Katie Kerr Bashford, Emma Cunnington, Rebeccah Small, Allan Pengelly and Harpreet Panesar from King Edward VI.

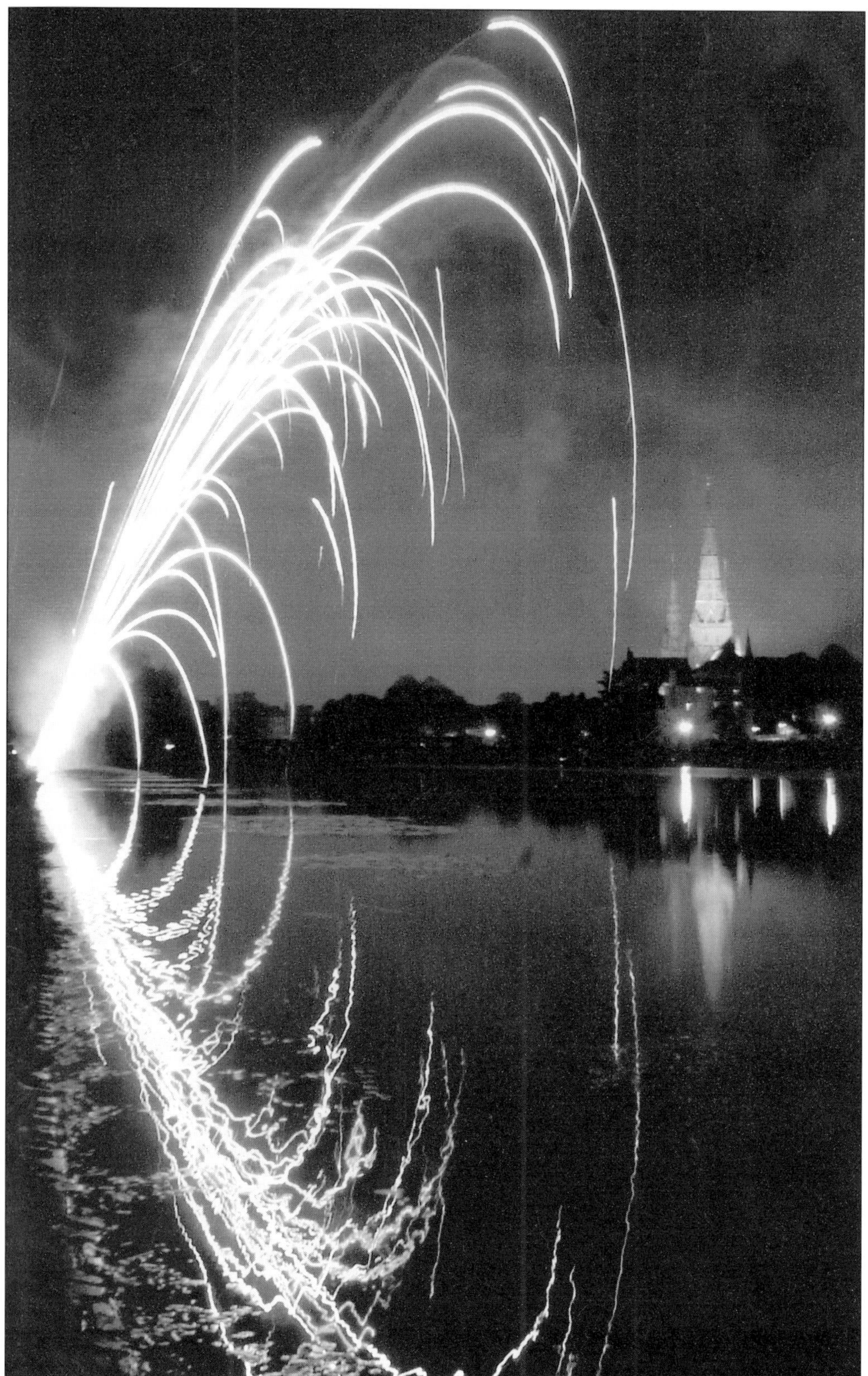

The Lichfield International Arts Festival Fireworks reflected in the still waters of Stowe Pool. A fitting finalé.

Index

Bibliography

Alfred Parker - *Lichfield*
Lichfield City Council - *Mother of the Midlands*
Helen Mullins - *History of the Friary School*
Julie A.Taylor - *History of King Edward VI School*
Pelham Books Ltd - *Pears Encyclopaedia*
Abbotsford Publishing - *Lichfield in Old Photographs*
Howard Clayton - *Cathedral City*
John Boyton - *Rails Around Walsall*
Lt Col M.B.Savage - *History of Naval & Military Effects in Lichfield Cathedral*
Neal Priestland - *Erasmus Darwin*

Picture of Erasmus Darwin by Joseph Wright of Derby (reproduced by kind permission of Darwin College, Cambridge)